John Henry Newman, Saint Athanasius

Select Treatises of Saint Athanasius in Controversy with the Arians

John Henry Newman, Saint Athanasius

Select Treatises of Saint Athanasius in Controversy with the Arians

ISBN/EAN: 9783337591106

Printed in Europe, USA, Canada, Australia, Japan

Cover: Foto ©Thomas Meinert / pixelio.de

More available books at **www.hansebooks.com**

SELECT TREATISES

OF

ST. ATHANASIUS

IN CONTROVERSY WITH THE ARIANS.

FREELY TRANSLATED

BY

JOHN HENRY CARDINAL NEWMAN,

Honorary Fellow of Trinity College, Oxford,
and late Fellow of Oriel.

VOL. II.

BEING AN APPENDIX OF ILLUSTRATOINS.

SEVENTH EDITION.

LONGMANS, GREEN, AND CO.

39 PATERNOSTER ROW, LONDON

NEW YORK AND BOMBAY

1897

CONTENTS.

Index of Annotations on Theological Subjects in the foregoing Treatises alphabetically arranged.

ADAM.

THOUGH the Fathers, in accordance with Scripture, hold that Adam was created sinless, they also hold that he could not have persevered in his state of innocence and uprightness without a special grace, which he lost upon his fall, and which is regained for us, (and that in far greater measure,) by our Lord's sufferings and merits.

¶ The Catholic doctrine is, that Adam innocent was mortal, yet in fact would not have died; that he had no principle of eternal life within his body naturally, but was sustained continually by divine power till such time as immortality should have been given him. Vid. Incarn. 4. "If God accorded to the garments and shoes of the Israelites," says S. Augustine, "that they should not wear out during so many years, how is it strange that to man obedient should by His power be accorded, that, whereas his body was animal and mortal, it was so constituted as to become aged without decay, and at such time as God willed might pass without the intervention of death from mortality to

immortality? For as the flesh itself, which we now
bear, is not therefore invulnerable, because it may be
preserved from wounding, so Adam's was not therefore
not mortal, because he was not bound to die. Such a
habit even of their present animal and mortal body I
suppose was granted also to them who have been
translated hence without death; for Enoch and Elias
too have through so long a time been preserved from
the decay of age." De Pecc. Mer. i. 3. Adam's body,
he says elsewhere, was "mortale quia poterat mori,
immortale quia poterat non mori;" and he goes on to
say that immortality was given him "de ligno vitæ,
non de constitutione naturæ." Gen. ad Lit. vi. 36.
This doctrine came into the controversy with Baius,
and Pope S. Pius V. condemned the assertion, "Im-
mortalitas primi hominis non erat gratiæ beneficium,
sed naturalis conditio."

Then, as to his soul, S. Augustine says, "An aid
was [given to the first Adam], but a more powerful
grace is given to the Second. The first is that by
which a man has justice if he will; the second does
more, for by it he also wills, and wills so strongly, and
loves so ardently, as to overcome the will of the flesh
lusting contrariwise to the will of the spirit," &c.
De Corr. et Grat. 31. And S. Cyril, "Our forefather
Adam seems to have gained wisdom, not in time, as
we, but appears perfect in understanding from the very
first moment of his formation, preserving in himself
the illumination, given him by nature from God, as
yet untroubled and pure, and leaving the dignity cf
his nature unpractised on," &c. In Joan. p. 75.

ALEXANDER'S ENCYCLICAL.

Vid. supr. vol. i. p. 1, *Prefatory Notice.*

I HERE set down the internal evidence in favour of this Letter having been written by Athanasius. A long letter on Arius and his tenets, addressed by Alexander to his namesake at Constantinople, has been preserved for us by Theodoret, and we can compare the Encyclical on the one hand with this Letter, and with the acknowledged writings of Athanasius on the other, and thereby determine for ourselves whether the Encyclical does not resemble in style what Athanasius has written, and does not differ from the style of Theodoret's Alexander. Athanasius is a great writer, simple in his diction, clear, unstudied, direct, vigorous, elastic, and above all characteristic; but Alexander writes with an effort, and is elaborate and exquisite in his vocabulary and structure of sentences.

Thus, the Encyclical before us, after S. Athanasius's manner in treating of sacred subjects, has hardly one scientific term; its words, when not Arius's own, are for the most part from Scripture, such as λόγος, σοφία, μονογενὴς, εἰκὼν, ἀπαύγασμα, just as they are found in Athanasius's controversial Treatises; whereas, in Alexander's etter in Theodoret, phrases are found, certainly not from Scripture, perhaps of Alexandrian theology,

perhaps peculiar to the writer, for instance, ἀχώριστα
πράγματα δύο· ὁ υἱὸς τὴν κατὰ πάντα ὁμοιότητα αὐτοῦ
ἐκ φύσεως ἀπομαξάμενος· δι᾽ ἐσόπτρου ἀκηλιδώτου καὶ
ἐμψύχου θείας εἰκόνος· μεσιτεύουσα φύσις μονογενής· τὰς
τῇ ὑποστάσει δύο φύσεις. And, instead of the οὐσία of
the Father, of the Son, of the Word, which is one of
the few, as well as familiar, scientific terms of Athanasius (Orat. i. § 45, ii. 7, 9, 11, 12, 13, 18, 22, 47, 56), and
which the Encyclical uses too, we read in the Letter of
Alexander, preserved by Theodoret, ὑπόστασις, and that
again and again; e.g., τὴν ἰδιότροπον αὐτοῦ ὑπόστασιν·
τῆς ὑποστάσεως αὐτοῦ ἀπεριεργαστοῦ· νεωτέραν τῆς
ὑποστάσεως γένεσιν· ἡ τοῦ μονογενοῦς ἀνεκδιήγητος
ὑπόστασις· τὴν τοῦ λόγου ὑπόστασιν, phrases quite out
of keeping with the style of the Encyclical. Nor is it
only in the expression of theological ideas that the
style of the Letter in Theodoret differs from the style of
the Encyclical; thus, when the latter speaks of φθορέας
τῶν ψυχῶν, the former uses the compound φθόροποιός·
Such, too, are ἡ φίλαρχος καὶ φιλάργυρος πρόθεσις·
χριστεμπορίαν· φρενοβλαβοῦς· ἰδιότροπον· ὁμοστοίχοις
συλλαβαῖς· θεηγόρους ἀποστόλους· ἀντιδιαστολὴν· τῆς
πατρικῆς μαιεύσεως· φιλόθεος σαφήνεια· ἀνοσιουργίας·
φληνάφων μύθων. It is very difficult to suppose that
the same hand wrote this Letter to the Bishop of Constantinople and the Encyclical which is the subject of
this note.

On the other hand, that Athanasius wrote the latter
becomes almost certain when, in addition to what has
been observed in Vol. i., supr., in the Prefatory Notice,
the following coincidence of words and phrases is

considered, on comparing the Encyclical with Athana·
sius's acknowledged writings :—

Encyclical, ap. Socr. Hist. i. § 6. (Oxf. Ed. 1844.)	Athan. Opp. (Ed. Benedict. Paris.)
1. p. 6, l. 2, ἐξῆλθον, 1 John ii. 19.	1. αἵρεσις νῦν ἐξελθοῦσα, Orat. i. § 1.
2. *ibid.* ἄνδρες παράνομοι.	2. παράνομοι, &c. Orat. iii. § 2; Ep. Æg. 16; Hist. Ar. 71, 75, 79.
3. *ibid.* l. 4, ἐξῆλθον διδάσκοντες ἀποστασίαν, πρόδρομον τοῦ 'Αντιχρίστου.	3. νῦν ἐξελθοῦσα, πρόδρομος τοῦ 'Αντιχρίστου, Orat. i. § 7
4. *ibid.* καὶ ἐβουλόμην μὲν σιωπῇ . . . ἐπειδὴ δέ, &c.	4. This form of apology, introductory to the treatment of a subject, is usual with Athan., e.g. Orat. i. § 23, *init.*, ii. 1, *init.*, iii. 1, *init.* ; Apol. c. Ar. 1, *init.* ; Decr. § 5 ; Serap. i. 1 and 16, ii. 1, *init.*, iii. 1, *init.*, iv. 8 ; Mon. 2 ; Epict. 3 fin. ; Max. 1 ; Apoll. i. 1, *init.*
5. *ibid.* l. 6, ῥυπώσῃ.	5. Orat. i. § 10 ; Decr. § 2 ; Hist. Ar. 3 ; Ep. Æg. 11.
6. *ibid.* τὰς ἀκοάς.	6. Orat. i. § 7 and 35 ; Hist. Ar. 56 ; Ep. Æg. 13.
7. *ibid.* ἀκεραίων.	7. Orat. i. § 8, ii. 34 ; iii. 16 ; Syn. § 20, 32, and 45 ; Ap. c. Ar. 1 ; Ep. Æg. 18 ; Epict. 1 ; Adelph. 2.
8. *ibid.* l. 14, ῥημάτια.	8. Orat. i. § 10 ; Decr. § 8 and 18 ; Sent. Dion. 23.
9. *ibid.* l. 15, κακόνοιαν.	9. Decr. § 1 ; Hist. Ar. § 75.
10. *ibid.* l. 22, &c. The enumeration of Arius's tenets.	10. runs with Orat. i. § 5 ; Decr. § 6 ; Ep. Æg. 12, more closely than with the Letter to Constantinople.
11. p. 7, l. 1, ἀναισχυντοῦντες.	11. Decr. § 20.
12. *ibid.* l. 7, τίς γὰρ ἤκουσε, &c.	12. Vid. similar form in Orat. i. § 8 ; Ep. Æg. 7 ; Epict. 2 ; Ap. c. Ar. 85 ; Hist. Ar. 46, 73, 74, &c.
13. *ibid.* l. 8, ξενίζεται.	13. Orat. i. § 35 and 42, ii. 34, 73, and 80, iii. 30, 48 ; Decr. § 22.

Encyclical, ap. Socr. Hist. l. § 6. (Oxf. Ed. 1844.)	Athan. Opp. (Ed. Benedict. Paris.)
14. p. 8, l. 27. The apology here made for the use of Mal. iii. 6, is	14. almost *verbatim* with that found in Orat. i. § 36.
15. p. 8, l. 12. The text 1 Tim. iv. 1 in this place, is	15. applied to Arians by Athan. also Orat. i. § 8. By whom besides?

ANGELS.

ANGELS were actually worshipped, in the proper sense of the word, by Gnostics and other heretics, who even ascribed to them a creative power; and certainly, to consider them the source of any good to man, and the acceptable channel intrinsically of approaching God, in derogation of our Lord's sole mediation, is idolatry. However, their presence in and about the Church, and with all of us individually, is an inestimable blessing, never to be slighted or forgotten; for, as by our prayers and our kind deeds we can serve each other, so Angels, but in a far higher way, serve us, and are channels of grace to us, as the Sacraments also are. All this would doubtless have been maintained by Athanasius had there been occasion for saying it. For instance, in commenting on Psalm 49, *Deus Deorum*, he says so in substance :—

"'He shall summon the heaven from above.' When the Saviour manifested Himself, He kindled in us the light of true religious knowledge : He converted that which had wandered ; He bound up that which was ailing ; as being the Good Shepherd, He chased away the wild beasts from the sheepfold ; He gave His people sanctification of the Spirit, and the protection of Angelic Powers, and He set those over them through the whole world who should be holy mystagogues. 'He will

summon,' He says, 'the Angels who are in heaven and
the men on earth chosen for the Apostolate, to judge
His people.' . . . That with those mystagogues and their
disciples Angels co-operate, Paul makes clear when he
says, Heb. i. 14," &c., &c.

¶ If it be asked why, such being his substantial teaching, his language in particular passages of his Orations
tends to discourage such *cultus Angelorum* as the Church
has since his time sanctioned, I answer first that he is
led by his subject to contrast the Angelic creation with
our Lord the Creator; and thus, while extolling Him as
Supreme, he comes to speak with disparagement of
those who were no more than works of His hands. And
secondly, the idolatrous honour paid to Angels by the
heretical bodies at that time made unadvisable, or
created a prepossession against, what in itself was
allowable. Moreover, the Church, as divinely guided,
has not formulated her doctrines all at once, but has
taken in hand, first one, and then another. As to S.
Athanasius, if he seemingly disparages the Angels, it
is in order to exalt our Lord. He is arguing against
the Arians somewhat in this manner: "You yourselves
allow that the Son is the Creator, and, as such, the
object of worship; but, if He be the Creator, how can
He be a creature? how can He be only a higher kind
of Angel, if it was He who created Angels? If so, He
must have created Himself. Why, it is the very
enormity of the Gnostics, that they ascribe creative
power and pay divine honours to Angels; how are you
not as bad as they?" Athanasius does not touch the
question whether, as Angels and Saints according to

him are (*improprie*) gods (vid. next paragraph), so in a corresponding sense worship may (*improprie*) be paid to them.

¶ "The sacred writer, with us in view, says, 'O God, who is like unto Thee?' and though he calls those creatures who are partakers (μετόχους) of the Word gods, still those who partake are not the same as, or like, Him who is partaken. For works are made, and make nothing," ad Afros 7. "Not one of things which come-to-be is an efficient cause," ποιητικὸν αἴτιον, Orat. ii. § 21; *ibid.* § 2, iii. 14, and contr. Gent. 9 init. "Our reason rejects the idea that the Creator should be a creature, for creation is by the Creator." Hil. Trin. xii. 5. πῶς δύναται τὸ κτιζόμενον κτίζειν; ἢ πῶς ὁ κτίζων κτίζεται; Athan. ad Afros, 4 fin. Vid. also Serap. i. 24, 6, iii. 4; Orat. ii. 21.

¶ As to Angels, vid. August. de Civ. Dei xii. 24; de Trin. iii. 13—18; Damasc. F. O. ii. 3; Cyril in Julian. ii. p. 62. "For neither would the Angels," says Athan., Orat. ii. § 21, "since they too are creatures, be able to frame, though Valentinus, and Marcion, and Basilides think so, and you are their copyists; nor will the sun, as being a creature, ever make what is not into what is; nor will man fashion man, nor stone devise stone, nor wood give growth to wood.' The Gnostics who attributed creation to Angels are alluded to in Orat. iii. 12; Epiph. Hær. 52, 53, 62, &c.; Theodor. Hær. i. 1 and 3. They considered the Angels consubstantial with our Lord, as the Manichees after them, seemingly from holding the doctrine of emanation. Vid. Bull. D. F. N. ii. 1, § 2, and

Beausobre, Manich. iii. 8. "If, from S. Paul saying
better than the Angels, they should therefore insist
that his language is that of comparison, and that
comparison in consequence implies oneness of kind, so
that the Son is of the nature of Angels, they will in
the first place incur the disgrace of rivalling and repeat-
ing what Valentinus held, and Carpocrates, and those
other heretics, of whom the former said that the Angels
were one in kind with the Christ, and Carpocrates that
Angels are framers of the world." Orat. i. § 56.

¶ As to the sins incident to created natures, all
creatures, says Athanasius, depend for their abidance
in good upon the Word, and without Him have no
stay. Thus, ad Afros 7, after, as in Orat. i. § 49,
speaking of ἀγγέλων μὲν παραβάντων, τοῦ δὲ Ἀδὰμ
παρακούσαντος, he says, "no one would deny that
things which are made are open to change (Cyril. in
Joan. v. 2), and since the Angels and Adam trans-
gressed, and all showed their need of the grace of the
Word, what is thus mutable cannot be like to the immutable God, nor the creature to the Creator." On the
subject of the sins of Angels, vid. Huet. Origen. ii. 5;
Petav. Dogm. t. iii. p. 73; Dissert. Bened. in Cyr.
Hier. iii. 5; Nat. Alex. Hist. Æv. i. Dissert. 7.

¶ So far Athanasius says nothing which the Church
has not taught up to this day; but he goes further.

"No one," he says, Orat. iii. § 12, "would pray
to receive aught from ' God and the Angels,' or from
any other creature, nor would he say ' May God and
the Angel give thee.'" Vid. Basil de Sp. S. c. 13
(t. ii. p. 585). Also, "There were men," says

Chrysostom on Col. ii., "who said, We ought not to have access to God through Christ, but through Angels, for the former is beyond our power. Hence the Apostle everywhere insists. on his teaching concerning Christ, 'through the blood of the Cross,'" &c. And Theodoret on Col. iii. 17, says : "Following this rule, the Synod of Laodicea, with a view to cure this ancient disorder, passed a decree against the praying to Angels, and leaving our Lord Jesus Christ." "All supplication, prayer, intercession, and thanksgiving is to be addressed to the Supreme God, through the High Priest who is above all Angels, the Living Word and God. . . . But Angels we may not fitly call upon, since we have not obtained a knowledge of them more than human." Origen. contr. Cels. v. 4, 5. Vid. also for similar statements Voss. de Idolatr. i. 9. These extracts are here made in illustration of the particular passage of Athan. to which they are appended, not as if they contain the whole doctrine of Origen, Theodoret, or S. Chrysostom, on the *cultus Angelorum.* Of course they are not really inconsistent with such texts as - 1 Tim. v. 21, Eccl. v. 4.

¶ Elsewhere Athan. says that "the Angel who delivered Jacob from all evil," from whom he asked a blessing, was not a created Angel, but the Angel of great Counsel, the Word of God Himself, Orat. iii. § 12; but he says shortly afterwards that the Angel that appeared to Moses in the Bush "was not the God of Abraham, but what was seen was an Angel, and in the Angel God spoke," § 14 ; vid. Monitum Bened. in Hilar. Trin. lib. iv. Thus Athan. does not differ from Augustine, vid. infr. art. *Scripture Passages,* No. i., p. 266.

¶ As to the word "worship," as denoting the *cultus Angelorum*, worship is a very wide term, and has obviously more senses than one. Thus we read in one passage of Scripture that "all the congregation . . . worshipped the Lord, and *the king* " [David]. S. Augustine, as S. Athanasius, Orat. ii. § 23, makes the characteristic of divine worship to consist in sacrifice. " No one would venture to say that sacrifice was due to any but God. Many are the things taken from divine worship and transferred to human honours, either through excessive humility or mischievous adulation; yet without giving us the notion that those to whom they were transferred were not men. And these are said to be honoured and venerated; or were worshipped, if much is heaped upon them; but whoever thought that sacrifice was to be offered, except to Him whom the sacrificer knew or thought or pretended to be God?" August. de Civ. Dei, x. 4. " Whereas you have called so many dead men gods, why are ye indignant with us, who do but honour, not deify the martyrs, as being God's martyrs and loving servants? . . . That they even offered libations to the dead, ye certainly know, who venture on the use of them by night contrary to the laws. . . . But we, O men, assign neither sacrifices nor even libations to the martyrs, but we honour them as men divine and divinely beloved." Theodor. contr. Gent. viii. pp. 908—910. It is observable that incense was burnt before the Imperial Statues, vid. art. *Imperial Titles*. Nebuchadnezzar offered an oblation to Daniel, after the interpretation of his dream.

ANTICHRIST.

As the early Christians, in obedience to our Lord's words, were ever looking out for His second coming, and for the signs of it, they associated it with every prominent disturbance, external or internal, which interfered with the peace of the Church; with every successive persecution, heretical outbreak, or schism which befell it. In this, too, they were only following the guidance of our Lord and His Apostles, who told them that "great tribulation," "false prophets," disunion, and "apostasy" and at length "Antichrist," should be His forerunners. Also, they recollected S. John's words, "Omnis Spiritus qui solvit Jesum, ex Deo non est, et hic est Antichristus de quo audistis, quoniam, venit," &c. Hence "forerunner of Antichrist" was the received epithet employed by them to designate the successive calamities and threatenings of evil, which one after another spread over the face of the *orbis terrarum*.

¶ Thus we have found S. Athanasius calling Arianism "the forerunner of Antichrist," Syn. § 5, πρόδρομος, præcursor; vid. also Orat. i. § § 1 and 7; Ap. c. Ar. fin.; Hist. Ar. 77; Cyr. Cat. xv. 9; Basil. Ep. 264; Hilar. Aux. 5, no distinction being carefully drawn between the apostasy and the Antichrist. Constantius is called Antichrist by Athan. Hist. Arian. 67; his acts are the προοίμιον καὶ παρασκευή of Antichrist, Hist. Arian. 70, fin., 71 and 80. Constantius is the image, εἰκὼν, of Antichrist, 74 and 80, and shows the likeness, ὁμοίωμα, of the malignity of Antichrist, 75. Vid. also 77. "Let Christ be expected, for Antichrist is in possession." Hilar. contr. Const. init., also 5. Speaking of Auxentius, the Arian Bishop of Milan, he says, "Of one thing I warn you, beware of Antichrist; it is ill that . . . your veneration for God's Church lies in houses and edifices. . . . Is there any doubt that Antichrist is to sit in these? Mountains, and woods, and lakes, and prisons, and pits are to me more safe," &c., Contr. Auxent. 12. Lucifer. calls Constantius "præcursor Antichristi," p. 89; possessed with the spirit of Antichrist, p. 219; friend of Antichrist, p. 259. Vid. also Basil, Ep. 264. Again, S. Jerome, writing against Jovinian, says that he who teaches that there are no differences of rewards is Antichrist, ii. 21. S. Leo, alluding to 1 John iv. 10, calls Nestorius and Eutyches, "Antichristi præcursores," Ep. 75, p. 1022; again, Antichrist is whoever withstood what the Church has once settled, with an allusion to opposition to the see of S. Peter, Ep. 156, c. 2. Anastasius speaks of the ten horns of Monophysitism, Hodeg. 8 and 24; and calls Severus Antichrist, for usurping the judicial powers of the Church, ibid. p. 92. Vid. also Greg. I. Ep. vii. 33.

¶ The great passage of S. Paul about the ἀποστασία, 1 Tim. iv. 1, 2, is taken to apply to the Arians in Orat. i. § 8, cf. ad Ægypt. § 20, 21; but the Fathers more commonly refer it to the Oriental sects of the early centuries, who fulfilled one or other of those con-

ditions which it specifies. It is predicated of the
Marcionists by Clement, Strom. iii. 6. Of the Valentinians, Epiph. Hær. 31, 34. Of the Montanists and
others, ibid. 48, 8. Of the Saturnilians (according
to Huet), Origen in Matt. xiv. 16. Of apostolic
heretics, Cyril. Cat. iv. 27. Of Marcionites, Valentinians, and Manichees, Chrysost. de Virg. 5. Of
Gnostics and Manichees, Theod. Hær. ii. præf. Of .
Encratites, ibid. v. fin. Of Eutyches, Ep. Anon. 190
(apud Garner. Diss. v. Theod. p. 901). Pseudo-Justin
seems to consider it fulfilled in the Catholics of the
fifth century, as being Anti-pelagians, Quæst. 22;
vid. Bened. note in loc. Besides Athanasius, no early
author by whom it is referred to the Arians, occurs
to the writer of this, except S. Alexander's Letter ap.
Socr. i. 6; and, if he may hazard the conjecture, there
is much in that letter like Athan.'s own writing. Vid.
supr. art. *Alexander*.

APOSTLE.

" THE Apostle " is the usual title of S. Paul in antiquity, as " the Philosopher " at a later date is appropriated to Aristotle. " When ' the Apostle ' is mentioned," says S. Augustine, " if it is not specified which, Paul only is understood, because he is more celebrated from the number of his Epistles, and laboured more abundantly than all the rest," ad Bonifac. iii. 3. E.g. " And this is what *Peter* has said, ' that ye may be partakers in a divine nature ; ' as says also *the Apostle*, ' know ye not that ye are the Temple of God,' " &c. Orat. i. § 16. Vid. also Enc. supr. vol. i. p. 6 ; Decr. §§ 15 and 17. " The Apostle himself, the Doctor of the Gentiles," Syn. §§ 28 and 39. " John saying and the Apostle," Orat. i. § 47.

However, S. Peter also is called the Apostle, Orat. i. § 47.

ARIUS.

It is very difficult to gain a clear idea of the character of Arius. Athanasius speaks as if his theological song, or Thalia, was but a token of his personal laxity; and certainly the mere fact of his having written it seems incompatible with any remarkable seriousness and strictness. "He drew up his heresy on paper," Athan. says, "and imitating, as if on a festive occasion (ὡς ἐν θαλίᾳ) no grave writer, but the Egyptian Sotades, in the character of his music, he writes at great length," &c. De Syn. § 15. Again, Orat. i. §§ 2—5, he calls him the Sotadean Arius; and speaks of the "dissolute manners," and "the effeminate tone," and the "jests" of the Thalia; a poem which, he says shortly before, "is not even found among the more respectable Greeks, but among those only who sing songs over their wine, with noise and revel." Vid. also de Sent. D. 6. Constantine also, after the Ἄρες Ἄρειε, proceeds, ἐπισχέτω δέ σε ἡ γοῦν Ἀφροδίτης ὁμιλία. Epiph. Hær. 69, 9 fin. Socrates too says that "the character of the book was gross and dissolute." Hist. i. 9. The Arian Philostorgius tells us that "Arius wrote songs for the sea, and for the mill, and for the road, and set them to suitable music," Hist. ii. 2. It is remarkable that Athanasius should say the *Egyptian* Sotades, as again in Sent. D. 6. There were two Poets of the

name; one a writer of the Middle Comedy, Athen.
Deipn. vii. 11; but the other, who is here spoken of,
was a native of Maronea in Crete, according to Suidas
(in voc.), under the successors of Alexander, Athen.
xiv. 4. He wrote in Ionic metre, which was of infamous
name from the subjects to which he and others applied
it. Vid. Suid. ibid. Some read "Sotadicos" for
"Socraticos," Juv. Satir. ii. 10. Vid. also Martial,
Ep. ii. 86. The characteristic of the metre was the
recurrence of the same cadence, which virtually
destroyed the division into verses, Turneb. in Quinct.
i. 8, and thus gave the composition that lax and
slovenly air to which Athanasius alludes. Horace's
Ode, "Miserarum est neque amori," &c., is a specimen of
this metre, and some have called it Sotadic ; but Bentley
shows in loc. that Sotades wrote in the Ionic à majore,
and that his verse had somewhat more of system than
is found in the Ode of Horace. Athenæus implies that
all Ionic metres were called Sotadic, or that Sotades
wrote in various Ionic metres. The Church adopted
the Doric music, and forbade the Ionic and Lydian.
The name "Thalia" commonly belonged to convivial
songs; Martial contrasts the "lasciva Thalia" with
"carmina sanctiora," Epigr. vii. 17. Vid. Thaliarchus,
"the master of the feast," Horat. Od. i. 9. This would
be the more offensive among Christians in Athan.'s day,
in proportion to the keener sensibilities of the South,
and the more definite ideas which music seems to have
conveyed to their minds; and more especially in a case
where the metre Arius employed had obtained so
shocking a reputation, and was associated in the minds

of Christians with the deeds of darkness, in the midst
of which in those heathen times the Church lived and
bore her witness.

Such is Athan.'s report, but Constantine and Epiphanius speak of Arius in very different terms, yet each
in his own way, as the following extracts show. It is possible that Constantine is only declaiming, for his whole
invective is like a school exercise or fancy composition.
Constantine too had not seen Arius at the time of this
invective, which was prior to the Nicene Council, and
his account of him is inconsistent with itself, for he
also uses the very strong and broad language about
Arius quoted above. " Look then," he says, " look all
men, what words of lament he is now professing, being
held with the bite of the serpent; how his veins and
flesh are possessed with poison, and are in a ferment of
severe pain; how his whole body is wasted, and is all
withered and sad and pale and shaking, and fearfully
emaciated. How hateful to see, how filthy is his mass
of hair, how he is half dead all over, with failing eyes,
and bloodless countenance, and woe-begone! so that
all these things combining in him at once, frenzy,
madness, and folly, for the continuance of the complaint, have made thee wild and savage. But not
having any sense what bad plight he is in, he cries
out, ' I am transported with delight, and I leap and
skip for joy, and I fly:' and again, with boyish im-
petuosity, ' Be it so,' he says, ' we are lost.' " Harduin.
Conc. t. i. p. 457. Perhaps this strange account may
be taken to illustrate the words " mania " and " Ariomaniacs." S. Alexander too speaks of Arius's melan-

c 2

cholic temperament, μελαγχυλικοῖς ἡρμοσμένης δόξης κενῆς. Theod. Hist. i. 3, p. 741. S. Basil also speaks of the Eunomians as εἰς λαμπρὰν μελαγχολίαν παρενεχθέντας. Contr. Eun. ii. 24. Elsewhere he speaks of the Pneumatomachists as worse than μελαγχολῶντες. De Sp. S. 41.

Epiphanius's account of Arius is as follows :—" From elation of mind the old man swerved from the mark. He was in stature very tall, downcast in visage, with manners like a wily serpent, captivating to every guileless heart by that same crafty bearing. For ever habited in cloak and vest, he was pleasant of address, ever persuading souls and flattering; wherefore what was his very first work but to withdraw from the Church in one body as many as seven hundred women who professed virginity?" Hær. 69, 3. Arius is here said to have been tall; Athanasius, on the other hand, would appear to have been short, if we may so interpret Julian's indignant description of him, μηδὲ ἀνὴρ, ἀλλ' ἀνθρωπίσκος εὐτελὴς, "not even a man, but a common little fellow." Ep. 51. Yet S. Gregory Nazianzen speaks of him as "high in prowess and humble in spirit, mild, meek, full of sympathy, pleasant in speech, more pleasant in manners, *angelical in person*, more angelical in mind, serene in his rebukes, instructive in his praises," &c. &c. Orat. 21. 9. There is no proof that S. Gregory had ever seen him.

THE ARIANS.

1. *Their Ethical Characteristics.*

WHEN we consider how grave and reverent was the temper of the Ante-Nicene Church, how it concealed its sacred mysteries from the world at large, how writers such as Tertullian make the absence of such a strict discipline the very mark of heresy, and that a vulgar ostentation and profaneness was the prominent charge brought against the heretic Paul of Samosata, Bishop of Antioch, we need no more ready evidence or note against the Arian party than our finding that the ethical character, which is in history so intimately associated with Paul and the heretics generally of the first three centuries, is the badge of Arianism also.

1. Athan. in various passages of his Theological Treatises refers to it, and it is one of the reasons why he speaks so familiarly of their "madness." "What pressed on us so much," he says of the Councils of Seleucia and Ariminum, "was that the whole world should be thrown into confusion, and those who then bore the profession of ecclesiastics should run about far and near, seeking forsooth how best to learn to believe in our Lord Jesus Christ. Certainly, if they were believers already, they would not have been seeking, as though they were not. And to the catechumens, this was no small scandal; but to the heathen, it was

something more than common, and even furnished broad merriment, that Christians, as if waking out of sleep at this time of day, should be making out how they were to believe concerning Christ, while their professed clergy, though claiming deference from their flocks, as teachers, were unbelievers on their own showing, in that they were seeking what they had not." Syn. § 2.

The heathen Ammianus supports this complaint in the well-known passage which tells of "the troops of Bishops hurrying to and fro at the public expense," and "the Synods, in their efforts to bring over the religion everywhere to their side, being the ruin of the posting establishments." Hist. xxi. 16. Again, "The spectacle proceeded to that pitch of indecency," says Eusebius, "that at length, in the very midst of the theatres of the unbelievers, the solemn matters of divine teaching were subjected to the basest mockery." In Vit. Const. ii. 61.

Also Athan., after speaking of the Arian tenet that our Lord was once on His probation and might have fallen, says, "This is what they do not shrink from conversing about in full market." Orat. i. § 37. And again, "When they commenced this heresy, they used to go about with dishonest crafty phrases which they had got together; nay, up to this time some of them, when they fall in with boys in the market-place, question them, not out of divine Scripture, but thus, as if bursting out with *the abundance of their heart*:—' He who is, did He, from Him who is, make him who·was not, or him who was?'" Orat. i. § 22.

Alexander speaks of the interference, even by legal process, against himself, of disobedient women, δι' ἐντυχίας γυναικαρίων ἀτάκτων ἃ ἠπάτησαν, and of the busy and indecent gadding about of the younger, ἐκ τοῦ περιτροχάζειν πᾶσαν ἀγυιὰν ἀσμένως. Ap. Theod. Hist. i. 3, p. 730; also p. 747; also of the men's buffoon conversation, p. 731. Socrates says that "in the Imperial Court the officers of the bedchamber held disputes with the women, and in the city in every house there was a war of dialectics." Hist. ii. 2. This mania raged especially in Constantinople; and S. Gregory Nazianzen speaks of these women as "Jezebels in as thick a crop as hemlock in a field." Orat. 35. 3. He speaks of the heretics as "aiming at one thing only, how to make good or refute points of argument," making "every market-place resound with their words, and spoiling every entertainment with their trifling and offensive talk." Orat. 27. 2. The most remarkable testimony of the kind, though not concerning Constantinople, is given by S. Gregory Nyssen, and often quoted, "Men of yesterday and the day before, mere mechanics, off-hand dogmatists in theology, servants too and slaves that have been flogged, runaways from servile work, are solemn with us and philosophical about things incomprehensible. . . . With such the whole city is full; its smaller gates, forums, squares, thoroughfares; the clothes-venders, the money-lenders, the victuallers. Ask about pence, and he will discuss the Generate and Ingenerate; inquire the price of bread, he answers, Greater is the Father, and the Son is subject; say that a bath would suit you, and he

defines that the Son is made out of nothing." t. 2, p.
898. (de Deitate Fil. &c.)

Arius set the example of all this in his Thalia;
Leontius, Eudoxius, and Aetius, in various ways,
followed it faithfully.

2. Another characteristic of the Arian party was
their changeableness, insincerity, and want of principle (vid. *Chameleons*). This was owing to their fear
of the Emperor and of the Christian populations, which
hindered them speaking out; also, to the difficulty of
keeping their body together in opinion, and the necessity they were in to deceive one party and to please
another, if they were to maintain their hold upon the
Church. Athanasius observes on their reluctance to
speak out, challenging them to present "the heresy
naked," de Sent. Dionys. 2, *init.* "No one," he says
elsewhere, "puts a light under a bushel; let them show
the world their heresy naked." Ad. Ep. Æg. 18. Vid.
ibid. 10. In like manner, Basil says that though Arius
was, in faith, really like Eunomius (contr. Eunom.
i. 4), Aetius his master was the first to teach openly
(φανερῶς) that the Father's substance was unlike,
ἀνόμοιος, the Son's. Ibid. i. 1. Epiphanius too, Hær.
76, p. 949, seems to say that the elder Arians held
the divine generation in a sense in which Aetius did
not; that is, they were not boldly consistent and definite
as he was. Athan. de Decret. § 7, enumerates some of
the attempts of the Arians to find some theory short of
orthodoxy, yet short of that extreme heresy, on the
other hand, which they felt ashamed to avow.

The Treatise *De Synodis*, above translated, supplies

abundant proof of their artifices and shuffling. (Vid. art. *Hypocrites.*)

3. Cruelty, as in the instance of George of Cappadocia and Macedonius of Constantinople, is another charge which falls heavily on both Arians and Semi-Arians. "In no long time," Athan. says, anticipating their known practice, de Decret. § 2, "they will be turning to outrage." As to the Council of Tyre, A.D. 335, he asks, Apol. contr. Arian. § 8, "How venture they to call that a Council in which a Count presided, and an executioner was present, and a registrar [or jailer] introduced us instead of the deacons of the Church?" Vid. also § 10 and 45; Orat. ii. § 43; Ep. Encycl. § 5. Against employing violence in religious matters, vid. Hist. Arian. § 33, 67. (Hil. ad Const. i. 2.) On the other hand, he observes, that at Nicæa, "it was not necessity which drove the judges to" their decision, "but all vindicated the truth from deliberate purpose." Ad Ep. Æg. 13.

4. They who did not scruple to use force were consistent in their use of bribes also. S. Athanasius speaks of them as δωρόδοκοι, and of the κέρδος τῆς φιλοχρηματίας which influenced them, and of the προστασίας φίλων. Orat. i. §§ 8, 10, and 53; also ii. § 43.

And so S. Hilary speaks of the exemptions from taxes which Constantius granted to the Clergy as a bribe for them to Arianize: "You concede taxes as Cæsar, thereby to invite Christians to a denial; you remit what is your own, that we may lose what is God's," contr. Const. 10. Again, he speaks of

Constantius as "hostem blandientem, qui non dorsa cædit, sed ventrem palpat, non proscribit ad vitam, sed ditat in mortem, non caput gladio desecat, sed animam auro occidit." Ibid. 5. Vid. Coustant. in loc. Liberius says the same, Theod. Hist. ii. 13. And S. Gregory Naz. speaks of φιλοχρύσους μᾶλλον ἢ φιλοχρίστους. Orat. 21. 21. It is true that, Ep. Æg. 22, Athan. contrasts the Arians with the Meletians in this respect, as if, unlike the latter, the Arians were not influenced by secular views. But there were, as was natural, two classes of men in the heretical party:—the fanatical class who began the heresy and were its real life, such as Arius, and afterwards the Anomœans, in whom mis-belief was a " mania ; " and the Eusebians, who cared little for a theory of doctrine or consistency of profession, compared with their own aggrandizement. With these must be included numbers who conformed to Arianism lest they should suffer temporal loss.

Athan; says, that after Eusebius (Nicomed.) had taken up the patronage of the heresy, " he made no pro-gress till he had gained the Court," Hist. Arian. 66, showing that it was an act of external power by which Arianism grew, not an inward movement in the Church, which indeed loudly protested against the Emperor's proceeding, &c. (Vid. *Catholic Church.*)

2. *The Arian Leaders.*

Arius himself refers his heresy to the teaching of Lucian, a presbyter of Antioch (Theod. Hist. i. 4 and

5), who seems to have been the head of a theological party, and a friend of Paulus the heretical Bishop, and out of communion during the time of three Bishops who followed. Eusebius of Nicomedia, who seems to have held the Arian tenets to their full extent, is claimed by Arius as his "fellow-Lucianist." Pronounced Arians also were the Lucianists Leontius and Eudoxius. Asterius, another of his pupils, did not go further than Semi-Arianism, without perhaps perfect consistency; nor did Lucian himself, if the Creed of the Dedication (A.D. 341) comes from him, as many critics have held. He died a martyr's death. (Vid. supr. vol. i. p. 96, Syn. § 23, and notes.)

Asterius is the foremost writer on the Arian side, on its start. He was by profession a sophist; he lapsed and sacrificed, as Athan. tells us, in the persecution of Maximian. His work in defence of the heresy was answered by Marcellus of Ancyra, to whom Eusebius of Cæsarea in turn replied. Athan. quotes or refers to it frequently in the treatises translated supr. Vid. Decr. § 8, 20; Syn. § 18—20; Orat. i. § 30, 31; ii. § 24. fin., 28, 37, 40; iii. § 2, 60; Nicen. 13, 28; Arim. 23 and 24; Disc. 47, 58, 60, 135, 139, 151, 155, 226, according to Bened. Ed., and according to this translation respectively. Asterius and Eusebius of Cæsarea seem to be Semi-Arians of the same level.

We must be on our guard against confusing the one Eusebius with the other. He of Nicomedia was an Arian, a man of the world, the head of the Arian party; he of Cæsarea was the historian to whom we are so much indebted—learned, moderate, liberal, the

private friend of Constantine, a Semi-Arian. (Vid.
infr., art. *Semi-Arianism* and *Eusebius*.)

The leading Arians at the time of the Nicenè Council,
besides Eusebius Nicom., were Narcissus, Patrophilus,
Maris, Paulinus, Theodotus, Athanasius of Nazarba,
and George (Syn. § 17).

Most of these original Arians were attacked in the
work of Marcellus which Eusebius (Cæsar.) answers.
" Now," says the Cæsarean Eusebius, " he replies to
Asterius, now to the great Eusebius," [of Nicomedia,]
" and then he turns upon that man of God, that indeed
thrice blessed person, Paulinus (of Tyre). Then he goes
to war with Origen. . . . Next he marches out against
Narcissus, and pursues the other Eusebius," i.e. himself.
" In a word, he counts for nothing all the Ecclesiastical
Fathers, being satisfied with no one but himself."
Contr. Marc. i. 4. Vid. art. *Marcellus*. There is little
to be said of Maris and Theodotus. Nazarba is more
commonly called Anazarbus, and is in Cilicia.

As is observed elsewhere, there were three parties
among the Arians from the first:—the Arians proper,
afterwards called Anomœans; the Semi-Arian reaction
from them; and the Court party, called Eusebians or
Acacians, from their leaders, Eusebius of Nicomedia
and Acacius of Cæsarea, which sometimes sided with
the Semi-Arians, sometimes with the Arians proper,
sometimes attempted a compromise of Scripture terms.
The six named by Athanasius as the chief movers in
the Bipartite Council of Seleucia and Ariminum, were
Ursacius, Valens, Germinius, Acacius, Eudoxius, and
Patrophilus. He numbers also among the Bishops at

Ariminum, Auxentius, Demophilus, and Caius. And at Seleucia, Uranius, Leontius, Theodotus, Evagrius, and George. Eusebius of Nicomedia was a kinsman of the Imperial family and tutor to Julian. He was, as has been already said, a fellow-disciple with Arius of Lucian. He was Bishop, first of Berytus, then of Nicomedia, and at length of Constantinople. He received Arius with open arms, on his expulsion from the Alexandrian Church, put himself at the head of his followers, corrected their polemical language, and used his great influence with Constantine and Constantius to secure the triumph of the heresy. He died about the year 343, and was succeeded in the political leadership of the Eusebians by Acacius and Valens.

George, whom Athanasius, Gregory Naz., and Socrates, call a Cappadocian, was born, according to Ammianus, in Epiphania of Cilicia, at a fuller's mill. He was appointed pork-contractor to the army, Syn. § 12, Hist. Arian. 75, Naz. Orat. 21. 16, and, being detected in defrauding the government, he fled to Egypt. Naz. Orat. 21. 16. How he became acquainted with the Eusebian party does not appear. Sozomen says he recommended himself to the see of Alexandria instead of Athan. by his zeal for Arianism and his τὸ δραστήριον; and Gregory calls him the hand of the heresy, as Acacius (?) was the tongue. Orat. 21. 21. He made himself so obnoxious to the Alexandrians, that in the reign of Julian he was torn to pieces in a rising of the heathen populace. He had laid capital informations against many persons of the place, and he tried to persuade Constantius that, as the successor of Alexander its founder, he was proprietor of the soil and had a claim upon the houses built on it. Ammian. xxii. 11. Epiphanius tells us, Hær. 76, 1, that he made a monopoly of the nitre of Egypt, farmed the beds of papyrus, and the salt lakes, and even contrived a profit from the undertakers. His atrocious cruelties to the Catholics are well known. Yet he seems to have collected a choice library of philosophers and poets and Christian writers, which Julian seized on. Vid. Pithæus in loc. Ammian.; also Gibbon, ch. 23.

Acacius was a pupil of Eusebius of Cæsarea, and succeeded him in the see of Cæsarea in Palestine. He inherited his library, and is ranked by S. Jerome among the most learned commentators on Scripture. Both Sozomen and Philostorgius speak, though in different ways, of his great talents. He seems to have taken up, as his weapon in controversy, the objection that the ὁμοούσιον was not a word of Scripture, which is in-directly suggested by Eusebius (Cæsar.) in his letter to his people, supr. vol. i. p. 59. His formula was the vague ὅμοιον (like), as the Anomœan was ἀνόμοιον (unlike), as the Semi-Arian was ὁμοιούσιον (like in sùb-stance), and the orthodox ὁμοούσιον (one in substance). However, like most of his party, his changes of opinion were considerable. At one time, after professing the κατὰ πάντα ὅμοιον, and even the τῆς αὐτῆς οὐσίας, Soz. iv. 22, he at length avowed the Anomœan doctrine. Ultimately, after Constantius's death, he subscribed the Nicene formula. Vid. "Arians of the Fourth Century," p. 275, 4th ed.

Valens, Bishop of Mursa, and Ursacius, Bishop of

Singidon, are generally mentioned together. They were pupils of Arius, and, as such, are called young by Athan. ad Episc. Æg. 7; and in Apol. contr. Arian. § 13, "young in years and mind;" by Hilary, ad Const. i. 5, "imperitis et improbis duobus *adolescentibus*;" and by the Council of Sardica, ap. Hilar. Fragm. ii. 12. They first appear at the Council of Tyre, A.D. 335. The Council of Sardica deposed them; in 349 they publicly retracted their charges against Athanasius, who has preserved their letters. Apol. contr. Arian. 58. Valens was the more prominent of the two; he was a favourite Bishop of Constantius, an extreme Arian in his opinions, and the chief agent at Ariminum in effecting the lapse of the Latin Fathers.

Germinius was made Bishop of Sirmium by the Eusebians in 351, instead of Photinus, whom they deposed for a kind of Sabellianism. However, in spite of his Arianism, he was obliged in 358 to sign the Semi-Arian formula of Ancyra; yet he was an active Eusebian again at Ariminum. At a later date he approached very nearly to Catholicism.

Eudoxius is said to have been a pupil of Lucian, Arius's master, though the dates scarcely admit of it. Eustathius, Catholic Bishop of Antioch, whom the Eusebians subsequently deposed, refused to admit him into orders. Afterwards he was made Bishop of Germanicia in Syria, by his party. He was present at the Council of Antioch in 341, the Dedication, vid. not. supr. vol. i. p. 94, and he carried into the West, in 345, the fifth Confession, called the Long, μακρόστιχος, Syn. § 26. He afterwards passed in succession

to the sees of Antioch and Constantinople, and baptised
the Emperor Valens into the Arian confession.

Patrophilus was one of the original Arian party, and
took share in all their principal acts, but there is nothing very distinctive in his history. Sozomen assigns
to the above six Bishops, of whom he was one, the
scheme of dividing the Council into two, Hist. iv. 16;
Valens undertaking to manage the Latins, Acacius the
Greeks.

There were two Arian Bishops of Milan of the name
of Auxentius, but little is known of them besides. S.
Hilary wrote against the elder; the other came into
collision with S. Ambrose. Demophilus, Bishop of
Berea, was one of those who carried the "Long Confession" into the West, though Athan. only mentions
Eudoxius, Martyrius, and Macedonius, Syn. § 26. He
was afterwards claimed by Aetius, as agreeing with him.
Of Caius, an Illyrian Bishop, nothing is known except
that he sided throughout with the Arian party.

Euzoius was one of the Arian Bishops of Antioch,
and baptised Constantius before his death. He had
been excommunicated with Arius in Egypt and at
Nicæa, and was restored with him to the Church at the
Council of Jerusalem. He succeeded at Antioch S.
Meletius, who, on being placed in that see by the Arians,
professed orthodoxy, and was forthwith banished by
them.

The leaders of the Semi-Arians, if they are on the
rise of the heresy to be called a party, were in the first
instance Asterius and Eusebius of Cæsarea, of whom I
have already spoken, and shall speak again. Semi-

Arianism was at first a shelter and evasion for pure Arianism, or at a later date it was a reaction from the Anomœan enormities. The leading Semi-Arians of the later date were Basil, Mark, Eustathius, Eleusius, Meletius, and Macedonius. Basil, who is considered their head, wrote against Marcellus, and was placed by the Arians in his see; he has little place in history till the date of the Council of Sardica, which deposed him. Constantius, however, stood his friend till the beginning of the year 360, when Acacius supplanted him in the Imperial favour, and he was banished into Illyricum. This was a month or two later than the date at which Athan. wrote his first draught or edition of his *De Synodis*. He was condemned upon charges of tyranny and the like, but Theodoret speaks highly of his correctness of life, and Sozomen of his learning and eloquence. Vid. Theod. Hist. ii. 20; Soz. ii. 33. A very little conscientiousness, or even decency of manners, would put a man in strong relief with the great Arian party which surrounded the Court, and a very great deal would not have been enough to secure him against their unscrupulous slanders. Athan. reckons him among those who " are not far from accepting even the phrase, ' One in substance,' in what he has written concerning the faith," vid. Syn. § 41. A favourable account of him will be found in " The Arians," &c., ed. 4, p. 300, &c., where vid. also a notice of the others. Of Macedonius little is known except his cruelties. Vid. " The Arians," p. 311.

The Anomœans, with whose history this work is scarcely concerned, had for their leaders Aetius and

Eunomius. Of these Aetius was the first to carry out Arianism in its pure logical form, as Eunomius was its principal apologist. He was born in humble life, and was at first a practitioner in medicine. After a time he became a pupil of the Arian Paulinus; then the guest of Athanasius of Nazarba; then the pupil of Leontius of Antioch, who ordained him deacon, and afterwards deposed him. This was in 350. In 351 he seems to have held a dispute with Basil of Ancyra, at Sirmium, as did Photinus; in the beginning of 360 he was formally condemned in that Council of Constantinople which confirmed the Creed of Ariminum, and at the time when Eudoxius had been obliged to anathematise his confession of faith. This was at the time Athan. wrote the *De Syn.*

3. *Arian Tenets and Reasonings.*

¶ The idea of Sonship includes in it two main relations viewed as regards paternity, non-priority of existence and community of nature. As used in theology, it is an analogous and indirect illustration (vid. *Illustrations*) of the Divine Truth which is the cardinal doctrine of Revelation, and what has to be determined is the special aspect under which we are intended to view it. For instance, it may be argued that, a son being junior in age to his father, and having a beginning, our Lord is not eternal, but a creature; or on the contrary, as the Catholic Church, as following Scripture, has ever taught, that, as the Son belongs to God's very essence and being, therefore, if God is from eternity uncreate, so is He.

¶ As God created the world out of nothing by an external, so He gave birth to the Son out of Himself by an internal; and if this divine generation be, as it is, incomprehensible, so also confessedly is the divine creation.

¶ The Arians refused to our Lord the name of God, except in the sense in which they called Him Word and Wisdom, not as denoting His nature and essence, but as epithets really belonging to the Supreme Being alone or to His attributes, though from grace or by privilege transferred by Him in an improper sense to the creature. In this sense the Son could claim to be called God, but in no other.

¶ The main argument of the Arians was that our Lord was a Son, and *therefore* was not eternal, but of a substance which had a beginning. With this Arius started in his dispute with Alexander. "Arius, a man not without dialectic skill, thinking that the Bishop was introducing the doctrine of Sabellius the Libyan, out of contention fell off into the opinion diametrically opposite, ... and he says, '*If* the Father begot the Son, he that was begotten had a beginning of existence; and from this it is plain that once the Son was not; and it follows of necessity that He had His subsistence out of nothing.'" Socr. i. 5. Accordingly, Athanasius says (in substance) early in his Decr., "Having argued with them as to the meaning of their own selected term, 'Son,' let us go on to others, which on their very face make for us, such as Word, Wisdom, &c."

¶ In what sense then was "Son" to be predicated of the Divine Nature? The Catholics said that the true

meaning of the word was consubstantiality (co-essenti-
ality) with the Father, whereas the point of posteriority
to the Father depended on a condition, *time*, which
could not exist in the instance of God.

¶ But the Arians persisted, maintaining that a son
has his origin of existence from his father; what has
an origin has a beginning; what has a beginning
is not from eternity; what is not from eternity is not
God; forgetting, first, that origination and beginning
are not convertible terms, and that the idea of a beginning is not bound up with the idea of an origin; and
secondly, that a son not only has his origin of existence
from his father, but also his nature, and all that is
proper to his nature.

¶ The Arians went on to maintain that to suppose a
true Son, was to think of God irreverently, as implying division, change, composition, &c. The Catholics
replied that the notion of materiality was quite as
foreign from the Divine Essence as time, and as a
Divine Sonship could be eternal, in like manner
it implied neither composition nor development,
συμβεβηκὸς, περιβολή or προβολή.

¶ The Arians, moreover, argued in behalf of their
characteristic tenet from the inferiority necessarily
involved in the very idea of a Son. But since He was
distinct from His Father, and inferior, He was not God;
and, if not God, then He was created, even though a
Son. Sonship was a mere quality or characteristic
bestowed upon a creature. The Catholics, in answer,
denied that a son was in his *nature* inferior to his father;
just the reverse; and the question here simply was about

our Lord's nature, whether it was divine, whether He was of one, of the same, nature with the Father.

¶ Though the Arians would not allow to Catholics that our Lord was Son *by nature*, and maintained that the word implied a *beginning of existence*, they were unwilling to say that He was Son merely in the sense in which we are sons, though, as Athan. contends, they necessarily tended to this conclusion, as soon as they receded from the Catholic view. Thus Arius said that He was a creature, " but not as one of the creatures." Orat. ii. § 19. Valens at Ariminum said the same. Jerom. adv. Lucifer. 18. Hilary says, that, not daring directly to deny that He was God, the Arians merely asked " whether He was a Son." De Trin. viii. 3.

¶ If once they could be allowed to deny our Lord's proper divinity, they cared not what high titles they heaped upon Him in order to cloak over their heresy, and to calm the indignation and alarm which it roused ; nay, in the case of many of the Semi-Arians, in order to hide the logical consequences of their misbelief from themselves. They did not like to call our Lord barely a creature ; certainly the political party did not, who had to carry the Emperor with them, and, if possible, the laity. Anyhow, in their preaching He was the first of creatures ; more than a creature, because a son, though they could not say what was meant by a son, as distinct from a creature : and so far they did in fact confess a mystery ; that is, the Semi-Arians, such as Eusebius, as shown in a passage quoted in art. *Son ;* though Arius and Arians proper, and the Anomœans, who spoke out, and had no fear of the Imperial Court, avowed their belief that our Lord, like other creatures, was capable of falling. However, as represented by their Councils and Creeds, they readily called Him "a creature not as other creatures, an offspring not as other offsprings," the primeval and sole work of God, the Creator, and created in order to create, the one Mediator, the one Priest, God of the world, Image of the Most Perfect, the Mystical Word and Wisdom of the Highest, and, as expressive of all this, the Only begotten.

¶ " What use is it," says Athan., " to pretend that He is a creature and not a creature? for though ye shall say, Not as ' one of the creatures,' I will prove this sophism of yours to be a poor one. For still ye pronounce Him to be one of the creatures; and whatever a man might say of the other creatures, such ye hold concerning the Son. For is any one of the creatures just what another is, that ye should predicate this of the Son as some prerogative?" Orat. ii. § 19. And so S. Ambrose, "Quæ enim creatura non sicut alia creatura non est? Homo non ut Angelus, terra non ut cœlum." De Fid. i. n. 130; and a similar passage in Nyss. contr. Eun. iii. p. 132, 3.

¶ The question between Catholics and Arians was whether our Lord was a true Son, or only called Son. " Since they whisper something about Word and Wisdom as only names of the Son," &c. ὀνόματα μόνον, Decr. § 16. " The title of Image too is not a token of a similar substance, but His name only," Orat. i. § 21 ; and so ii. § 38, where τοῖς ὀνόμασι is synonymous with κατ ἐπίνοιαν, as Sent. D. 22, vid. also ibid. § 39 ; Orat.

iii. § 11, 18; "not named Son, but ever Son," iv. § 24, fin.; Ep. Æg. 16. "We call Him so, and mean truly what we say; they say it, but do not confess it." Chrysost. in Act. Hom. 33, 4. Vid. also νόθοις ὥσπερ ὀνόμασι, Cyril. de Trin. ii. p. 418. "Non hæc nuda nomina," Ambros. de Fid. i. 17. Yet, though the Arians denied the reality of the Sonship, so it was that since Sabellianism went beyond them, as denying the divine Sonship in any sense, Orat. iv. 2, they were able to profess that they believed that our Lord was "true Son." E.g., this is professed by Arius, Syn. § 16; by Euseb. in Marc. pp. 19, 35, 161; by Asterius, Orat. ii. § 37; by Palladius and Secundianus in the Council of Aquileia ap. Ambros. Opp. t. 2, p. 791 (ed. Bened.); by Maximinus ap. August. contr. Max. i. 6. As to their sense of "real," it was no more than the sense in which Athan. uses the word of us, when he says υἱοποιούμεθα ἀληθῶς.

¶ When the Nicene controversialists maintained, on the contrary, that He was "true God," because He was "of true God," as the Creed speaks (vid. art. Son); of one nature with God as the offspring of man is of one nature with man, and of one essence as well as of one nature, because God is numerically one, the Arians in answer denied that, by reason of His being true Son therefore He was true God. They said that in order to be a true Son it was sufficient to partake of the Father's nature, that is, to have a certain portion of divinity, μετουσία; this all holy beings had, and without it they could not be holy; of this S. Peter speaks; but as this participation of the divine nature does not make holy beings who possess it God, neither is the Son God, though He be Son κυρίως καὶ ἀληθῶς. And it must be granted that the words κυρίως and ἀληθῶς are applied by the Fathers themselves to the sonship conveyed in the gifts of regeneration and santification. (Arts. *Father* and *Grace.*)

¶ The Catholics would reply that it was not a question of the use of terms: anyhow, to have a μετουσία of divinity, as creatures have, is not to have the divine οὐσία, as our Lord has. No μετουσία is a proper *gennesis.* "When God is *wholly* partaken, this," says Athanasius, and we may add, this only, "is equivalent to saying He begets." In this sense Augustine says, "'As the Father has life in Himself, so hath He given also to the Son to have life in Himself,' *not by participating,* but *in* Himself. For we men have not life in ourselves, but in our God. But that Father, who has life in Himself, begat a Son such, as to have life in Himself, not to become partaker of life, but *to be Himself life; and of that life to make us partakers.*" Serm. 127, de Verb. Evang. 9. It was plain, then, that, though the Arians professed to accept the word "Son" in its first and true sense, they did not understand it in its literal fulness, but in only a portion or aspect of its true sense, that is, figuratively.

¶ Hence it stands in the Nicene Creed, "from the Father, *that is,* from the substance of the Father." Vid. Eusebius's Letter (Decr. App.). According to the received doctrine of the Church, all rational beings, and in one sense all beings whatever, are "from God," over and above the fact of their creation; and of this truth the Eusebians made use to deny our Lord's proper divinity. Athan. lays down elsewhere that nothing continues in consistence and life, except from a participation of the Word, which is to be considered a gift from Him, additional to that of creation, and separable in idea from it. Vid. art. *Grace.* Thus he says that " the all-powerful and all-perfect, Holy Word of the Father, pervading all things, and developing everywhere His power, and illuminating all things visible and invisible, gathers them within Himself and knits them in one, leaving nothing destitute of His power, but quickening and preserving all things and through all, and each by itself, and the whole altogether." Contr. Gent. 42. Again, " God *not only* made us of nothing, *but also* vouchsafed to us a life according to God, *by the grace of the Word.* But men, turning from things eternal to the things of corruption at the devil's counsel, have brought on themselves the corruption of death, who were, as I said, *by nature corrupted,* but by *the grace of the participation (μετουσίας) of the Word,* would have escaped their natural state, had they remained good." Incarn. 5. Man thus considered is, in his first estate, a son of God and born of God, or, to use the term which occurs so frequently in the Arian controversy, in the number, not only of the creatures, but of *things generate, γενητά.* This was the sense in which the Arians said that our Lord was Son of God ; whereas, as Athan. says, " things generate, *being works* (δημιουργήματα,) cannot be called generate, except so far as, *after* their making, they partake of the begotten Son, and are therefore *said* to have been generated also; not at all in their own *nature*, but because of their participation of the Son in the Spirit." Orat. i. 56. The question then was, as to the *distinction* of the Son's divine generation over that of holy men; and the Catholics answered that He was ἐξ οὐσίας, from the substance of God; not by participation of grace, not by resemblance, not in any limited sense, but really and simply from Him, and therefore by an internal divine act. Vid. Decr. § 22.

¶ The Arians availed themselves of certain texts as objections, argued keenly and plausibly from them, and would not be driven from them. Orat. ii. § 18; Epiph. Hær. 69, 15. Or rather they took some words of Scripture, and made their own deductions from them; viz., " Son," " made," " exalted," &c. " Making their private impiety as if a rule, they misinterpret all the divine oracles by it." Orat. i. § 52. Vid. also Epiph. Hær. 76. 5, fin. Hence we hear so much of their θρυλληταὶ φωναὶ, λέξεις, ἔπη, ῥητά, sayings in general circulation, which were commonly founded on some particular text; e.g., Orat. i. § 22, " amply providing themselves with words of craft, they used to go about, &c." περιήρχοντο. Vid. vol. i. p. 29, note. Also ἄνω καὶ κάτω περιφέροντες, De Decr. § 13; τῷ ῥήτῳ τεθρυλλήκασι τὰ πανταχοῦ, Orat. ii. § 18; τὸ πολυθρύλλητον σόφισμα, Basil. contr. Eunom. ii. 14; τὴν πολυθρύλλητον διαλεκτικὴν, Nyssen contr. Eun. iii. p. 125; τὴν θρυλλουμένην ἀπορροήν, Cyril. Dial. iv. p. 505; τὴν πολυθρυλλητὸν φωνὴν, Socr. ii. 43.

¶ Eusebius's letter to Euphration, mentioned Syn. § 17, illustrates their sharp and shallow logic—" If they

co-exist, how shall the Father be Father and the Son
Son ; or how the One first, the Other second ? and the
One ingenerate and the Other generate ? " Acta Conc.
7, p. 1015, Ed. Ven. 1729. Hence Arius, in his Letter
to Eusebius Nic., complains that Alexander says, ἀεὶ ὁ
θεὸς, ἀεὶ ὁ υἱός· ἅμα πατὴρ, ἅμα υἱός. Theod. Hist.
i. 4. "Then their profaneness goes farther," says
Athan. ; Orat. i. § 14. "'If it never was, that the Son
was not,' say they, 'but He is eternal, and co-exists
with the Father, call Him no more the Father's Son,
but brother.'" As the Arians here object that the
First and Second Persons of the Holy Trinity are
ἀδελφοὶ, so did they say the same in the course of the
controversy of the Second and Third. Vid. Athan.
Serap. i. 15 ; iv. 2.

¶ "They contend that the Son and the Father are
not in such wise One or Like as the Church preaches,
but . . . they say, since what the Father wills, the
Son wills also, in all respects concordant, . . . therefore it is that He and the Father are one." Orat. iii. § 10.

¶ "The Arians reply, 'So are the Son and the Father
One, and so is the Father in the Son, and the Son in
the Father, as we too may become one in Him.'"
Orat. iii. § 17.

¶ In the Arian Creed of Potamius, Bishop of Lisbon,
our Lord is said " hominem suscepisse per quem
compassus est," which seems to imply that He had no
soul distinct from His Divinity. "Non passibilis Deus
Spiritus," answers Phœbadius, "licet in homine suo
passus." The Sardican confession also seems to impute
this heresy to the Arians. Vid. supr. vol. i. note, p.
116, and infr. art. *Eusebius*, fin.

¶ They did not admit into their theology the notion
of mystery.   In vain might Catholics urge the *ne sutor
ultra crepidam*.   It was useless to urge upon them that
they were reasoning about matters upon which they
had no experimental knowledge; that we had no means
of determining whether or how a spiritual being, really
trine, could be numerically one, and therefore can only
reason by means of our conceptions, and as if nothing
were a fact which was inconceivable.   It is a matter of
faith that Father and Son are one, and reason does not
therefore contradict it, because experience does not
show us how to conceive of it.   To us, poor creatures
of a day,—who are but just now born out of nothing,
and have everything to learn even as regards human
knowledge,—that such truths are incomprehensible to
us, is no wonder.

¶ The Anomœan Arians, who arose latest and went
farthest, had no scruple in answering this consideration
by denying that God was incomprehensible.   Arius
indeed says in his Thalia that the Son cannot know
the Father by comprehension, κατὰ κατάληψιν: "to
that which has origin, to conceive how the Unoriginate
is, is impossible."   Syn. § 15; but on the other hand
the doctrine of the Anomœans, who in most points
agreed with Arius, was, that all men could know God
as He knows Himself; according to Socrates, who
says, "Not to seem to be slandering, listen to
Eunomius himself, what words he dares to use in
sophistry concerning God; they run thus:—'God
knows not of His own substance more than we do;
nor is it known to Him more, to us less; but whatso-

ever we may know of it, that He too knows; and what
again He, that you will find without any difference in
us.'" Hist. iv. 7.

¶ Κατάληψις was originally a Stoical word, and even
when the act was perfect, it was considered attribu-
table only to an imperfect being. For it is used in
contrast to the Platonic doctrine of ιδέαι, to express
the hold of things obtained by the mind through the
senses; it being a Stoical maxim, "nihil esse in
intellectu quod non fuerit prius in sensu." In this
sense it is also used by the Fathers, to mean real and
certain knowlege after inquiry, though it is also
ascribed to Almighty God. As to the position of
Arius, since we are told in Scripture that none
"knoweth the things of a man save the spirit of man
which is in him," if κατάληψις be an exact and complete knowledge of the object of contemplation, to
deny that the Son comprehended the Father, was
to deny that He was in the Father, that is, to deny
the doctrine of the περιχώρησις,—vid. in the Thalia,
Syn. § 15, the word ανεπίμικτοι; or to maintain that
He was a distinct, and therefore a created, being.
On the other hand, Scripture asserts that, as the Holy
Spirit which is in God, "searcheth all things, yea, the
deep things," of God, so the Son, as being, "in the
bosom of the Father," alone "hath declared Him."
Vid. Clement. Strom. v. 12. And thus Athan., speaking
of Mark xiii. 32, "If the Son is in the Father, and the
Father in the Son, and the Father knows the day
and the hour, it is plain that the Son too, being in the
Father, and knowing the things in the Father, Himself

also knows the day and the hour." Orat. iii. 44, vid. also Matt. xi. 27.

4. *Historical Course of Arianism.*

There seems to have been a remarkable anticipation of this heresy in the century before its rise; and it is notable as showing in consequence the early date of a formal development of Catholic theology, which we are apt to assign to the fourth and fifth centuries. Vid. note on p. 47 in the present work, ed. Oxf. The controversy which called for this development arose in the middle of the third century, and incurred the vigilant protest of the Pope of the day as being the issue of a dangerous opinion, founded apparently on the Stoic distinction between the λογος ἐνδιάθετος and προφορικὸς, and looked on with favour in some Catholic quarters, vid. Tracts Theol., &c., art. iii. p. 137. And thus we are brought to Arianism.

¶ When this conclusion was reached by a number of men sufficient in position and influence to constitute a party, the first Ecumenical Council was held in A.D. 325 at Nicæa for its condemnation.

The Nicene Fathers, in the first place, defined the proper divinity of the Son of God, introducing into their creed the formulas ἐξ οὐσίας and ὁμοούσιος, as tests of orthodoxy, and next they anathematised the heretical propositions: and this with the ready adhesion of Constantine. He died in 337.

¶ During his later years he had softened towards the Arians, and on his death they gained his son Constantius, who tyrannised over Christendom, persecuting the orthodox Bishops, and especially Athanasius, till his immature death in 361.

¶ The Arians regained political power on the accession of Valens, in 364, who renewed the persecutions of Constantius.

¶ They came to an end, as far as regards any influence on the State, upon the accession of Theodosius and the Second Ecumenical Council, 381.

In the controversies and troubles they occasioned, while the orthodox *formulas* were, as has been said, the ἐξ οὐσίας and the ὁμοούσιος, (viz., that our Lord was from and in the Divine Essence,) the Semi-Arians maintained the ὁμοιούσιον, or that He was like the Divine Essence, the political and worldly party of Eusebius, Acacius, and Eudoxius, professed vaguely the ὅμοιον κατὰ πάντα, or that our Lord was like God in all things, and the fanatical Anomœans gained their name because they denied any likeness in Him to God at all.

ASTERIUS.

This writer, already noticed in art. *Arian Leaders*, seems according to Athan. to have been hired to write upon the Arian side, and argued on the hypothesis of Semi-Arianism. He agrees very much in doctrine with Eusebius, and in moderation of language, judging by the extracts which Athan. has preserved. (Vid. also Epiph. Hær. 72, 6.)

¶ Like Eusebius, he held (Orat. ii. § 24) that the God of all created His Son as an instrument or organ, or ὑπουργὸς, of creation, by reason of the necessary incapacity in the creature, as such, to endure the force and immediate presence of a Divine Hand (vid. art. ἄκρατος), which, while It created, would have annihilated. (Euseb. Demonstr. iv. 4; Eccl. Th. i. 8, 13; Præp. vii. 15; Sabell. p. 9.)

¶ But, says Athanasius, it is contrary to all our notions of religion to suppose God is not sufficient for Himself, and cannot create, enlighten, address, and unite Himself to His creatures immediately. "The Word has with His Father the oneness of Godhead indivisible. Else, why does the Father through Him create, and in Him reveal Himself to whom He will, &c. . . . If they say that the Father is not all-sufficient, their answer is impious." Orat. ii. § 41. And such an answer seems to be implied in saying that the Son was created for creation, illumination, &c., &c.; vid. art. *Mediation*.

¶ He considered that our Lord was taught to create, and without teaching could not by His mere nature have acquired the skill. "Though He is a creature, and has been brought into being," Asterius writes, "yet as from Master and Artificer has He learned to frame things, and thus has ministered to God who taught Him," Orat. ii. § 28, vid. art. *Eusebius*, who speaks of the Word in the poetical tone of Platonism.

¶ Also he distinguishes after the manner of the Semi-Arians, between the γεννητικὴ and the δημιουργικὴ δύναμις. Again, the illustration of the Sun (Syn. § 19) is another point of agreement with Eusebius; vid. Demonstr. iv. 5.

¶ And he, like Eusebius, is convicted of Arianism beyond mistake, in whatever words he might cloak his heresy, by his rejection of the doctrine of the περιχώρησις. "He is in the Father," he says, "and the Father again in Him, because neither the word on which He is discoursing is His own, but the Father's, nor the works, but the Father's who gave Him the power." Orat. iii. § 2.

¶ He defined the ἀγέννητος, or "Ingenerate, to mean that which never came into being, but was always" (Orat. i. § 30); and then he would argue, that God being ἀγέννητος, and a Son γεννητὸς, our Lord could not be God.

¶ While, with the other Arians, he introduced philosophical terms into theology, he with them explained away Scripture. They were accustomed to interpret our Lord's titles, "Son," "Word," "Power," by the secondary senses of such terms, as they belong to us, God's children by adoption; and so Asterius, perhaps flippantly, answered such arguments, as "Christ God's Power and Wisdom," by objecting that the locust was called by the prophet "God's great power." Syn. § 19.

¶ He argues, in behalf of our Lord's *gennesis* following upon an act of Divine counsel and will, that we must determine the point by inquiring whether it is more worthy of God to act with deliberation or not. Now the Creator acted with such counsel and will in the work of creation; therefore so to act is most worthy of Him; it follows that will should precede the *gennesis* also. But in that case the Son is posterior to the Father.

ATHANASIUS.

THIS renowned Father is in ecclesiastical history the special doctor of the sacred truth which Arius denied, bringing it out into shape and system so fully and luminously that he may be said to have exhausted his subject, as far as it lies open to the human intellect. But, besides this, writing as a controversialist, not primarily as a priest and teacher, he accompanies his exposition of doctrine with manifestations of character which are of great interest and value. Here some of the more prominent of these traits shall be set down, as they are seen in various of his Treatises.

1. The fundamental idea with which he starts in the controversy is a deep sense of the authority of Tradition, which he considers to have a definitive jurisdiction even in the interpretation of Scripture, though at the same time he seems to consider that Scripture, thus interpreted, is a document of final appeal in inquiry and in disputation. Hence, in his view of religion, is the magnitude of the evil which he is combating, and which exists prior to that extreme aggravation of it (about which no Catholic can doubt) involved in the characteristic tenet of Arianism itself. According to him, opposition to the witness of the Church, separation from its communion, private judgment overbearing the authorised catechetical teaching, the fact of a denomination, as men now speak, this is a self-condemnation; and the heretical tenet, whatever it may happen to be,

which is its formal life, is a spiritual poison and nothing
else ; the sowing of the evil one upon the good seed, in
whatever age and place it is found; and he applies to
all separatists the Apostle's words, "They went out
from us, for they were not of us." Accordingly, speaking of one Rhetorius, an Egyptian, who, as S. Austin
tells us, taught that "all heresies were in the right
path and spoke truth," he says that "the impiety of
such doctrine is frightful to mention." Apoll. i. § 6.

This is the explanation of the fierceness of his
language, when speaking of the Arians, which to a
modern reader may seem superfluous and painful; the
heretics were simply, as Elymas, "full of all guile and
of all deceit, children of the devil, enemies of all
justice," θεομάχοι,—by court influence, by violent
persecution, by sophistry, seducing, unsettling, per-
verting, the people of God.

2. It was not his way to be fierce, as a matter of
course, with those who opposed him; his treatment of
the Semi-Arians is a proof of this. Eusebius of
Cæsarea indeed he did not favour, for he discerned in
that eminent man what, alas, was genuine Arianism ;
and Eusebius's conduct towards him, and his partisan-
ship with the heretics, and his antagonism to the Nicene
Council, confirmed his judgment; but with the Semi-
Arian body, who rose up against the pure Arians, he was
very gentle, considering them, or at least many of them,
of good promise, as the event proved them to be. He
calls some of them "brethren" and ἀγαπητοί (Syn.
§§ 41, 43), as Hilary calls them "Sanctissimi viri,"
(Syn. 80, vid. art. *Semi-Arianism* infr.) Nor is there

any violence in his treatment of Marcellus, Apollinaris, Hosius, or Liberius. Vid. art. 'Αλήθεια.

3. And so in the account he has left us of the death of Arius (de Mort. Ar.), which he considers, and truly, as an awful judgment of God, there is no triumph in his tone, though he held him in holy horror; not those fierce expressions, which certainly are to be found in his Orations. "I was not at Constantinople," he says, "when he died, but Macarius the Presbyter was, and I heard the account of it from him. Arius had been summoned by the Emperor Constantine, through the interest of the Eusebians, and, when he entered the presence, the Emperor inquired of him, whether he held the faith of the Catholic Church, and he declared upon oath that he held the right faith. . . The Emperor dismissed him saying, 'If thy faith be right, thou hast done well to swear; but if thy faith be impious, and thou hast sworn, God judge thee according to thy oath.' When he thus came from the presence of the Emperor, the Eusebians, with their accustomed violence, desired to bring him into the Church; but Alexander the Bishop . . . . was greatly distressed, and, entering into the Church, he stretched forth his hands to God, and bewailed himself; and, casting himself upon his face, in the chancel, he prayed upon the pavement. Macarius also was present and prayed with him, and heard his words. And he sought these two things, saying, 'If Arius is brought to communion to-morrow, let me Thy servant depart, ... but, if Thou wilt spare Thy Church . . . take off Arius, lest the heresy may seem to enter with him.' . . . A wonderful and extra-

ordinary circumstance took place. While the Eusebians threatened, the Bishop prayed; but Arius, who had great confidence in the Eusebians, and talked very wildly, seized by indisposition withdrew, and suddenly, in the language of Scripture, *falling headlong, burst asunder in the midst*, and immediately expired as he lay, and was deprived both of communion and of his life together." Then he adds, "Such was the end of Arius; and the Eusebians, overwhelmed with shame, buried their accomplice, while the blessed Alexander, amid the rejoicing of the Church, celebrated the Synaxis with piety and orthodoxy, praying with all the brethren and greatly glorifying God; not as exulting in his death (God forbid), for it is appointed unto all men once to die, but . . . that the Lord Himself judged between the threats of the Eusebians and the prayer of Alexander, and condemned the Arian heresy."

4. His language, in speaking of Constantius, gives opportunity for more words. Up to the year 356, Athanasius had treated Constantius as a member of the Church; but at that date the Eusebian or Court party abandoned the Semi-Arians for the Anomœans. George of Cappadocia was placed as Bishop in Alexandria, Athanasius was driven into the desert, S. Hilary and other Western Bishops were sent into banishment. Hosius was persecuted into signing an Arian confession, and Pope Liberius into communicating with the Arians. Upon this Athanasius changed his tone, and considered that he had to deal with an Antichrist. In his Apol. contr. Arian. init. (A.D. 350), ad Ep. Æg. 5 (356), and his Apol. ad Constant. passim. (356), he calls the

Emperor most pious, religious, &c. At the end of the last-mentioned work, § 27, the news comes to him, while in exile, of the persecution of the Western Bishops and the measures against himself. He still in the peroration calls Constantius "blessed and divinely favoured Augustus," and urges on him that he is a "Christian Emperor, φιλόχριστος." In the works which follow, Apol. de fuga, § 26 (357), he calls him a heretic; and Hist. Arian. § 45, &c. (358), speaking with indignation of the treatment of Hosius, &c., he calls him "Ahab," "Belshazzar," "Saul," "Antichrist." The passage at the end of the Apol. contr. Arian., in which he speaks of the "much violence and tyrannical power of Constantius," is an addition of Athan.'s at a later date. Vid. Montfaucon's note on § 88, fin. This is worth mentioning, as it shows the unfairness of the following passage in Gibbon, ch. xxi. note 116: "As Athanasius dispersed secret invectives against Constantius, see the Epistle to the monks" [i.e., Hist. Arian. ad Monach. A.D. 358], "at the same time that he assured him of his profound respect, we might distrust the professions of the Archbishop, tom. i. p. 677" [i.e., apparently Apol. ad Const. A.D. 356]. Again, in a later part of the chapter, "In his public Apologies, which he addressed to the Emperor himself, he sometimes affected the praise of moderation; whilst at the same time in secret and vehement invectives he exposed Constantius as a weak and wicked prince, the executioner of his family, the tyrant of the republic, and the Antichrist of the Church." He offers no proof of this assertion. It may be added that S. Greg. Naz.

praises Constantius, but it is in contrast to Julian.
Orat. 4. 3, and 5. 6. And S. Ambrose, but it is for his
enmity to paganism. Ep. i. 18, n. 32.

5. It is the same prudent, temperate spirit and practical good sense, which leads Athanasius, though the
prime champion of the Nicene Homoüsion, to be so loth
to use that formula, much less abruptly to force it upon
his adversaries in the first instance, and to content
himself with urging and inculcating our Lord's Divinity
in other language and by casual explanations, when prejudice or party-spirit made it difficult to get a hearing
for the terms which the Church had determined.
Hence in his Three Orations he hardly names the
Homoüsion, though the doctrine which it upholds is
never out of his thoughts. He accepted the Semi-Arian
Homœiüsion, though he is so often represented by the
shallow ignorance of modern times to have waged war
with other theologians whose views did not differ from
his own except by a single letter. "Those," he says,
"who accept everything else that was determined at
Nicæa, and quarrel only with the Homoüsion, must not
be received as enemies, nor do we here attack them as
Ariomaniacs, nor as opposers of the Fathers, but we
discuss the matter with them, as brothers with brothers,
who mean what we mean, and dispute only about the
word." Syn. § 41. (*Arim.* n. 47.) Vid. arts. ὅμοιος,
Semi-Arians, &c.

¶ 6. It arises from the same temper of mind that he is
so self-distrustful and subdued in his comments on Scripture and in his controversial answers; he, the foremost
doctor of the Divine Sonship, being the most modest as

well as the most authoritative of teachers. Thus, "They had best have been silent," i.e., in so sacred a matter, he says, "but since it is otherwise, after many prayers that God would be gracious to us, thus we might ask them in turn," &c., Orat. i. § 25. (_Disc._ n. 39.) "Against their profaneness I wish to urge a further question, bold indeed, but with a religious intent,—be propitious, O Lord! (_Disc._ n. 50, p. 197.) "The unwearied habits of the religious man is to worship the All (τὸ πᾶν) in silence, and to hymn God his benefactor with thankful cries . . . . but since," &c., Apoll. i. init.

¶ And especially in his letter to the Monks, " I thought it needful to represent to your piety what pains the writing of these things has cost me, in order that you may understand thereby how truly the Blessed Apostle has said, O, the depth, &c., and may kindly bear with a weak man, such as I am by nature. For the more I desired to write and endeavoured to force myself to understand the Divinity of the Word, so much the more did the knowledge thereof withdraw itself from me, and in proportion as I thought that I apprehended it, in so much I perceived myself to fail of doing so. Moreover, I was also unable to express in writing even what I seemed to myself to understand, and that which I wrote was unequal to the imperfect shadow of the truth which existed in my conceptions," ad Monach. i. Vid. also Serap. i. 15—17, 20; ii. init., iv. 8, 14; Epict. 12 fin.; Max. init.; Ep. Æg. 11 fin. Once more: " It is not safe for the writings of an individual to be published, especially if they relate to the highest and chief

doctrines, lest what is imperfectly expressed, through
infirmity or the obscurity of language, do hurt to the
reader," &c. Mort. Ar. § 5.

¶ He set the example of modesty to others. Vid. Basil.
in Eunom. ii. 17; Didym. Trin. iii. 3, p. 341; Ephr.
Syr. adv. Hær. Serm. 55 init. (t. 2, p. 557); Facund.
Tr. Cap. iii. 3 init.

¶ 7. And his repetitions of statements in these Treatises are not without a place in the evidences of his religious caution. Often indeed they must be accounted
purely accidental, arising from forgetfulness, as he
wandered or travelled about, what it was that he had
written the day before; often, too, they may have
subserved the purpose of cathechetical instruction; but
sometimes they would seem to be owing to his anxiety
to confine himself to words which had stood the test of
time or of readers, or at least were existing forms which
he could improve upon or at least reconsider and appeal to, as after his time is instanced in S. Leo.

¶ 8. As to his acquirements, they were considerable.
Gregory only says that he had a knowledge τῶν ἐγκυκ-
λίων, but Sulpitius speaks of him as a jurisconsult (vid.
philosophy and οὐσία). His earliest works, written when
perhaps he was not more than twenty-one, give abundant evidence of a liberal education. He had a knowledge of Homer and Plato, and his early style, though
it admits of pruning, is graceful and artistic. I cannot,
with Gibbon, talk of its "rude eloquence," though it
has not the refined and elaborate elegance of Basil.
And Gibbon grants that his writings are "clear, for-
cible, and persuasive." Erasmus seems to prefer him, as

a writer, to all the Fathers, and certainly, in my own judgment, no one comes near him but Chrysostom and Jerome. "Habebat," says Erasmus, "vere dotem illam quam Paulus in Episcopo putat esse præcipuam, τὸ διδακτικόν; adeo dilucidus est, acutus, sobrius, adtentus, breviter omnibus modis ad docendum appositus. Nihil habet durum, quod offendit in Tertulliano, nihil ἐπιδεικτικὸν, quod vidimus in Hieronymo, nihil operosum, quod in Hilario, nihil laciniosum, quod est in Augustino, atque etiam Chrysostomo, nihil Isocraticos numeros aut Lysiæ compositionem redolens, quod est in Gregorio Nazianzeno, sed totus est in explicandâ re." ap. Montfaucon, t. 1. p. xxi. ed. Patav.

Photius's praise of Athan.'s style and matter is quoted supr. in the Notice prefixed to the Orations.

THE VICARIOUS ATONEMENT.

¶ "FORMERLY the world, as guilty, was under judgment from the Law; but now the Word has taken on Himself the judgment, and, having suffered in the body for all, has bestowed salvation on all." Orat. i. § 60.

¶ "When the Father willed that ransom should be paid for all, and to all grace should be given, then truly the Word . . . did take earthly flesh . . . that, as a high priest . . . He might offer Himself to the Father and cleanse us all from sins in His own blood." Orat. ii. § 7.

¶ The perfect Word of God puts around Him an imperfect body, and is said to be created for the creatures, that, paying the debt in our stead (ἀνθ ἡμῶν τὴν ὀφειλὴν ἀποδιδούς), He might by Himself perfect what was wanting in man. Now immortality was wanting to him, and the way to paradise." Orat. ii. § 66.

¶ "How, were the Word a creature, had He power to undo God's sentence, and to remit sin?" Orat. ii. § 67. Our Lord's death is λύτρον πάντων, Incarn. V. D. 25, et passim; λύτρον καθάρσιον, Naz. Orat. 30, 20 fin.

¶ "Therefore was He made man, that what was as though given to Him, might be transferred to us; for a mere man had not merited this, nor had the Word

Himself needed it. He was united therefore to us,"
&c. Orat. iv. § 6. Vid. also iii. § 33 init. and *In
Illud Omnia*, § 2 fin.

¶ " There was need He should be both man and God ;
for unless He were man, He could not be slain; unless
He were God. He would have been thought, (not, unwilling to be what He could, but) unable to do what He
would." August. Trin. xiii. 18. " Since Israel could
become sold under sin, he could not redeem himself
from iniquities. He only could redeem, who could not
sell Himself, who did no sin; He is the redeemer from
sin." Id. in Psalm. 129, n. 12. "In this common
overthrow of all mankind, there was but one remedy,
the birth of some son of Adam, a stranger to the
original prevarication and innocent, to profit the rest
both by his pattern and his merit. Since natural
generation hindered this, .. the Lord of David became
his son." Leon. Serm. 28, n. 3. " Seek neither a
' brother ' for thy redemption, but one who surpasses
thy nature ; nor a mere 'man,' but a man who is God,
Jesus Christ, who alone is able to make propitiation for
us all ... One thing has been found sufficient for all
men at once, which was given as the price of ransom of
our soul, the holy and most precious blood of our Lord
Jesus Christ, which He poured out for us all." Basil. in
Psalm. 48, n. 4. " One had not been sufficient instead
of all, had it been simply a man ; but if He be understood as God made man, and suffering in His own
flesh, the whole creation together is small compared to
Him, and the death of one flesh is enough for the
ransom of all that is under heaven." Cyril. de rect.

fid. p. 132. Vid. also Theod. Eran. iii. pp. 196-8, &c. Procl. Orat. i. p. 63 (ed. 1630); Vigil. contr. Eutych. v. 9 fin. § 15, &c.; Greg. Moral. xxiv. init.; Job. ap. Phot. 222, p. 583.

¶ Pardon, however, could have been bestowed without an Atonement such as our Lord made, though not renovation of nature. Vid. art. *Incarnation.*

CATECHISING.

ATHANASIUS lays much stress on this practice, as in fact supplying the evidence of Tradition as to the doctrine which Arius blasphemed.

E.g. "Let them tell us, by what teacher or by what tradition they have derived these notions concerning the Saviour?" de Decr. § 13 init.

"For who was ever yet a hearer of such a doctrine? or whence or from whom did the abettors and hirelings of the heresy gain it? who thus expounded to them when they were at school? who told them, 'Abandon creature worship, and then draw near and worship a creature and a work?' But if they themselves own that they have heard it now for the first time, how can they deny that this heresy is foreign, and not from our fathers? But what is not from our fathers, but has come to light in this day, how can it be but that of which the blessed Paul has foretold, that *in the latter times some shall depart from the sound faith*," &c.? Orat. i. § 8.

"Who is there, who when he heard, upon his first catechisings, that God had a Son, and had made all things in His proper Word, did not understand it in that sense which we now intend? who, when the vile Arian heresy began, but at once, on hearing its teachers, was startled, as if they taught strange things?" Orat. ii. § 34.

¶ Hence too Athan.'s phrases μαθὼν ἐδίδασκεν, de Decr. § 7, Orat. iii. 9, ἐρωτῶντες ἐμάνθανον, Orat. ii. § 1, after S. Paul, 1 Cor. xv. 3. And so "What Moses taught, that Abraham observed, that Noe and Enoch acknowledged," &c., de Decr. § 6. Vid. art. *Rule of Faith.*

CATHOLIC: THE NAME AND THE CLAIM.

For the adoption into Christianity, and the sense and force of the word " Catholic," not a very obvious word, we must refer to the Creed. The articles of the Creed are brief enunciations and specimens of some, and of the chief, of the great mercies vouchsafed to man in the Gospel. They are truths of pregnant significance, and of direct practical bearing on Christian life and conduct. Such, for instance, obviously is " one Baptism for the remission of sins," and " the resurrection of the body." Such then must be our profession of " catholicity." And, thus considered, the two, " the Catholic Church " and " the Communion of Saints," certainly suggest an explanation of each other ; the one introducing us to our associates and patrons in heaven, and the other pointing out to us where to find the true teaching and the means of grace on earth. Indeed, what else can be the meaning of insisting on the " *One* Holy Catholic Apostolic Church "? does it not imply a contrast to other so-called Churches? Now this plain sense of the Article, this its obvious or rather its only sense, is abundantly confirmed by such passages of the Fathers as the following, taken in connection and illustration of each other.

Thus, to begin with what is implied and introduced to us by the name " Christian." Orat. i. §§ 2, 3. " Though the blessed Apostles have become our teachers, and have ministered the Saviour's Gospel, yet not from

them have we our *title*, but from Christ we are and are
named Christians. But for those who derive the faith
which they profess from others, good reason is it they
should bear their *name*, whose property they have become." Also, "Let us become His disciples and learn
to live according to Christianity; for whoso is called
by other name beside this, is not of God." Ignat. ad
Magn. 10. Hegesippus speaks of "Menandrians, and
Marcionites, and Carpocratians, and Valentinians, and
Basilidians, and Saturnilians," who "each in his own way,
and that a different one, brought in his own doctrine."
Euseb. Hist. iv. 22. "There are, and there have been,
my friends, many who have taught atheistic and blas-
phemous words and deeds, coming in the Name of
Jesus ; and they are called by us from the appellation
of the men, whence each doctrine and opinion began.
. . . . Some are called Marcians, others Valentinians,
others Basilidians, others Saturnilians," &c. Justin.
Tryph. 35. "They have a name from the author of
that most impious opinion, Simon, being called Simonians." Iren. Hær. i. 23. "When men are called
Phrygians, or Novatians, or Valentinians, or Marcionites, or Anthropians, or by any other name, they
cease to be Christians ; for they have lost Christ's
name, and clothe themselves in human and foreign
titles." Lact. Inst. iv. 30. "*A.* How are you a Christian, to whom it is not even granted to bear the *name*
of Christian ? for you are not called Christian, but
Marcionite. *M.* And you are called of the Catholic
Church ; therefore ye are not Christians either.
A. Did we profess man's name, you would have spoken

to the point, but, if we are so called for being all over
the world, what is there bad in this?" Adamant.
Dial. § 1, p. 809. "We never heard of Petrines, or
Paulines, or Bartholomeans, or Thaddeans, but from
the first there was ·one preaching of all the Apostles,
not preaching themselves, but Christ Jesus the Lord.
Wherefore also they all gave one *name* to the Church,
not their own, but that of their Lord Jesus Christ,
since they began to be called Christians first at
Antioch; which is the *sole* Catholic Church, having
naught else but Christ's, being a Church of Christians,
not of Christs, but of Christians; He being one, they
from that one being called Christians. After this
Church and her preachers, all others are no longer
of the same character, making show by their own
epithets, Manichæans, and Simonians, and Valentinians,
and Ebionites." Epiph. Hær. 42, p. 366. "This is
the fearful thing, that they change the *name* of
Christians of the Holy Church, which hath no epithet
but the name of Christ alone, and of Christians, to be
called by the name of Audius," &c. Ibid. 70, 15. Vid.
also Hær. 75, 6 fin. "If you ever hear those who are
called Christians, *named*, not from the Lord Jesus
Christ, but from some one else, say Marcionites,
Valentinians, Mountaineers, Campestrians, know that
it is not Christ's Church, but the synagogue of Antichrist." Jerom. adv. Lucif. fin.

¶ Having thus laid down the principle that the
name, given to a religious body, is a providential
or divine token, they go on to instance it in
the word "Catholic." "Since one might pro-

perly and truly say that there is a 'Church of evil doers,' I mean the meetings of the heretics, the Marcionists, and Manichees, and the rest, the faith hath delivered to thee by way of security the Article, 'And in *One* Holy Catholic Church,' that thou mayest avoid their wretched meetings; and ever abide with the Holy Church Catholic, in which thou wast regenerated. And if ever thou art sojourning in any city, inquire not simply where the Lord's House is, (for the sects of the profane also make an attempt to call their own dens houses of the Lord,) nor merely where the Church is, but where is the *Catholic* Church. For this is the *peculiar name* of this Holy Body," &c. Cyril Cat. xviii. 26. "Were I by chance to enter a populous city, I should in this day find Marcionites, Apollinarians, Cataphrygians, Novatians, and other such, who called themselves Christian; by what *surname* should I recognise the congregation of my own people, were it not called Catholic? . . . . Certainly that word 'Catholic' is not borrowed from man, which has survived through so many ages, nor has the sound of Marcion or Apelles or Montanus, nor takes heretics for its authors . . Christian is my *name*, Catholic my *surname*." Pacian. Ep. 1.

¶ Athan. seems to allude, Orat. i. § 2, to Catholics being called Athanasians; supr., vol. i. p. 157. Two distinctions are drawn between such a title in controversy as applied to Catholics, and then again to heretics, when they are taken by Catholics as a *note* against them. S. Augustine says, "*Arians* call Catholics Athanasians or Homoüsians, *not other heretics call them so.* But ye not only by Catholics *but also by heretics*, those who agree with you and those who disagree are called Pelagians; as *even by heretics* are Arians called Arians. But ye, and ye only, call us Traducianists, as Arians call us Homoüsians, as Donatists Macarians, as Manichees Pharisees, and as the other heretics use various titles." Op. imp. i. 75. It may be added that the heretical name *adheres*, the Catholic dies away. S. Chrysostom draws a second distinction, " Are we divided from the Church? have we heresiarchs? are we called from man? is there any leader to us, as to one there is Marcion, to another Manichæus, to another Arius, to another some other author of heresy? for if we too have the name of any, still it is not those who began a heresy, but our superiors and governors of the Church. We have not ' teachers upon earth,' " &c., in Act. Ap. Hom. 33 fin.

¶ Athan. says that after Eusebius had taken up the patronage of the heresy, he made no progress till he had gained the Court, (Hist. Arian. 66,) showing that it was an act of external power by which Arianism grew, not an inward movement in the Church, which indeed loudly protested against the Emperor's proceeding. " If Bishops are to judge," he says, ibid. § 52, " what has the Emperor to do with this matter? if the Emperor is to threaten, what need of men styled Bishops? where in the world was such a thing heard of? where had the Church's judgment its force from the Emperor, or his sentence was at all recognised?" Vid. art. *Heretics.*

¶ " Many Councils have been before this, many judg-

ments of the Church, but neither the Fathers ever argued
with the Emperor about them, nor the Emperor meddled
with the concerns of the Church. Paul the Apostle had
friends of Cæsar's household, and in his Epistle he
saluted the Philippians in their name; but he took them
not to him as partners in his judgments. But now a
new spectacle, and this the discovery of the Arian
heresy," &c. § 52. Again, " In what then is he behind
Antichrist? What more will he do when he comes? or
rather, on his coming will he not find the way prepared for him by Constantius unto his deceiving
without effort? for he is claiming to transfer causes to
the Court instead of the Churches, and presides at them
in person." Hist. Arian. § 76. And so also Hosius to
Constantius, " Cease, I charge thee, and remember that
thou art a mortal man. Fear the day of judgment;
keep thyself clear against it. Interfere not with
things ecclesiastical, nor be the man to charge us in
a matter of the kind; rather learn thou thyself from
us. God has put into thy hand the kingdom; to us
He hath entrusted the things of the Church,—and as
he who is traitorous to thy rule speaks against God
who has thus ordained, so fear thou, lest drawing to
thyself the things of the Church, thou fallest beneath
a great accusation." ap. Athan. ibid. 44.

CHAMELEONS.

THE Arians were ever shifting their ground or changing their professions, in order to gain either the favour of the State, or of local bishops, or of populations, or to perplex their opponents. Hence Athan. calls them chameleons, as varying their colours according to their company, Decr. § 1, and Alexander, Socr. i. 6. Cyril, however, compares them to "the leopard which cannot change his spots." Dial. ii. init.; vid. also Naz. Orat. 28, 2. Athan. says, "When confuted, they are confused, and when questioned, they hesitate; and then they lose shame and betake themselves to evasions." Decr. § 1. "What wonder that they fight against their fathers, when they fight against themselves?" Syn. § 37. "They have collisions with their own principles, and conflict with each other, at one time saying that there are many wisdoms, at another maintaining one," &c. Orat. ii. § 40. He says, Æg. Ep. 6, that they treated creeds as yearly covenants, and as State Edicts, Syn. § 3, 4. He calls also the Meletians chameleons, Hist. Ar. § 79; indeed the Church alone and her children are secure from change.

THE COINHERENCE,

περιχώρησις, circumincessio or coinherence of the
Divine Three with each other, is the test at once
against Arianism and Tritheism. Arius denies it
in his Thalia, ἀνεπίμικτοὶ ἑαυτοῖς αἱ ὑποστάσεις.
It is the point of doctrine in which Eusebius so
seriously fails. Vid. art. *Eusebius.* When Gibbon
called this doctrine "perhaps the deepest and
darkest corner of the whole theological abyss," he
made as irrelevant and feeble a remark as could
fall from an able man; as if any Catholic pretended
that it was on any side of it comprehensible, and as
if this was not the very enunciation in which the incomprehensibility lies; as we profess in the Creed,
"neque confundentes personas, neque substantiam
separantes." This doctrine is not the deepest part of
the whole, but it is the whole, other statements being
in fact this in other shapes. Each of the Three who
speak to us from heaven is simply, and in the full
sense of the word, God, yet there is but one God; this
truth, as a statement, is enunciated most intelligibly
when we say the Father, Son, and Holy Ghost, being
one and the same Spirit and Being, are in each other,
which is the doctrine of the περιχώρησις.

¶ "They next proceed," says Athanasius, "to disparage our Lord's words, *I in the Father and the Father
in Me,* saying 'How can the One be contained in the

Other and the Other in the One?' &c.; and this state
of mind is consistent with their perverseness, who
think God to be material, and understand not what
is True Father and True Son. . . When it is said, *I in
the Father and the Father in Me,* They are not therefore, as these suppose, discharged into Each Other,
filling the One the Other, as in the case of empty
vessels, so that the Son fills the emptiness of the
Father and the Father that of the Son, and Each of
Them by Himself is not complete and perfect, (for
this is proper to bodies, and therefore the mere assertion of it is full of impiety,) for the Father is full and
perfect, and the Son is the Fulness of Godhead. Nor
again, as God, by coming into the Saints, strengthens
them, is He also thus in the Son. For He is Himself
the Father's Power and Wisdom, and, by partaking
($\mu\epsilon\tau o\chi\tilde{\eta}$) of Him, things generate are sanctified in the
Spirit; but the Son Himself is not Son by participa-
tion ($\mu\epsilon\tau o\upsilon\sigma\acute{\iota}\alpha$, vid. art. *Arian Tenets,* supr. pp. 39—42),
but is the Father's proper Offspring. Nor again is
the Son in the Father, in the sense of the passage, *In
Him we live and move and have our being;* for He, as
being from the Fountain of the Father, is the Life, in
which all things are both quickened and consist; for
the Life does not live in Life, else it would not be
Life, but rather He gives life to all things." Orat. iii.
§ 1. And again: " The Father is in the Son, since
the Son is what is from the Father and proper to Him,
as in the radiance the sun, and in the word the thought,
and in the stream the fountain: for whoso thus contemplates the Son, contemplates what belongs to the

Father's Substance, and knows that the Father i·· in the Son. For whereas the essential character (εἶδος) and Godhead of the Father is the Being of the Son, it follows that the Son is in the Father and the Father in the Son." ibid. § 3.

¶ In accordance with the above, Thomassin observes that by the mutual coinherence or indwelling of the Three Blessed Persons is meant "not a commingling as of material liquids, nor as of soul with body, nor as the union of our Lord's Godhead and humanity, but it is such that the whole power, life, substance, wisdom, essence, of the Father, should be the very essence, substance, wisdom, life, and power of the Son." de Trin. 28, 1. S. Cyril adopts Athan.'s language to express this doctrine. "The Son in one place says, that He is in the Father and has the Father again in Him; for what is simply proper (ἴδιον) to the Father's substance, by nature coming to the Son, shows the Father in Him," in Joan. p. 105. "One is contemplated in the other, and is truly, according to the connatural and consubstantial." de Trin. vi. p. 621. "He has in Him the Son, and again is in the Son, because of the identity of substance." in Joan. p. 168. Vid. art. *Trinity*; also, *Spirit of God*.

¶ The περιχώρησις is the test of orthodoxy, as regards the Holy Trinity, against Arianism. This is seen clearly in the case of Eusebius, whose language approaches to Catholic more nearly than that of Arians in general. After all his strong assertions, the question recurs, Is our Lord a distinct being from God, as we are, or not? he answers in the affirmative, vid.

infra. art. *Eusebius*, whereas Catholics hold that He is literally and numerically one with the Father, and therefore His Person dwells in the Father's Person by an ineffable unity. And hence the strong language of Pope Dionysius, supr. vol. i. p. 45, "the Holy Ghost must repose and dwell in God," ἐμφιλοχωρεῖν τῷ θεῷ καὶ ἐνδιαιτᾶσθαι. And hence the strong figure of S. Jerome (in which he is followed by S. Cyril, Thesaur. p. 51), "Filius locus est Patris, sicut et Pater locus est Filii." in Ezek. 3, 12. Hence Athan contrasts creatures, who are ἐν μεμερισμένοις τόποις, with the Son. vid. Serap. iii. 4. Accordingly, one of the first symptoms of reviving orthodoxy in the second school of Semi-Arians is the use, in the Macrostich Creed, of language of this character, viz., "All the Father embosoming the Son," they say, "and all the Son hanging and adhering to the Father, and alone resting on the Father's breast continually," supr. vol. i. p. 107.

¶ St. Jerome's figure above might seem inconsistent with S. Athanasius's disclaimer of material images; but Athan. only means that such illustrations cannot be taken literally, as if spoken of physical subjects. The Father is the τόπος or locus of the Son, because when we contemplate the Son in His fulness as ὅλος θεὸς, we only view the Father as Him in whom God the Son is; our mind for the moment abstracting His Substance which is the Son from Him, and regarding Him merely as Father. Thus Athan. τὴν θείαν οὐσίαν τοῦ λογοῦ ἡνωμένην φύσει τῷ ἑαυτοῦ πατρί. in illud Omn. 4. It is, however, but a mode of speaking in theology, and not a real emptying of Godhead from the Father,

if such words may be used. Father and Son are both
the same God, though really and eternally distinct from
each other; and Each is full of the Other, that is, their
Substance is one and the same. This is insisted on by S
Cyril: "We must not conceive that the Father is held in
the Son as body in body, or vessel in vessel; . . . for
the One is in the Other." ὡς ἐν ταὐτότητι τῆς οὐσίας
ἀπαραλλάκτῳ, καὶ τῇ κατα φύσιν ἑνότητί τε καὶ ὁμοιότητι.
in Joan. p. 28. And by S. Hilary: "Material natures
do not admit of being mutually in each other, of having
a perfect unity of a nature which subsists, of the abiding nativity of the Only-begotten being inseparable
from the verity of the Father's Godhead. To God the
Only-begotten alone is this proper, and this faith
attaches to the mystery of a true nativity, and this is
the work of a spiritual power, that to be, and to be in,
differ nothing; to be in, yet not to be one in another
as body in body, but so to be and to subsist, as to be
in the subsisting, and so to be in, as also to subsist,"
&c. Trin. vii. fin.; vid. also iii. 23. The following
quotation from S. Anselm is made by Petavius, de Trin.
iv. 16 fin.: "Though there be not many eternities,
yet if we say eternity in eternity, there is but one
eternity. . . And so whatever is said of God's Essence,
if repeated in itself, does not increase quantity, nor
admit number. . . Since there is nothing out of God,
when God is born of God. . . He will not be born out
of God, but remains in God."

¶ "There is but one Face (εἶδος, character) of Godhead,
which is also in the Word, and One God, the Father,
existing by Himself according as He is above all; and

appearing in the Son according as He pervades all things; and in the Spirit according as in Him He acts in all things through the Word. And thus we confess God to be One through the Trinity." Orat. iii. § 15. And so: "The Word is in the Father, and the Spirit is given from the Word." iii. § 25. "That Spirit is in us which is in the Word which is in the Father." ibid. "The Father in the Son taketh the oversight of all." § 36 fin.; vid. art. *The Father Almighty*, 2. "The sanctification which takes place from Father through Son in Holy Ghost." Serap. i. § 20; vid. also ibid. 28, 30, 31, iii. 1, 5 init. et fin., also Hil. Trin. vii. 31. Eulogius says, "The Holy Ghost, proceeding from the Father, having the Father as an Origin, and proceeding through the Son unto the creation." ap. Phot. cod. p. 865. Damascene speaks of the Holy Spirit as δύναμιν τοῦ πατρὸς προερχομένην καὶ ἐν τῷ λόγῳ ἀναπαυομένην, F. O. i. 7; and in the beginning of the ch. he says that "the Word must have Its Breath (Spirit) as our word is not without breath, though in our case the breath is distinct from our substance." "The way to knowledge of God is from One Spirit through the One Son to the One Father." Basil. de Sp. S. 47. "We preach One God by One Son with the Holy Ghost." Cyr. Cat. xvi. 4. "The Father through the Son with the Holy Ghost bestows all things." ibid. 24. "All things have been made from Father through the Son in Holy Ghost." Pseudo-Dion. de Div. Nom. i. p. 403. "Through Son and in Spirit God made all things consist, and contains and preserves them." Pseudo-Athan. c. Sab. Greg. 10.

¶ Since the Father and the Son are the numerically
One God, it is but expressing this in other words to
say that the Father is in the Son, and the Son in the
Father, for all They have and all They are is common
to Each, excepting their being Father and Son. A
περιχώρησις of Persons is implied in the Unity of
Substance. This is the connection of the two texts so
often quoted: "the Son is in the Father and the
Father in the Son," because "the Son and Father are
one." And the cause of this unity and περιχώρησις is
the Divine γέννησις. Thus S. Hilary: "The perfect
Son of a perfect Father, and of the Ingenerate God
the Only-generate Offspring, (who from Him who hath
all hath received all, God from God, Spirit from Spirit,
Light from Light,) says confidently 'The Father in
Me and I in the Father,' for as the Father is Spirit so
is the Son, as the Father God so is the Son, as the
Father Light so is the Son. From those things therefore which are in the Father, are those in which is the
Son; that is, of the whole Father is born the whole
Son; not from other, &c. . . . not in part, for in the
Son is the fulness of Godhead. What is in the Father,
that too is in the Son; One from the Other and Both
One (unum); not Two One Person ('unus,' vid. however the language of the Athan. Creed, which expresses
itself differently after S. Austin,) but Either in Other,
because not Other in Either. The Father in the Son
because from Him the Son . . . the Only-begotten in
the Ingenerate, because from the Ingenerate the Only-
generate," &c. Trin. iii. 4.

¶ And so ἐργαζομένου τοῦ πατρὸς, ἐργάζεσθαι καὶ τὸν

υἱόν. in illud Omn. 1. "Cum luce nobis prodeat, In Patre totus Filius, et totus in Verbo Pater." Hymn. Brev. in fer. 2. Ath. argues from this oneness of operation the oneness of substance. And thus S. Chrysostom thinks it right to argue that if the Father and Son are one κατὰ τὴν δύναμιν, They are one also in οὐσία. in Joan. Hom. 61, 2. Tertullian in Prax. 22, and S. Epiphanius, Hær. 57, p. 488, seem to say the same on the same text. Vid. Lampe, Joan. x. 35. And so S. Athan. τριὰς ἀδιαίρετος τῇ φύσει, καὶ μία ταύτης ἡ ἐνέργεια. Serap. i. 28; ἓν θέλημα πατρὸς καὶ υἱοῦ καὶ βούλημα, ἐπεὶ καὶ ἡ φύσις μία. in illud Omn. 5. Various passages of the Fathers to the same effect, (e.g. of S. Ambrose, "si unius voluntatis et operationis, unius est essentiæ," de Sp. ii. 12 fin., and of S. Basil, ὧν μία ἐνέργεια, τούτων καὶ οὐσία μία, of Greg. Nyss. and Cyril. Alex.) are brought together in the Lateran Council. Concil. Hard. t. 3, p. 859; &c. The subject is treated at length by Petavius, Trin. iv. 15, § 3.

As to the very word περιχώρησις, Petavius observes, de Trin. iv. 16, § 4, that its first use in ecclesiastical writers was one which Arianism would admit of; its use to express the Catholic doctrine was later.

CURSUS PUBLICUS.

ON the Cursus Publicus, vid. Gothofred, in Cod. Theod. viii. tit. 5. It was provided for the journeys of the Emperor, for parties whom he summoned, for magistrates, ambassadors, and such private persons as the Emperor indulged in the use of it. The use was granted by Constantine to the Bishops summoned to Nicæa, as far as it went. Euseb. Constant. iii. v. 6. The Cursus Publicus brought the Bishops to the Council of Tyre, ibid. iv. 43. In the conference between Liberius and Constantius, Theod. Hist. ii. 13, it is objected that the Cursus Publicus is not sufficient to convey Bishops to the Council which Liberius contemplates. Constantius answers that the Churches are rich enough to convey their Bishops as far as the sea. Thus S. Hilary was compelled ("datâ evectionis ·opiâ," Sulp. Hist. ii. 57) to attend at Seleucia, and Athan. at Tyre. Julian complains of the abuse of the Cursus Publicus, perhaps with an allusion to these Councils of Constantius, vid. Cod. Theod. viii. 5, § 12, where Gothofred quotes Libanius's Epitaph in Julian. t. i. p. 569, ed. Reize. Vid. the passage in Ammianus, who speaks of the Councils being the ruin of the *res vehicularia*, Hist. xxi. 16. The Eusebians at Philippopolis say the same thing. Hil. fragm. iii. 25. The Emperor provided board and perhaps lodging for the Bishops at

Ariminum, which the Bishops of Aquitaine, Gaul and Britain declined, excepting three British by reason of poverty, Sulp. ii. 56. Hunneric in Africa, after assembling 466 Bishops at Carthage, dismissed them without conveyances, provision or baggage. Vict. Ut. iv. fin. In the Emperor's letter before the sixth Ecumenical Council, A.D. 678 (Hard. Conc. t. 3, p. 1048 fin.), he says he has given orders for the conveyance and maintenance of its members. Pope John VIII. (A.D. 876) reminds Ursus, Duke of Venice, of the same duty of providing for the members of a Council, "secundum pios principes, qui in talibus munificè semper erant intenti." Colet. Concil. t. xi. p. 14, Venet. 1730.

Gibbon says that by the Government conveyances "it was easy to travel 100 miles in a day," ch. ii.; but the stages were of different lengths, sometimes a day's journey, Coust. in Hilar. Psalm. 118, Lit. 5, 2 (as over the Delta to Pelusium, and then coasting all the way to Antioch), sometimes half a day's journey, Herman. ibid. Vid. also Ambros. in Psalm. 118, Serm. 5, 5. The halts were called μοναὶ or mansiones, and properly meant the building where soldiers or other public officials rested at night; hence applied to monastic houses, a statement which, if correct, disconnects the word from μόνος. Such buildings included granaries, stabling, &c. Vid. Cod. Theod. t. 1, p. 47, t. 2, p. 507; Ducange, Gloss. t. 1, p. 426, col. 2.

DEFINITIONS.

FROM the first the Church had the power, by its
divinely appointed representatives, to declare the truth
upon such matters in the revealed message or gospel-
tidings as from time to time came into controversy
(for, unless it had this power, how could it be the
" columna et firmamentum veritatis " ?) ; and these representatives, of course, were the Rulers of the Christian people who received, as a legacy, the depositum
of doctrine from the Apostles, and by means of it, as
need arose, exercised their office of teaching. Each
Bishop was in his own place the Doctor Ecclesiæ for
his people; there was an appeal, of course, from his
decision to higher courts; to the Bishops of a province,
of a nation, of a partriarchate, to the Roman Church, to
the Holy See, as the case might be; and thus at length
a final determination was arrived at, which in consequence was the formal teaching of the Church, and as
far as it was direct and categorical, was, from the
reason of the case, the Word of God. And being such,
was certain, irreversible, obligatory on the inward belief
and reception of all subjects of the Church, or what is
called *de fide.*

All this could not be otherwise if Christianity was
to teach divine truth in contrast to the vague opinions
and unstable conjectures of human ' philosophers and

moralists, and if, as a plain consequence, it must have authoritative organs of teaching, and if true doctrines never can be false, but what is once true is always true. What the Church proclaims as true never can be put aside or altered, and therefore such truths are called ὁρισθέντα or ὅροι, *definitions*, as being boundaries or landmarks. Vid. Athan. Decret. § 2.

¶ Decrees or definitions of Councils come to us as formal notices or memoranda, setting forth in writing what has ever been held orally or implicitly in the Church. Hence the frequent use of such phrases as ἐγγράφως ἐξετέθη with reference to them. Thus Damasus, Theod. Hist. v. 10, speaks of that "apostolical faith, which was *set forth in writing* by the Fathers in Nicæa." On the other hand, Ephrem of Antioch speaks of the doctrine of our Lord's perfect humanity being "inculcated by our Holy Fathers, but not as yet [i.e. till the Council of Chalcedon] being *confirmed* by the decree of an Ecumenical Council." Phot. 229, p. 801. (ἐγγράφως, however, sometimes relates to the act of the Bishops in subscribing, Phot. *ibid.*, or to Scripture, Clement. Strom, i. init. p. 321.) Hence Athan. says, ad Afros 1 and 2, that "the Word of the Lord, which was given through the Ecumenical Council in Nicæa *remaineth for ever;*" and uses against its opposers the texts, "Remove not the ancient landmark which thy fathers have set" (vid. also Dionysius in Eus. Hist. vii. 7), and "He that curseth his father or his mother shall surely be put to death." Prov. 22, 28, Ex. 21, 17; vid. also Athan. ad Epict. 1. And the Council of Chalcedon professes to "drive away the doctrines of erroi by a common decree, and *renew* the unswerving faith of the Fathers," Act. v. p. 452, "according as from of old the prophets spoke of Christ, and He Himself instructed us, and the creed of the Fathers has delivered to us," whereas "other faith it is not lawful for any to bring forth, or to write, or to draw up, or to hold, or to teach," p. 456.

¶ And so S. Leo *passim* concerning the Council of Chalcedon, "Concord will be easily established, if the hearts of all concur in that faith, which, &c., *no discussion* being allowed whatever with a view to retractation," Ep. 94. He calls such an act "magnum sacrilegium." Ep. 157, c. 3. "To be seeking for what has been perfected, to tear up what has been laid down (definita), what is this but to be unthankful for what we gained?" Ep. 162, vid. the whole of it. He says that the attempt is "no mark of a peacemaker but a rebel," Ep. 164, c. 1 fin.; vid. also Epp. 145 and 156, where he says, none can assail what is once determined, but "aut antichristus aut diabolus," c. 2.

¶ When at Seleucia Acacius said, "If the Nicene faith has been altered once and many times since, no reason why we should not dictate another faith now," Eleusius the Semi-Arian answered, "This Council is convoked, not to learn what it does not know, not to receive a faith which it does not possess, but walking in the faith of the Fathers," (meaning the Semi-Arian Council of the Dedication, A.D. 341, vid. supr. vol. i. p. 96), "it swerves not from it in life or death." On this Socrates (Hist. ii. 40) observes, "How call you those, who met at Antioch, Fathers, O Eleusius, you who deny *their*

Fathers? for those who met at Nicæa, and who unani-
mously professed the Consubstantial, might more
properly receive the name, &c. But if the Bishops at
Antioch set at nought their own fathers, those who
come after are blindly following parricides; and how
did they receive a valid ordination from them, whose
faith they set at nought as reprobate? But if those
had not the Holy Ghost, which cometh through laying
on of hands, neither did these receive the priesthood;
for did they receive from those who have not where-
with to give?"

¶ This reconsideration of points once settled Athan.
all through his works strenuously resists, and with
more consistency than the Semi-Arians at Seleucia.
And so in their Letter the Fathers at Ariminum observe that the Emperor had commanded them "to treat
of the faith," to which ambiguous phrase they reply that
they mean rather to "adhere" to the faith, and to
reject all novelties. At Sardica indeed the Council
writes to Pope Julius, that the Emperors Constantius
and Constans had proposed three subjects for its consideration: first, "that all points in discussion should
be debated afresh (de integro), and above all concerning
the holy faith and the integrity of the truth which [the
Arians] had violated." Hil. Fragm. ii. 11. Enemies of
the Arians too seem to have wished this as well as
themselves; but the Council got into difficulty in consequence. · Hosius the president and Protogenes
Bishop of the place wrote to the Pope to explain,
"from fear," says Sozomen, "lest some might think
that there was any innovation upon the Nicene de-

crees." iii. 12. However, from his way of stating the matter, Sozomen seems to have himself believed that the Council did publish a creed. And, in fact, a remarkable confession, and a confession attributed to the Council, does exist. Accordingly Athanasius, Eusebius of Vercellæ, and the Council of Alexandria, A.D. 362, protest against the idea of a treatment *de integro.* " It is true," they say, " that certain persons wished to add to the Nicene Council as if there was something wanting, but the Holy Council was displeased," &c. Tom. ad Antioch. § 5. However, Vigilius of Thapsus repeats the report. contr. Eutych. v. init.

¶ This, however, did not interfere with their *adding* without *undoing.* " For," says Vigilius, " if it were unlawful to receive aught further after the Nicene statutes, on what authority venture we to assert that the Holy Ghost is of one substance with the Father, which it is notorious was there omitted?" contr. Eutych. v. init. He gives other instances, some in point, others not; vid. also Eulogius, apud Phot. Cod. 23, pp. 829, 853. Yet to add to the *confession* of the Church is not to add to the *faith*, since nothing can be added to the faith. Leo, Ep. 124, p. 1237. Nay, Athan. says that the Nicene faith is sufficient to refute every heresy, ad Max. 5, fin., also Leo, Ep. 54, p. 956, and Naz. Ep. 102 init., *excepting, however,* the doctrine of the Holy Spirit; which explains his meaning. The Henoticon of Zeno says the same, but with the intention of dealing a blow at the Council of Chalcedon. Evagr. iii, 14, p. 345,

¶ Aetius of Constantinople at Chalcedon says that at Ephesus and Chalcedon the Fathers did not profess to draw up an exposition of faith, and that Cyril and Leo did but *"interpret the Creed."* Conc. Hard. t. 2, p. 428. Leo even says that the Apostles' Creed is sufficient against all heresies, and that Eutyches erred on a point " of which our Lord wished no one of either sex in the Church to be ignorant," and he wishes Eutyches to take the plentitude of the Creed " puro et simplici corde." Ep. 31, p. 857, 8.

DEIFICATION.

THE titles which belong to the Divine Word by nature, are by grace given to us, a wonderful privilege, of which the Arians showed their sense, not by teaching the elevation of the creature to the Son of God, but by lowering the Son to the level of the creature. The means by which these titles become ours are our real participation (μετοχή) of the Son by His presence within us, a participation so intimate that in one sense He can be worshipped in us as being His temple or shrine. Vid. arts. *In-dwelling* and μετουσία.

Athanasius insists on this doctrine again and again.

¶ "The Word was made flesh in order to offer up this body for all, and that we, partaking of His Spirit, might be made gods." Decr. § 14.

¶ "While all things which are made, have by participation (ἐκ μετουσίας) the grace of God, He is the Father's Wisdom and Word, of whom all things partake. It follows that He, being the deifying and enlightening power of the Father, in which all things are deified and quickened, is not alien in substance from the Father, but one in substance." Syn. § 51.

¶ "He was not man, and then became God, but He was God, and then became man, and that to make us gods." Orat. i. § 39.

¶ "This is our grace and high exaltation, that even

when He became man, the Son of God is worshipped, and the heavenly powers are not startled at all of us, who are one body with Him, being introduced into their realms." ibid. § 42.

¶ "Because of our relationship to His body, we too have become God's Temple, and in consequence are made God's Sons, so that even in us the Lord is now worshipped, and beholders report, as the Apostle says, that 'God is in them of a truth.'" ibid. § 43.

¶ "God created Him for our sakes, because of us, preparing for Him that created body, that in Him we might be capable of being renewed and made gods." Orat. ii. § 47.

¶ "Therefore did He assume the body generate and human, that, having renewed it as its framer, He might make it god. . . . For man had not been made god, if joined to a creature, . . . the union was of this kind, . . . that his salvation and deification might be sure." ibid. § 70.

"Although there be but one Son by nature, True and Only-begotten, we too become sons, . . . and, though we are men from the earth, we are yet called gods . . . as has pleased God who has given us that grace." Orat. iii. § 19.

¶ "As we are sons and gods, because of the Word in us, so shall we be in the Son and in the Father, because the Spirit is in us." ibid. § 25.

¶ "We men are made gods by the Word, as being joined to Him through His flesh." ibid. § 34.

¶ "That He might redeem mankind . . . that He

might hallow them and make them gods, the Word became flesh." ibid. § 39.

¶ " What is this advance but the deifying and grace imparted from Wisdom to men ? " ibid. § 53.

Vid. also Adelph. 4; Serap. i. 24; Cyr. in Joann. p. 74; Theod. Hist. p. 846 init.

ECONOMICAL LANGUAGE.

¶ By "Economical," I mean language relating to matters beyond the direct apprehension of those to whom it is addressed, and which, in order to have a chance of conveying to them any idea, however faint, of the fact, must be more or less of an analogous or figurative character, as viewed relatively to the truths which it professes to report, instead of a direct and literal statement of the things which have to be conveyed. Thus a child's idea of a king is that of a man richly dressed with a crown and sceptre, sitting on a throne; thus an attempt might be made to convey to a blind man the character of scarlet contrasted with other colours by telling him that it is like the sound of a trumpet; thus, since none of us can imagine to ourselves a spirit and its properties, it is a received economy to represent Angels as bright beings with wings. Hence, again, it is an economy to speak of our Lord as sitting on the right hand of God, as if right and left were possible in Him; and, indeed, Scripture is necessarily full of economies, when speaking of heavenly things, because there is no other way of introducing into our minds even a rude idea, even any idea at all, of matters so utterly out of our experience. About such economies in the statement of revealed truths, two rules must be observed.

First, while aware of their imperfection as informations, still we must keep strictly to what is told us in them, because we cannot know more exactly what is told us in them than they tell us. Thus we read, " God is a consuming fire; " now fire is a material substance, and cannot literally belong to the Divine Nature ; but it is the only, or at least the truest, mode in which His nature, in a certain relation to us, can be brought home to us, and we must accept it and believe it as a substantial truth, in spite of its not being the whole truth or the exact impress of the truth. Secondly, it must be recollected that we cannot argue and deduce freely from economical language as if it were adequate and complete, and that in revealed matters we may fall into serious error, if we argue and deduce except under the *magisterium* of the Church. Thus it is that some Calvinists have argued against freewill from St. Peter's words in his first Epistle ("Ye, as living *stones*, are built up a spiritual house,") thus, "This is giving freewill a stab under the fifth rib, for can stones build themselves?" Copleston *on Predestinat.* p. 129. And thus it was, that Arius argued, from the economical word Son, (given us as the nearest approximation in human language to the ineffable truth itself,) that our Lord was not the everlasting God, because human sons have a beginning of existence.

Hence it is that mystery is the necessary note of divine revelation, that is, mystery subjectively to the human mind: because, when the mind goes on freely to reason from language which only partially corresponds to eternal truths, and which cannot be adequately expressed in human words, it draws from one revealed information what is inconsistent with what it draws from another, and instead of saying, "This collision of deductions arises from the imperfection of our knowledge," it refuses to accept premisses which are serviceable only in the sense and to the extent in which they are intended. This is acting like a reasoner who, having learned some geometrical truths by means of arithmetic or algebra, and having found that by multiplying a quantity into itself, and again into itself, he could reach a number which in its properties was parallel to a geometrical cube, should in consequence go on to multiply once more, and then should consider that he had been brought to the absurdity of a fourth dimension in space, and should forthwith withdraw his faith from algebraical deductions altogether. Vid. art. *Trinity*, also *Illustrations*, and others.

¶ "Such illustrations and such images," says Athanasius, "has Scripture proposed, that, considering the inability of human nature to comprehend God, we might be able to form ideas even from these, however poorly and dimly, as far as is attainable." Orat. ii. 32, ἀμυδρῶς, vid. also ἀμυδρὰ ; ii. 17.

¶ Elsewhere, after adducing the illustration of the sun and its light, he adds, "From things familiar and ordinary we may use some poor illustration, and represent intellectually what is in our mind, since it were presumptuous to intrude upon the incomprehensible Nature." in Illud Omnia 3 fin. Vid. also 6; also Serap. i. 20, and Decr. § 12. And S. Austin, after an

illustration from the nature of the human mind, proceeds: " Far other are these Three and that Trinity. . .
When a man hath discovered something in them and
stated it, let him not at once suppose that he has discovered what is above him," &c. Confess. xiii. 11.
And again, " Ne hanc imaginem ita comparet Trinitati,
ut omni modo existimet similem." Trin. xv. 39. And
S. Basil says, "Let no one urge against what I say,
that the illustrations do not in all respects answer to
the matters in question. For it is not possible to
apply with exactness what is little and low to things
divine and eternal, except so far as to refute," &c.
contr. Eunom. ii. 17.

¶ Scripture is full of mysteries, but they are mysteries of *fact*, not of words. Its dark sayings or
ænigmata are such, because in the nature of things they
cannot be expressed clearly. Hence contrariwise,
Orat. ii. § 77 fin. he calls Prov. 8, 22 an enigma, with an
allusion to Prov. 1, 6, Sept. In like manner S. Ambrose
says, " Mare est scriptura divina, habens in se sensus
profundos, et altitudinem propheticorum *ænigmatum*,"
&c. Ep. ii. 3. What is commonly called " explaining
away " Scripture, is the transference of this obscurity
from the subject to the words used.

¶ Nothing is more common in theology than large
comparisons which are only parallel to a certain point as
regards the matter in hand, especially since many
doctrines do not admit of exact illustrations. Our
Lord's real manhood and imputed sinfulness were alike
adjuncts to His Divine Person, which was of an Eternal
and Infinite Nature; and therefore His Manhood may

be compared to an Attribute, or to an accident, without meaning that it really was either. The Athan. Creed compares the Hypostatic Union to that of soul and body in one man, which, as taken literally by the Monophysites, became their heresy. Again S. Cyril says, " As the Bread of the Eucharist, after the invocation of the Holy Ghost, is mere bread no longer, but the body of Christ, so also this holy ointment is no more simple ointment," &c. Catech. xxi. 3, Oxf. Tr.; but no Catholic thinks that S. Cyril held either a change in the chrism, or no change in the bread. Hence again we find the Arians arguing from John xvii. 11, that our union with the Holy Trinity is *as* that of the Adorable Persons with Each Other; vid. Euseb. Eccl. Theol. iii. 19, and Athanasius replying to the argument, Orat. iii. 17—25. And so " *As* we, receiving the Spirit, do not lose our own proper substance, *so* the Lord, when made man for us and bearing a body, was no less God," Decr. § 14; yet He was God made man, and we are but the temple of God. And again Athanasius compares the Incarnation to our Lord's presence in the world of nature. Incarn. 41, 42.

ECUMENICAL.

THIS name was given from the first to Councils of the whole Church, whose definitions could not be altered, vid. art. *Definitions.* Athan. twice in his Decr. calls the Nicene by this name, viz. § 4 and § 27. " Are they not committing a crime to gainsay so great and ecumenical a Council ? " § 4, and " the devil alone persuades you to slander the ecumenical Council," § 27 ; vid. also Orat. i. § 7; ad Afros 2 twice ; Apol. contr. Arian. 7 ; ad Ep. Æg. 5; Epiph. Hær. 70, 9 ; Euseb. Vit. Const. iii. 6. The second General Council, A:D. 381, took the name of ecumenical, vid. Can. 6 fin.; but incidentally· The Council of Ephesus so styles itself in the opening of its Synodical Letter.

EUSEBIUS.

Vɪᴅ. arts. *Semi-Arianism* and *Asterius* for a notice of the symbol of the ὁμοιούσιον, in opposition to the orthodox ὁμοούσιον and ἐξ οὐσίας on the one hand, and to ἀνόμοιον on the other. Eusebius is one of the special supporters of this form of heresy. Asterius is another (vid. art. *Arian Leaders*); the statements set down here and under the title "Asterius" are mainly taken from what we find in their controversial works.

¶ In his Letter to his people, supr. vol. i. p. 55, &c., Eusebius scarcely commits himself to any positive sense in which the formula "of the substance" (ἐξ οὐσίας), is to be interpreted, but only says what it does not mean. His comment on it is "of the Father, but not as a part;" where, what is not negative, instead of being an explanation, is but a recurrence to the original words of Scripture, "of the Father," of which ἐξ οὐσίας itself is the explanation; a curious inversion. He says, that the Son is not like the radiance of light so far as this, that the radiance is an inseparable accident of substance, whereas the Son is by the Father's will, κατὰ γνώμην καὶ προαίρεσιν, Dem. Ev. iv. 3. (vid. art. Βούλησις). And though he insists on our Lord being *alone* ἐκ ᾁου, yet he

means in the sense which Athan. refutes, Decr. § 7, viz.
that He alone was created immediately from God. It
is true that he plainly condemns with the Nicene Creed
the ἐξ οὐκ ὄντων of the Arians, "the Son was out of
nothing," but an evasion was at hand here also; for
he not only adds, according to Arian custom, "not as
others," but he has a theory that no being whatever
is out of nothing, for non-existence cannot be the
cause of existence. God, he says, "proposed His own
will and power as *a sort of matter and substance* of the
production and constitution of the universe, so that it
is not reasonably said, that anything is out of nothing.
For what is from nothing cannot be at all. How
indeed can nothing be to anything a cause of being?
but all that is, takes its being *from One* who only
is and was, who also said, 'I am that I am.' " Dem.
Ev. iv. 1. Again, speaking of our Lord, "He who
was from nothing would not truly be Son of God, *as
neither is any other of things generate*." Eccl. Theol.
i. 9 fin.   ·

¶ He distinctly asserts, Dem. Ev. iv. 2, that our Lord
is a creature. "This offspring," he says, "did He
first produce Himself from Himself as a foundation of
those things which should succeed; the perfect handiwork, δημιούργημ a of the Perfect, and the wise structure
ἀρχιτεκτόνημα, of the Wise," &c. It is true in his Lett.
§ 6, he grants that "He was not a work resembling the
things which through Him came to be;" but this again
is only the ordinary Arian evasion of "an offspring, not
as the offsprings." E.g. "It is not without peril to
say recklessly that the Son is generate out of nothing

similarly to the other generates." Dem. Ev. v. 1; vid.
also Eccl. Theol. i. 9, iii. 2. And he considers our Lord
the only Son by a divine provision similar to that by
which there is only one sun in the firmament, as a
centre of light and heat. "Such an Only-begotten
Son, the excellent artificer of His will and operator,
did the supreme God and Father of that operator
Himself first of all beget, through Him and in Him
giving subsistence to the operative words (ideas or
causes) of things which were to be, and casting in Him
the seeds of the constitution and governance of the
universe; . . . Therefore the Father being one, it
behoved the Son to be one also; but should any one
object that He did not constitute more, it is fitting for
such a one to complain that He constituted not more
suns, and moons, and worlds, and ten thousand other
things." Dem. Ev. iv. 5 fin.; vid. also iv. 6.

¶ He does not say that our Lord is *from the substance
of* the Father, but that He has *a substance from* the
Father, " not from other substance, but from the Father."
This is the Semi-Arian doctrine, which, whether confessing the Son from the substance of the Father or
not, implied that His substance was not the Father's
substance, but a second substance. The same doctrine
is found in the Semi-Arians of Ancyra, though they
seem to have confessed, " of the substance." And
this is one object of the ὁμοούσιον, to hinder the confession " of the substance" from implying a second
substance, which was not obviated or was even
encouraged by the ὁμοιούσιον. The Council of Ancyra,
quoting the text " As the Father hath life in Himself,

H 2

so," &c., says "since the life which is in the Father
means substance, and the life of the Only-begotten
who is begotten from the Father means substance,
the word 'so' implies a likeness of substance to substance." Epiph. Hær. 73, 10 fin. Hence Eusebius does
not scruple to speak of "two substances," and other
writers of three substances, contr. Marcell. i. 4, p. 25.
He calls our Lord "a second substance," Dem. Ev.
vi. Præf.; Præp. Ev. vii. 12, p. 320, and the Holy Spirit
a third substance, ibid. 15, p. 325. This it was that made
the Latins so suspicious of three hypostases, because
the Semi-Arians, as well as they, understood ὑπόστασις
to mean substance. Eusebius in like manner calls our
Lord "another God," "a second God," Dem. Ev. v.
4, p. 226, v. fin.; "second Lord," ibid. 3 init. 6 fin.;
"second cause," Dem. Ev. v. Præf.; "not the True
God." Syn. § 17, Concil. vii. art. 6, p. 409. Vid.
also ἕτερον ἔχουσα τὸ κατ' οὐσίαν ὑποκείμενον, Dem. Ev.
v. 1, p. 215; καθ' ἑαυτὸν οὐσιωμένος, ibid. iv. 3. And
so ἕτερος παρὰ τὸν πατέρα, Eccl. Theol. i. 20, p. 90;
and ζωὴν ἰδίαν ἔχων, ibid.; and ζῶν καὶ ὑφεστὼς καὶ τοῦ
πατρὸς ὑπάρχων ἔκτος, ibid. Hence Athan. insists so
much on our Lord *not* being external to the Father.
Once admit that He is *in* the Father, and we may call
the Father, the *only* God, for then the Son is included.
And so again as to the Ingenerate, the term does not
exclude the Son, for He is generate in the Ingenerate. Vid. Ἀγένητος and *Marcellus*.

¶ The Semi-Arians, however, considering the Son as
external to the Father, and this as a necessary truth,
maintained, in order logically to escape Sabellianism,

that the ὁμοούσιον implied a separation or divulsion of
the Divine Substance into two, following the line of argument of Paul of Samosata, who seems to have stopped
the reception of that formula at Antioch in the third
century by arguing that it involved either Sabellianism
(vid. Hilary) or materialism (vid. Athan. and Basil).
E.g. Euseb. Demonstr. iv. 3, p. 148, p. 149, v. 1, p.
213—215; contr. Marcell. i. 4, p. 20; Eccl. Theol.
i. 12, p. 73; in laud. Const. p. 525; de Fide i. ap.
Sirmond. tom. i. p. 7; de Fide ii. p. 16; and apparently
his de Incorporali. And so the Semi-Arians at Ancyra,
Epiph. Hær. 73, 11, p. 858. And so Meletius, ibid.
p. 878 fin., and Cyril Hier. Catech. vii. 5, xi. 18.
οὐ πάθει πατὴρ γενόμενος, οὐκ ἐκ συμπλοκῆς, οὐ κατ᾽
ἄγνοιαν, οὐκ ἀπορρεύσας, οὐ μειωθεὶς, οὐκ ἀλλοιωθείς.
Vid. also Eusebius's letter to his people as given by
Athan. Cyril, however, who had friends among the
Semi-Arians and apparently took their part, could not
be stronger on this point than the Nicene Fathers.

¶ The only sense then in which the word ὁμοούσιον
could be received by such as Eusebius, would seem
to be negative, unless it should rather be taken as
a mere formula of peace; for he says, "We assented
&c. . . . without declining even the term 'Consubstantial,' peace being the object which we set before
us, and maintenance of the orthodox view. . . 'Consubstantial with the Father' suggests that the Son of
God bears no resemblance to the creatures which have
been made, but that He is in every way after the
pattern of His Father alone who begat Him." Euseb.
Lett. § 7. These last words can hardly be called an

interpretation of ὁμοούσιον, for it is but saying that
ὁμοούσιον means ὁμοιούσιον, whereas the two words
notoriously were antagonistic to each other.

¶ It must be observed too that, though the Semi-Arian
ὁμοιούσιον may be taken, as it is sometimes by Athan.,
as satisfying the claims of theological truth, especially
when it is understood in the sense of ἀπαράλλακτος
εἰκὼν, "the exact image" of the Father, (vid. Decr.
§ 20, Theod. Hist. i. 4,) yet it could easily be explained
away. It need mean no more than a likeness of Son
to Father, such as a picture to its original, while
differing from it in substance. "Two men are not of
like nature, but of the same nature; tin is like silver,
but not of the same nature." Syn. § 47—50. Also
Athan. notices that "like" applies to qualities rather
than to substance. Also Basil. Ep. 8, n. 3; "While in
itself," says the same Father, "it is frequently used
of faint similitudes, and falling very far short of the
original." Ep. 9, n. 3. But the word ὁμοούσιον implies
"*the same* in likeness," ταὐτὸν τῇ ὁμοιώσει, that the
likeness may not be considered analogical. vid. Cyril.
in Joan. iii. 5, p. 302. Eusebius makes no concealment
that it is in this sense that he uses the word ὁμοιούσιον,
for he says, "Though our Saviour Himself teaches
that the Father is the only True, still let me not be
backward to confess Him also the true God, *as in an
Image*, and as possessed; so that the addition of
'only' may belong to the Father alone as Archetype
of the Image. . . . As supposing one king held sway,
and his image was carried about into every quarter,
no one in his right mind would say .that those who

held sway were two, but one, who was honoured through his image." de Eccl. Theol. ii. 23; vid. ibid. 7, pp. 109, 111.

¶ Accordingly, instead of ἐξ οὐσίας, which was the Nicene formula, he held μετουσίᾳ, that is, "like to the Father by participation of qualities," as a creature may be; ἐξ αὐτῆς τῆς πατρικῆς [not οὐσίας, but] μετουσίας, ὥσπερ ἀπὸ πηγῆς, ἐπ᾽ αὐτὸν προχεομένης πληρούμενον. Eccl. Theol. i. 2. Whereas Athan. says, οὐδὲ κατὰ μετουσίαν αὐτοῦ, ἀλλ᾽ ὅλον ἴδιον αὐτοῦ γέννημα. Orat. iii. § 4. Disc. n. 228.) "If γe speak of the Son as being merely such by participation, μετουσίᾳ, then call Him ὁμοιούσιον," Syn. 53; but no, it is for creatures to possess God μετουσίᾳ, but when God is said to beget, this is all one with enunciating the ἐξ οὐσίας, and a *whole* participation. Vid. Orat. i. § 16.

¶ Hence St. Austin says, as quoted supr. *Arian tenets*, "As the Father has life in Himself, so hath He given also to the Son to have life in Himself, *not by participating*, but in Himself. For we have not life in ourselves, but in our God. But that Father, who has life in Himself, begat a Son such, as to have life in Himself, not to become partaker of life, but *to be Himself life; and of that life to make us partakers*." Serm. 127, de Verb. Evang. 9.

¶ In Eusebius's Letter to Euphration, as quoted in the seventh Ecum. Council, he introduced the usual Arian argument against the Son's Eternity. "If they co-exist, how shall the Father be Father and the Son Son? or how the One first, and the Other second? and the

One ingenerate and the Other generate?" Vid. supr. *Arian tenets.*

¶ And further he explained away what Catholics held of the eternity of the *gennesis* by insisting that God was a Father *in posse* from eternity, not in fact. "Our religious Emperor did at the time," at Nicæa, "prove in a speech, that our Lord was in being even according to His Divine generation, which is before all ages, since even before He was generated in fact He was in virtue with the Father ingenerately, the Father being always Father, as King always and Saviour always, being all things in virtue, and having all things in the same respects and in the same way." Eus. Lett. § 10.

Theognis too, another of the Nicene Arians, says the same, according to Philostorgius; viz. "that God even before He begat the Son was a Father, as having the power, δύναμις, of being so," Hist. ii. 15, 16; and Asterius. They are answered by Catholics, on the ground that Father and Son are words of nature, but Creator, King, Saviour, are external, or what may be called accidental to Him. Thus Athanasius observes, that Father actually implies Son, but Creator only the power to create, as expressing a δύναμις; "a maker is before his works, but he who says Father, forthwith in Father implies the existence of the Son." Orat. iii. 6. (*Disc.* n. 231, supr. vol. i. p. 364.) Vid. Cyril too, Dial. ii. p. 459; Pseudo-Basil. contr. Eun. iv. 1 fin. On the other hand Origen argues the reverse way, that since God is eternally a Father, therefore eternally Creator also. "As one cannot be father without a son, nor lord

without possession, so neither can God be called All-
powerful, without subjects of His power," Periarch.
i. 2, n. 10; hence he argued for the eternity of creation,
which Suarez, after St. Thomas, allows to be abstract-
edly possible. Vid. Theol. Tracts ii. § 11 circ. fin.

¶ Athan. distinguishes as follows: that, as it is of
the *essence* of a son to be *of the nature* of the father,
so is it of the *essence* of a creature to be *of nothing*,
ἐξ οὐκ ὄντων; therefore, while it was *not* impossible,
from the nature of the case, for Almighty God to be
always Father, it *was* impossible for the same reason
that He should be always a Creator, impossible from
incapacity, not in the Infinite, but in the finite. Orat.
i. 29. Vid. ibid. § 58, where he takes "They shall
perish," in the Psalm, not as a fact, but as the definition of the *nature* of a creature. Also ii. § 1, where
he says, "It is proper to creatures and works to have
said of them, ἐξ οὐκ ὄντων and οὐκ ἦν πρὶν γεννηθῇ."
Vid. Cyril. Thesaur. 9, p. 67. Dial. ii. p. 460.

It has been above shown that Eusebius held with
Arians generally that our Lord was created by the God
of all in order that He might create all else. And this
was because the creation could not bear the Divine Hand,
as the Arians also said. Vid. a clear and eloquent
passage in his Eccl. Theol. i. 8, also 13, to show that
our Lord was brought into being before all creation, ἐπὶ
σωτηρίᾳ τῶν ὅλων. Vid. also Demonstr. iv. 4; Præp. vii.
15; but especially his remark, "not because the Father
was not able to create, did He beget the Son, but
because those things which were made were not able
to sustain the power of the Ingenerate, therefore

speaks He through a Mediator," contra Sabell. i.
p. 9.

There is another peculiarity of Eusebius's view of the
creative office of the Divine Word, in contrast with
the Catholic doctrine. It is that the Word does not
create from His own designs, as being Himself really
the τύπος, εἰκὼν, and ὑπόγραμμα of those things which
He is creating, but that He copies the Father's
patterns as an external minister. " The Father *designed*
(διετύπου) and prepared with consideration, *how,*· and
of *'what shape, measure,* and *parts*. . . . And He
watching (ἐνατενίζων) the Father's thoughts, and alone
beholding the depths in Him, went about the work,
subserving the Father's orders (νεύμασι) . . . As a
skilful painter, *taking the archetypal ideas from* the
Father's thoughts, He transferred them to the substances of the works." Eccl. Theol. iii. 3, pp. 164, 5.

In this Eusebius follows the Platonists; so he does,
when he attributes our Lord's Priesthood to His
Divine Nature, as the Word, in which case His human
sufferings have no part in it.

Moreover, it is doubtful whether he held that our
Lord, in becoming incarnate, took on Him a human soul
as well as body. In his work against Marcellus, p. 54,
he seems to grant his opponent's doctrine, when he
says, εἰ μέν ψυχῆς δίκην (δίχα) οἰκῶν ἐν αὐτῷ τῷ σώματι ;
and at p. 55 he seems to say that, if the Word retired
from the ζωοποιὸς σὰρξ, the σὰρξ would be left ἄλογος ;
vid. also ibid. p. 91.

THE FATHER ALMIGHTY.

1. The idea of an Almighty, All-perfect Being, in its fulness involves the belief of His being the Father of a co-equal Son, and this is the first advance which a habit of devout meditation makes towards the intellectual apprehension of the doctrine of the Holy Trinity, as soon as that doctrine has been received with the claim and the sanction of its having been revealed.

¶ The Fathers speak as if it were nothing short of a necessary truth, involved in the nature of things, that One who is infinite in His attributes should subsist over again in an infinite perfect Image, Impress, Likeness, Word, or Son, for these names denote the same sacred truth. A redundatio in imaginem or in Verbum is synonymous with a generatio Filii. "Naturam et essentiale Deitatis," says Thomassin, "in suo Fonte assentiuntur omnes esse plenitudinem totius Esse. At hæc necesse est ut statim exundet nativâ fœcunditate suâ. Infinitum enim illud Esse non Esse tantum est sed Esse totum est; vivere id ipsum est intelligere, sapere; opulentiæ suæ, bonitatis, et sapientiæ rivulos undique spargere; nec rivulos tantum, sed et fontem et plenitudinem ipsam suam diffundere. Hæc enim demum fœcunditas Deo digna, Deo par est, ut a Fonte bonitatis non rivulus sed flumen effluat, nec extra effluat, sed in ipsomet, cùm extra nihil sit, quo illa plenitudo capi possit." de Trin. 19, 1.

Thus Athan. says, " Let them dare to say openly . . that the Fountain failed to beget Wisdom, whence it would follow that there is no longer a Fountain, but a sort of pool, as if receiving water from without, yet usurping the name of Fountain." Decr. § 15; vid. also Orat. i. § 14 and 19. And so πηγὴ ξηρὰ, Serap. ii. 2; Orat. i. § 14 fin.; also καρπογόνος ἡ οὐσία, ii. § 2, where Athanasius speaks as if those who deny that Almighty God is Father cannot really believe in Him as a Creator. "If our Lord be not a Son, let Him be called a work .. and let God be called, not Father, but Framer only and Creator, .. and not of a generative nature. But if the Divine substance be not fruitful (καρπογόνος), but barren, as they say, as a light which enlightens not, and a dry fountain, are they not ashamed to maintain that He possesses the creative energy?" Vid. also πηγὴ θεότητος, Pseudo-Dion. Div. Nom. ii. 4; πηγὴ ἐκ πηγῆς, of the Son, Epiphan. Ancor. 19. And Cyril, "If thou take from God His being Father, thou wilt deny the generative power (καρπογόνον) of the divine nature, so that It no longer is *perfect*. This then is a token of its perfection, and the Son who went forth from Him apart from time, is a pledge (σφραγὶς) to the Father that He is perfect." Thesaur. p. 37. Vid. also γεννητικὸς, Orat. ii. § 2, iii. § 66, iv. § 4 fin.; ἄγονος, i. 14, 19, and Sent. Dion. 15 and 19; ἡ φυσικὴ γονιμότης, Damasc. F.O. i. 8; ἄκαρπος, Cyr. Thes. p. 45; Epiph. Hær. 65, p. 609; also the γέννησις and the κτίσις connected together, Orat. i. 29. · This doctrine is briefly expressed in Orat. iv. 4, εἰ ἄγονος, καὶ ἀνενέργητος. So much at least is plain at first sight, that a divine *gennesis* is not more difficult to our imagination than a creation out of nothing.

This is the first conclusion which we are in a position to draw under the sanction given to our reasonings by the revelation of the doctrine of the Holy Trinity in Unity.

2. A second conclusion is suggested by Thomassin's words towards the end of the above quotation, " ut effluat nec extra effluat." It is the first of truths that there is but one only Supreme Almighty Being. The Arians and others accused Catholics, in their maintenance of our Lord's Divinity, of virtually contravening this initial doctrine of all faith ; as Euseb. Eccl. Theol. i. 10, p. 69; and accordingly they insisted on His being external, and thereby subordinate and inferior to God. But this was in fact to admit that He was not born from God at all, but κεκολλῆσθαι τῷ πατρὶ λόγον, Orat. iv. § 3; and Marcellus, according to Eusebius, spoke of Him as ἡνωμένον τῷ θεῷ λόγον (vid. συμβεβηκὸς), Athan. protesting on the other hand against the notion " that the Fountain begat not wisdom from Itself, but acquired it from without," vid. supr. Decr. § 15, and Orat. iv. § 4, and laying down the principle οὐδὲν ἐν πρὸς τὸν πατέρα, εἰ μὴ τὸ ἐξ αὐτοῦ. Orat. iv. 17.

¶ But the Son still was *in* as well as *from* the Father, and this union of distinct characteristics in the Son was signified by S. John by the word πρὸς, i. 1, whereas the Sabellians preferred to say ἐν τῷ θεῷ. Hence

Basil, ὁ ἐν ἀνθρώπῳ λόγος οὐ πρὸς αὐτὸν εἶναι λέγεται ἀλλ' ἐν αὐτῷ, c. Sabell. 1, fin., but the Divine Son was πρὸς τὸν θεὸν, not ἐν τῷ θεῷ. It was in this sense and with this explanation that Catholics held and insisted on the Divine Unity; or, as they then called it, the *Monarchia:* and thence they went on to the second great doctrine associated in theology with the Eternal Father, and signified by Thomassin in the above extract in the words, "ut effluat flumen Deitatis nec extra effluat." The Infinite Father of an Infinite Son must necessarily be con-terminus (so to speak) with Him. A second self (still to use inaccurate language) cannot be a second God. The *Monarchia* of the Father is not only the symbol of the Divine Unity, but of the Trinity in that Unity, for it implies the presence of Those who, though supreme, are not ἀρχαί. This was especially its purpose in the first centuries, when polytheistic errors prevailed. The Son and Spirit were then viewed relatively to the Father, and the Father as the absolute God. Even now statements remain in the Ritual of the old usage, as in the termination of Collects, and as in the Sunday Preface in the Mass: "Pater Omnipotens, qui cum Unigenito Filio tuo et Spiritu Sancto, Unus es Deus" instead of the "Pater, Filius, Spiritus Sanctus, Unus Deus" of the Psalmus *Quicunque.*

And so, "The Word," says Athan., "being the Son of the One God, is *referred* to Him *of whom* also He is." Orat. iv. § 1. εἰς αὐτὸν ἀναφέρεται. vid. also Nazianz. Orat. 20. 7; Damasc. F. O. i. 8, p. 140; Theod. Abuc. Opusc. 42, p. 542. And so ἀνάγεται, Naz. Orat. 42. 15; and ἵνα ἡμᾶς ἀναπέμψῃ ἐπὶ τὴν τοῦ πατρὸς αὐθεντίαν, Euseb. Eccl. Theol. i. 20, p. 84, though in an heretical sense. (Vid. a remarkable illustration of this, under *Ignorance* in Basil on Mark xiii. 32.) This, then, is the Catholic doctrine of the Monarchia, in opposition to the Three Archical Hypostases of Plato and others. The Son and the Spirit were viewed as the Father's possession, as one with Him yet as really distinct from Him as a man's hands are one and not one with himself; but still, in spite of this, as being under the conditions of a nature at once spiritual and infinite, therefore, in spite of this ana-logy, not inferior, even if subordinate to the Father. The word "parts" belongs to bodies, and implies magnitude; but as the soul has powers and properties, conscience, reason, imagination, and the like, but no parts, so each Person of the Holy Trinity must either be altogether and fully God, or not God at all.

¶ By the Monarchy is meant the doctrine that the Second and Third Persons in the Ever-blessed Trinity are ever to be referred in our thoughts to the First as the Fountain of Godhead. It is one of the especial senses in which God is said to be one. "We are not introducing three origins or three Fathers, as the Marcionites and Manichees, just as our illustration is not of three suns, but of sun and its radiance." Orat. iii. § 15; vid. also iv. § 1. Serap. i. 28 fin. Naz. Orat. 23. 8. Bas. Hom. 24, init. Nyssen. Orat. Cat. 3, p. 481. "The Father is *unition, ἕνωσις*," says S. Greg. Naz., "from whom and unto whom are the other Two." Orat. 42. 15: also Orat. 20. 7,

and Epiph. Hær. 57, 5. Tertullian, and Dionysius of
Alexandria after him (Athan. Decr. § 26), uses the word
Monarchia, which Praxeas had perverted into a kind
of Unitarianism or Sabellianism, in Prax. 3. Irenæus
too wrote on the Monarchy, i.e. against the doctrine
that God is the author of evil. Eus. Hist. v. 20. And
before him was Justin's work " de Monarchiâ," where
the word is used in opposition to Polytheism. The
Marcionites, whom Dionysius also mentions, are
referred to by Athan. de Syn. § 52; vid. also Cyril.
Hier. Cat. xvi. 4. Epiphanius says that their three
origins were God, the Creator, and the evil spirit,
Haer. 42, 3, or as Augustine says, the good, the just,
and the wicked, which may be taken to mean nearly
the same thing. Hær. 22. The Apostolical Canons
denounce those who baptise into Three Unoriginate;
vid. also Athan. Tom. ad Antioch. 5; Naz. Orat. 20. 6.
Basil denies τρεῖς ἀρχικαὶ ὑποστάσεις, de Sp. S. § 38.

¶ When characteristic attributes and prerogatives
are ascribed to God, or to the Father, this is done only
to the exclusion of creatures, or of false Gods, not to
the exclusion of His Son who is implied in the mention
of Himself. Thus when God is called only wise, or
the Father the only God, or God is said to be ingenerate, ἀγένητος, this is not in contrast to the Son, but to
all things which are distinct from God, vid. Athan.
Orat. iii. 8 ; Naz. Orat. 30. 13; Cyril. Thesaur. p. 142.
" The words 'one' and 'only' ascribed to God in
Scripture," says S. Basil, " are not used in contrast
to the Son or the Holy Spirit, but with reference to
those who are not God, and falsely called so." Ep. 8,

ι.. 3. On the other hand, when the Father is mentioned, the other Divine Persons are implied in Him. "The Blessed and Holy Trinity," says S. Athan., "is indivisible and one with Itself; and when the Father is mentioned, His Word is present too ($\pi\rho\acute{o}\sigma\epsilon\sigma\tau\iota$), and the Spirit in the Son; and if the Son is named, in the Son is the Father, and the Spirit is not external to the Word." ad Serap. i. 14. "I have named the Father," says S. Dionysius, "and before I mention the Son, I have already signified Him in the Father; I have mentioned the Son, and though I had not yet named the Father, He had been fully comprehended in the Son," &c. Sent. D. 17, vid. art. *Coinherence.*

¶ Passages like these are distinct from that in which Athan. says that "Father implies Son," Orat. iii. § 6, for there the question is of words, but here of fact. That the words are correlative, even Eusebius does not scruple to admit in Sabell. i. (ap. Sirm. t. i. p. 8.) "Pater statim, ut dictus fuit pater, *requirit ista vox* filium," &c.; but in that passage no $\pi\epsilon\rho\iota\chi\acute{\omega}\rho\eta\sigma\iota\varsigma$ is implied, which *is* the orthodox doctrine. Yet Petavius observes as to the very *word* $\pi\epsilon\rho\iota\chi\acute{\omega}\rho\eta\sigma\iota\varsigma$ that one of its first senses in ecclesiastical writers was this which Arians would not disclaim; its use to express the Catholic doctrine here spoken of was later. Vid. de Trin. iv. 16.

3. Thirdly, from what has been said, since God, although He is One and Only, nevertheless is Father because He is God, we are led to understand that He is Father in a sense of His own, not in a mere human sense; for a Father, who was like other fathers,

would of course impart to a Son that which he was himself, and thus God would have a Son who could be a father, and, as God, would in His Son commence a θεογονία; this was the objection of the Arians; but His Son is His Image, not as Father, but as God; and to be Father is not the accident of His Person, as in the case of men, but belongs necessarily to it; and His personality in the Godhead consists, as far as we know it, in His being Father and in nothing else, and can only so be defined or described; and so in a parallel way as regards the Son. The words "Father" and "Son" have a high archetypical sense, and human fathers and sons have but the shadow of it.

¶ With us a son becomes a father because our nature is ῥευστή, transitory and without stay, ever shifting and passing on into new forms and relations: but God is perfect and ever the same; what He is once, that He continues to be; God the Father remains Father, and God the Son remains Son. Moreover, men become fathers by detachment and transmission, and what is received is handed on in a succession; thus Levi before his birth was in the loins of Abraham; whereas it is by imparting Himself wholly that the Father begets the Son; and a perfect *gennesis* finds its termination in itself. The Son has not a Son, because the Father has not a Father. Thus the Father is the only true Father, and the Son the only true Son; the Father only a Father, the Son only a Son; being really in Their Persons what human fathers are but by function, circumstance, accident, and name. And since the Father is unchangeable as Father, in nothing does the Son more fulfil the idea of a perfect Image than in being unchangeable too. Thus S. Cyril. also, Thesaur. 4, pp. 22, 23 ; 13, p. 124, &c.

Men differ from each other as being individuals, but the characteristic difference between Father and Son is, not that they are separate individuals, but that they *are* Father and Son. In these extreme statements it must be ever borne in mind that we are contemplating divine things according to *our notions*, not *in re*: i.e. we are speaking of the Almighty Father, *as such*; there being no real separation between His Person and His Substance.

¶ Thus Athanasius: " ' If the Son is the Father's offspring and image, and is like in all things to the Father,' say the Arians, ' then it necessarily holds that as He is begotten, so He begets, and He too becomes father of a son. And again, he who is begotten from Him, begets in his turn, and so on without limit; for this is to make the Begotten like Him that begat Him.' Authors of blasphemy! . . if God be as man, let Him be also a parent as man, so that His Son should be father of another, and so in succession one from another, till the series they imagine grows into a multitude of gods. But if God be not as man, as He is not, we must not impute to Him the attributes of man. For brutes and men after that a Creator has begun their line, are begotten by succession; and the son, having been begotten of a father who was a son, becomes accordingly in his turn a father to a son, in inheriting from his father that by which he himself has come into being. Hence in such instances there is not, properly

I 2

speaking, either father or son, nor do the father and the son stay in their respective characters, for the son himself becomes a father, being son of his father, and father of his son. But it is not so in the Godhead; for not as man is God; for the Father is not from father; therefore doth He not beget one who shall beget; nor is the Son from effluence of the Father, nor is He begotten from a father that was begotten; therefore neither is He begotten so as to beget. Thus it belongs to the Godhead alone, that the Father is properly (κυρίως) father, and the Son properly son, and in Them, and Them only, does it hold that the Father is ever Father and the Son ever Son. Therefore he who asks why the Son has not a son, must inquire why the Father had not a father. But both suppositions are indecent and impious exceedingly. For as the Father is ever Father and never could be Son, so the Son is ever Son and never could be Father. For in this rather is He shown to be the Father's Impress and Image, remaining what He is and not changing, but thus receiving from the Father to be one and the same." Orat. i. § 21, 22. Presently he says, "For God does not make men His pattern, but rather, because God is properly and alone truly Father of His Son, we men also are called fathers of our own children, for 'of Him is every fatherhood in heaven and on earth named.'" § 23. The Semi-Arians at Ancyra quote the same text for the same doctrine. Epiphan. Hær. 73, 5. As do Cyril. in Joan. iii. p. 24; Thesaur. 32, p. 281; and Damascene de Fid. Orth. i. 8.

Again: "As men create not as God creates, as their

being is not such as God's being, so men's generation
is in one way, and the Son is from the Father in
another. For the offspring of men are portions of
their fathers, since the very nature of bodies is to
be dissoluble, and composed of parts; and men lose
their substance in begetting, and again they gain
substance from the accession of food. And on this
account men in their time become fathers of many
children; but God, being without parts, is Father of
the Son without partition or passion; for of the Immaterial there is neither effluence nor accession from
without, as among men; and being uncompounded in
nature, He is Father of One Only Son. This is why the
Son is Only-begotten, and alone in the Father's bosom,
and alone is acknowledged by the Father to be from
Him, saying, *This is My beloved Son in whom I am
well pleased.*" de Decr. § 11. The parallel, with which
this passage begins, as existing between creation and
generation, is insisted on by Isidor. Pel. Ep. iii. 355;
Basil. contr. Eun. iv. 1, p. 280, A; Cyril. Thesaur. 6,
p. 43; Epiph. Hær. 69, 36; and Gregor. Naz. Orat. 20.
9, who observes that God creates with a *word*, Ps. 148,
5, which evidently transcends human creations. (Vid.
also supr. 1st part of this art.) Theodorus Abucara,
with the same object, draws out the parallel of life, ζωὴ,
as Athan. that of being, εἶναι. Opusc. iii. p. 420—422.

The word κυρίως, used in the first of these passages,
also occurs on the same subject in Serap. i. § 16.
" The Father, being one and only, is Father of a Son
one and only; and in the instance of Godhead only
have the names Father and Son a stay and a perpetuity;

for of men if any one be called father, yet he has been
son of another ; and if he be called son, yet is he called
father of another; so that in the case of men the
names father and son do not properly (κυρίως) hold."
Vid. the whole passage.   Also ibid. iv. 4 fin. and 6 ;
vid. also κυρίως, Greg. Naz. Orat. 29. 5 ; ἀληθῶς,
Orat. 25. 16 ; ὄντως, Basil. contr. Eunom. i. 5, p.
215.

¶ Ὁ μὲν πατήρ, πατήρ ἐστι. Orat. iii. § 11. And so,
" In the Godhead only, ὁ πατήρ κυρίως ἐστὶ πατήρ,
καὶ ὁ υἱὸς κυρίως υἱός." Serap. i. 16. He speaks of
"receding from things generate, casting away created
images, and ascending to the Father." Again of men
" not being in nature and truth benefactors," Almighty
God being Himself the type and pattern, &c.   Vid.
Nic. § xi.; Syn. § 51; Orat. iii. § 19.   And so S.
Cyril, τὸ κυρίως τίκτον ἐξ ἑαυτοῦ τὸ θεῖόν ἐστιν, ἡμεῖς
δὲ κατὰ μίμησιν.   Thesaur. 13, p. 133, πατήρ κυρίως,
ὅτι μὴ καὶ υἱός· ὥσπερ καὶ υἱὸς κυρίως, ὅτι μὴ καὶ
πατήρ.   Naz. Orat. 29. 5; vid. also 23, 6 fin. 25,
16; vid. also the whole of Basil. adv. Eun. ii. 23.
" One must not say," he observes, " that these names
properly and primarily, κυρίως καὶ πρώτως, belong to
men, and are given by us but by a figure καταχρησ-
τικῶς (vol. i. p. 19, note 2) to God.   For our Lord Jesus
Christ, referring us back to the Origin of all and True
Cause of beings, says, ' Call no one your father upon
earth, for One is your Father, which is in heaven.' " He
adds, that if He is properly and not metaphorically the
Father even of us, much more is He the πατήρ τοῦ κατὰ
φύσιν υἱοῦ.   Vid. also Euseb. contr. Marc. i. 4, p. 22. Eccl.

Theol. i. 12 fin.; ii. 6. Marcellus, on the other hand, contrasting Son and Word, said that our Lord was κυρίως λόγος, not κυρίως υἱός. ibid. ii. 10 fin.

S. Basil says in like manner that, though God is Father κυρίως (properly), yet it comes to the same thing though we were to say that He is τροπικῶς and ἐκ μεταφορᾶς, figuratively, Father; contr. Eun. ii. 24; for in that case we must, as in other metaphors used of Him (anger, sleep, flying), take that part of the human sense which can apply to Him. Now γέννησις implies two things—passion, and relationship, οἰκείωσις φύσεως; accordingly we must take the latter as an indication of the divine sense of the term. On the terms Son, Word, &c., being figurative, or illustrative, and how to use them, vid. also de Decr. § 12; Orat. i. § 26, 27, ii. § 32, iii. § 18, 67; Basil. contr. Eunom. ii. 17; Hil. de Trin. iv. 2. Vid. also Athan. ad Serap. i. 20, and Basil. Ep. 38, n. 5, and what is said of the office of faith in each of these.

THE FLESH.

WE know that our Lord took our flesh and in it by
His death atoned for our sins, and by the grace communicated to us through that Flesh, renews our nature;
but the question arises whether He took on Him our
flesh as it was in Adam before the fall, or as it is now.
To this the direct and broad answer is,—He assumed it
as it is after the fall,—though of course some explanations have to be made.

¶ It was usual to say against the Apollinarians, that,
unless our Lord took on Him our nature, *as it is*, He
had not purified and changed it, as it is, but another
nature; "The Lord came not to save Adam as free
from sin, that unto him He should become like; but
as, in the net of sin and now fallen, that God's mercy
might raise him up with Christ." Leont. contr. Nestor.
&c. ii. t. 9, p. 692, Bibl. Max. Accordingly Athan. says,
"He took a servant's form, putting on that flesh, which
was enslaved to sin." Orat. i. § 43. And, "Had not
Sinlessness appeared *in the nature which had sinned,*
how was sin condemned in the flesh?" in Apoll. ii. 6.
"It was necessary for our salvation," says S. Cyril,
"that the Word of God should become man, that
human flesh *subject to corruption* and *sick with the lust
of pleasures*, He might make His own; and, *whereas He
is life and life-giving*, He might *destroy the corruption*

&c. . . . . For by this means might sin in our flesh become dead." Ep. ad Success. i. p. 138. And S. Leo, "Non alterius naturæ erat ejus caro quam nostra, nec alio illi quam cæteris hominibus anima est inspirata principio, quæ excelleret, non diversitate generis, sed sublimitate virtutis." Ep. 35 fin.; vid. also Ep. 28, 3; Ep. 31, 2; Ep. 165, 9; Serm. 22, 2, and 25, 5. If indeed sin were *of the substance* of our fallen nature, as some heretics have said, then He could not have taken our nature without partaking our sinfulness; but if sin be, as it is, a fault of the *will*, then the Divine Power of the Word could sanctify the human will, and keep it from swerving in the direction of evil. Hence S. Austin says, "We say not that it was by the *felicity of a flesh* separated from sense that Christ *could not* feel the desire of sin, but that *by perfection of virtue*, and by a flesh not begotten through concupiscence of the flesh, He had not the desire of sin." Op. Imperf. iv. 48. On the other hand, S. Athanasius expressly calls it Manichean doctrine to consider τὴν φύσιν of the flesh ἁμαρτίαν, καὶ οὐ τὴν πρᾶξιν, contr. Apoll. i. 12 fin., or φυσικὴν εἶναι τὴν ἁμαρτίαν, ibid. i. 14 fin. His argument in Apoll. i. 15 is on the ground that all *natures* are from God, but God made man upright nor· can be the author of evil (vid. also Vit. Anton. 20); "not as if," he says, "the devil wrought in man a nature, (God forbid!) for of a nature the devil cannot be maker (δημιουργὸς), as is the impiety of the Manichees, but he wrought a bias of nature by transgression, and 'so death reigned over all men.' Wherefore, saith He, 'the Son of God came to destroy the works of the devil;' what works? that nature, which God made sinless, and the devil biassed to the transgression of God's command and the assault of sin which is death, that nature did God the Word raise again so as to be secure from the devil's bias and the assault of sin. And therefore the Lord said, 'The prince of this world cometh and findeth nothing in Me.'" vid. also § 19. Ibid. ii. 6, he speaks of the devil having introduced "the *law* of sin." vid. also § 9.

¶ " As, since the flesh has become the all-quickening Word's, it overbears the might of corruption and death, so, I think since the soul became His who knew not error, it has an unchangeable condition for all good things established in it, and far more vigorous than the sin that of old time tyrannised over us. For, first and only of men on the earth, Christ did not sin, nor was guile found in His mouth; and He is laid down as a root and firstfruit of those who are re-fashioned unto newness of life in the Spirit, and unto immortality of body, and He will transmit to the whole human race the firm security of the Godhead, as by participation and by grace." Cyril. de Rect. Fid. p. 18. Vid. art. *Specialties.*

USE OF FORCE IN RELIGION.

"IN no long time," says Athan., "they will turn to outrage; and next they will threaten us with the band and the captain." Vid. John xviii. 12. Elsewhere he speaks of tribune and governor, with an allusion perhaps to Acts xxiii. 22, 24, &c. Hist. Arian. § 66 fin. and 67; vid. also § 2. "How venture they to call that a Council, in which a Count presided," &c. Apol. c. Ar. 8; vid. also 10, 45; Ep. Enc. 5. And so also doctrinally, "Our Saviour is so gentle that He teaches thus, *If any man wills to come after Me,* and *Whoso wills to be My disciple;* and coming to each, He does not force them, but knocks at the door and says, *Open unto Me, My sister, My spouse;* and, if they open to Him, He enters in, but if they delay and will not, He departs from them. For *the Truth* is not preached with swords or with darts, nor by means of soldiers, but by persuasion and counsel." Ar. Hist. § 33; vid. also 67, and Hilar. ad Const. i. 2. On the other hand he observes of the Nicene Fathers, "It was not necessity which drove the judges" to their decision, "but all vindicated the truth of deliberate purpose." Ep. Æg. 13.

As to the view taken in early times of the use of force in religion, it seems to have been that that was a bad cause which depended upon it; but that, when a cause was good, there was nothing wrong in using secular means in due subordination to argument; that it was as lawful to urge religion by such means on individuals who were incapable of higher motives, as by inducements of temporal advantage. Our Lord's kingdom was not of this world, in that it did not depend on this world; but means of this world were sometimes called for in order to lead the mind to an act of faith in that which was not of this world. The simple question was, whether a cause depended on force for its success. S. Athanasius declared, and the event proved, that Arianism was thus dependent. When Emperors ceased to persecute, Arianism ceased to be; it had no life in itself. Again, active heretics were rightly prevented by secular means from spreading the poison of their heresy. But all exercise of temporal pressure, long continued or on a large scale, was wrong, as arguing an absence of moral and rational grounds in its justification. Again, the use of secular weapons in ecclesiastical hands was a scandal, as *negotiatio* would be. And further there is an abhorrence of cruelty, just and natural to us, which may easily be elicited, unless the use of the secular arm is directed with much discretion and charity. For a list of passages from the Fathers on the subject, vid. Limborch on the Inquisition, vol. i. and ii. 2 and 5; Bellarmin. de Laicis, c. 21, 22. For authors who defend its adoption, vid. Gerhard de Magistr. Polit. p. 741. So much as to the question of principle, which even Protestants act on and have generally acted; in this day and here, State interference would so simply tell against the Catholic cause, that it would be a marvel to find any Catholic advocating it.

In that day it was a thought which readily arose in the minds of zealous men. Thus:

¶ " Who comprehends not the craft of these God-assailants? who but would stone such madmen? οὐκ ἂν καταλιθώσειεν." Decr. § 28.

" If then they thus conceive of the Son, let all men throw stones at them, considering, as they do, the Word a part of this universe, and a part insufficient without the rest for the service committed to Him. But if this be manifestly impious, let them acknowledge that the Word is not in the number of things made, but the sole and proper Word of the Father, and their Framer. His words are βαλλέσθωσαν παρὰ πάντων," Orat. ii. § 28. Vid. also i. 38, and iii. 41.

¶ There is an apparent allusion in such passages to the punishment of blasphemy and idolatry under the Jewish Law. Vid. art. *Definition*, supra, Ex. xxi. 17. Thus, for instance, Nazianzen: " While I go up the mount with good heart, . . that I may become within the cloud, and may hold converse with God, (for so God bids,) if there be any Aaron, let him go up with me and stand near. . . And if there be any Nadab or Abiud, or any of the elders, let him go up, but stand far off, according to the measure of his purification. . . . But if any one is an evil and savage beast, and quite incapable of science and theology . . let him stand off still further, and depart from the mount ; *or he will be stoned* and crushed ; for the wicked shall be miserably destroyed. For *as stones for the bestial are true words and strong.* Whether he be leopard, let him die, spots and all," &c. Orat. 28. 2. The stoning then was

metaphorical; the stones were strong words. In the
same way S. Dionysius speaks of the charges of heterodoxy brought against him before the Roman See.
"By two words taken out of their context, as with
stones, they sling at me from a distance." Athan. de
Sent. D. § 18.

¶ "Are they not deserving of many deaths?" Orat.
ii. § 4. "You *ought* (ὤφειλες) to have your impious
tongue cut out," the Arian Acacius says to Marcellus,
ap. Epiph. Hær. 72, 7. "If Eutyches thinks otherwise
than the decrees of the Church, he *deserves* (ἄξιος) not
only punishment, but the fire," says the Monophysite.
Dioscorus ap. Concil. Chalced. (Hard. t. 2, p. 100.)
In time they advanced from accounting to doing. The
Emperor Justin proposes to cut out the heretic Severus's
tongue, Evagr. iv. 4; and "blasphemiis lapidasti,"
Theodor. ap. Concil. 6. (Labbe, t. 6, p. 88.) Afterwards we find an advance from allegory to fact.
Sometimes it was a literalism deduced from the doctrine
in dispute; as the heretics at the Latrocinium cried,
"Cut in two those who assert two Natures." Concil.
Hard. t. 2, p. 81. Palladius relates a case in which a
sort of ordeal became a punishment: Abbot Copres
proposed to a Manichee to enter a fire with him. After
Copres had come out unharmed, the populace forced
the Manichee into it, and then cast him, burnt as he
was, out of the city. Hist. Lausiac. 54. S. Gregory
mentions the case of a wizard, who had pretended to
be a monk, and had used magical arts against a nun,
being subsequently burned by the Roman populace.
Dial. i. 4.

FREEDOM OF OUR MORAL NATURE.

THIS, it need hardly be said, is one of the chief blessings which we have secured to us by the Incarnation. We are by nature the captives and prisoners of our inordinate and unruly passions and desires; we are not our own masters, till our Lord sets us free; and the main question is, how does He set us free, and by what instrumentality?

1. Here we answer, first, by bringing home to us the broad and living law of liberty and His own pattern which He has provided for us. "Whereas," Athan. says, " of things made the nature is alterable, . . therefore there was here need of One who was unalterable, that men might have the immutability of the righteousness of the Word as an image and type for virtue." Orat. i. § 51. (*Disc.* n. 84.)

¶ Vid. Athan. de Incarn. § 13, 14; vid. also Gent. 41 fin. "Cum justitia nulla esset in terrâ, doctorem misit, quasi vivam legem." Lactant. Instit. iv. 25. "The Only-begotten was made man like us, . . . as if lending us His own steadfastness." Cyril. in Joann. lib. v. 2, p. 473; vid. also Thesaur. 20, p. 198; August. de Corr. et Grat. 10—12; Damasc. F. O. iv. 4. And this pattern to us He is, not only through His Incarnation, but as manifested in a measure by His glory, as πρωτότοκος, in the visible universe.

Vid. a beautiful passage, contr. Gent. 42, &c. Again, "He made them [men] after His own image, imparting to them of the power of His own Word, that, having as it were *certain shadows of the* Word, and becoming rational, λογικοὶ, they might be enabled to continue in blessedness." Incarn. 3; vid. also Orat. ii. § 78, (*Disc.* n. 215,) where he speaks of Wisdom as being infused into the world on its creation, that the world might possess "an impress and semblance of Its Image."

So again, "He is the truth, and we by imitation become virtuous and sons; .. that, as He, being the Word, is in His own Father, so we too, taking Him as an exemplar, might live in unanimity," &c. &c. Κατὰ μίμησιν. Orat. iii. § 19. (*Disc.* n. 252;) Clem. Alex. τῶν εἰκόνων τὰς μὲν ἐκτρεπομένους, τὰς δὲ μιμουμένους. Pædag. i. 3, p. 102, ed. Pott. and μιμήσει τοῦ νοὸς ἐκείνου. Naz. Ep. 102, p. 95 (ed. Ben.). Vid. Leo. in various places, infra, p. 190, art. *Incarnation;* ut imitatores operum, factores sermonum, &c. Iren. Hær. v. 1; exemplum verum et adjutorium. August. Serm. 101, 6; mediator non solum per adjutorium, verùm etiam per exemplum. August. Trin. xiii. 22, also ix. 21, and Eusebius, though with an heretical meaning, κατὰ τὴν αὐτοῦ μίμησιν. Eccl. Theol. iii. 19.

2. But of course an opportunity of imitation is not enough: a powerful internal grace is necessary, however great the beauty of the Moral Law and its Author, in order to set free and convert the human heart. "Idly do ye imagine to be able to work in yourselves newness of the principle which thinks (φρονοῦντος) and

actuates the flesh, expecting to do so by imitation . . .
for if men could have wrought for themselves newness
of that actuating principle without Christ, and if what
is actuated follows what actuates, what need was there
of Christ's coming?." Apoll. i. § 20 fin. And again:
"The Word of God," he says, "underwent a sort of
creation in the Incarnation, in order to effect thereby
our new creation. If He was not thus created for us,"
but was absolutely a creature, which is the Arian
doctrine, "it follows that we are not created in Him;
and if not created in Him, we have Him not in ourselves, but externally, as, for instance, receiving instruction from Him as from a teacher. And, it being
so with us, sin has not lost its reign over the flesh,
being inherent and not cast out of it." Orat. ii. § 56.
(*Disc.* n. 180.) And this is necessary, he goes on to
say, "that we might have ἐλεύθερον τὸ φρόνημα."

¶ He speaks, contr. Gent., of man "having the
grace of the Giver, and his own virtue from the
Father's Word;" of the mind "seeing the Word,
and in Him the Word's Father also," § 2; of "the way
to God being, not as God Himself, above us and far
off, or external to us, but in us," 30, &c. &c.; vid. also
Basil. de Sp. S. n. 19. This is far more than mere
teaching. "Rational creatures receiving light," says
Cyril, "enlighten by imparting principles, which are
poured from their own minds into another intellect;
and such an illumination may be justly called teaching
rather than revelation. But the Word of God en-
lighteneth every man that cometh into the world, not
iu the way of a teacher, as for instance Angels do or

men, but rather as God, in the way of a Framer, doth He sow in each whom He calls into being the seed of Wisdom, that is, of divine knowledge, and implant a root of understanding," &c. Cyril. in Joan. xix. p. 75. Athan. speaks of this seed sometimes as natural, sometimes as supernatural, and indeed the one order of grace is parallel to the other, and not incompatible with it. Again, he speaks of "a reason combined and connatural with everything that came into being, which some are wont to call seminal, inanimate · indeed and unreasoning and unintelligent, but operating only by external art according to the science of Him who sowed it." contr. Gent. 40. Thus there are three supernatural aids given to men of which the Word is the ἀρχὴ, that of instinct, of reason, and the "gratia Christi."

3. Even this is not all which is given us over and above nature. The greatest and special gift is the actual presence, as well as the power within us of the Incarnate Son as a principle or ἀρχὴ (vid. art. ἀρχὴ) of sanctification, or rather of deification. (vid. art. Deif.) On this point Athan. especially dwells in too many passages to quote or name.

E.g. "The Word of God was made man in order to sanctify the flesh." Orat. ii. § 10. (Disc. n. 114 fin.) "Ye say, 'He destroyed [the works of the devil] by not sinning;' but this is no destruction of sin. For not in Him did the devil in the beginning work sin, that by His coming into the world and not sinning sin was destroyed; but whereas the devil had wrought sin by an after-sowing in the rational and spiritual nature of man, therefore it became impossible for nature, which was rational and had voluntarily sinned, and fell under the penalty of death, to recover itself into freedom (ἐλευθερίαν). . . . Therefore came the Son of God by Himself to establish [the flesh] in His own nature from a new beginning (ἀρχὴ) and a marvellous generation." Apoll. ii. § 6.

¶ "True, without His incarnation at all, God was able to speak the Word only and undo the curse. . . but then the power indeed of Him who gave command had been shown, but man would have fared but as Adam before the fall by receiving grace only from without, not having it united to the body. . . Then, had he been again seduced by the serpent, a second need had arisen of God's commanding and undoing the curse; and thus the need had been interminable, and men had remained under guilt just as before, being in slavery to sin," &c. Orat. ii. § 68. (*Disc.* n. 200); vid. arts. *Incarnation* and *Sanctification.* And so in Incarn. § 7, he says that repentance might have been pertinent, had man merely offended, without *corruption* following; but that that *corruption* involved the necessity of the Word's vicarious sufferings and intercessory office.

¶ "If the works of the Word's Godhead had not taken place through the body, man had not been made god; and again, had not the belongings of the flesh been ascribed to the Word, man had not been thoroughly delivered from them; but though they had ceased for a little while, as I said before, still sin had remained in man and corruption, as was the case with mankind before He came; and for this reason :—

Many, for instance, have been made holy and clean from all sin; nay, Jeremias was hallowed, even from the womb, and John, while yet in the womb, leapt for joy at the voice of Mary Mother of God; nevertheless *death reigned from Adam to Moses, even over those that had not sinned after the similitude of Adam's transgression*; and thus men remained mortal and corruptible as before, liable to the affections proper to their nature. But now the Word having become man and having appropriated the affections of the flesh, no longer do these affections touch the body, because of the Word who has come in it, but they are destroyed by Him, and henceforth men no longer remain sinners and dead according to their proper affections, but, having risen according to the Word's power, they abide ever immortal and incorruptible. Whence also, whereas the flesh is born of Mary Mother of God, He Himself is said to have been born, who furnishes to others a generation of being; in order that, by His transferring our generation into Himself, we may no longer, as mere earth, return to earth, but as being knit into the Word from heaven, may be carried to heaven by Him." Orat. iii. 33. (*Disc.* n. 270.)

¶ "We could not otherwise," says S. Irenæus, "receive incorruption and immortality, but by being united to incorruption and immortality. But how could this be, unless incorruption and immortality had first been made what we are? that corruption might be absorbed by incorruption and mortal by immortality, that we might receive the adoption of Sons." Hær. iii. 19, n. 1. "He took part of flesh and blood, that

is, He became man, whereas He was Life by nature,
. . . that uniting Himself to the corruptible flesh
according to the measure of its own nature, ineffably,
and inexpressibly, and as He alone knows, He might
bring it to His own life, and render it partaker through
Himself of God and the Father. . . . For He bore our
nature, re-fashioning it into His own life ; . . . He is
in us through the Spirit, turning our natural corruption into incorruption, and changing death to its
contrary." Cyril. in Joan. lib. ix. cir. fin. pp. 883, 4.
This is the doctrine of S. Athanasius and S. Cyril,
one may say, *passim*.

¶ Vid. Naz. Epp. ad Cled. 1 and 2 (101, 102, ed.
Ben.) ; Nyssen. ad Theoph. in Apoll. p. 696. " Generatio
Christi origo est populi Christiani," says S. Leo ; " for
whoso is regenerated in Christ," he continues, " has
no longer the propagation from a carnal father, but the
germination of a Saviour, who therefore was made Son
of man, that we might be sons of God." Serm. 26,
2. " Multum fuit a Christo recepisse formam, sed plus
est in Christo habere substantiam. Suscepit nos in
suam proprietatem illa natura," &c. &c. Serm. 72, 2 ;
vid. Serm. 22, 2 ; " ut corpus regenerati fiat caro Cruci-
fixi." Serm. 63, 6. " Hæc est nativitas nova dum homo
nascitur in Deo ; in quo homine Deus natus est, carne
antiqui seminis susceptâ, sine semine antiquo, ut illam
novo semine, id est, spiritualiter, reformaret, exclusis
antiquitatis sordibus, expiatam." Tertull. de Carn.
Christ. 17 ; vid. Orat. iii. § 34.

¶ Such is the channel and mode in which spiritual
life and freedom is given to us. Our Lord Himself,

according to the Holy Fathers, is the ἀρχὴ of the new
creation to each individual Christian. If it be asked
of them, What real connection can there possibly be
between the sanctification of Christ's manhood and
ours? how does it prove that human nature is sanctified because a particular specimen of it was sanctified
in Him? S. Chrysostom explains: " He is born of our
substance; you will say, ' This does not pertain to
all;' yea, to all. He mingles (ἀναμίγνυσιν) Himself
with the faithful individually, through the mysteries,
and whom He has begotten those He nurses from
Himself, not puts them out to other hands," &c. Hom.
82. 5. in Matt. And just before, " It sufficed not for
Him to be made man, to be scourged, to be sacrificed;
but He unites Himself to us (ἀναφύρει ἑαυτὸν ἡμῖν),
not merely by faith, but really, has He made us His
body." Again, " That we are commingled (ἀνακερασ-
θῶμεν) into that flesh, not merely through love, but
really, is brought about by means of that food which
He has bestowed upon us." Hom. 46. 3. in Joann.
And so S. Cyril writes against Nestorius: " Since we
have proved that Christ is the Vine, and we branches
as adhering to a communion with Him, not spiritual
merely but bodily, why clamours he against us thus
bootlessly, saying that, since we adhere to Him, not
in a bodily way, but rather by faith and the affection
of love according to the Law, therefore He has called,
not His own flesh the vine, but rather the Godhead? "
in Joann. 10, p. 863, 4. And Nyssen: " As they who
have taken poison, destroy its deadly power by some
other preparation . . . so when we have tasted what

destroys our nature, we have need of that instead
which restores what was destroyed. . . . But what is
this? nothing else than that Body which has been
proved to be mightier than death, and was the beginning, κατήρξατο, of our life. For a little leaven,"
&c. Orat. Catech. 37. "Decoctâ quasi per ollam carnis
nostræ cruditate, sanctificavit in æternum nobis cibum
carnem suam." Paulin. Ep. 23. 7. Of course in such
statements nothing simply *material* is implied. But
without some explanation really literal, language such
as S. Athanasius's in the text seems a mere matter of
words. Vid. infr. p. 225.

GRACE OF GOD.

IT is a doctrine much insisted on by S. Athanasius, that, together with the act of creation, there was, on the part of the Creator, a further act conservative of the universe which He was creating. This was the communication to it of a blessing or grace, analógous to the grace and sonship purchased for us by our Lord's incarnation, though distinct in kind from it and far inferior to it; and in consequence the universe is not only γενητὸν but γεννητὸν, not only made, but in a certain sense begotten or generated, and, being moulded on the Pattern supplied by the Divine Nature, is in a true sense an Image or at least a Semblance of the Creator. (Vid. art. γεννητόν.)

In controversy with the Arians, he explains with great care the nature of this gift, because it was their device to reduce our Lord's Sonship, in which lay the proof of His Divinity, to the level of the supernatural adoption which has been accorded by the Creator to the whole world, first on its creation, and again through the redemption upon the cross of the fallen race of man.

This grace of adoption was imparted in both cases by the ministration of the Eternal Son, in capacity of Primogenitus or First-born, (as through His Incarnation in the Gospel Economy, so through His συγκατάβασις, or the coming of His Personal

Presence into the world in the beginning,) and was His type and likeness stamped upon the world, physical and moral, and a fulness of excellence enriching it from the source of all excellence. (Vid. πρωτότοκος.) " Since God is self-existing and not composed of parts," says Athan., "such too is His Word also, being One Only-begotten God, who from a Father, as a Fount of Good, has gone forth (προελθών) Himself Good, and put into order and into consistency all things. The reason for this is truly admirable, and evidently befitting. For the nature of creatures, as coming into subsistence out of nothing, is dissoluble, and feeble, and, taken by itself, is mortal, but the God of the universe is good and of surpassing beauty in His nature. (vid. ρευστός) . . Beholding then that all created nature was in respect of its own laws dissoluble and dissolving, lest this should happen to it, and the whole world fall back again into nothing, having made all things by His own Eternal Word, and having given substance to the creation, He refused to let it be carried away and wrecked (χειμάζεσθαι) by stress of its own nature, and, as a Good God, He governs and sustains it all by His own Word, who is Himself God, . . . through whom and in whom all things consist, visible and invisible," &c. contr. Gent. § 41.

Again, " In order that what came into being might not only be, but be good, it pleased God that His own Wisdom should condescend (συγκαταβῆναι) to the creatures, so as to introduce an impress and semblance of Its Image on all in common and on each, that what was made might be manifestly wise works and worthy of God. For as

of the Son of God, considered as the Word, our word
is an image, so of the same Son considered as Wisdom
is the wisdom which is implanted in us an image; in
which wisdom we, having the power of knowledge and
thought, become recipients of the All-framing Wisdom,
and through It we are able to know Its Father."
Orat. ii. 78. (*Disc.* n. 215.)

¶ S. Cyril, using another figure, says that the universe is grafted on the Word: " He is Only-begotten
according to nature, as being alone from the Father,
God from God, Light kindled from Light; and He is
First-born for our sakes, that, *as if on some immortal
root*, the whole creation might be ingrafted and might
bud forth from the Everlasting. For all things were
made by Him, and *consist* for ever and are *preserved in
Him*." Thesaur. 25, p. 238.

Moreover, Athan. goes so far as to suggest that the
universe does not evidence the Creator, except as being
inhabited by the Son, and that what we see divine in
it is His Presence. " He has said, ' The invisible
things of Him from the creation of the world are
clearly seen, being understood by the things that are
made, His eternal Power and Divinity.' . . . Study the
context, and ye will see that it is the Son who is
signified. For after making mention of the creation,
he naturally speaks of the Framer's Power as seen in
it, which Power, I say, is the Word of God, by whom
all things were made. *If indeed* the creation be sufficient of itself alone, without the Son, to make God
known, see that you fall not into the further opinion
that without the Son it came to be. But if through

the Son it came to be, and *in Him all things consist*, it must follow that he who contemplates the creation rightly, is contemplating also the Word who framed it, and *through Him* begins to apprehend the Father. And on Philip's asking, *Show us the Father*, He said not, 'Behold the creation,' but, *He that hath seen Me, hath seen the Father.*" Orat. i. § 11, 12. (*Disc.* n. 17.)

2. It is then the original συγκατάβασις of the Son, making Himself the First-begotten of the creation in the beginning, which breathes, and which stamps a sort of divinity upon the natural universe, and prepares us for that far higher grace and glory which is given to human nature by means of the Incarnation; this evangelical grace being not merely a gift from above, as resulting from the συγκατάβασις, but an inhabitation of the Giver in man, a communication of His Person, and a participation, as it may be called, of the Virtue of that Person, similar to that which, when He came upon earth, He bestowed on individuals by contact with His hands or His garments for their deliverance from bodily ailments or injuries.

¶ Our Lord, then, came on earth, not merely as the physician of our souls, but as the First-born and the Parent of a new Family, who should be the principle of propagation of a new birth in a fallen world. "The flesh being first sanctified in Him, we have the sequel of the Spirit's grace, receiving out of His fulness." Orat. i. § 50 fin. (*Disc.* n. 83 fin.) "Therefore did He assume the body created and human, that, having renewed it as its Framer, He might make it God in Himself, and thus might introduce us all into the

kingdom of heaven after His likeness." Orat. ii. § 70.
"How could we be partakers of that adoption of sons,
unless through the Son we had received from Him
that communion with Him, unless His Word had been
made flesh, and had communicated it to us?" Iren.
Hær. iii. 18, 7.

¶ Hence it is that the adoption of sons which is
the gift which we gain by the Incarnation, is far more
than an adoption in the ordinary sense of that word,
and far stronger terms are used of it. Athan. says
that we are made sons "truly," υἱοποιούμεθα ἀληθῶς.
Decr. § 31. (Nic. n. 45.) Again S. Basil says, that we
are sons, κυρίως, "properly," and πρώτως, "primarily,"
in opposition to ἐκ μεταφορᾶς and τροπικῶς, "figuratively," contr. Eunom. ii. 23, 24. S. Cyril too says that
we are sons "naturally," φυσικῶς, as well as κατὰ χάριν,
vid. Suicer. Thesaur. v. υἱὸς, i. 3. Of these words,
ἀληθῶς, φυσικῶς, κυρίως, and πρώτως, the first two
are commonly reserved for our Lord; e.g. τὸν ἀληθῶς
υἱὸν, Orat. ii. § 37. (Disc. n. 150 fin.) ἡμεῖς υἱοὶ, οὐκ ὡς
ἐκεῖνος φύσει καὶ ἀληθείᾳ, Orat. iii. § 19. (Disc. n. 251.)
Hilary indeed seems to deny us the title of "proper"
sons, de Trin. xii. 15; but his "proprium" is a translation of ἴδιον, not κυρίως.

¶ The true statement is, that, whereas there is a
primary and secondary sense in which the word Son is
used,—the primary, when it has its formal meaning of
continuation of nature, and the secondary, when it is
used nominally, or for an external resemblance to the
first meaning,—it is applied to the regenerate, not in the
secondary sense, but in the primary. S. Basil and S.

Gregory Nyssen consider Son to be a "a term of *rela-tionship* according to *nature*" (vid. art. *Son*), also Basil, in Psalm. 28, 1. The actual presence of the Holy Spirit in the regenerate in *substance* (vid. Cyril. Dial. 7, p. 638) constitutes this relationship of nature; and hence after the words quoted from S. Cyril above, in which he says, that we are sons φυσικῶς, he proceeds "naturally, because *we are in Him*, and in Him alone," vid. Athan.'s words which follow in the text at the end of Decr. § 31. And hence Nyssen lays down as a received truth, that "to none does the term 'proper,' κυριώτατον, apply, but to one in whom the name responds with truth to the nature." contr. Eunom. iii. p. 123. And he also implies, p. 117, the intimate association of our sonship with Christ's, when he con-nects together regeneration with our Lord's eternal generation, neither being διὰ παθοῦς, or, of the will of the flesh. If it be asked what the *distinctive* words are which are incommunicably the Son's, since so much is man's, it is obvious to answer, first, ἴδιος υἱὸς and μονογενὴς, which are in Scripture; and, next, the symbols "Of the substance," and "One in substance," of the Council; and this is the value of the Council's phrases, that, while they guard the Son's divinity, they allow full scope, without risk of trenching on that divinity, to the Catholic doctrine as to the fulness of the Christian privileges.

THE DIVINE HAND.

GOD, the Creative Origin and Cause of all beings, acts by the mediation, ministration, or agency of His co-equal Son. To symbolise His numerical oneness with that Son, the Son is called His Hand.

E.g. by Athan. Dec. § 7, 17. Orat. ii. § 31, 71. iv. 26. Also Incarn. c. Ar. 12.

Also by Clem. Recogn. viii. 43. Hom. xvi. 12. Method ap. Phot. cod. 235, p. 937. Iren. Hær. iv. præf. 20, v. 1 and 5 and 6. Clem. Protr. (brachium) p. 93. Potter. Tertull. Herm. 45. Cyprian. Test. ii. 4. Euseb. in Psalm. 108, 27. Hilar. Trin. viii. 22. Basil. Eunom. v. p. 297. Cyril. in Joann. 476, 7, et *alibi*. Thesaur. p. 154. Job. ap. Phot. p. 582. August. in Joan. 48, 7 (though he prefers another use of the word), p. 323.

This image is in contrast with that of *instrument*, ὄργανον, which the Arians would use to express the relation of the Son to the Father, as implying separateness and subservience, whereas the word *Hand* implies His consubstantiality; vid. art. *Mediation*.

HERESIES.

¶ HERESIES are *partial* views of the truth, starting
from some truth which they exaggerate, and disowning
and protesting against other truth, which they fancy
inconsistent with it.

¶ All heresies are partial views of the truth, and are
wrong, not so much in what they directly say as in
what they deny.

¶ All heresies seem connected together and to run
into each other. When the mind has embraced one,
it is almost certain to run into others, apparently
the most opposite, it is quite uncertain which.
Thus Arians were a reaction from Sabellians, yet
did not the less consider than they that God was but
one Person, and that Christ was a creature. Apollinaris was betrayed into his heresy by opposing the
Arians, yet his heresy started with the tenet in which
the Arians ended, that Christ had no human soul.
His disciples became, and even naturally, some of
them Sabellians, some Arians. Again, beginning with
denying our Lord a soul, Apollinaris came to deny Him
a body, like the Manichees and Docetæ. The same
passages from Athanasius will be found to refute both
Eutychians and Nestorians, though diametrically opposed to each other: and these agreed together, not
only in considering nature and person identical, but,

strange to say, in holding (and the Apollinarians too,)
that our Lord's manhood existed before its union with
Him, which is the special heresy of Nestorius. Again,
the Nestorians were closely connected with the Sabellians
and Samosatenes, and the latter with the Photinians
and modern Socinians. And the Nestorians were connected with the Pelagians; and Aerius, who denied
Episcopacy and prayers for the dead, with the Arians;
and his opponent the Semi-Arian Eustathius with the
Encratites. One reason of course of this peculiarity
of heresy is, that when the mind is once unsettled, it
may fall into any error. Another is that it *is* heresy;
all heresies being secretly connected, as in temper, so
in certain primary principles. And lastly, the Truth
only is a *real* doctrine, and therefore stable; everything false is of a transitory nature and has no stay,
like reflections in a stream, one opinion continually
passing into another, and creations being but the first
stages of dissolution. Hence so much is said in the
Fathers of orthodoxy being a narrow way. Thus S.
Gregory speaks of the middle and "royal" way.
Orat. 32, 6, also Damasc. contr. Jacob. iii. t. 1, p. 398;
vid. also Leon. Ep. 85, 1, p. 1051; Ep. 129, p. 1254,
" brevissimâ adjectione corrumpitur ; " also Serm. 25, 1,
p. 83 ; also Vigil. in Eutych. i. init. " Quasi inter duos
latrones crucifigitur Dominus," &c. Novat. Trin. 30.
vid. the promise, " Thine ears shall hear a word behind
thee, saying, This is the way, walk ye in it, and go
not aside either to the right hand, or to the left."
Is. xxx. 21.

¶ Heresies run into each other, (one may even say,)

logically. No doctrines were apparently more opposed, whether historically or ethically, than the Arian and the Apollinarian or the Monophysite; nay, in statement, so far as the former denied that our Lord was God, the latter that He was man. But their agreement lay in this compromise, that strictly speaking He was neither God nor man. Thus in Orat. ii. § 8, Athan. hints that if the Arians gave the titles (such as Priest) which really belonged to our Lord's manhood, to His pre-existent nature, what were they doing but removing the evidences of His manhood, and so far denying it? Vid. the remarkable passage of the Council of Sardica against Valens and Ursacius quoted supr. vol. i. p. 116. In the Arian Creed No. vii. or second Sirmian, it is implied that the Divine Son is passible, the very doctrine against which Theodoret writes one of his Anti-monophysite Dialogues called Eranistes. He writes another on the ἄτρεπτον of Christ, a doctrine which was also formally denied by Arius, and is defended by Athan. Orat. i. § 35. Vid. art. *Eusebius*, who speaks of our Lord's taking a *body*, almost to the prejudice of the doctrine of His taking a perfect *manhood*; εἰ μὲν ψυχῆς δίκην, &c., supr. p. 106. Hence it is that Gibbon throws out (ch. 47, note 34), after La Croze, Hist. Christ. des Indes, p. 11, that the Arians invented the term θεοτόκος, which the Monophysites, in their own sense strenuously held, vid. Garner in Mar. Merc. t. 2, p. 299. If the opposites of connected heresies are in fact themselves connected together, then the doctrinal connection of Arianism and Apollinarianism is shown in their respective opposition to the heresies of Sabellius and Nestorius. Salig (Eutych. ant. Eut. 10) denies the connection, but with very little show of reason. La Croze calls Apollinarianism "Arianismi tradux," Thes. Ep. Lacroz. t. 3, p. 276.

¶ It was the tendency of all the heresies concerning the Person of Christ to explain away or deny the Atonement. The Arians, after the Platonists, insisted on the pre-existing Priesthood, as if the incarnation and crucifixion were not of its essence. The Apollinarians resolved the Incarnation into a manifestation, Theod. Eran. i. The Nestorians denied the Atonement, Procl. ad Armen. p. 615. And the Eutychians, Leon. Ep. 28, 5.

¶ It is remarkable that the Monophysites should have been forced into their circumscription of the Divine Nature by the limits of the human, considering that Eutyches their Patriarch began with asserting for reverence-sake that the Incarnate Word was not under the *laws* of human nature, vid. infra art. *Specialties,* &c. This is another instance of the running of opposite heresies into each other. Another remarkable instance will be found in art. *Ignorance,* viz. the Agnœtæ, a sect of those very Eutychians, who denied or tended to deny our Lord's manhood with a view of preserving His Divinity, yet who were characterised by holding that He was ignorant as man.

¶ "This passage of the Apostle," Rom. i. 1, "[Marcellus] I know not why perverts, instead of *declared*, ὁρισθέντος, making it *predestined*, προορισθέντος, that the Son may be such as they who are predestined according to foreknowledge." Euseb. contr. Marc. i. 2.

Paul of Samosata also considered our Lord Son by foreknowledge, προγνώσει. vid. Routh, Reliqu. t. 2, p. 466; and Eunomius, Apol. 24.

¶ In spite of their differing diametrically from each other in their respective heresies about the Holy Trinity, that our Lord was not really the Divine Word was a point in which Arians and Sabellians agreed. vid. infr. Orat. iv. init.; also ii. § 22, 40, also Sent. D. 25. Ep. Æg. 14 fin. Epiph. Hær. 72, p. 835.

¶ Heretics have frequently assigned reverence as the cause of their opposition to the doctrine of the Church; and if even Arius was obliged to affect it, the plea may be expected in any others. "O stultos et impios metus," says S. Hilary, "et irreligiosam de Deo sollicitudinem." de Trin. iv. 6. It was still more commonly professed in regard to the Catholic doctrine of the Incarnation. Thus Manes, "Absit ut Dominum nostrum Jesum Christum per naturalia mulieris descendisse confitear; ipse enim testimonium dat, quia de sinibus Patris descendit." Archel. Disp. t. iii. p. 601. "We, as saying that the Word of God is incapable of defilement, even by the assumption of mortal and vulnerable flesh, fear not to believe that He is born of a Virgin; ye," Manichees, "because with impious perverseness ye believe the Son of God to be capable of it, dread to commit Him to the flesh." August. contr. Secund. 9. Faustus "is neither willing to receive Jesus of the seed of David, nor made of a woman . . . nor the death of Christ itself, and burial, and resurrection," &c. August. contr. Faust xi. 3. As the Manichees denied our Lord a body, so the Apollinarians denied Him a rational soul, still under pretence of reverence, because, as they said, the soul was necessarily sinful. Leontius makes this their main argument, ὁ νοῦς ἁμαρτητικός ἐστι, de Sect. iv. p. 507 vid. also Greg. Naz. Ep. 101, ad Cledon. p. 89; Athan. in Apoll. i. 2, 14; Epiph. Ancor. 79, 80. Athan. and others call the Apollinarian doctrine Manichean in con-sequence. vid. in Apoll. ii. 8, 9, &c. Again, the Era-nistes in Theodoret, who advocates a similar doctrine, will not call our Lord *man*. "I consider it important to acknowledge an assumed *nature*, but to call the Saviour of the world *man* is to impair our Lord's glory." Eranist. ii. p. 83. Eutyches, on the other hand, would call our Lord *man*, but refused to admit His human *nature*, and still with the same profession. "Ego," he says, "sciens sanctos et beatos patres nostros refutantes *duarum naturarum* vocabulum, et non *audens* de naturâ tractare Dei Verbi, qui in carnem venit, in veritate non in phantasmate *homo* factus," &c. Leon. Ep. 21, 1 fin. "Forbid it," he says at Constantinople, "that I should say that the Christ was of two natures, or should discuss the nature, φυσιολογεῖν, of my God." Concil. t. 2, p. 157. And so in this day popular Tracts have been published, ridiculing St. Luke's account of our Lord's nativity under pretence of reverence towards the God of all, and interpreting Scripture allegorically on Pantheistic principles. A modern argument for Universal Resti-tution takes the same form: "Do not *we* shrink from the notion of another's being sentenced to eternal punishment; *are we more merciful than God?*" vid. Matt. xvi. 22, 23.

¶ That heresies before the Arian appealed to Scripture we learn from Tertullian, de Præscr. 42, who warns Catholics against indulging themselves in their own view of isolated texts against the voice of the Catholic Church. vid. also Vincentius, who specifies *obiter* Sabellius and Novatian. Commonit. 2. Still Arianism was contrasted with other heresies on this point, as in these two respects : (1.) they appealed to a *secret tradition,* unknown even to most of the Apostles, as the Gnostics, Iren. Hær. iii. 1 ; or they professed a gift of prophecy introducing fresh *revelations,* as Montanists, Syn. § 4, and Manichees, Aug. contr. Faust. xxxii. 6. (2.) The Arians availed themselves of certain texts as objections, argued keenly and plausibly from them, and would not be driven from them. Orat. ii. § 18, c.; Epiph. Hær. 69, 15. Or rather they took some words of Scripture, and made their own deductions from them ; viz. " Son," " made," " exalted," &c.

HERETICS.

REVEALED truth, to be what it professes, must have an uninterrupted descent from the Apostles; its teachers must be unanimous, and persistent in their unanimity; and it must bear no human master's name as its designation.

On the other hand, first novelty, next discordance, vacillation, change, thirdly sectarianism, are consequences and tokens of religious error.

These tests stand to reason; for what is over and above nature must come from divine revelation; and, if so, it must descend from the very date when it was revealed, else it is but matter of opinion; and opinions vary, and have no warrant of permanence, but depend upon the relative ability and success of individual teachers, one with another, from whom they take their names.

The Fathers abound in passages which illustrate these three tests.

¶ "Who are you?" says Tertullian, "whence and when came ye? what do ye on my property, being none of mine? by what right, O Marcion, cuttest thou my wood? by what licence, O Valentinus, turnest thou my springs? by what power, O Apelles, movest thou my landmarks? Mine is possession. . . . I possess of old, I have prior possession. . . . I am heir of the Apostles." Tertull. de Præscr. 37. "Tardily for me hath this time of day put forth these, in my judgment, most impious doctors. Full late hath that faith of mine, which Thou hast taught me, encountered these Masters. Before these names were heard of, I thus believed in Thee, I·thus was new born by Thee, and thenceforth I thus am Thine." Hil. de Trin. vi. 21. "What heresy hath ever burst forth, but under the name of some certain men, in some certain place, and at some certain time? who ever set up any heresy, but first divided himself from the consent of the universality and antiquity of the Catholic Church?" Vincent. Lir. Commonit. 24. "I will tell thee my mind briefly and plainly, that thou shouldest remain in that Church which, being founded by the Apostles, endures even to this day. When thou hearest that those who are called Christ's, are named, not after Jesus Christ, but after some one, say Marcionites, Valentinians, &c., know then it is not Christ's Church, but the synagogue of Antichrist. For by the very fact that they are formed afterwards, they show that they are those who the Apostle foretold should come." Jerom. in Lucif. 27. "If the Church was not . . . whence hath Donatus appeared? from what soil has he sprung? out of what sea hath he emerged? from what heaven hath he fallen?" August. de Bapt. contr. Don. iii. 2. vid. art. *Catholic*, &c.

¶ "However the error was, certainly," says Tertullian ironically, "error reigned so long as heresies were not. Truth needed a rescue, and looked out for Marcionites and Valentinians." "Meanwhile, gospelling was nought, faith was nought, nought was the baptism of so many thousand thousand, so many works of faith performed, so many virtues, so many gifts displayed, so many priesthoods, so many ministries exercised, nay, so many martyrdoms crowned." Tertull. Præscr. 29. "'Profane novelties,' which if we receive, of necessity the faith of our blessed ancestors, either all or a great part of it, must be overthrown; the faithful people of all ages and times, all holy saints, all the chaste, all the continent, all the virgins, all the Clergy, the Deacons, the Priests, so many thousands of confessors, so great armies of martyrs, so many famous populous cities and commonwealths, so many islands, provinces, kings, tribes, kingdoms, nations, to conclude, almost now the whole world, incorporated by the Catholic Faith to Christ their head, must needs be said, so many hundred years, to have been ignorant, to have erred, to have blasphemed, to have believed they knew not what." Vinc. Comm. 24. "O the extravagance! the wisdom, hidden until Christ's coming, they announce to us to-day, which is a thing to draw tears. For if the faith began thirty years since, while near four hundred are past since Christ was manifested, nought hath been our gospel that long while, and nought our faith, and fruitlessly have martyrs been martyred, and fruitlessly have such and so great rulers ruled the people." Greg. Naz. ad Cledon. Ep. 102, p. 97.

¶ "They know not to be reverent even to their leaders. And this is why commonly schisms exist not among heretics; because while they exist, they are not visible. Schism is their very unity. I am a liar if they do not dissent from their own rules, while every man among them equally alters at his private judgment (suo arbitrio) what he has received, just as he who gave to them composed it at his private judgment. The progress of the thing is true to its nature and its origin. What was a right to Valentinus, was a right to Valentinians, what to Marcion was to the Marcionites, to innovate on the faith at their private judgment. As soon as any heresy is thoroughly examined, it is found in many points dissenting from its parent. Those parents for the most part have no Churches; they roam about without mother, without see, bereaved of the faith, without a country, without a home." Tertull. Præscr. 42. "He writes," says Athan. of Constantius, "and while he writes repents, and while he repents is exasperated; and then he grieves again, and not knowing how to act, he shows how bereft the soul is of understanding." Hist. Arian. 70; vid. also ad Ep. Æg. 6.

¶ "Faith is made a thing of dates rather than Gospels, while it is written down by years, and is not measured by the confession of baptism." Hil. ad Const. ii. 4. "We determine yearly and monthly creeds concerning God, we repent of our determinations; we defend those who repent, we anathematise those whom we have defended; we condemn our own doings in those of others, or others in us, and gnawing each other, we are well-nigh devoured one of another." ibid. 5. "It happens to thee," says S. Hilary to Constantius, "as to unskilful builders, always to be dissatisfied with what thou hast done; thou art ever destroying what thou art ever building." contr. Constant. 23.

¶ " The Emperor [Theodosius] had a conversation with Nectarius, Bishop [of Constantinople], in
what way to make Christendom concordant, and to
unite the Church. . . This made Nectarius anxious; but
Sisinnius, a man of ready speech and of practical experience, and thoroughly versed in the interpretation
of the sacred writings and in the doctrines of philosophy, having a conviction that disputation would but
aggravate the party-spirit of the heretics instead of
reconciling schisms, advised him to avoid dialectic
engagements, and to appeal to the statements of the
ancients, and to put the question to the heresiarchs
from the Emperor, whether they made any sort of
account of the doctors who belonged to the Church
before the division, or came to issue with them as
aliens from Christianity; for if they made their authority null, therefore let them venture to anathematise
them. But if they did venture, then they would be
driven out by the people." Socr. v. 10.

¶ " They who do not pertinaciously defend their
opinion, false and perverse though it be, especially
when it does not spring from the audacity of their
own presumption, but has come to them from parents
seduced and lapsed into error, while they seek the
truth with cautious solicitude, and are prepared to
correct themselves when they have found it, are by no
means to be ranked among heretics." August. Ep.
43, init.; vid. also de Bapt. contr. Don. iv. 20.

HIERACAS.

HIERACAS was a Manichæan. He compared the Two
Divine Persons to the two lights of one lamp, where
the oil is common and the flame double, thus implying
a third substance distinct from Father and Son, or to
a flame divided into two by (for instance) the papyrus
which was commonly used instead of a wick. vid.
Hilar. de Trin. vi. 12.

¶ This doctrine is also imputed to Valentinus,
though in a different sense, by Nazianzen, Orat. 33.
16. vid. also Clement, Recogn. i. 69.

HOMOUSION, HOMŒUSION.

Vid. ὁμοούσιον, *Nicene Tests, Semi-Arians,* &c.

HYPOCRISY, HYPOCRITES.

THIS is almost a title of the Arians, (with an apparent allusion to 1 Tim. iv. 2. vid. Socr. i. p. 13. Athan. Orat. i. § 10, ii. § 1 and § 19, iii. § 16. Syn. § 32. Ep. Enc. 6. Ep. Æg. 18. Epiph. Hær. 73, 1,) and that in various senses. The first meaning is that, being heretics, they nevertheless used orthodox phrases and statements to deceive and seduce Catholics. The term is thus used by Alexander in the beginning of the controversy. vid. Theod. Hist. i. 3, pp. 729, 746. Again, it implies that they agreed with Arius, but would not confess it; professed to be Catholics, but would not anathematise him. vid. Athan. ad Ep. Æg. 20, or alleged untruly the Nicene Council as their ground of complaint, ibid. § 18. Again, it is used of the hollowness and pretence of their ecclesiastical proceedings, with the Emperor at their head; which were a sort of make-belief of spiritual power, or piece of acting, δραματούργημα. Ep. Encycl. 2 and 6. It also means general insincerity, as if they were talking about what they did not understand, and did not realise what they said, and were blindly implicating themselves in evils of a fearful character. Thus Athan. calls them (as cited supr.) τοὺς τῆς Ἀρείου ἀνίας ὑποκριτάς, Orat. ii. § 1, init.; and he speaks of the evil spirit making them his sport, τοῖς ὑποκρινομένοις τὴν μανίαν αὐτοῦ, ad Serap. i. 1. And hence further it is applied, at Syn. § 32, as though with severity, yet to those who were near the truth, and who, though in sin, would at length come to it or not, according as the state of their hearts was. He is here anticipating the return into the Church of those whom he thus censures. In this sense, though with far more severity in what he says, the writer of a Tract imputed to Athan. against the Catholicising Semi-Arians of 363, entitles it "On the *hypocrisy* of Meletius and Eusebius of Samosata." It is remarkable that what Athan. here predicts was fulfilled to the letter, even of the worst of these "hypocrites." For Acacius himself, who in 361 signed the Anomœan Confession above recorded (vid. vol. i. supr. p. 121, note), was one of those very men who accepted the Homoùsion with an explanation in 363.

HYPOSTASIS.

ὑπόστασις, subsistence, person. It is remarkable how seldom this word occurs in Athanasius except as found in Hebr. i. 3 ; and the more so because it is a term little known outside Christian theology, and within that theology after Athan.'s time so important and authentic. It is not found, I believe, in his first two Orations ; twice in the third ; in the fourth, which seems a distinct work from the three, by contrast five times, and often in S. Alexander's Letter in Theodoret, to his namesake at Constantinople. Vid. art. εἶδος and οὐσία, which Athan. seems to use instead of it.

It would seem as if there were a class of words which, in the first age, before the theological terminology was fixed by ecclesiastical determinations, admitted of standing either for the Divine Being or a Divine Person according to the occasion ; and this, as being one of them, was not definite or precise enough for a mind so clear as Athan.'s ; vid. Orat. iii. § 66, iv. § 1, 25, 33, 35. Vid. art. οὐσία.

IDOLATRY OF ARIANISM.

ARIANS considered our Lord a creature, with a beginning of existence, with a probation, and during it a liability to fall. Yet it was one of their fundamental tenets that He was Creator of the universe, and created in order to create. Accordingly Athan. and the other Fathers rightly charge them with idol worship.

"We must take reverent heed," says Athanasius, "lest transferring what is proper to the Father to what is unlike Him, and expressing the Father's godhead by what is unlike in kind and alien, we introduce another being foreign to Him, as if capable of the properties of the first, and lest we be silenced by God Himself, saying, *My glory I will not give to another,* and be discovered worshipping this alien God." Syn. § 50. "Who told them, after abandoning the worship of creatures, after all to draw near and to worship a creature and a work?" Orat. i. § 8. vid. also Orat. ii. § 14. Ep. Ægypt. 4 and 13. Adelph. 3. Serap. i. 29.

This point, as might be expected, is insisted on by other Fathers, vid. Cyril. Dial. iv. p. 511, &c. v. p. 566. Greg. Naz. Orat. 40. 42. Hil. Trin. viii. 28. Ambros. de Fid. i. n. 69 and 104. Theod. in Rom. i. 25.

¶ The Arians were in the dilemma of holding two Gods, or worshipping the creature, unless they denied to the Lord both divinity and worship. Hence Athan.

says, φάσκοντες, οὐ λέγομεν δύο ἀγένητα, λέγουσι· δύο θεούς, Orat. iii. 16. But "every substance," says S. Austin, "which is not God, is a creature, and which is not a creature, is God," de Trin. i. 6. And so S. Cyril, "We see God and creation and besides nothing; for whatever falls external to God's nature has certainly a maker; and whatever is clear of the definition of creation, is certainly within the definition of the Godhead." In Joan.. p. 52. vid. also Naz. Orat. 31. 6. Basil. contr. Eunom. ii. 31.

¶ Petavius gives a large collection of passages, de Trin. ii. 12, § 5, from other Fathers in proof of the worship of Our Lord evidencing His Godhead.

IGNORANCE ASSUMED ECONOMICALLY BY OUR LORD.

"IT is plain that He knows the hour of the end of all things," says Athan., "as the Word, though as man He is ignorant of it, for ignorance belongs to man." Orat. iii. § 43, and Serap. ii. 9.

¶ S. Basil, on the general question being asked him, of our Lord's infirmities, by S. Amphilochius, says that he shall give him the answer he had "heard from boyhood from the fathers," but which was more fitted for pious Christians than for cavillers, and that is, that "Our Lord says many things to men in His human aspect, as 'Give Me to drink,' . . . yet He who asked was not flesh without a soul, but Godhead using flesh which had one." Ep. 236, 1. He goes on to suggest another explanation about His ignorance which is mentioned below. And S. Cyril, "Let them [the heretics] strip the Word openly of the flesh and what it implies, and destroy outright the whole Economy [Incarnation], and then they will clearly see the Son as God; or, if they shudder at this as impious and absurd, why blush they at the conditions of the manhood, and determine to find fault with what especially befits the economy of the flesh?" Trin. pp. 623, 4. Vid. also Thes. p. 220. "As He submitted as man to hunger and thirst, so . . . to be ignorant," p. 221. Vid. also Naz.

Orat. 30. 15. Theodoret expresses the same opinion very strongly, speaking of a gradual revelation to the manhood from the Godhead, but in an argument when it was to his point to do so, in Anath. 4, t. v. p. 23, ed. Schulze. Theodore of Mopsuestia also speaks of a revelation made by the Word. ap. Leont. iii. c. Nest. (Canis. i. p. 579).

¶ Though our Lord, as having two natures, had a human as well as a divine knowledge, and though that human knowledge was not only limited because human, but liable to ignorance in matters in which greater knowledge was possible; yet it is the received doctrine, that *in fact* He was not ignorant even in His human nature, according to its capacity, since it was from the first taken out of its original and natural condition, and "deified" by its union with the Word. As then (infra art. *Specialties*, part 5) His manhood was created, yet He may not be called a creature even in His manhood, and as *(ibid.* part 6) His flesh was in its abstract nature a servant, yet He is not a servant in fact, even as regards the flesh; so, though He took on Him a soul which left to itself would have been partially ignorant, as other human souls, yet as ever enjoying the Beatific Vision from its oneness with the Word, it never was ignorant in fact, but knew all things which human soul can know. vid. Eulog. ap. Phot. 230, p. 884. As Pope Gregory expresses it, "Novit in naturâ, non ex naturâ humanitatis." Epp. x. 39. However, this view of the sacred subject was not received by the Church till after S. Athanasius's day, and it cannot be denied that he and others of the most eminent

Fathers use language which *primâ facie* is inconsistent with it. They certainly seem to impute ignorance to our Lord as man, as Athan. in the passage cited above. Of course it is not meant that our Lord's soul had the same perfect knowledge which He has as God. This was the assertion of a General of the Hermits of S. Austin at the time of the Council of Basil, when the proposition was formally condemned, "animam Christi Deum videre tam clarè et intensè quàm clarè et intensè Deus videt seipsum." vid. Berti Opp. t. 3, p. 42. Yet Fulgentius had said, "I think that in no respect was full knowledge of the Godhead wanting to that Soul, whose Person is one with the Word,—whom Wisdom did so assume that it is itself that same Wisdom," ad Ferrand. Resp. iii. p. 223, ed. 1639; though, ad Trasimund. i. 7, he speaks of ignorance attaching to our Lord's human nature.

¶ S. Basil takes the words οὐδ᾽ ὁ υἱὸς, εἰ μὴ ὁ πατήρ, to mean, "nor does the Son know except the Father knows," or "nor would the Son but for," &c., or "nor does the Son know, except as the Father knows." "The cause of the Son's knowing is from the Father." Ep. 236, 2. S. Gregory alludes to the same interpretation, οὐδ᾽ ὁ υἱὸς ἢ ὡς ὅτι ὁ πατήρ, "Since the Father knows, therefore the Son." Naz. Orat. 30. 16. S. Irenæus seems to adopt the same when he says, "The Son was not ashamed to *refer* the knowledge of that day to the Father;" Hær. ii. 28, n. 6, as Naz. supr. uses the words ἐπὶ τὴν αἰτίαν ἀναφερέσθω. And so Photius distinctly, εἰς ἀρχὴν ἀναφέρεται. "'Not the Son, but the Father,' that is, whence knowledge

M 2

comes to the Son as from a fountain." Epp. p. 342, ed. 1651.

¶ Origen considers such answer an economy. "He who knows what is in the heart of men, Christ Jesus, as John also has taught us in his Gospel, asks, yet is not ignorant. But since He has now taken on Him man, He adopts all that is man's, and among them the asking questions. Nor is it strange that the Saviour should do so, since the very God of all, accommodating Himself to the habits of man, as a father might to his son, inquires, for instance, 'Adam, where art thou?' and 'Where is Abel, thy brother?'" in Matt. t. 10, § 14; vid. also Pope Gregory and Chrysost. infr.

¶ S. Chrysostom, S. Ambrose, and Pope S. Gregory in addition to the instances in Orat. iii. § 50, refer to "I will go down now, and see whether they have done, &c. and if not, I will know." Gen. xviii. 21. "The Lord came down to see the city and the tower," &c. Gen. xi. 5. "God looked down from heaven upon the children of men to see," &c. Ps. liii. § 3. "It may be they will reverence My Son." Matt. xxi. 37. Luke xx. 13. "Seeing a fig tree afar off, having leaves, He came, if haply He might find," &c. Mark xi. 13. "Simon, lovest thou Me?" John xxi. 15. Vid. Ambros. de Fid. v. c. 17. Chrys. in Matt. Hom. 77, 3. Greg. Epp. x. 39. Vid. also the instances Athan. Orat. iii. § 37. Other passages may be added, such as Gen. xxii. 12. vid. Berti Opp. t. 3, p. 42. But the difficulty of Mar. xiii. 32 lies in its signifying that there is a sense in which the Father knows what the Son knows not. Petavius, after S. Augustine, meets this by explaining it to mean that our Lord, *as sent* from the Father on a mission, was not to reveal all things, but to observe a silence and profess an ignorance on those points which it was not good for His brethren to know.   *As* Mediator and Prophet He was ignorant.   He refers in illustration of this view to such texts as, " I have not *spoken of Myself;* but the Father which sent Me, He gave Me commandment *what* I should say and *what* I should speak. . . . . *Whatsoever* I speak therefore, even as the Father said unto Me, *so* I speak." John xii. 49, 50.

¶ It is a question to be decided, whether our Lord speaks of actual ignorance in His human Mind or of the natural ignorance of that Mind considered as human; ignorance " in " or " ex naturâ ; " or, which comes to the same thing, whether He spoke of a real ignorance, or of an economical or professed ignorance, in a certain view of His incarnation or office, as when He asked, " How many loaves have ye ? " when " He Himself knew what He would do," or as He is called sin, though sinless.   Thus Ath. seems, Orat ii. § 55 fin., to make His infirmities altogether imputative, not real; " He is said to be infirm, not being infirm Himself," as if showing that the subject had not in his day been thoroughly worked out.   In like manner S. Hilary, who, if the passage be genuine, states so clearly our Lord's ignorance, de Trin. ix. fin., yet, as Petavius observes, seems elsewhere to deny to Him those very affections of the flesh to which he has there paralleled it.   And this view of Athan.'s meaning is favoured by the turn of his expressions.   He says, such a defect belongs to " *that human nature* whose property it is to be ignorant;" Orat. iii. § 43; that "since He was made man, He is not *ashamed*, because of the flesh which is ignorant, *to say* 'I know not;'" ibid. And § 45, that "as *showing* His manhood, in that to be ignorant is *proper* to man, and that He had *put on* a flesh *that was ignorant*, being in which, He *said* according to the flesh, 'I know not;'" "that He might *show* that as man He knows not," § 46; viz. *as* man, (i.e. on the *ground* of being man, not in the *capacity* of man,) "He knows not," ibid.; and that "He asks about Lazarus humanly," even when "He was *on His way* to raise him," which implied surely knowledge in His human nature. The reference to the parallel of S. Paul's professed ignorance when he really knew, § 47, leads us to the same suspicion. And so, "for *our profit*, as I think, did He this." § 48—50.

The natural want of precision on such questions in the early ages was shown or fostered by such words as οἰκονομικῶς, which, in respect of this very text, is used by S. Basil to denote both our Lord's Incarnation, Ep. 236, 1 fin., and His gracious accommodation of Himself and His truth, Ep. 8, 6; and with the like variety of meaning, with reference to the same text, by Cyril. Trin. p. 623; and Thesaur. p. 224. (And the word *dispensatio* in like manner, Ben. note on Hil. Trin. x. 8.) In the latter Ep. S. Basil suggests that our Lord "economises by a feigned ignorance." And S. Cyril. in Thesaur. l. c. (in spite of his strong language ibid. p. 221), "The Son knows all things, though economically He says He is ignorant of something," Thesaur. p. 224. And even in de Trin. vi. he seem to recognise the distinction laid down just now between the natural and actual state of our Lord's humanity : " God would not make it known even to the Son Himself, were He a *mere* man upon earth, as they say, and not having it in His nature to be God." p. 629. And S. Hilary arguing that He must as man know the day of judgment, for His then coming is as man, says, " Since He is Himself a sacrament, let us see whether He be ignorant in the things which He knows not. For if in the other respects a profession of ignorance is not an intimation of not knowing, so here too He is not ignorant of what He knows not. For since His ignorance, in respect that all treasures of knowledge lie hid in Him, is rather an economy (dispensation) than an ignorance, you have a cause why He might be ignorant without an actual intimation of not knowing." Trin. ix. 62. And he gives reasons why He professed ignorance, n. 67, viz. as S. Austin words it, " Christum se dixisse nescientem, in quo alios facit occultando nescientes." Ep. 180. 3. S. Austin follows Hilary, saying, " Hoc nescit quod nescientes facit." Trin. i. n. 23. Pope Gregory says that the text " is most certainly to be referred to the Son not as He is Head, but as to His body which we are." Ep. x. 39. And S. Ambrose distinctly : " The Son which took on Him the flesh, assumed our affections, so as to say that He knew not with our ignorance ; not that He was ignorant of anything Himself, for, though He seemed to be man in truth of body, yet He was the life and light, and virtue went out of Him," &c. de Fid. v. 222. And so Cæsarius, Qu. 20. and Photius Epp. p. 336, &c. Chrysost. in Matth. Hom. 77, 3. Theodoret, however, but in controversy, is very severe on the principle of Economy. "If He knew the day, and wishing to conceal it, said He was ignorant, see what a blasphemy is the result. Truth tells an untruth." l. c. pp. 23, 24.

¶ The expression, Orat. iii. § 48, &c. "for our sake," which repeatedly occurs, surely implies that there was something economical in our Lord's profession of ignorance. He used it with a purpose, not as a mere plain fact or doctrine. And so S. Cyril, "He says that He is ignorant, *for our sake* and among us, as man," Thes. p. 221: "economically effecting, οἰκονομῶν, something profitable and good." ibid. And again, after stating that there was an objection, and paralleling His words with His question to S. Philip about the loaves, he says, "Knowing as God the Word, He *can*, as man, be ignorant." p. 223. "It is not a sign of ignorance, but of wisdom, for it was inexpedient that we should know it." Ambros. de Fid. v. 209. S. Chrysostom seems to say the same, denying that the Son was ignorant, Hom. 77, 1. And Theophylact, "Had He said, 'I know, but I will not tell you,' they had been cast down, as if despised by Him; but now in saying 'not the Son but the Father only,' He hinders their asking . . . . for how can the Son be ignorant of the day?" Theophyl. in loc. Matt. "Often little children see their fathers holding something in their hands, and ask for it, but they will not give it. Then the children cry as not receiving it. At length the fathers hide what they have got and show their empty hands to their children, and so stop their crying.. . . .

For our profit hath He hid it." ibid. in loc. Marc.
"For thee He is ignorant of the hour and day of judgment, though nothing is hid from the Very Wisdom.
. . . . But He economises this because of thy infirmity," &c. supr. Basil, Ep. 8, 6.

¶ It is the doctrine of the Church that Christ, as man,
was perfect in knowledge from the first, as if ignorance
were hardly separable from sin, and were the direct
consequence or accompaniment of original sin. "That
ignorance," says S. Austin, "I in nowise can suppose
existed in that Infant, in whom the Word was made
flesh to dwell among us; nor can I suppose that that
infirmity of the mind belonged to Christ as a babe,
which we see in babes. For in consequence of it,
when they are troubled with irrational emotions, no
reason, no command, but pain sometimes and the
alarm of pain restrains them," &c. de Pecc. Mer. ii. 48.

¶ As to the limits of Christ's perfect knowledge as
man, we must consider "that the soul of Christ knew all
things that are or ever will be or ever have been, but
not what are only *in posse*, not in fact." Petav. Incarn.
xi. 3, 6.

¶ Leporius, in his Retractation, which S. Augustine
subscribed, writes, "That I may in this respect also
leave nothing to be cause of suspicion to any one, I
then said, nay I answered when it was put to me, that
our Lord Jesus Christ was ignorant as He was man
(secundùm hominem). But now not only do I not
presume to say so, but I even anathematise my former
opinion expressed on this point, because it may not be
said, that the Lord of the Prophets was ignorant even

as He was man." ap. Sirmond. t. i. p. 210. A subdivision also of the Eutychians were called by the name of Agnoetæ from their holding that our Lord was ignorant of the day of judgment. " They said," says Leontius, " that He was ignorant of it, as we say that He underwent toil." de Sect. 5 circ. fin. Felix of Urgela held the same doctrine according to Agobard's testimony, as contained adv. Fel. 6, Bibl. Patr. Max. t. xiv. p. 244. The Ed. Ben. observes, Ath. Orat. iii. § 44, that the assertion of our Lord's ignorance " seems to have been condemned in no one in ancient times, unless joined to other error." And Petavius, after drawing out the authorities for and against it, says, " Of these two opinions, the latter, which is now received both by custom and by the agreement of divines, is deservedly preferred to the former. For it is more agreeable to Christ's dignity, and more befitting His character and office of Mediator and Head, that is, Fountain of all grace and wisdom, and moreover of Judge, who is concerned in knowing the time fixed for exercising that function. In consequence, the former opinion, though formerly it received the countenance of some men of high eminence, was afterwards marked as a heresy." Incarn., xi. 1. § 15.

¶ The mode in which Athan. expresses himself, is as if he only ascribed apparent ignorance to our Lord's soul, and not certainly in the broad sense in which heretics have done so:—as Leontius, e.g. reports of Theodore of Mopsuestia, that he considered Christ " to be ignorant so far, as not to know, when He was tempted, who tempted Him;" contr. Nest. iii. (Canis. t. i. p. 579,)

and Agobard of Felix the Adoptionist that he held
"Our Lord Jesus Christ according to the flesh *truly* to
have been ignorant of the sepulchre of Lazarus, when
He said to his sisters, 'Where have ye laid him?'
and was *truly* ignorant of the day of judgment; and
was *truly* ignorant what the two disciples were saying
as they walked by the way, of what had been done at
Jerusalem; and was *truly* ignorant whether He was
more loved by Peter than by the other disciples, when
He said, 'Simon Peter, lovest thou Me more than
these?'" Bibl. Patr. Max. t. xiv. p. 244. The
Agnoetæ have been noticed above.

¶ It is remarkable, considering the tone of his
statements, Orat. iii. § 42—53, that there and in what
follows upon them, Athan. should resolve our Lord's
advance in wisdom merely into its gradual manifestation through the flesh; and it increases the
proof that his statements are not to be taken in the
letter, and as if fully brought out and settled.
Naz. says the same, Ep. ad Cled. 101, p. 86, which
is the more remarkable since he is chiefly writing
against the Apollinarians, who considered a φανέρωσις
the great end of our Lord's coming; and Cyril. c.
Nest. iii. p. 87. Theod. Hær. v. 13. On the other
hand, S. Epiphanius speaks of Him as growing in
wisdom as man. Hær. 77, pp. 1019-24, and S. Ambrose,
Incarn. 71—74. Vid. however Ambr. de Fid. as quoted
supr. p. 167. The Ed. Ben. in Ambr. Incarn. considers the advancement of knowledge spoken of to
be that of the "scientia experimentalis" alluded to in
Hebr. v. 8, which is one of the three kinds of know-

ledge possessed by Christ as man. vid. Berti Opp. t. 3, p. 41. Petavius, however, omits the consideration of this knowledge, (which S. Thomas at first denied in our Lord, and in his Summa ascribes to Him,) as lying beyond his province. "De hac lite neutram in partem pronuntiare audeo," says Petavius, "hujusmodi enim quæstiones ad Scholas relegandæ sunt; de quibus nihil apud antiquos liquidi ac definiti reperitur." Incarn. xi. 4, § 9.

ILLUSTRATIONS.

¶ "Is there any cause of fear," says Athan., "lest, because the offspring from men are one in substance, the Son, by being called One in substance, be Himself considered as a human offspring too? perish the thought! not so; but the explanation is easy. For the Son is the Father's Word and Wisdom; whence we learn the impassibility ($\dot{a}\pi a\theta\grave{e}\varsigma$) and indivisibility ($\dot{a}\mu\acute{e}\rho\iota\sigma\tau o\nu$) of such a generation from the Father. For not even is man's word part of him, nor proceeds from him according to passion; much less God's Word; whom the Father has declared to be His own Son: lest, on the other hand, if we merely heard of 'Word,' we should suppose Him, such as is the word of man, unsubsistent ($\dot{a}\nu\upsilon\pi\acute{o}\sigma\tau a\tau o\nu$); therefore we are told that He is Son, that we may acknowledge Him to be a living Word and a substantive ($\dot{e}\nu o\acute{u}\sigma\iota o\nu$) Wisdom. Accordingly as in saying 'Offspring,' we have no human thoughts, and, though we know God to be a Father, we entertain no material ideas concerning Him, but while we listen to these illustrations and terms, we think suitably of God, for He is not as man, so in like manner, when we hear of 'consubstantial,' we ought to transcend all sense, and, according to the Proverb, *understand by the understanding that is set before us;* so as to know, that not by the Father's will, but in eternal truth, is

He genuine Son of the Father, as Life from Fountain, and Radiance from Light. Else why should we understand 'Offspring' and 'Son,' in no corporeal way, while we conceive of 'One in substance' as after the manner of bodies? especially since these terms are not here used about different subjects, but of whom 'offspring' is predicated, of Him is predicated 'one in substance also.'" Syn. § 41, 42.

"For whereas men beget with passion, so again when at work they work upon an existing subject matter, and otherwise cannot make. Now if we do not understand creation in a human way, when we attribute it to God, much less seemly is it to understand generation in a human way, or to give a corporeal sense to Consubstantial; instead, as we ought, of receding from things generate, casting away human images, nay, all things sensible, and ascending to the Father, lest in ignorance we rob the Father of the Son and rank Him among His own creatures." Syn. § 51.

¶ S. Athanasius's doctrine is, that, God containing in Himself all perfection, whatever is excellent in one created thing above another, is found in its perfection in him. If then such generation as radiance from light is more perfect than that of children from parents, that belongs, and transcendently, to the All-perfect God.

¶ The question is not, whether in matter of fact, in the particular case, the rays would issue after, and not with, the initial existence of the luminous body; for the illustration is not used to show *how* such a thing may be, or to give an *instance* of it, but to convey to the mind a correct *idea* of what it is proposed to teach in the Catholic doctrine.

¶ Athanasius guards against what is defective in his illustration, Orat. iii. § 5, (e.g. of an Emperor and his image,) but, even independent of such explanation, a mistake as to his meaning would be impossible; and the passage affords a good instance of the imperfect and partial character of all illustrations of the Divine Mystery. What it is taken to symbolise is the unity of the Father and Son, (for the Image is not a Second Emperor but the same, vid. Sabell. Greg. 6,) still no one who bowed before the Emperor's Statue can be supposed to have really worshipped it; whereas our Lord is the Object of supreme worship, which terminates in Him, as being really one with Him whose Image He is.

¶ " Whoso uses the particle *as*, implies, not identity, nor equality, but a likeness of the matter in question, viewed in a certain respect. This we may learn from our Saviour Himself, when He says ' As Jonas,' " &c. Orat. iii. 22, 23. " Even when the analogy is solid and well founded," says a Protestant writer, " we are liable to fall into error, if we suppose it to extend farther than it really does. . . . Thus because a just analogy has been discerned between the metropolis of a country, and the heart in the animal body, it has been sometimes contended that its increased size is a disease, that it may impede some of its most important functions, or even be the means of its dissolution." Copleston on Predestination, p. 129. The principle here laid down, in accordance with S. Athan., of course *admits* of being made an

excuse for denying the orthodox meaning of "Word,
Wisdom, &c.," under pretence that the figurative terms
are not confined by the Church within their proper
limits; but here the question is about the *matter of
fact, which* interpretation is right, the Church's or the
objector's? Thus another writer says, "The most
important words of the N. T. have not only received an
indelibly false stamp from the hands of the old Schoolmen, but those words having, since the Reformation,
become common property in the language of the
country, are, as it were, thickly incrusted with the
most vague, incorrect, and vulgar notions. . . . . Any
word . . . . if habitually repeated in connection with
certain notions, will appear to reject all other signi-
fications, as it were, by a natural power." Heresy and
Orthod. pp. 21, 47. Elsewhere he speaks of words
"which were used in a language now dead to represent
objects . . . . which are now supposed to express
figuratively something spiritual and quite beyond the
knowledge and comprehension of man." P. 96. Of
course Athan. assumes that *since* the figures and
parallels given us in Scripture have but a partial
application, *therefore* there is given us from above
also an interpreter in order to apply them. Vid. art.
Economical.

¶ Again, just as S. Athan. says, "A figure is but a
parallel, . . hence if we too become one, *as* the Son in
the Father, we shall not therefore be *as* the Son, nor
equal to Him, for He and we are but parallel," so
again Dr. Copleston thus proceeds, "Analogy does not
mean the similarity of two things, but the similarity

or sameness of two relations. . . . . Things most unlike and discordant in their nature may be strictly analogous to one another. Thus a certain *proposition* may be called the *basis* of a system . . . . it serves a similar *office* and *purpose* . . . . the system *rests* upon it; it is *useless to proceed* with the argument till this is well established: if this were *removed*, the system must fall." On Predest. pp. 122, 123.

IMAGE

Is used to signify our Lord's relation to the Eternal
Father: and first in Scripture,—

1. We find Him called εἰκὼν, imago, in 2 Cor. iv. 4;
and Col. i. 15. In a verse following the former of
these passages it is said in like manner that the glory
of God is in the face of Jesus Christ. This carries us
to Heb. i. 3, where we read of Him as the ἀπαύγασμα
of God's glory, and find in the word χαρακτὴρ, figura,
impress, a synonym for the word *Image*. St. John
confirms St. Paul; he speaks of our Lord's glory
" quasi Unigeniti a Patre," and says that the " Son who
is in the bosom of the Father, hath declared Him."

These modes of expressing the nature and office of
the Son as the revealed and revealing God, as the
Light, the Glory, the Image, the Impress, the Face of
the Almighty, are exemplified with still greater variety
and fulness of language in the Book of Wisdom, ch.
vii., in a passage too long to quote, in which, among
other attributes and prerogatives, Wisdom, that is, our
Lord, is called a πνεῦμα ἅγιον, μονογενής, φιλάγαθος,
φιλάνθρωπος, the ἀπόρροια τῆς τοῦ παντοκράτορος δόξης,
the ἀπαύγασμα φωτὸς ἀϊδίου, the ἔσοπτρον ἀκηλίδωτον
τῆς τοῦ θεοῦ ἐνεργείας, and the εἰκὼν τῆς ἀγαθότητος
αὐτοῦ.

It is impossible that the Holy Apostles, when they

spoke of our Lord as the Word, Image, and Splendour of God, should not have had in mind this passage, so overpowering in its force and significance, and were not investing with personality and substance what they thus viewed as all-perfect, immutable, co-eternal, consubstantial with Him.

2. S. Athanasius and the other Fathers take up and insist upon this definite theology, thus found in Scripture.

"We must conceive of necessity," says Athan., "that in the Father is the eternal, the everlasting, the immortal; and in Him, not as foreign to Him, but as in a Fount abiding (ἀναπαυόμενα) in Him, and also in the Son. When then you would form a conception of the Son, learn what are the things in the Father, and believe that they are in the Son too. If the Father is creature or work, these attributes are also in the Son, &c. . . . He who honours the Son, is honouring the Father who sent Him, and he who receives the Son, is receiving with Him the Father," &c. In illud Omn. 4. "As the Father is I am (ὁ ὢν) so His Word is I Am and God over all." Serap. i. 28. "Altogether, there is nothing which the Father has, which is not the Son's; for therefore it is that the Son is in the Father, and the Father in the Son; because the things of the Father, these are in the Son, and still the same are understood as being in the Father. Thus is understood, 'I and the Father are One;' since not these things are in Him and those in the Son, but the things which are in the Father those are in the Son, and what thou seest in the Father, because thou seest in the Son, thereby is

N 2

rightly understood 'He that hath seen Me, hath seen the Father.'" Serap. ii. 2.

Again: "Such as the parent, such of necessity is the offspring; and such as is the Word's Father, such must be also His Word . . . God is not as man, as Scripture has said, but is existing (ὤν ἐστι) and is ever, therefore His Word also is existing, and is everlastingly with the Father as radiance with light. . . . As radiance from light, so is He perfect offspring from perfect. Hence He is also God, as being God's Imáge." Orat. ii. § 35. "It was fitting that, whereas God is One, that His Image should be One also, and His Word One, and One His Wisdom." Ibid. § 36.

¶ "He is likeness and image of the sole and true God, being Himself sole also," § 49. μόνος ἐν μόνῳ, Orat. iii. § 21. ὅλος ὅλου εἰκών, Serap. i. 16. "The Offspring of the Ingenerate," says S. Hilary, "is One from One, True from True, Living from Living, Perfect from Perfect, Power of Power, Wisdom of Wisdom, Glory of Glory," de Trin. ii. 8; τέλειος τέλειον γεγέννηκεν, πνεῦμα πνεῦμα. Epiph. Hær. lxxvi. p. 945. "As Light from Light, and Life from Life, and Good from Good; so from Eternal Eternal." Nyss. contr. Eunom. i. p. 164. App. "De Deo nascitur Deus, de Ingenito Unigenitus, de Solo Solus, de Toto Totus, de Vero Verus, de Perfecto Perfectus, Totum Patris habens, nihil derogans Patri." Zenon. Serm. ii. 3.

¶ "A man will see the extravagance of this heresy still more clearly, if he considers that the Son is the Image and Radiance of the Father, and Impress and Truth. For if, when Light exists, there be withal its Image, viz. Radiance,—and a Subsistence existing, there be of it the entire Impress,—and a Father existing, there be His true representation,—let them consider what depths of impiety they fall into, who make time the measure of the Image and Countenance of the Godhead. For if the Son was not before His generation, Truth was not always in God, which it were a sin to say; for, since the Father was, there was ever in Him the Truth, which is the Son, who says, *I am the Truth.* And the Subsistence existing, of course there was forthwith its Impress and Image; for God's Image is not delineated from without, but God Himself hath begotten It; in which seeing Himself, He has delight, as the Son Himself says, *I was His delight.* When then did the Father not see Himself in His own Image? or when had He not delight in Him, that a man should dare to say, ' The Image is out of nothing,' and ' The Father had not delight before the Image was generated?' and how should the Maker and Creator see Himself in a created and generated substance? for such as is the Father, such must be the Image. Proceed we then to consider the attributes of the Father, and we shall come to know whether this Image is really His. The Father is eternal, immortal, powerful, light, King, Sovereign, God, Lord, Creator, and Maker. These attributes must be in the Image, to make it true, that *he that hath seen* the Son, *hath seen the Father.*" Orat. i. § 20, 21.

¶ " If God be ingenerate, His Image is not generate [made,] but an Offspring, which is His Word and His Wisdom," ibid. § 31.

¶ Athan. argues from the very name Image for our
Lord's eternity. An Image, to be really such, must be
an impress from the Original, not an external and
detached imitation. It was attempted to secure this
point before Nicæa by the epithets *living* and ἀπαράλλακτος, unsucessfully, vid. Decr. § 20. Thus S. Basil:
" He is an Image not made with the hand, or a work of
art, but a living Image," &c. vid. art. ἀπαράλλακτον,
also contr. Eunom. ii. 16, 17. Epiph. Hær. 76, 3.
Hilar. Trin. vii. 41 fin. Origen observes that man, on
the contrary, is an example of an external or improper image of God. Periarch. i. 2, § 6. vid. Theod.
Hist. i. 3, pp. 737, 742.

¶ S. Gregory Naz. argues from the name of Image
to our Lord's consubstantiality. "He is Image as
ὁμοούσιον . . . for this is the nature of an image to be
a copy of the archetype." Orat. 30. 20.

¶ Vid. S. Athan.'s doctrine concerning Wisdom,
Orat. ii. § 80, &c. He says, Gent. 34, "The soul as in a
mirror, contemplates the Word the Image of the Father,
and in Him considers the Father, whose Image the
Saviour is . . . or if not . . . yet from the things that
are seen, the creation is such, as if by letters signifying
and heralding its Lord and Maker by means of its
order and harmony." And "As by looking up to the
heaven . . . we have an idea of the Word who set it
in order, so considering the Word of God, we cannot
but see God His Father." 45. And Incarn. 11, 41, 42,
&c. Vid. also Basil. contr. Eunom. ii. 16.

¶ On the Arian objection, that if our Lord be the
Father's Image, He ought to resemble Him in being

a Father, vid. article, "Father Almighty." The
words "like" and much more "image," would be in-
appropriate, if the Second Divine Person in nothing
differed from the First. Sonship is just that one
difference which allows of likeness being predicated
of Him.

IMPERIAL TITLES AND HONOURS.

¶ EUSEBIUS was emphatically the court bishop, but he did not observe the ecclesiastical rule in calling Constantine "most pious," § 14, Lett. App. Decr. "most wise and most religious," § 4, "most religious," § ˙8, § 10. (*Nic.* n. 47, &c.) He goes in his Vit. Const. further than this, and assigns to him the office of determining the faith (Constantine being as yet unbaptised). E.g. "When there were differences between persons of different countries, the Emperor, as if some common bishop appointed by God, convened Councils of God's ministers; and, not disdaining to be present, and to sit amid their conferences," &c. i. 44. When he came into the Nicene Council, "it was," says Eusebius, "as some heavenly Angel of God," iii. 10, alluding to the brilliancy of the imperial purple. He confesses, however, he did not sit down until the Bishops bade him. Again, at the same Council, "with pleasant eyes, looking serenity itself into them all, collecting himself, and in a quiet and gentle voice," he made an oration to the Fathers upon peace. Constantine had been an instrument in conferring such vast benefits, humanly speaking, on the Christian body, that it is not wonderful that other writers of the day besides Eusebius should praise him. Hilary speaks of him as "of sacred memory," Fragm. 5, init.

Athanasius calls him "most pious," Apol. contr.
Arian. 9, "of blessed memory," Ep. Æg. 18, 19.
Epiphanius "most religious and of ever-blessed
memory," Hær. 70, 9. Posterity, as was natural, was
still more grateful.

¶ Up to the year 356, when Constantius took up the
Anomœans, this was Athan.'s tone in speaking of him
also. In his Apol. contr. Arian. init. (A.D. 350,) ad Ep.
Æg. 5, (356,) and his Apol. ad Constant. passim (356,)
he calls the Emperor most pious, religious, &c. At
the end of the last-mentioned work, § 27, the news
comes to him while in exile of the persecution of the
Western Bishops and the measures against himself.
He still in the peroration calls Constantius, "blessed
and divinely favoured Augustus," and urges on him
that he is a "Christian, φιλόχριστος, Emperor." Vid.
supr. art. *Athanasius*.

¶ The honour paid to the Imperial Statues is well
known. "He who crowns the Statue of the Emperor
of course honours him whose image he has crowned."
Ambros. in Psalm. 118, x. 25. vid. also Chrysost. Hom. on
Statues, Oxf. Tr. pp. 355, 6, &c. Fragm. in Act. Conc. vii.
(t. 4, p. 89, Hard.) Chrysostom's second persecution
arose from his interfering with a statue of the Empress,
which was so near the Church that the acclamations
of the people before it disturbed the services. Socr.
vi. 18. The Seventh Council speaks of the images
sent by the Emperors into provinces instead of their
coming in person; Ducange in v. Lauratum. Vid. a
description of the imperial statues and their honours
in Gothofred, Cod. Theod. t. 5, pp. 346, 347, and in

Philostorg. ii. 18, xii. 10. vid. also Molanus de Imaginibus ed. Paquot, p. 197.

¶ From the custom of paying honour to the Imperial Statues, the Cultus Imaginum was introduced into the Eastern Church. The Western Church, not having had the civil custom, resisted. vid. Döllinger, Church History, vol. iii. p. 55. E. Tr. Certain Fathers, e.g. S. Jerome, set themselves against the civil custom, as idolatrous, comparing it to that paid to Nebuchadnezzar's statue, vid. Hieron. in Dan. iii. 18. Incense was burnt before those of the Emperors; as afterwards before the Images of the Saints.

THE INCARNATION.

1. *Considered in its purpose.*

"THE need of man preceded His becoming man," says Athan., "apart from which He had not put on flesh. And what the need was for which He became man, He Himself thus signifies, *I came down from heaven . . . to do the will of Him that sent Me. And this is the will of Him that sent Me, that of all which He hath given Me, I should lose nothing; but, &c. &c.* (John vi. 38—40), and again, *I am come a Light into the World, &c.,* and again, *To this end was I born, &c., that I should bear witness unto the truth* (John xviii. 37), and John hath written, *For this was manifested the Son of God, that he might destroy the works of the devil* (1 John iii. 8). To give a witness, then, and for our sakes to undergo death, to raise men up and loose the works of the devil, the Saviour came, and this is the reason of His Incarnate Presence." Orat. ii. § 54.

¶ However, there are theologians of great name, who consider that the decree of the Incarnation was independent of Adam's fall; and certainly by allowing that it was not absolutely necessary (vid. infra) for the divine forgiveness of sin, and that it was the actual and immediate means of the soul's renewal and sanctification, as we shall see presently, Athan. goes far towards countenancing that belief. "Dico ex vi præentis decreti," says Viva (Curs. Theol. de Incarn. p. 74,) "Adamo non peccante Verbum fuisse incarnatum; atque adeo motivum Incarnationis non fuit sola redemptio, sed etiam et principalius ipsa Christi excellentia ac *humanæ naturæ exaltatio*. Ita Scotistæ, Suar. Martinon. et alii contra Thomistas. Angelicus vero qu. 1 a. 3 sententiam nostram censet probabilem, quamvis probabiliorem putet oppositam."

¶ It is the general teaching of the Fathers in accordance with Athan., that our Lord would not have been incarnate had not man sinned. "Our cause was the occasion of His descent, and our transgression called forth the Word's love of man. Of His incarnation we became the ground." Athan. de Incarn. V. D. 4. vid. Thomassin, at great length, de Incarn. ii. 5—11, also Petav. de Incarn. ii. 17, 7—12. Vasquez. in 3 Thom. Disp. x. 4 and 5.

¶ "Without His sojourning here at all, God was able to speak the word only and undo the curse . . . . but then the power indeed of Him who gave command had been shown, but man, though restored to what Adam was before the fall, would have received grace only from without, not had it united to his body. . . . Then, had he been again seduced by the serpent, a second need had arisen of God's commanding and undoing the curse; and this had gone on without limit, and men had remained under guilt just as before, being in slavery to sin; and ever sinning, they had ever needed pardon, and never been made free, being in themselves carnal, and ever defeated by the Law by reason of the infirmity of the flesh." Orat. ii. 68. And so in Incarn. 7, he says that repentance might have been pertinent, had man merely offended, without *corruption* following (supra *Freedom*). vid. also 14. Athan. is supported by Naz. Orat. 19. 13; Theod. adv. Gent. vi. p. 876-7. Aug. de Trin. xiii. 13. The contrary view is taken by St. Anselm, but St. Thomas and the Schoolmen side with the Fathers. vid. Petav. Incarn. ii. 13.

¶ On the subject of God's power, as contrasted with His acts, vid. Petav. de Deo, v. 6.

¶ There were two reasons then for the Incarnation, viz. atonement for sin, and renewal in holiness, and these are ordinarily associated with each other by Athanasius.

These two ends of our Lord's Incarnation, that He might die for us, and that He might renew us, answer nearly to those specified in Rom. iv. 25, " who was delivered for our offences and raised again for our justification." The general object of His coming, including both of these, is treated of by Athanasius in Incarn. 4—20, or rather in the whole Tract, and in the two books against Apollinaris. It is difficult to make accurate references under the former head, (vid. supr. art. *Atonement*,) without including the latter. "Since all men had to pay the debt of death, on which account especially He came on earth, therefore after giving proofs of His Divinity from His works, next He offered a sacrifice for all," &c., and then the passage runs on into the other fruit of His death. Incarn. 20. Vid. also Orat. ii. § 7—9, where he speaks of our Lord as offering Himself, as offering His flesh to God; also Decr. § 14. And Orat. iv. § 6, he says, "When He is said to hunger, to weep and weary, and to cry Eloi, which are human affections, He receives them from us and offers to His Father, interceding for us, that in Him they may be annulled." And so Theodoret, "Whereas He had an immortal nature, He willed according to the law of equity to put a stop to death's power, taking first on Himself from those who were exposed to death a first-fruit; and, preserving this nature immaculate and guiltless of sin, He surrenders it for death to seize upon as well as upon others, and to satiate its insatiableness; and then on the ground of its want of equity against that first-fruit, He put a stop to its iniquitous tyranny over others." Eran. iii. p. 196, 7. Vigil. Thaps. contr. Eutych. i. § 9, p. 496 (Bibl. Patr. ed. 1624).

And S. Leo speaks of the whole course of redemption, i.e. incarnation, atonement, regeneration, justification, &c., as one sacrament, not drawing the line distinctly between the several agents, elements, or stages in it, but considering it to lie in the intercommunion of Christ's person and ours. Thus he says that our Lord "took on Him all our infirmities which come of sin without sin;" and "the most cruel pains and death," because "none could be rescued from mortality, unless He, in whom our common nature was innocent, allowed Himself to die by the hands of the impious;" "unde," he continues, "in se credentibus et *sacramentum* condidit et exemplum, ut unum apprehenderent *renascendo*, alterum sequerentur imitando." Serm. 63, 4. He speaks of His fortifying us against our passions and infirmities, both "*sacramento susceptionis*" and "exemplo." Serm. 65, 2, and of a "duplex remedium cujus aliud in

sacramento, aliud in exemplo." Serm. 67, 5, also 69, 5.
Elsewhere he makes the strong statement, "The
Lord's passion is continued on [producitur] even to
the end of the world; and as in His Saints He is
honoured Himself, and Himself is loved, and in the
poor He Himself is fed, is clothed Himself, so in all who
endure trouble for righteousness' sake, does He Himself suffer together [compatitur]," Serm. 70, 5. vid.
also more or less in Serm. pp. 76, 93, 98, 99, 141, 249,
257, 258, 271, fin. and Epist. pp. 1291, 1363, 1364. At
other times, however, the atonement is more distinctly
separated from its circumstances, pp. 136, 198, 310;
but it is very difficult to draw the line. The tone of
his teaching is throughout characteristic of the
Fathers, and very like that of S. Athanasius. vid. arts.
Atonement and *Freedom.*

2. *Considered in itself.*

THE Two natures, the divine and human, both perfect,
though remaining distinct, are in the Christ intimately
and for ever one.

" Two natures," says S. Leo, "met together in our
Redeemer, and, while what belonged to each remained,
so great a unity was made of either substance, that from
the time that the Word was made flesh in the Blessed
Virgin's womb, we may neither think of Him as God
without that which is man, nor as man without that
which is God," &c. Vid. art. *Two Natures.*

¶ And the principle of unity, viz. that in which they
were united, was the Person of the Son. From this

unity of Person it comes to pass, first, that one and the same act on the part of our Lord may be both divine and human; (e.g. His curing with a touch, this is called the θεανδρικὴ ἐνέργεια;) and secondly, that the acts and attributes of one nature may safely be ascribed as personal to the other; this is called the ἀντίδοσις ἰδιωμάτων. Thus it is true that " the Creator is the Lamb of God," though there can be no intrinsic union of attribute or act in Him who both in the beginning created and in the fulness of time suffered.

That Person which our Lord is after the Incarnation, He was before; His human nature is not a separate being; that is the heresy of the Nestorians.   vid. *Unity*, &c.   It has no personality belonging to it; but that human nature, though perfect as a nature, lives in and belongs to and is possessed by Him, the second Person of the Trinity, as an attribute or organ or inseparable accident of being, not as what is substantive, independent, or co-ordinate.   Vid. articles ὄργανον and παραπέτασμα.

¶ Personality is not necessary in order to a nature being perfect, as we see in the case of brute animals.

¶ Nothing then follows from the union of the two natures, which circumscribes or limits the Divine Son; so to teach was the heresy of the Monophysites, who held that the Divinity and Manhood of Christ made up together one nature, as soul and body in man are one compound nature; from which it follows that neither of them is perfect.   Vid. article Μία φύσις.

THE DIVINE INDWELLING.

Our Lord, by becoming man, has found a way whereby to sanctify that nature, of which His own manhood is the pattern specimen. He inhabits us personally, and this inhabitation is effected by the channel of the Sacraments.

"Since the Word bore our body," says Athanasius, "and came to be in us (γέγονεν), therefore, by reason of the Word in us, is God called our Father." Decr. § 31. Vid. τὸν ἐν ἡμῖν υἱόν. Orat. ii. § 59, ὁ λόγος θεὸς ἐν σαρκὶ . . . ἕνεκα τοῦ ἁγιάζειν τὴν σάρκα γέγονεν ἄνθρωπος. ibid. § 10, also § 56, and τὸν ἐν αὐτοῖς οἰκοῦντα λόγον, § 61. Also Orat. i. § 50, iii. 23—25, iv. § 21. "We rise from the earth, the curse of sin being removed, because of Him who is in us," iii. § 33.

¶ In thus teaching Athan. follows the language of Scripture, in which ἐν means *in* our nature, though sometimes *among* us; vid. ὄντως ἐν ἡμῖν θεὸς, 1 Cor. xiv. 25. ἐν ἐμοὶ, Gal. i. 24. ἐντὸς ὑμῶν, Luke xvii. 21. ἐσκήνωσεν ἐν ἡμῖν, John i. 14; also xiv. 17, 23; 1 Cor. vi. 20; 1 John iii. 24, &c.

By this indwelling our Lord is the immediate ἀρχὴ of spiritual life to each of His elect individually. Οὐκ ὁ λόγος ἐστὶν ὁ βελτιούμενος, εἶχεν γὰρ πάντα, ἀλλ' οἱ ἄνθρωποι οἱ ἀρχὴν ἔχοντες τοῦ λαμβάνειν ἐν αὐτῷ καὶ δἰ αὑτοῦ. Orat. i. 48. Vid. also what he says on the phrase ἀρχὴ ὅδων. Orat. ii. 48, &c. Also the note of the Benedictine editor on Justin's Tryphon. 61, referring to Tatian. c. Gent. S. Athenag. Apol. 10. Iren. Hær. iv. 20, n. 4. Origen in Joan. tom. i. 39. Tertull. Prax. 6, and Ambros. de Fid. iii. 7.

¶ "Flesh being first sanctified in Him," says Athan., "and He being said on account of it to have received as man [the anointing], we have the sequel of the Spirit's grace receiving *out of His fulness.*" Orat. i. 50. vid. art. *Grace.* Other Fathers use still stronger language. S. Chrysostom explains, "He is born of our Substance: you will say, 'This does not pertain to all;' yea, to all. He mingles (ἀναμίγνυσιν) Himself with the faithful individually, through the mysteries, and whom He has begotten those He nurses from Himself, not puts them out to other hands," &c. Hom. 82, 5, in Matt., &c., &c. vid. art. *Freedom.*

In Orat. iii. § 33 S. Athanasius uses the strong phrase λογωθείσης τῆς σαρκὸς, of regenerate human nature. Damascene speaks of the λόγωσις of the flesh, but he means principally our Lord's flesh, F. O. iv. 18, p. 286, ed. Ven. For the words θεοῦσθαι, &c. vid. supr. art. *Deification;* also vid. *The Flesh.*

¶ Nor is this all; we must go on to the results of this doctrine, as indicated in the following passages of Scripture which are referred to above: "Know ye not that ye are the temple of God, and that the Spirit of God dwelleth in you?" 1 Cor. iii. 16, 17; vi. 15—20. 2 Cor. vi. 16, &c. It is plain that there is a special presence of God in those who are real members of our Lord. To this St. Paul seems to refer when he says, "They glorified God in me," Gal. i. 24. To this and to other passages noted supr. Athanasius refers, when he says, "Because of our relationship to His Body we too have become God's temple, and in consequence are made God's sons, so that even in us the Lord is now worshipped, and beholders report, as the Apostle says, that God is in them of a truth." Orat. i. § 43. And S. Basil, arguing for the worship of the Holy Spirit, says, "Man in common is crowned with glory and honour, and glory and honour and peace are reserved in the promises for every one who doeth good. And there is a certain glory of Israel peculiar, and the Psalmist speaks of a glory of his own, 'Awake up my glory;' and there is a glory of the sun, and according to the Apostle even a ministration of condemnation with glory. So many then being glorified, choose you that the Spirit alone of all should be without glory?" de Sp. S. c. 24.

¶ We are led on to a farther remark:—If even while we are in the flesh, soul and body become, by the indwelling of the Word, so elevated above their natural state, so sacred, that to profane them is a sacrilege, is it wonderful that the Saints above should so abound in prerogatives and privileges, and should claim a religious *cultus*, when once in the *pleroma*, and in the sight as in the fruition of the exuberant infinitude of God?

MARCELLUS.

¶ MARCELLUS was Bishop of Ancyra in Galatia. In the early years of S. Athanasius's episcopate, he wrote his Answer to the Arian Asterius and others, which was the occasion, and forms the subject of Eusebius's "contra Marcellum" and "Ecclesiastica Theologia," and which is the only authentic existing document recording his opinions. "Now he replies to Asterius," says Eusebius, "now to the great Eusebius [of Nicomedia], and then he turns upon that man of God, that indeed thrice blessed person, Paulinus [of Tyre]. Then he goes to war with Origen. . . Next he marches out against Narcissus, and pursues the other Eusebius," himself. "In a word, he counts for nothing all the Ecclesiastical Fathers, being satisfied with no one but himself." contr. Marc. i. 4. He was in consequence condemned in several Arian Councils, and retired to Rome, as did S. Athanasius, about the year 341, when both of them were formally acquitted of heterodoxy by the Pope in Council. Both were present, and both were again acquitted, at the Council of Sardica in 347. From this very date, however, the charges against him, which had hitherto been confined to the Arians, begin to find a voice among the Catholics. S. Cyril in his Catechetical Lectures, A.D. 347, speaks of the heresy which had lately arisen in Galatia, which denied Christ's

eternal reign, a description which both from country
and tenet is evidently levelled at Marcellus. He is
followed by S. Paulinus at the Council of Arles, and
by S. Hilary, in the years which follow; but S.
Athanasius seems to have acknowledged him down to
about A.D. 360. At length the latter began to own
that Marcellus "was not far from heresy," vid. below,
and S. Hilary and S. Sulpicius say that he separated
from his communion. S. Hilary adds (Fragm. ii. 21)
that Athanasius was decided in this course, not by
Marcellus's work against Asterius, but by publications
posterior to the Council of Sardica. Photinus, the
disciple of Marcellus, who had published the very
heresy imputed to the latter before A.D. 345, had
now been deposed for some years, with the unanimious
consent of all parties.

¶ Thus for ten years Marcellus was disowned by the
Saint with whom he had shared so many trials; but in
the very end of S. Athanasius's life a transaction took
place between himself, S. Basil, and the Galatian school,
which issued in his being induced again to think more
favourably of Marcellus, or at least to think it right in
charity to consider him in communion with the Church.
S. Basil had taken a strong part against him, and wrote
to S. Athanasius on the subject, Ep. 69, 2, thinking
that Athanasius's apparent countenance of him did
harm to the Catholic cause. Upon this the accused
party sent a deputation to Alexandria, with a view of
setting themselves right with Athanasius. Eugenius,
deacon of their Church, was their representative, and
he, in behalf of his brethren, subscribed a statement in

vindication of his and their orthodoxy, which was counter-
signed by the clergy of Alexandria and apparently by S.
Athanasius, though his name does not appear among the
extant signatures. This important document, which was
brought to light and published by Montfaucon, speaks
in the name of "the Clergy and the others assembled
in Ancyra of Galatia, with our father Marcellus." He,
as well as Athanasius himself, died immediately after
this transaction, Marcellus in extreme age, being at
least twenty years older than Athanasius, who himself
lived till past the age of seventy. One might trust
that the life of the former was thus prolonged, till he
really recanted the opinions which go under his name;
yet viewing him historically, and not in biography, it
still seems right, and is in accordance with the usage
of the Church in other cases, to consider him rather in
his works and in his school and its developments, than
in his own person and in his penitence.

¶ Whether S. Athanasius wrote the controversial
passages which form Orat. iv. against him or against
his school, in either case it was prior to the date of the
explanatory document signed by Eugenius; nor is its
interpretation affected by that explanation. As to S.
Hilary's statement, that S. Athanasius did not condemn
the particular work of Marcellus against Asterius, of
which alone portions remain to us, his evidence in
other parts of the history is not sufficiently exact for
us to rely on his evidence in Marcellus's favour,
against the plainly heretical import of the statements
made in that work. Those statements were as follows:—

Marcellus held, according to Eusebius, that (1) there

was but one person, πρόσωπον, in the Divine Nature;
but he differed from Sabellius in maintaining, (2) not
that the Father was the Son and the Son the Father,
(which is called the doctrine of the υἱοπάτωρ,) but that
(3) Father and Son were mere names or titles, and
(4) not expressive of essential characteristics,—names
or titles given to Almighty God and (5) to His Eternal
Word, on occasion of the Word's appearing in the
flesh, in the person, or subsistence (ὑπόστασις) of Jesus
Christ the Son of Mary. The Word, he considered,
was from all eternity in the one God, being analogous
to man's reason within him, or the ἐνδιάθετος λόγος of
the philosophical schools. (6) This One God or μόνας,
has condescended to extend or expand Himself,
πλατύνεσθαι, to effect our salvation. (7 and 8) The
expansion consists in the action, ἐνεργεία, of the λόγος,
which then becomes the λόγος προφορικὸς or voice of
God, instead of His inward Reason. (9) The incarnation is a special divine expansion, viz. an expansion in
the flesh of Jesus, Son of Mary; (10) in order to
which the Word went forth, as at the end of the
dispensation He will return. Consequently the λόγος
is not (11) the Son, nor (12) the Image of God, nor
the Christ, nor the First-begotten, nor King, but
Jesus is all these; and if these titles are applied to the
Word in Scripture, they are applied prophetically, in
anticipation of His manifestation in the flesh. (13)
And when He has accomplished the object of His
coming, they will cease to apply to Him; for He
will leave the flesh, return to God, and be merely the
Word as before; and His Kingdom, as being the

Kingdom of the flesh or manhood, will come to an end.

This account of the tenets of Marcellus comes, it is true, from an enemy, who was writing against him, and moreover from an Arian or Arianiser, who was least qualified to judge of the character of tenets which were so opposite to his own. Yet there is no reason to doubt its correctness on this account. Eusebius supports his charges by various extracts from Marcellus's works, and he is corroborated by· the testimony of others. Moreover, if Athanasius's account of the tenets against which he himself writes in his fourth Oration, answers to what Eusebius tells us of those of Marcellus, as in fact they do, the coincidence confirms Eusebius as well as explains Athanasius. And further, the heresy of Photinus, the disciple of Marcellus, which consisted in the very doctrines which Eusebius deduces from the work of Marcellus, gives an additional weight to such deductions.

¶ He wrote his work against Asterius not later than 335, the year of the Arian Council of Jerusalem, which at once took cognisance of it, and cited Marcellus to appear before them. The same year a Council held at Constantinople condemned and deposed him, about the time that Arius came thither for re-admission into the Church. From that time his name is frequently introduced into the Arian anathemas, vid. Macrostich, Syn. § 26. By adding in that document "those who communicate with him," the Eusebians intended to strike at the Roman see, which had acquitted Marcellus in a Council held in June of the same year.

¶ The Arians of Alexandria, writing to Alexander, (Syn. § 16) speak of the Son "not as existing before, and afterwards generated or new created into a Son." One school of theologians may be aimed at, who held our Lord's συγκατάβασις to create the world was His γέννησις, and certainly such language as that of Hippol. contr. Noet. § 15, favours the supposition. But a class of the Sabellians may more probably be intended, who held that the Word became the Son, on His incarnation, such as Marcellus, vid. Euseb. Eccles. Theol. i. 1. contr. Marc. ii. 3. vid. also Eccles. Theol. ii. 9, p. 114. b. μηδ' ἄλλοτε ἄλλην κ. τ. λ. Also the Macrostich says, "We anathematise those who call Him the mere Word of God, . . . not allowing Him to be Christ and Son of God before all ages, but from the time He took on Him our flesh . . . such are the followers of Marcellus and Photinus, &c." Syn. § 26. Again, Athanasius, Orat. iv. 15, says that of those who divide the Word from the Son, some called our Lord's manhood the Son, some the two Natures together, and some said "that the Word Himself became the Son when He was made man." It makes it the more likely that Marcellus is meant, that Asterius seems to have written against him before the Nicene Council, and that Arius in other of his writings borrowed from Asterius, vid. de Decret. § 8; though it must not be forgotten that some of the early Fathers spoke unadvisedly on this subject, vid. the author's *Theological Tracts.*

¶ In the fourth (Arian) Confession of Antioch (supr. vol. i. p. 101) words are used which answer to those added in the second General Council (381) to the Creed, and are directed against the doctrine of Marcellus, who taught that the Word was but a divine energy, manifested in Christ and retiring from Him at the consummation of all things, when the manhood or flesh of Christ would consequently no longer reign. "How can we admit," says Marcellus in Eusebius, "that that flesh, which is from the earth and profiteth nothing, should co-exist with the Word in the ages to come as serviceable to Him?". de Eccl. Theol. iii. 8. Again, "If He has received a beginning of His Kingdom not more than four hundred years past, it is no paradox that He who gained that kingdom so short a while since, should be said by the Apostle to deliver it up to God. What are we to gather about the human flesh, which the Word bore for us, not four hundred years since? will the Word have it in the ages to come, or only to the judgment season?" iii. 17. And, "Should any ask whether that flesh which is in the Word has become immortal, we say to him, that we count it not safe to pronounce on points of which we learn not for certain from divine Scripture." Ibid. 10.

¶ Pope Julius acquitted Marcellus, Athan. Apol. Ar. 32, A.D. 341, but it would seem that he did not eventually preserve himself from heresy, even if he deserved a favourable judgment at that time. Athan. also sides with him, de Fug. 3. Hist. Arian. 6, but Epiphanius records, that, once on his asking Athan. what he (Athan.) thought of Marcellus, a smile came on his face, as if he had an opinion of him which he did not like to express, or which Epiphanius ought not to have asked for. Hær. 72, 4. And S. Hilary says that

Athan. separated Marcellus from his communion, because he agreed with his disciple, Photinus. He is considered heretical by Epiphanius, l.c.; by Basil, Epp. 69, 125, 263, 265 ; Chrysost. in Heb. i. 8 ; Theod. Hær. ii. 10 ; by Petavius. far more strongly by Bull. Montfaucon defends him, Tillemont, and Natal. Alex.

THE BLESSED MARY.

1. *Mary Ever-Virgin.*

THIS title is found in Athan. Orat. ii. § 70. " Let
those who deny that the Son is from the Father by
nature and proper to His substance, deny also that He
took true human flesh of Mary Ever-Virgin." Vid. also
Athan. Comm. in Luc. in Collect. Nov. t. 2, p. 43.
Epiph. Hær. 78, 5. Didym. Trin. i. 27, p. 84. Rufin.
Fid. i. 43. Lepor. ap. Cassian. Incarn. i. 5. Leon. Ep.
28, 2. Pseudo-Basil, t. 2, p. 598. Cæsarius has
ἀεπιαῖς. Qu. 20. On the doctrine itself, vid. the controversial Tract of S. Jerome against Helvidius; also
a letter of S. Ambrose and his brethren to Siricius,
and the Pope's letter in response. Coust. Ep. Pont.
t. i. p. 669—682.

¶ Pearson, Bishop of Chester, writes well upon this
subject. Creed, Art. 3. (A passage from him is also
incidentally quoted infr. art. εὐσέβεια.) He says here,
" As we are taught by the predictions of the Prophets
that a Virgin was to be Mother of the promised
Messias, so are we assured by the infallible relation of
the Evangelists, that this Mary ' was a Virgin when
she bare Him.' .... Neither was her act of parturition
more contradictory to virginity than that former [act]
of conception. Thirdly, we believe the Mother of our

Lord to have been, not only before and after His nativity, but also for ever, the most immaculate and blessed Virgin. . . . . The peculiar eminency and unparalleled privilege of that Mother, the special honour and reverence due unto her Son and ever paid by her, the regard of that Holy Ghost who came upon her, the singular goodness and piety of Joseph to whom she was espoused, have persuaded the Church of God in all ages to believe that she still continued in the same virginity, and therefore is to be acknowledged as the Ever-Virgin Mary." Creed, Art. 3.

He adds that "many have taken the boldness to deny this truth, because not recorded in the sacred writ," but "with no success." He replies to the argument from "until" in Matt. i. 25 by referring to Gen. xxviii. 15, Deut. xxxiv. 6, 1 Sam. xv. 35, 2 Sam. vi. 23, Matt. xxviii. 20.

He might also have referred to Psalm cix. 1 and 1 Cor. xv. 25, which are the more remarkable because they were urged by the school of Marcellus as a proof that our Lord's kingdom would have an end, and are explained by Euseb. himself, Eccl. Theol. iii. 13, 14. Vid. also Cyr. Cat. 15, 29, Naz. Orat. 30. 4, where the true force of "until" is well brought out,—"He who is King *before* He subdued His enemies, how shall He not *the rather* be King after He has got the mastery over them ? "

¶ I have said in a note on the word in the *Aurea Catena*, that the word "till" need not imply a termination at a certain point of time, but may be given as information up to a certain point from which onwards there is

already no doubt. Supposing an Evangelist thought
the very notion shocking that Joseph should have considered the Blessed Virgin as his wife, *after* he was
witness of her bearing the Son of God, he would only
say that the vision had its effect upon him up to that
date, when the idea was monstrous. If one said of
a profligate, that, in consequence of some awful warn-
ing, he had said a prayer for grace every night up to
the time of his conversion, no one would gather thence
that he left off praying on being converted. "Michal
the daughter of Saul had no child *to* the day of her
death;" had she children after it? This indeed is
one of Pearson's references. Vid. also Suicer de Symb.
Niceno-Const. p. 231. Spanheim, Dub. Evang. part i.
28, 11.

¶ Athan. elsewhere compares the Virgin's flesh to the
pure earth of Paradise out of which Adam was formed.
She is ἀνέργαστος γῆ. Orat. ii. § 7, and so Iren. Hær.
iii. 21 fin., and Tertullian, "That virgin earth, not yet
watered by rains, nor impregnated by showers, from
which man was formed in the beginning, from which
Christ is now born according to the flesh from a Virgin." Adv. Jud. 13, vid. de Carn. Christ 17. "Ex
terra virgine Adam, Christus ex virgine." Ambros. in
Luc. lib. iv. 7. Vid. also the parallel drawn out t. v. Serm.
147. App. S. August. and in Proclus, Orat. 2, pp. 103,
4, ed. 1630, vid. also Chrysost. t. 3, p. 113, ed. Ben.
and Theodotus at Ephesus, "O earth unsown, yet
bearing a salutary fruit, O Virgin, who didst surpass the
very Paradise of Eden," &c. Conc. Eph. p. 4 (Hard.
t. i. p. 1643). And so Proclus again, "She, the

flowering and incorruptible Paradise, in whom the Tree of Life," &c. Orat. 6, p. 227. And Basil of Seleucia, " Hail, full of grace, the amaranthine Paradise of purity, in whom the Tree of Life," &c. Orat. in Annunc. p. 215. And p. 212, "Which, think they, is the harder to believe, that a virgin womb should be with child, or the ground should be animated?" &c. And Hesychius, "Garden unsown, Paradise of immortality." Bibl. Patr. Par. 1624. t. 2, pp. 421, 423.

¶ Vid. the well-known passage in S. Ignatius, ad Eph. 19, where the devil is said to have been ignorant of the Virginity of Mary, and of the Nativity and the Death of Christ; Orig. Hom. 6, in Luc. Basil, (if Basil,) Hom. in t. 2, App. p. 598, ed. Ben. and Jerome in Matt. i. 18, who quote it; vid. also Leon. Serm. 22, 3. Clement. Eclog. Proph. p. 1002, ed. Potter.

¶ "Many," says Athanasius, "have been made holy and clean from all sin; nay, Jeremias was hallowed even from the womb, and John, while yet in the womb, leapt for joy at the voice of Mary Mother of God." Orat. iii. § 33. vid. Jer. i. 5. And so S. Jerome, S. Leo, &c. as mentioned in Corn. à. Lap. in loc. who adds that S. Ephrem considers Moses also sanctified in the womb, and S. Ambrose Jacob. S. Jerome implies a similar gift in the case of Asella (ad Marcell. Ep. 24, 2). And of S. John Baptist, Maldon. in Luc. i. 15.

¶ It is at first strange that these instances of special exemptions should be named by early writers, without our Lady also being mentioned; or rather it would be strange, unless we bore in mind how little is

said of her at all by Scripture or the Fathers up to the
Council of Ephesus, A.D. 431. It would seem as if,
till our Lord's glory called for it, it required an effort
for the reverent devotion of the Church to speak much
about her or to make her the subject of popular
preaching; but, when by her manifestation a right
faith in her Divine Son was to be secured, then the
Church was to be guided in a contrary course. It
must be recollected that there was a *disciplina
arcani* in the first centuries, and, if it was exercised,
as far as might be, as regards the Holy Trinity and
the Eucharist, so would it be as regards the Blessed
Virgin.

I have insisted upon this deep sentiment of reverence
in matters of sacred doctrine in my "History of the
Arians," written long before I was a Catholic, and I
may fairly quote here one of several passages contained
in it, in solution of a difficulty with which at that
time I was not concerned. For instance, I say, ch. 2,
§ 1:—"The meaning and practical results of deep-
seated religious reverence were far better understood
in the primitive times than now, when the infidelity
of the world has corrupted the Church. Now, we
allow ourselves publicly to canvass the most solemn
truths in a careless or fiercely argumentative way;
truths, which it is as useless as it is unseemly to discuss
before men, as being attainable only by the sober and
watchful, by slow degrees, with dependence on the
Giver of wisdom, and with strict obedience to the light
which has already been granted. Then, they would
scarcely express in writing, what now is not only

preached to the mixed crowds who frequent our churches, but circulated in prints among all ranks and classes of the unclean and the profane, and pressed upon all who choose to purchase. Nay, so perplexed is the present state of things, that *the Church is obliged to change her course of acting*, after the spirit of the alteration made at Nicæa, and unwillingly to take part in the theological discussions of the day, as a man crushes venomous creatures of necessity, powerful to do it, but loathing the employment." I am corroborated in my insistence on this principle by the words of Sozomen, who says, " I formerly deemed it necessary to transmit the confession drawn up by the unanimous consent of the Nicene Council, in order that posterity might possess a public record of the truth; but subsequently I was persuaded to the contrary by some godly and learned men, who represented that such matters ought to be kept secret, as only requisite to be known by disciples and their instructors." Hist. i. 20.

In an Anglican Sermon of a later date, I apply this instinctive feeling to the fact of the silence of Scripture about the Blessed Virgin in its narrative of the Resurrection. " Here perhaps," I say, " we learn a lesson from the deep silence which Scripture observes concerning the Blessed Virgin after the Resurrection; as if she, who was too pure and holy a flower to be more than seen here on earth, even during the season of her Son's humiliation, was altogether drawn by the Angels into paradise on His Resurrection," &c. Par. Serm. vol. iv. 23. And I refer in a note to the following passage in the Christian Year:

> " God only, and good angels, look
> Behind the blissful screen,—
> As when, triumphant o'er His woes,
> The Son of God by moonlight rose,
> By all but Heaven unseen;
> As when the Holy Maid beheld
> Her risen Son and Lord,
> Thought has not colours half so fair,
> That we to paint that hour may dare,
> In silence best adored."

Such doubtless were the spirit and the tone of the Church till Nestorius came forward to deny that the Son of God was the Son of Mary. Thenceforward her title of Theotocos, already in use among Christian writers, became dogmatic.

2. *Mary Theotocos.*

Mater Dei. Mother of God. Vid. art. ἀντίδοσις ἰδιωμάτων. Athanasius gives the title to the Blessed Virgin, Orat. iii. § 14, § 29, § 33. Orat. iv. 32. Incarn. c. Ar. 8, 22.

¶ As to the history of this title, Theodoret, who from his party would rather be disinclined towards it, says that " *the most ancient* (τῶν πάλαι καὶ πρόπαλαι) heralds of the orthodox faith taught the faithful to name and believe the Mother of the Lord θεοτόκος, according to *the Apostolical tradition.*" Hær. iv. 12. And John of Antioch, whose championship of Nestorius and quarrel

with S. Cyril are well known, writes to the former, "This
title no ecclesiastical teacher has put aside; those who
have used it are many and eminent, and those who have
not used it have not attacked those who used it."
Concil. Eph. part i. c. 25. (Labb.) And Alexander,
the most obstinate or rather furious of all Nestorius's
adherents, who died in banishment in Egypt, fully
allows the ancient reception of the word, though only
into popular use, from which came what he considers
the doctrinal corruption. "That in festive solemnities,
or in preaching and teaching, θεοτόκος should be un-
guardedly said by the orthodox without explanation,
is no blame, because such statements were not dogmatic, nor said with evil meaning. But now after the
corruption of the whole world," &c. Lup. Ephes. Epp.
94. He adds that it, as well as ἀνθρωποτόκος, "was used
by the great doctors of the Church." Socrates, Hist.
vii. 32, says that Origen, in the first tome of his Commentary on the Romans (vid. de la Rue in Rom. lib. i. 5,
the original is lost), treated largely of the word; which
implies that it was already in use. "Interpreting," he
says, "how θεοτόκος is used, he discussed the question
at length." Constantine implies the same, with an
allusion to pagan mythology of an unpleasant kind; he
says, "When He had to draw near to a body of this
world, and to tarry on earth, the need so requiring, He
contrived a sort of irregular birth of Himself, νόθην
τινὰ γένεσιν; for without marriage was there conception, and childbirth, εἰλείθυια, from a pure Virgin, and
a maid, the Mother of God, θεοῦ μήτηρ κόρη." Ad. Sanct.
Cœt. p. 480. The idea must have been familiar to

P 2

Christians before Constantine's date to be recognised by him, a mere catechumen, and to be virtually commented on by such a parallelism.

¶ For instances of the word θεοτόκος, besides Origen. ap. Socr. vii. 32, vid. Euseb. V. Const. iii. 43, in Psalm. cix. 4, p. 703, Montf. Nov. Coll.; Alexandr. Ep. ad Alex. ap. Theodor. Hist. i. 3, p. 745; Athan. (supra); Cyril. Cat. x. 19; Julian Imper. ap. Cyril. c. Jul. viii. p. 262; Amphiloch. Orat. 4, p. 41 (if Amphil.) ed. 1644; Nyssen. Ep. ad Eustath. p. 1093; Chrysost. apud Suicer Symb. t. ii. p. 240; Greg. Naz. Orat. 29. 4; Ep. 101, p. 85, ed. Ben. Antiochus and Ammon. ap. Cyril. de Recta Fid. pp. 49, 50; Pseudo-Dion. contr. Samos. 5, p. 240; Pseudo-Basil. Hom. t. 2, p. 600, ed. Ben.

¶ Pearson on the Creed (notes on Art. 3), arguing from Ephrem. ap. Phot. Cod. 228, p. 775, says the phrase *Mater Dei* originated with St. Leo. On the contrary, besides in Constantine's Oration as above, it is found, before S. Leo. in Ambros. de Virg. ii. 7; Cassian. Incarn. ii. 5, vii. 25; Vincent. Lir. Commonit. 21. It is obvious that θεοτόκος, though framed as a test against Nestorians, was equally effective against Apollinarians and Eutychians, who denied that our Lord had taken human flesh at all, as is observed by Facundus Def. Trium Cap. i. 4. And so S. Cyril, "Let it be carefully observed, that nearly this whole contest about the faith has been created against us for our maintaining that the Holy Virgin is Mother of God; now, if we hold," as was the calumny, "that the Holy Body of Christ our common Saviour was from heaven, and not born of her, how can she be considered as

Mother of God?" Epp. pp. 106, 7. Yet these sects, as the Arians, maintained the term. Vid. supr. *Heresies.*

¶ As to the doctrine, which the term implies and guards, the following are specimens of it. Vid. S. Cyril's quotations in his de Recta Fide, p. 49, &c. "The fleshless," says Atticus, "becomes flesh, the impalpable is handled, the perfect grows, the unalterable advances, the rich is brought forth in an inn, the coverer of heaven with clouds is swathed, the king is laid in a manger." Antiochus speaks of Him, our Saviour, "with whom yesterday in an immaculate bearing Mary travailed, the Mother of life, of beauty, of majesty, the Morning Star," &c. "The Maker of all," says S. Amphilochius, "is born to us to-day of a Virgin." "She did compass," says S. Chrysostom, "without circumscribing the Sun of righteousness. To-day the Everlasting is born, and becomes what He was not. He who sitteth on a high and lofty throne is placed in a manger, the impalpable, incomposite, and immaterial is wrapped around by human hands; He who snaps the bands of sin, is environed in swathing bands." And in like manner S. Cyril himself, "As a woman, though bearing the body only, is said to bring forth one who is made up of body and soul, and that will be no injury to the interests of the soul, as if it found in flesh the origin of its existence, so also in the instance of the Blessed Virgin, though she is Mother of the Holy Flesh, yet she bore God of God the Word, as being in truth one with it." Adv. Nest. i. p. 18. "God dwelt in the womb, yet was not circumscribed; whom the heaven containeth not, the Virgin's frame did not

straiten." Procl. Orat. i. p. 60. When thou hearest
that God speaks from the bush, and Moses falling on
his face worships, believest thou, not considering the
fire that is seen, but God that speaks? and yet, when
I mention the Virgin womb, dost thou abominate and
turn away? . . . In the bush seest thou not the Virgin,
in the fire the loving-kindness of Him who came?"
Theodotus of Ancyra ap. Conc. Eph. (p. 1529, Labb.)
"Not only did Mary bear her Elder," says Cassian in
answer to an objector, "but her Author, and giving
birth to Him from whom she received it, she became
parent of her Parent. Surely it is as easy for God to
give nativity to Himself, as to man; to be born of
man, as to make men ·born. For God's power is not
circumscribed in His own Person, that He should not
do in Himself what He can do in all." Incarn. iv. 2.
"The One God Only-begotten, of an ineffable origin
from God, is introduced into the womb of the Holy
Virgin, and grows into the form of a human body.
He who contrives all . . . is brought forth according
to the law of a human birth; He at whose voice Arch-
angels tremble . . and the world's elements are dis-
solved, is heard in the wailing of an infant," &c. Hil.
Trin. ii. 25. "'My beloved is white and ruddy;'
white truly, because the Brightness of the Father,
ruddy, because the Birth of a Virgin. In Him shines
and glows the colour of each nature; . . He did not
begin from a Virgin, but the Everlasting came into a
Virgin." Ambros. Virgin. i. n. 46. "Him, whom,
coming in His simple Godhead, not heaven, not
earth, not sea, not any creature had endured,

Him the inviolate womb of a Virgin carried."
Chrysost. ap. Cassian. Incarn. vii. 30. "Happily do
some understand by the 'closed gate,' by which only
'the Lord God of Israel enters,' that Prince on whom
the gate is closed; to be the Virgin Mary, who both before and after her bearing remained a Virgin." Jerom.
in Ezek. 44. init. "Let them tell us," says Capreolus of
Carthage, "how is that Man from Heaven, if He be
not God conceived in the womb?" ap. Sirm. Opp. t. i.
p. 216. "He is made in thee," says S. Austin, "who
made thee . . . nay, through whom heaven and earth
is made ; . . the Word of God in thee is made flesh,
receiving flesh, not losing Godhead. And the Word
is joined, is coupled to the flesh, and of this so high
wedding thy womb is the nuptial chamber," &c. Serm.
291, 6. "Say, O blessed Mary," says S. Hippolytus,
"what was It which by thee was conceived in the
womb, what carried by thee in that virgin frame? It
was the Word of God," &c. ap. Theod. Eran. i. p. 55.
"There is one physician," says S. Ignatius, "fleshly
and spiritual, generate and ingenerate, God come in
the flesh, in death true life, both from Mary and
from God, first passible, then impassible, Jesus Christ
our Lord." Ep. ad Eph. 7.

MEDIATION.

God, the Origin and Cause of all things, acts by the
mediation, ministration, or operation of His Son, as
signified by the Son's names of Word and Wisdom.
Vid. art. *Eternal Son.*

"It belongs to the Son," says Athanasius, "to
have the things of the Father; and to be such that
the Father is seen in Him, and that through Him
all things were made, and that the salvation of all
comes to pass and consists in Him." Orat. ii. § 24.
"Men were made through the Word, when the Father
Himself willed." Orat. i. § 63. "Even if God compounded the world out of materials, . . . still allow the
Word to work those materials, say at the bidding and
in the service of God, προστατrόμενος καὶ ὑπουργῶν;
but if by His own Word He calls into existence things
which existed not, then the Word is not in the number
of things not existing," &c. Orat. ii. § 22. "With whom
did God speak," (saying *Let us make,* &c.) "so as even
to speak with a command," προστάττων? "He bids,
προστάττει, and says, *Let us make* men. . . . Who was
it but His Word?" c. Gent. § 46. "A Word then
must exist, to whom God gives command, ἐντέλλεται ὁ
θεός," de Decr. § 9.

¶ The language of Catholics and heretics is very much
the same on this point of the Son's ministration, with

this essential difference of sense, that Catholic writers
mean a ministration internal to the divine substance and
an instrument connatural with the Father, and Arius
meant an external and created medium of operation.
vid. arts. *The Divine Hand* and ὄργανον. Thus S. Clement
calls our Lord " the All-harmonious Instrument (ὄργανον)
of God." Protrept. p. 6. Eusebius, "an animated and
living instrument, (ὄργανον ἔμψυχον,) nay, rather divine
and . . . vivific of every substance and nature."
Demonstr. iv. 4. S. Basil, on the other hand, insists
that the Arians reduced our Lord to "an inanimate
instrument," ὄργανον ἄψυχον, though they called Him
ὑπουργὸν τελειότατον, most perfect minister or under-
worker." adv. Eunom. ii. 21. Elsewhere he says, " the
nature of a cause is one, and the nature of an instrument, ὄργανον, another; . . . foreign then in nature
is the Son from the Father, as an instrument is from
the artist who uses it." de Sp. S. n. 6 fin. vid. also
n. 4. fin. and n. 20. Afterwards he speaks of our
Lord as " not intrusted with the ministry of each work
by particular injunctions in detail, for this were ministration," λειτουργικὸν, but as being "full of the
Father's excellences," and " fulfilling not an instrumental, ὀργανικὴν, and servile ministration, but accom-
plishing the Father's will like a Maker, δημιουργικῶς."
ibid. n. 19. And so S. Gregory, "The Father signifies, the Word accomplishes, not servilely nor igno-
rantly, but with knowledge and sovereignty, and, to-
speak more suitably, in the Father's way, πατρικῶς."
Orat. 30. 11. And S. Cyril, " There is nothing abject
in the Son, as in a minister, ὑπουργῷ, as they say ; for

the God and Father enjoins not [ἐπιτάττει] on His
Word, 'Make man,' but as one with Him, by nature,
and inseparably existing in Him as a co-operator,"
&c., in Joann. p. 48. Explanations such as these
secure for the Catholic writers some freedom in their
modes of speaking; e.g. we have seen supr. that Athan.
seems to speak of the Son as being directed, and minis-
tering," προστατόμενος, καὶ ὑπουργῶν, Orat. ii. § 22.
Thus S. Irenæus speaks of the Father being well-pleased
and commanding, κελεύοντος, and the Son doing and
framing. Hær. iv. 38, 3. S. Basil too, in the same
treatise in which are some of the foregoing protests,
speaks of " the Lord ordering, [προστάσσοντα,] and the
Word framing." de Sp. S. n. 38. S. Cyril of Jerusalem, of " Him who bids, [εντέλλεται,] bidding to one
who is present with Him," Cat. xi. 16. vid. also
ὑπηρετῶν τῇ βουλῇ, Justin. Tryph. 126, and ὑπουργὸν,
Theoph. ad Autol. ii. 10 (Galland. t. 2, p. 95), ἐξυπη-
ρετῶν θελήματι, Clem. Strom. vii. p. 832.

¶ As to those words προστατόμενος καὶ ὑπουργῶν,
it is not quite clear that Athan. accepts them· in
his own person, as has been assumed supr. Vid.
de Decr. § 7, and Orat. ii. § 24 and 31, which, as
far as they go, are against such use. Also S. Basil
objects to ὑποῦργος, contr. Eunom. ii. 21, and S.
Cyril in Joan. p. 48, though S. Basil speaks of τὸν
προστάττοντα κύριον, as noticed above, and S. Cyril of
the Son's ὑποταγὴ, Thesaur. p. 255. Vid. " minister-
ing, ὑπηρετοῦντα, to the Father of all." Just. Tryph.
n. 60. " The Word become minister, ὑπηρέτης, of the
Creator," Origen in Joan. t. 2, p. 67, also Constit.

Ap. viii. 12, but Pseudo-Athan. objects to ὑπηρετῶν, de Comm. Essent. 30, and Athan. apparently, Orat. ii. § 28. Again, "Whom did He order, præcepit?" Iren. Hær. iii. 8, n. 3. "The Father bids [ἐντέλλεται] (allusion to Ps. 33, 9), the Word accomplishes . . . He who commands, κελεύων, is the Father, He who obeys, ὑπακούων, the Son . . . the Father willed, ἠθέλησεν, the Son did it." Hippol. c. Noet. 14, on which vid. Fabricius's note. S. Hilary speaks of the Son as "subditus per obedientiæ obsequelam," Syn. 51. Origen contr. Cels. ii. 9. Tertul. adv. Prax. 12, fin. Patres Antioch. ap. Routh t. 2, p. 468. Prosper in Psalm 148. Hilar. Trin. iv. 16. "That the Father speaks and the Son hears, or contrariwise, that the Son speaks and the Father hears, are expressions for the sameness of nature and the agreement of Father and Son." Didym. de Sp. S. 36. "The Father's· bidding is not other than His Word ; so that 'I have not spoken of Myself,' He perhaps meant to be equivalent to 'I was not born from Myself.' For if the Word of the Father speaks, He pronounces Himself, for He is the Father's Word," &c. August. de Trin. i. 26. On this mystery vid. Petav. Trin. vi. 4.

¶ Athan. says that it is contrary to all our notions of religion that Almighty God cannot create, enlighten, address, and unite Himself to His creatures immediately. This seems to be implied when it was said by the Arians that the Son was created for creation, illumination, &c.; whereas in the Catholic view the Son is simply that Divine Person, who in the economy of grace is Creator, Enlightener, &c. God is represented as All-perfect, but acting according to a certain divine order. Here the remark is in point about the right and wrong sense of the words "commanding," "obeying," &c.

Hence our Lord is the βούλησις and the βουλή, and ζῶσα βουλή, of the Father. Orat. iii. 63 fin. and so Cyril Thes. p. 54, who uses βουλή expressly, (as it is always used by implication,) in contrast to the κατὰ βούλησιν of the Arians, though Athan. uses κατὰ τὸ βούλημα, e.g. Orat. iii. 31. And so αὐτὸς τοῦ πατρὸς θέλημα, Nyss. contr. Eunom. xii. p. 345.

¶ The bearing of the above teaching of the early Fathers on the relation of the Second to the First Person in the Holy Trinity, is instructively brought out by Thomassinus in his work, de Incarnatione, from which I have made a long extract in one of my Theological Tracts:—part of it I will make use of here.

"It belongs to the Father to be without birth, but to the Son to be born. Now innascibility is a principle of concealment, but birth of exhibition. The former withdraws from sight, the latter comes forth into open day; the one retires into itself, lives to itself, and has no outward start; the other flows forth and extends itself and is diffused far and wide. It corresponds then to the idea of the Father, as being ingenerate, to be self-collected, remote, unapproachable, invisible, and in consequence to be utterly alien to an incarnation. But to the Son, considered as once for all born, and ever coming to the birth, and starting into view, it especially belongs to display Himself, to

be prodigal of Himself, to bestow Himself as an object
for sight and enjoyment, because in the fact of being
born He has burst forth into His corresponding act of
self-diffusion. . . .

"Equally . . . incomprehensible is in His nature the
Son as the Father. Accordingly we are here considering a personal property, not a natural. It is
especially congenial to the Divine Nature to be good,
beneficent, and indulgent; and for these qualities
there is no opening at all without a certain manifestation of their hiding-place, and outpouring of His
condescending Majesty. Wherefore, since the majesty
and goodness of God, in the very bosom of His
nature, look different ways, and by the one He retires into Himself, and by the other He pours Himself out, it is by the different properties of the Divine
Persons that this contrariety is solved," &c., &c. vid.
Thomassin. Incarn. ii. 1, p. 89, &c.

MELETIUS.

MELETIUS was Bishop of Lycopolis in the Thebais, in the first years of the fourth century. He was convicted of sacrificing to idols in the persecution, and deposed by a Council under Peter, Bishop of Alexandria and (subsequently) a martyr. Meletius separated from the communion of the Church and commenced a schism; at the time of the Nicene Council it included as many as twenty-eight or thirty Bishops; in the time of Theodoret, a century and a quarter later, it included a number of monks. Though not heterodox, they supported the Arians on their first appearance, in their contest with the Catholics. The Council of Nicæa, instead of deposing their Bishops, allowed them on their return a titular rank in their sees, but forbade them to exercise their functions.

¶ The Meletian schismatics of Egypt formed an alliance with the Arians from the first. Athan. imputes the alliance to ambition and avarice in the Meletians, and to zeal for their heresy in the Arians. Ep. Æg. 22, vid. also Hist. Arian. 78. In like manner after Sardica the Semi-Arians attempted a coalition with the Donatists of Africa. Aug. contr. Cresc. iii. 34 (n. 38).

¶ Epiphanius gives us another account of the circumstances under which Meletius's schism originated.

¶ There was another Meletius, Bishop of Antioch, in the latter part of the same century. He at one time belonged to the Semi-Arian party, but joined the orthodox, and was the first president of the second Ecumenical Council.

TWO NATURES OF EMMANUEL.

¶ "Two natures," says S. Leo, "met together in our Redeemer, and, while what belonged to each respectively remained, so great a unity was made of either substance, that from the time that the Word was made flesh in the Blessed Virgin's womb, we may neither think of Him as God without that which is man, nor as man without that which is God. Each nature certifies its own reality under distinct actions, but neither of them disjoins itself from connection with the other. Nothing is wanting from either towards other; there is entire littleness in majesty, entire majesty in littleness; unity does not introduce confusion, nor does what is special to each divide unity. There is what is passible, and what is inviolable, yet He, the Same, has the contumely whose is the glory. He is in infirmity who is in power; the Same is both the subject and the conqueror of death. God then did take on Him whole man, and so knit Himself into man and man into Himself in His mercy and in His power, that either nature was in other, and neither in the other lost its own attributes." Serm. 54, 1. "Suscepit nos in suam proprietatem illa natura, quæ nec nostris sua, nec suis nostra consumeret," &c. Serm. 72, p. 286. vid. also Ep. 165, 6. Serm. 30, 5. Cyril. Cat. iv. 9. Amphiloch. ap. Theod. Eran. i. p. 66, also pp. 60, 87, 88.

¶ "All this belongs to the Economy, not to the Godhead. On this account He says, 'Now is My soul

troubled,' . . . . so troubled as to seek for a release, if
escape were possible. . . . . As to hunger is no blame,
nor to sleep, so is it none to desire the present life.
Christ had a body pure from sins, but not exempt from
physical necessities, else it had not been a body."
Chrysost. in Joann. Hom. 67, 1 and 2. "He used His
own flesh as an instrument for the works of the flesh,
and for physical infirmities and for other infirmities
which are blameless," &c. Cyril. de Rect. Fid. p. 18.
"As a man' He doubts, as a man He is troubled; it is
not His power (virtus) that is troubled, not His
Godhead, but His soul," &c. Ambros. de Fid. ii. n.
56. Vid. a beautiful passage in S. Basil's Hom. iv. 5
(de Divers.), in which he insists on our Lord's having
wept to show us how to weep neither too much nor
too little.

"Being God, and existing as Word, while He remained what He was, He became flesh, and a child,
and a man, no change profaning the mystery. The
Same both works wonders, and suffers; by the
miracles signifying that He is what He was, and
by the sufferings giving proof that He had become what He had framed." Procl. ad Armen.
p. 615. "Without loss then in what belongs to
either nature and substance" (salvâ proprietate, and
so Tertullian, "Salva est utriusque proprietas substantiæ," &c., in Prax. 27), "yet with their union in one
Person, Majesty takes on it littleness, Power infirmity,
Eternity mortality, and, to pay the debt of our estate,
an inviolable Nature is made one with a nature that is
passible; that, as was befitting for our cure, One and

the Same Mediator between God and man, the man Jesus Christ, might both be capable of death from the one, and incapable from the other." Leo's Tome (Ep. 28, 3), also Hil. Trin. ix. 11 fin. "Vagit infans, sed in cælo est," &c., ibid. x. 54. Ambros. de Fid. ii. 77. "Erat vermis in cruce sed dimittebat peccata. Non habebat speciem, sed plenitudinem divinitatis," &c. Id. Epist. i. 46, n. 5. Theoph. Ep. Pasch. 6, ap. Conc. Ephes. p. 1404. Hard.

¶ Athanasius, Orat. iv. § 33, speaks of the Word as "putting on the first-fruits of our nature, and being blended (ἀνακραθείς) with it;" vid. note on Tertull. Oxf. Tr. vol. i. p. 48; and so ἡ καινὴ μίξις, θεὸς καὶ ἄνθρωπος, Greg. Naz. as quoted by Eulogius ap. Phot. Bibl. p. 857; "immixtus," Cassian. Incarn. i. 5; "commixtio," Vigil. contr. Eutych. i. 4, p. 494 (Bibl. Patr. 1624); "permixtus," August. Ep. 137, 11; "ut naturæ alteri altera misceretur," Leon. Serm. 23, 1 (vid. supr. p. 134). There is this strong passage in Naz. Ep. 101, p. 87 (ed. 1840), κιρναμένων ὥσπερ τῶν φύσιων, οὕτω δὴ καὶ τῶν κλήσεων, καὶ περιχωρουσῶν εἰς ἀλλήλας τῷ λόγῳ τῆς συμφυΐας; Bull says that in using περιχωρουσῶν Greg. Naz. and others "minùs propriè loqui." Defens. F. N. iv. 4, § 14. Petavius had allowed this, but proves the doctrine intended amply from the Fathers. De Incarn. iv. 14. Such oneness is not "confusion," for οὐ σύγχυσιν ἀπεργασάμενος, ἀλλὰ τὰ δύο κεράσας εἰς ἕν, says Epiph. Ancor. 81 fin. and so Eulog. ap. Phot. Bibl. p. 831 fin. οὐ τῆς κράσεως σύγχυσιν αὐτῷ δηλούσης. Vid. also on the word μίξις, &c. Zacagn. Monum. p. xxi.—xxvi. Thomassin. de Incarn. iii. 5, iv. 15.

THE NICENE TESTS OF ORTHODOXY.

WHAT were the cardinal additions, made at Nicæa, to the explicit faith of the Church, will be understood by comparing the Creed, as there recorded and sanctioned, with that of Eusebius, as they both are found (vol. i. supr. pp. 55—57) in his Letter to his people. His Creed is distinct and unexceptionable, as far as it goes; but it does not guard against the introduction of the Arian heresy into the Church, nor could it, as being a creed of the primitive age, and drawn up before the heresy. On the other hand, we see by the anathematisms appended to the Nicene Creed what it was that had to be excluded, and by the wording of the additions to the Creed, and by Eusebius's forced explanation of them, how they acted in effecting its exclusion. The following are the main additions in question:—

1. The Creed of Eusebius says of our Lord, ἐκ τοῦ πατρὸς γεγεννημένον; but the Nicene says, γεννηθέντα οὐ ποιηθέντα, because the Arians considered generation a kind of creation, as Athan. says, Orat. ii. § 20, "Ye say that an offspring is the same as a work, writing ' generated or made.' " And more distinctly, Arius in his Letter to Eusebius uses the words, πρὶν γεννηθῇ ἤτοι κτισθῇ ἢ ὁρισθῇ ἢ θεμελιωθῇ. Theodor. Hist. i. 4, p. 750. And to Alexander, ἀχρόνως γεννηθεὶς καὶ πρὸ αἰώνων κτισθεὶς καὶ θεμελιωθείς. De Syn. § 16.

And Eusebius to Paulinus, κτιστὸν καὶ θεμελιωτὸν καὶ γεννητόν. Theod. Hist. i. 5, p. 752. These different words profess to be scriptural, and to explain each other; "created" being in Prov. viii. 22; "made" in the speech of St. Peter, Acts ii. 22; "appointed" or "declared" in Rom. i. 4; and "founded" or "established" in Prov. viii. 23; vid. Orat. ii. § 72, &c., vid. also § 52.

2. We read in the Nicene Creed, "from the Father, *that is*, from the substance of the Father,' whereas in Eusebius's Letter it is only "God from God." According to the received doctrine of the Church, all rational beings, and in one sense all beings whatever, are "from God," over and above the fact of their creation, and in a certain sense sons of God, vid. supr. *Arian tenets, Adam,* and *Eusebius.* And of this undeniable truth the Arians availed themselves to explain away our Lord's proper Sonship and Divinity.

3. But the chief test at Nicæa was the word ὁμοούσιον, its special force being that it excludes the maintenance of *more than one* divine οὐσία or substance, which seems to be implied or might be insinuated even in Eusebius's creed; "We believe," he says, "each of these [Three] to be and to exist, the Father *truly* Father, the Son *truly* Son, the Holy Ghost *truly* Holy Ghost;" for if there be Three substances or *res* existing, either there are Three Gods or two of them are not God. The ἐξ οὐσίας, important and serviceable as it was, did not exclude the doctrine of a divine emanation, and was consistent with Semi-Arianism, and with belief in two or in three substances; vid. the art

ὁμοούσιον. "It is the precision of this phrase," says
Athan., "that detects their pretence, whenever they
use the phrase 'from God,' and that excludes all the
subtleties with which they seduce the simple. For,
whereas they contrive to put a sophistical construction
on all other words at their will, this phrase only, as
detecting their heresy, do they dread, which the Fathers
did set down as a bulwark against their impious
speculations one and all," de Syn. § 45. And Epiphanius calls it σύνδεσμος πίστεως, Ancor. 6. And again
he says, "Without the confession of the 'One in
substance' no heresy can be refuted; for as a serpent
hates the smell of bitumen, and the scent of sesame-
cake, and the burning of agate, and the smoke of
storax, so do Arius and Sabellius hate the notion of the
sincere profession of the 'One in substance.'" And
Ambrose, "That term did the Fathers set down in their
formula of faith, which they perceived to be a source
of dread to their adversaries; that they themselves
might unsheathe the sword which cut off the head of
their own monstrous heresy." de Fid. iii. 15.

This is very true, but a question arises whether another
and a better test than the *homoüsion* might not have
been chosen, one eliciting less opposition, one giving
opportunities to fewer subtleties; and on this point a
few words shall be said here.

Two ways, then, lay before the Fathers at Nicæa of
condemning and eliminating the heresy of Arius, who
denied the proper divinity of the Son of God. By
means of either of the two a test would be secured for
guarding the sacred truth from those evasive profes-

sions and pretences of orthodoxy, which Arius himself,
to do him justice, did not ordinarily care to adopt.
Our Lord's divinity might be adequately defined either
(1) by declaring Him to be in and of the essence of
the Father, or (2) to be with the Father from everlasting, that is, by defining Him to be either consubstantial or co-eternal with God. Arius had denied
both doctrines; "He is not eternal," he says, "or
co-eternal, or co-ingenerate with the Father, nor has
He His being together with Him." And "The Son
of God is not consubstantial with God." Syn. § 15,
16 (vid. also Epiph. Hær. 69, 7). Either course then
would have answered the purpose required: but the
Council chose that which at first sight seems the less
advisable, the more debatable of the two; it chose
the "Homoüsion" or "Consubstantial," not the
Co-eternal.

Here it is scarcely necessary to dwell on a statement of Gibbon, which is strange for so acute and
careful a writer. He speaks as if the enemies of Arius
at Nicæa were at first in a difficulty how to find a test
to set before the Council which might exclude him
from the Church, and then accidentally became aware
that the *Homoüsion* was such an available term. He
says that in the Council a letter was publicly read
and ignominiously torn, in which the Arian leader,
Eusebius of Nicomedia, "*ingenuously* confessed that
the admission of the Homoüsion, a word already
familiar to the Platonists, was incompatible with the
principles of his theological system. The *fortunate
opportunity* was eagerly embraced by the bishops who

governed the resolutions of the Synod," &c., ch. **xxi.**
He adds in a note, " We are indebted to Ambrose (vid.
de Fid. iii. 15,) for the knowledge of this *curious*
anecdote." This comes of handling theological subjects with but a superficial knowledge of them; it is
the way in which foreigners judge of a country which
they enter for the first time. Who told Gibbon that
Arius's enemies and the governing bishops did not
know from the first of the Arian rejection of this word
" consubstantial "? who told him that there were not
other formulæ which Arius rejected quite as strongly
as it, and which would have served as a test quite as
well ? As I have quoted above, he had publicly said,
" The Son is not equal, no, nor consubstantial with
God," and " Foreign to the Son in substance is the
Father;" and, as to matter already provided by him
for other tests, he says in that same Thalia, " When
the Son was not yet, the Father was already God;"
" Equal, or like Himself, He [the Father] has
none " (vid. Syn. § 15), &c., &c. S. Ambrose too was
not baptised till A.D. 374, a generation after the
Nicene Council, and his report cannot weigh against
contemporary documents; nor can his words at that
later date receive Gibbon's interpretation. It was not
from any dearth of tests that the Fathers chose the
Homoüsion; and the question is, why did they prefer
it to συναΐδιον, ἄναρχον, ἀγένητον, &c., &c.?

The first difficulty attached to " consubstantial"
was that it was not in Scripture, which would have been
avoided had the test chosen been " from everlasting,"
" without beginning," &c.; a complaint, however, which

came with a bad grace from the Arians, who had begun the controversy with phrases of their own devising, and not in Scripture. But, if the word was not Scriptural, it had the sanction of various Fathers in the foregoing centuries, and was derived from a root, ὁ ὤν, which was in Scripture. Nor could novelty be objected to the word. Athanasius, ad Afros 6, speaks of the use of the word ὁμοούσιον "by ancient Bishops, about 130 years since;" and Eusebius, supr. Decr. App. § 7, confirms him as to its ancient use in the Church: and, though it was expedient to use the words of Scripture in enunciations of revealed teaching, it would be a superstition in the Council to confine itself to them, as if the letter could be allowed to supersede the sense.

A more important difficulty lay in the fact that some fifty or sixty years before, in the Councils occasioned by the heretical doctrine of Paulus, Bishop of Antioch, the word had actually been proposed in some quarter as a *tessera* against his heresy, and then withdrawn by the Fathers as if capable of an objectionable sense. Paulus, who was a sharp disputant, seems to have contended that the term either gave a material character to the Divine nature, or else, as he wished himself to hold, that it implied that there was no real distinction of Persons between Father and Son. Anyhow, the term was under this disadvantage, that in some sense it had been disowned in the greatest Council which up to the Nicene the Church had seen. But its inexpedience at one time and for one purpose was no reason why it should not be expedient at another time and for another purpose, and its imposition at

Nicæa showed by the event that it was the fitting word, and justified those who selected it. But true as this is, still the question recurs why it was that the Nicene Fathers selected a term which was not in Scripture, and had on a former occasion been considered open to objection, while against " co-eternal " or " from everlasting " no opposition could have been raised short of the heretical denial of its truth; and further, whether it was not rather a test against Tritheism, of which Arius was not suspected. " Consubstantial " was a word needing a definition ; " co-eternal " spoke for itself.

Arius, it is true, had boldly denied the " consubstantial," but he had still more often and more pointedly denied the " co-eternal." The definition of the Son's eternity *a parte ante* would have been the destruction of the heresy. Arius had said on starting, according to Alexander, that " God was not always a Father ; " " the Word was not always." " He said," says Socrates, " if the Father begot the Son, he that was begotten had a beginning of existence." Arius himself says to his friend Eusebius, " Alexander has driven us out of our city for dissenting from his public declaration, ' As God is eternal, so is His Son.' " Again, to Alexander himself, as quoted supr., " The Son is not eternal, or co-eternal, or co-ingenerate with the Father." Vid. also Decr. § 6. Would it not, then, have avoided all the troubles which, for a long fifty or sixty years, followed upon the reception of the Homoüsion by the Nicene Council, would it not have been a far more prudent handling of the Creed of the Church, to have said " begotten *from everlasting,* not made," instead of introducing into it a word of doubtful meaning, already discredited, and at best unfamiliar to Catholics? This is what may be asked, and, with a deep feeling of our defective knowledge of the ecclesiastical history of the times, I answer, under correction, as follows:—

There are passages, then, in the writers of the Ante-Nicene times which suggest to us that the leading bishops in the Council were not free to act as they might wish, or as they might think best, and that the only way to avoid dangerous disputes in an assemblage of men good and orthodox, but jealous in behalf of their own local modes of thought and expression and traditional beliefs, was to meet with the utmost caution a heresy which all agreed to condemn, which all aimed at destroying. So it was, that various writers, some of them men of authority and influence, and at least witnesses to the sentiments of their day, had, in the course of the three centuries past, held the doctrine of the temporal *gennesis*, a doctrine which afterwards gave an excuse and a sort of shelter to the Arian misbelief. (Vid. supr. art. *Arians*, 3.) I am not denying that these men held with the whole Catholic Church that our Lord was in personal existence from eternity as the Word, connatural with the Father, and in His bosom; but they also held, with more or less distinctness, that He was not fully a Son from eternity, but that when, according to the Divine counsels, the creation was in immediate prospect, and with reference to it, the Word was born into Sonship, and became the Creator, the Pattern, and the Conservative Power of all

that was created.   These writers were such as Tatian,
Theophilus, Tertullian, and Hippolytus; and if the
Fathers of the Nicene Council had defined uncon-
ditionally and abruptly the Son's eternity, they would
have given an opening to the Arians, who disbelieved
in the eternity of the Personal Word, to gain over to
their side, and to place in opposition to the Alexandrians,
many who substantially were orthodox in their belief.
They did not venture then, as it would seem, to pronounce categorically that the *gennesis* was from everlasting, lest they should raise unnecessary questions :—
at the same time, by making the " consubstantial " the
test of orthodoxy, they provided for the logical and
eventual acceptance of the Son's *à parte ante* eternity,
on the principle, (which Athan. is continually insisting
on,) " What God is, that He ever was ; " and, by including among the parties anathematised at the end of
the Creed " those who said that our Lord ' was not in
being before He was born,'" they both inflicted an
additional blow upon the Arians, and indirectly
recognised the orthodoxy, and gained the adhesion, of
those who, by speaking of the temporal *gennesis*,
seemed at first sight to ascribe to our Lord a beginning
of being.

OMNIPRESENCE OF GOD.

¶ ATHAN. says, Decr. § 11, "Men being incapable of self-existence, are inclosed in place, and consist in the Word of God; but God is self-existent, inclosing all things, and inclosed by none,—within all according to His own goodness and power, yet outside all in His own nature." Vid. also Incarn. § 17. This contrast is not commonly found in ecclesiastical writers, who are used to say that God is present everywhere, in substance as well as by energy or power. Clement, however, expresses himself still more strongly in the same way: "In substance far off (for how can the generate come close to the Ingenerate?), but most close in power, in which the universe is embosomed." Strom. ii. 2, but the parenthesis explains his meaning. Vid. Cyril. Thesaur. 6, p. 44. The common doctrine of the Fathers is, that God is present everywhere in *substance*. Vid. Petav. de Deo, iii. 8 and 9. It may be remarked that S. Clement continues, "*neither inclosing* nor inclosed."

¶ Athan., however, explains himself in Orat. iii. 22, saying that when our Lord, in comparing the Son and creatures, "uses the word 'as,' He signifies those who become from afar *as* He is *in* the Father; . . for in place nothing is far from God, but only in nature all things are far from Him." When, then, he says "outside all in His nature," he must mean as here "far from all things considered in His nature." He says here distinctly, "in place nothing is far from God." S. Clement, loc. cit., gives the same explanation, as above noticed. It is observable that the Tract Sab. Greg. (which the Benedictines consider not Athan.'s) speaks as Athan. does supr., "not by being co-extensive with all things, does God fill all; for this belongs to bodies, as air; but He comprehends all as a power, for He is an incorporeal, invisible power, not encircling, not encircled." 10. Eusebius says the same thing, "Deum circumdat nihil, circumdat Deus omnia non corporaliter; virtute enim incorporali adest omnibus," &c. De Incorpor. i. init. ap. Sirm. Op. t. i. p. 68. Vid. S. Ambros. "Quomodo creatura in Deo esse potest," &c. de Fid. i. 16.

PAUL OF SAMOSATA.

MENTION of this Paul and of his sect is frequently made by Athan. There is some difficulty in determining what his opinions were. As far as the fragments of the Antiochene Acts state or imply, he taught, more or less, as follows:—that the Son's pre-existence was only in the divine foreknowledge, Routh. Rell. t. 2, p. 466; that to hold His substantial pre-existence was to hold two Gods, ibid. p. 467; that He was, if not an instrument, an impersonal attribute, p. 469; that His manhood was not "unalterably made one with the Godhead," p. 473; "that the Word and Christ were not one and the same," p. 474; that Wisdom was in Christ as in the prophets, only more abundantly, as in a temple; that He who appeared was not Wisdom, p. 475; in a word, as it is summed up, p. 484, that "Wisdom was born with the manhood, not substantially, but according to quality." vid. also p. 476, 485. All this plainly shows that he held that our Lord's personality was in His Manhood, but does not show that he held a second personality as being in His Godhead; rather he considered the Word impersonal, though the Fathers in Council urge upon him that he ought with his views to hold two Sons, one from eternity, and one in time, p. 485.

Accordingly the Synodal Letter after his deposition

speaks of him as holding that Christ came not from heaven, but from beneath. Euseb. Hist. vii. 30. S. Athanasius's account of his doctrine is altogether in accordance, (vid. vol. i. supr. p. 25, note 1,) viz., that Paul taught that our Lord was a mere man, and that He was advanced to His Divine power, ἐκ προκοπῆς.

However, since there was much correspondence between Paul and Nestorius, (except in the doctrine of the personality and eternity of the Word, which the Arian controversy determined and the latter held,) it was not unnatural that reference should be made to the previous heresy of Paul and its condemnation when that of Nestorius was on trial. Yet the Contestatio against Nestorius which commences the Acts of the Council of Ephesus, Harduin. Conc. t. i. p. 1272, and which draws out distinctly the parallel between them, says nothing to show that Paul held a double personality. And though Anastasius tells us, Hodeg. c. 7, p. 108, that the "holy Ephesian Council showed that the tenets of Nestorius agreed with the doctrine of Paul of Samosata," yet in c. 20, p. 323, 4, he shows us what he means, by saying that Artemon also before Paul "divided Christ in two." Ephrem of Antioch too says that Paul held that "the Son before ages was one, and the Son in the last time another," ap. Phot. p. 814; but he seems only referring to the words of the Antiochene Acts, quoted above. Again, it is plain from what Vigilius says in Eutych. t. v. p. 731, Ed. Col. 1618, (the passage is omitted in Ed. Par. 1624,) that the Eutychians considered that Paul and Nestorius differed; the former holding that our Lord was a mere man, the latter a mere man only till He was united to the Word. And Marius Mercator says, "Nestorius circa Verbum Dei, *non* ut Paulus sentit, qui non substantivum, sed prolatitium potentiæ Dei efficax Verbum esse definit." Part 2, p. 17. Ibas, and Theodore of Mopsuestia, though more suspicious witnesses, say the same. Vid. Facund. vi. 3, iii. 2, and Leontius de Sectis, iii. p. 504. To these authorities may be added Nestorius's express words, Serm. 12, ap. Mar. Merc. t. 2, p. 87, and Assemani takes the same view, Bibl. Orient. t. 4, p. 68, 9.

The principal evidence in favour of Paul's Nestorianism consists in the Letter of Dionysius to Paul and his answer to Paul's Ten Questions, which are certainly spurious, as on other grounds, so on some of those urged against the professed Creed of Antioch, (in my "Theol. Tracts,") but which Dr. Burton in his excellent remarks on Paul's opinions, Bampton Lectures, Note 102, admits as genuine. And so does the accurate and cautious Tillemont, who in consequence is obliged to believe that Paul held Nestorian doctrines; also Bull, Fabricius, Natalis Alexander, &c. In holding these compositions to be certainly spurious, I am following Valesius, Harduin, Montfaucon, Pagi, Mosheim, Cave, Routh, and others.

PERSONAL ACTS AND OFFICES OF OUR LORD.

THERE are various (and those not the least prominent and important) acts and offices of our Lord, which, as involving the necessity of both His natures in concurrence and belonging to His Person, may be said to be either θεανδρικὰ (vid. art. under that heading), or instances of ἀντίδοσις ἰδιωμάτων (vid. also art. on it). Such are His office and His acts as Priest, as Judge, &c., in which He can be viewed neither as simply God, nor as simply man, but in a third aspect, as Mediator, the two natures indeed being altogether distinct, but the character, in which He presents Himself to us by the union of these natures, belonging rather to His Person, which is composite.

¶ Athanasius says, Orat. ii. § 16, "Since we men would not acknowledge God through His Word, nor serve the Word of God our natural Master, it pleased God to show in man His own Lordship, and so to draw all men to Himself. But to do this by a mere man beseemed not; lest, having man for our Lord, we should become worshippers of man. Therefore the Word Himself became flesh, and the Father called His Name Jesus, and so 'made' Him Lord and Christ, as much as to say, 'He made Him to rule and to reign,' that while in the name of Jesus, whom ye

crucified, every knee bows, we may acknowledge as
Lord and King both the Son and through Him the
Father." Here the renewal of mankind is made to
be the act, primarily indeed of the Word, our natural
Master, but not from Him, as such, simply, but as
given to Him to carry out by the Father, when He
became incarnate, by virtue of His *Persona composita.*

¶ He says again that, though none could be "a
beginning" of creation, who was a creature, yet still
that such a title belongs not to His essence. It is the
name of an *office* which the Eternal Word alone can
fill. His Divine Sonship is both superior and necessary to that office of a " Beginning." Hence it is
both true (as he says) that "if the Word is a creature,
He is not a beginning; " and yet that that " beginning" is "in the number of the creatures." Though
He becomes the "beginning," He is not "a beginning
as to His *substance;* " vid. Orat. ii. § 60, where he says,
"He who is *before all,* cannot be a *beginning of all,*
but is other than all." He is the beginning in the
sense of *Archetype.*

¶ And so again of His Priesthood (vid. art. upon it),
the Catholic doctrine is that He is Priest, neither as
God nor as man simply, but as being the Divine Word
in and according to His manhood.

¶ Again S. Augustine says of judgment: "He
judges by His divine power, not by His human, and
yet man himself will judge, as ' the Lord of Glory' was
crucified." And just before, "He who believes in Me,
believes not in that which he sees, lest our hope
should be in a creature, but in Him who has taken

on Him the creature, in which He might appear to human eyes." Trin. i. 27, 28.

¶ And so again none but the Eternal Son could be πρωτότοκος, yet He is so called only when sent, first as Creator, and then as Incarnate. Orat. ii. § 64.

¶ The phrase λόγος, ᾗ λόγος ἐστί, is frequent in Athan., as denoting the distinction between the Word's original nature and His offices. vid. Orat. i. § 43, 44, 47, 48. ii. § 8, 74. iii. § 38, 39, 41, 44, 52. iv. § 23.

PHILOSOPHY.

ATHAN. says, speaking of ἀγέννητον, "I am *told* the word has different senses." Decr. § 28.

And so de Syn. § 46, "we have on *careful inquiry* ascertained," &c. Again, "I have acquainted myself on their account [the Arians'] with the meaning of ἀγένητον." Orat. i. § 30. This is remarkable, for Athan. was a man of liberal education. In the same way S. Basil, whose cultivation of mind none can doubt, speaks slightingly of his own philosophical knowledge. He writes of his "neglecting his own weakness, and being utterly unexercised in such disquisitions;" contr. Eunom. init. And so in de Sp. S. n. 5, he says, that "they who have given time" to vain philosophy, "divide causes into principal, co-operative," &c. Elsewhere he speaks of having "expended much time on vanity, and wasted nearly all his youth in the vain labour of pursuing the studies of that wisdom which God has made foolishness." Ep. 223, 2. In truth Christianity has a philosophy of its own. Thus at the commencement of his Viæ Dux, Anastasius says, "It is a first point to be understood that the tradition of the Catholic Church does not proceed upon, or follow, the philosophical definitions in all respects of the Greeks, and especially as regards the mystery of Christ and the doctrine of the Trinity, but a certain rule of its own, evangelical and apostolical;" p. 20. In like manner, Damascene, speaking of the Jacobite use of φύσις and ὑπόστασις, says, "Who of holy men ever thus spoke? unless ye introduce to us your St. Aristotle as a thirteenth Apostle, and prefer the idolater to the divinely inspired." contr. Jacob. .0, p. 399; and so again Leontius, speaking of Philoponus, who from the Monophysite confusion of nature and hypostasis was led into Tritheism. "He thus argued, taking his start from Aristotelic principles; for Aristotle says that there are of individuals particular substances as well as one common." de Sect. v. fin.

¶ "What our Fathers have delivered," says Athan., "this is truly doctrine; and this is truly the token of doctors, to confess the same thing with each other, and to vary neither from themselves nor from their fathers; whereas they who have not this character, are not to be called true doctors but evil. Thus the Greeks, as not witnessing to the same doctrines, but quarrelling one with another, have no truth of teaching; but the holy and veritable heralds of the truth agree together, not differ. For though they lived in different times, yet they one and all tend the same way, being prophets of the one God, and preaching the same Word harmoniously." Decr. § 4.

S. Basil says the same of the Grecian Sects: "We have not the task of refuting their tenets, for they suffice for the overthrow of each other." Hexaem. i. 2. vid. also Theod. Græc. Affect. i. p. 707, &c. August. Civ. Dei. xviii. 41, and Vincentius's celebrated Commonitorium *passim*.

PRIESTHOOD OF CHRIST.

"THE expressions *He became* and *He was made*," says Athanasius, on Hebr. iii. 2, (vid. Orat. ii. § 8,) "must not be understood as if the Word, considered as the Word, were *made*, (vid. art. *Personal Acts*, &c.,) but because the Word, being Framer of all, afterwards was made High Priest, by putting on a body which was made."

¶ In a certain true sense our Lord may be called a Mediator before He became incarnate, but the Arians, even Eusebius, seem to have made His mediatorship consist essentially in His divine nature, instead of holding that it was His office, and that He was made Mediator when He came in the flesh. Eusebius, like Philo and the Platonists, considers Him as made in the beginning the "Eternal Priest of the Father." Demonst. v. 3. de Laud. C. p. 503 fin. "an intermediate divine power," p. 525, "mediating and joining generated substance to the Ingenerate," p. 528.

¶ The Arians considered that our Lord's Priesthood preceded His Incarnation, and belonged to His Divine Nature, and was in consequence the token of an inferior divinity. The notice of it therefore in Heb. iii. 1, 2, did but confirm them in their interpretation of the words *made*, &c. For the Arians, vid. Epiph. Hær. 69, 37. Eusebius too had distinctly declared, "Qui

videbatur, erat agnus Dei; qui occultabatur sacerdos
Dei." advers. Sabell. i. p. 2, b. vid. also Demonst. i. 10,
p. 38, iv. 16, p. 193, v. 3, p. 223, vid. contr. Marc.
pp. 8 and 9, 66, 74, 95.   Even S. Cyril of Jerusalem
makes a similar admission, Catech. x. 14.   Nay, S.
Ambrose calls the Word, "plenum justitiæ sacerdota-
lis," de fug. Sæc. 3, 14.   S. Clement Alex. before them
speaks once or twice of the λόγος ἀρχιερεὺς, e.g.
Strom. ii. 9 fin. and Philo still earlier uses similar language, de Profug. p. 466 (whom S. Ambrose follows),
de Somniis, p. 597. vid. Thomassin. de Incarn. x. 9.
Nestorius on the other hand maintained that the Man
Christ Jesus was the Priest; Cyril adv. Nest. p. 64.
And Augustine and Fulgentius may be taken to countenance him, de Consens. Evang. i. 6, and ad Thrasim.
iii. 30.   The Catholic doctrine is, that the Divine
Word is Priest *in* and *according to* His manhood. vid.
the parallel use of πρωτότοκος infr. art. in voc.   "As He
is called Prophet and even Apostle for His humanity,"
says S. Cyril Alex., "so also Priest."   Glaph. ii. p. 58.
And so Epiph. loc. cit.   Thomassin. loc. cit. makes a
distinction between a divine Priesthood or Mediatorship, such as the Word may be said to sustain between
the Father and all creatures, and an earthly and sacri-
ficial for the sake of sinners.   vid. also Huet. Origenian.
ii. 3, § 4, 5.

PRIVATE JUDGMENT ON SCRIPTURE.

(Vid. art. *Rule of Faith.*)

THE two phrases by which Athan. denotes private
judgment on religious matters, and his estimate of it,
are τὰ ἴδια and ἃ ἤθελον, e.g.

¶ "Laying down their private (τὴν ἰδίαν) impiety
as some sort of rule (ὡς κανόνα τινὰ, i.e. as a Rule of
Faith), they wrest all the divine oracles into accordance with it." Orat. i. § 52. And so ἰδίων κακονοιῶν,
Orat. ii. § 18. ταῖς ἰδίαις μυθοπλαστίαις. Orat. iii.
§ 10, and, "they make the language of Scripture their
pretence; but, instead of the true sense, sowing upon
it (Matt. xiii. 25, vid. art. ἐπίσπειρας) the private (τὸν
ἴδιον) poison of their heresy." Orat. i. § 53. And so,
κατὰ τὸν ἴδιον νοῦν. Orat. i. § 37. τῆν ἰδίαν ἀσέβειαν.
iii. § 55. And, "He who speaketh of his own, ἐκ τῶν
ἰδίων, speaketh a lie." contr. Apoll. i. fin.

¶ And so other writers: "They used to call the
Church a virgin," says Hegesippus, "for it was not
yet defiled by profane doctrines . . . the Simonists,
Dositheans, &c. . . . each privately (ἰδίως) and separately has brought in a private opinion." ap. Euseb.
Hist. iv. 22. Ruffinus says of S. Basil and S.
Gregory, "Putting aside all Greek literature, they
are said to have passed thirteen years together
in studying the Scriptures alone, and followed out

their *sense*, not *from their private opinion*, but by the writings and authority of the Fathers," &c. Hist. ii. 9. Sophronius at Seleucia cried out, "If to ,publish day after day our own private (ἰδίαν) will, be a profession of faith, accuracy of truth will fail us." Socr. ii. 40.

"We must not make an appeal to the Scriptures, nor take up a position for the fight, in which victory cannot be, or is doubtful, or next to doubtful. For though this conflict of Scripture with Scripture did not end in a drawn battle, yet the true order of the subject required that that should be laid down first, which now becomes but a point of debate, viz. *who* have a claim to the faith itself, *whose* are the Scriptures." Tertull. de Præscr. 19. "Seeing the Canon of Scripture is perfect, &c., why need we join unto it the authority of the Church's understanding and interpretation? because the Scripture being of itself so deep and profound, all men do not understand it in one and the same sense, but *so many men, so many opinions* almost may be gathered out of it; for Novatian expounds it one way, Photinus another, Sabellius," &c., Vincent. Comm. 2. Hippolytus has a passage very much to the same purpose, contr. Noet. 9 fin.

As to the phrase ὡς οὗτοι θέλουσι, vid. λέγοντες μὴ οὕτως . . ὡς ἡ ἐκκλησία κηρύσσει, ἀλλ' ὡς αὐτοὶ θέλουσι. Orat. iii. § 10, words which follow ἰδίαις μυθοπλαστίαις, quoted just above. Vid. also iii. § 8 and 17. This is a common phrase with Athan. ὡς ἐθέλησεν, ἅπερ ἐθέλησαν, ὅταν θέλωσι, οὓς ἐθέλησαν, &c., &c., the proceedings of the heretics being self-willed from first to

last. Vid. Sent. Dion. 4 and 16. Mort. Ar. fin. Apoll.
ii. 5 init. in contrast with the εὐαγγελικὸς ὅρος. Also
Decr. § 3. Syn. § 13. Ep. Æg. § 5, 19, 22. Apol.
Arian. § 2, 14, 35, 36, 73, 74, 77. Apol. Const. § 1.
de Fug. § 2, 3, 7. Hist. Arian. § 2, 7, 47, 52, 54, 59,
60.

In like manner ἃ βούλονται, &c. Ep. Enc. 7. Ap.
Arian. § 82, 83. Ep. Æg. § 6. Apol. Const. § 32.
de Fug. § 1. Hist. Ar. 15, 18.

THE RULE OF FAITH.

THE recognition of this rule is the basis of St. Athanasius's method of arguing against Arianism. Vid. art. *Private Judgment*. It is not his aim ordinarily to *prove* doctrine by Scripture, nor does he appeal to the private judgment of the individual Christian in order to determine what Scripture means; but he assumes that there is a tradition, substantive, independent, and authoritative, such as to supply for us the true sense of Scripture in doctrinal matters—a tradition carried on from generation to generation by the practice of catechising, and by the other ministrations of Holy Church. He does not care to contend that no other meaning of certain passages of Scripture besides this traditional Catholic sense is possible or is plausible, whether true or not, but simply that any sense inconsistent with the Catholic is untrue, untrue because the traditional sense is apostolic and decisive. What he was instructed in at school and in church, the voice of the Christian people, the analogy of faith, the ecclesiastical φρόνημα, the writings of saints; these are enough for him. He is in no sense an inquirer, nor a mere disputant; he has received, and he transmits. Such is his position, though the expressions and turn of sentences which indicate it are so delicate and indirect, and so scattered about his pages, that it is difficult to collect them and to analyse what they imply. Perhaps the most obvious proof that what I have stated is substantially true, is that on any other supposition he seems to argue illogically. Thus he says: " The Arians, looking at what is human in the Saviour, have judged Him to be a creature. . . . But let them learn, however tardily, that *the Word became flesh;* " and then he goes on to show that he does not rely simply on the inherent, unequivocal force of St. John's words, satisfactory as that is, for he adds, " Let us, as possessing τὸν σκόπον τῆς πίστεως, acknowledge that this is the right (ὀρθὴν, orthodox) understanding of what they understand wrongly." Orat. iii. § 35.

Again : " What they now allege from the Gospels they explain in an unsound sense, as we may easily see *if we will but avail ourselves* of τὸν σκόπον τῆς καθ᾽ ἡμᾶς πίστεως, and using this ὥσπερ κανόνι, apply ourselves, as the Apostle says, to the reading of inspired Scripture." Orat. iii. 28.

And again : " Since they pervert divine Scripture in accordance with their own private (ἴδιον) opinion, we must *so far* (τοσοῦτον) answer them as (ὅσον) to justify its word, and to show that its sense is orthodox, ὀρθήν." Orat. i. 37.

For other instances, vid. art. ὀρθός; also vid. supr. vol. i. pp. 36, 237 note, 392, fin. 409; also Serap. iv. § 15, Gent. § 6, 7, and 33.

¶ In Orat. ii. § 5, after showing that "made " is used in Scripture for " begotten," in other instances besides that of our Lord, he says, " Nature and truth

draw the meaning to themselves" of the sacred text—
that is, while the style of Scripture *justifies* us in thus
interpreting the word " made," doctrinal truth *obliges*
us to do so. He considers the Regula Fidei the
principle of interpretation, and accordingly he goes on
at once to apply it.

¶ It is his way to start with some general exposition
of the Catholic doctrine which the Arian sense of the
text in dispute opposes, and thus to create a *præju-
dicium* or proof against the latter; vid. Orat. i. 10, 38,
40 init. 53, ii. § 12 init. 32—34, 35, 44 init., which
refers to the whole discussion, (18—43,) 73, 77, iii. 18
init. 36 init. 42, 51 init. &c. On the other hand
he makes the ecclesiastical sense the rule of interpretation, τούτῳ (τῷ σκοπῷ, the general drift of Scripture
doctrine) ὥσπερ κανόνι χρησάμενοι, as quoted just
above. This illustrates what he means when he says
that certain texts have a " good," " pious," " orthodox " sense, i.e. they can be interpreted (in spite, if
so be, of appearances) in harmony with the Regula
Fidei.

¶ It is with a reference to this great principle that he
begins and ends his series of Scripture passages, which
he defends from the misinterpretation of the Arians.
When he begins, he refers to the necessity of interpreting them according to that sense which is not the
result of private judgment, but is orthodox. " This,"
he says, " I conceive is the meaning of this passage,
and that a meaning *especially ecclesiastical*." Orat. i.
§ 44. And he ends with : " Had they dwelt on these
thoughts, and recognised the ecclesiastical scope as an

anchor for the faith, they would not of the faith have made shipwreck." Orat. iii. § 58.

¶ It is hardly a paradox to say that in patristical works of controversy the conclusion in a certain sense proves the premisses. As then he here speaks of the ecclesiastical scope "as an anchor for the faith;" so when the discussion of texts began, Orat. i. § 37, he introduces it as already quoted by saying, "Since they allege the divine oracles and force on them a misinterpretation *according to their private sense*, it becomes necessary to meet them *so far* as to do justice to these passages, and to show that they bear an orthodox sense, and that our opponents are in error." Again, Orat. iii. 7, he says, "What is the *difficulty*, that one *must need* take such a view of such passages?" He speaks of the σκόπος as a κανὼν or rule of interpretation, supr. iii. § 28. vid. also § 29 init. 35 Serap. ii. 7. Hence too he speaks of the "ecclesiastical sense," e.g. Orat. i. 44, Serap. iv. 15, and of the φρόνημα, Orat. ii. 31 init. Decr. 17 fin. In ii. § 32, 3, he makes the general or Church view of Scripture supersede inquiry into the force of particular illustrations.

SABELLIUS.

EUSEBIUS, Eccles. Theol. i. 20, p. 91, as well as the Macrostich Confession, supr. vol. i. p. 106, says that Sabellius held the Patripassian doctrine. Epiph. however, Hær. p. 398, denies it, and imputes the doctrine to Noetus. Whatever Sabellius taught, it should be noticed, that, in the reason which the Arian Macrostich alleges against his doctrine, it is almost implied that the divine nature of the Son suffered on the Cross. The Arians would naturally fall into this notion directly they gave up their belief in our Lord's absolute divinity. It would as naturally follow to hold that our Lord had no human soul, but that His pre-existent nature stood in the place of it:—also that His Priesthood was not dependent on His Incarnation.

¶ It is difficult to decide what Sabellius's doctrine really was; nor is this wonderful, considering the perplexity and vacillation which is the ordinary consequence of abandoning Catholic truth. Also we must distinguish between him and his disciples. He is considered by Eusebius, Eccl. Theol. i. p. 91, Patripassian, i.e. as holding that the Father was the Son; also by Athan. Orat. iii. 36 init. de Sent. Dion. 5 and 9. By the Eusebians of the Macrostich Creed ap. Athan. de Syn. 26 vol. i. supr. By Basil. Ep. 210, 5. By Ruffin. in

Symb. 5. By Augustine de Hær. 41. By Theodor. Hær. ii. 9. And apparently by Origen. ad Tit. t. 4, p. 695. And by Cyprian. Ep. 73. On the other hand, Epiphanius seems to deny it, ap. August. l. c. and Alexander, by comparing Sabellianism to the emanation doctrine of Valentinus, ap. Theod. Hist. i. 3, p. 743.

¶ Sabellians, as Arians, denied that the Word was a substance, and as the Samosatenes, who, according to Epiphanius, considered our Lord the internal, ἐνδιάθετος, Word and Thought, Hær. 65.

All Sabellians, except Patripassians, mainly differed from Arians only at this point, viz. *when* it was that our Lord came into being. Both parties considered Him a creature, and the true Word and Wisdom but attributes or energies of the Almighty. This Lucifer well observes to Constantius, with the substitution of Paulus and Photinus for Sabellius, "Quid interesse arbitraris inter te et Paulum Samosatenum, vel eum tum ejus discipulum tuum conscotinum, nisi quia tu 'ante omnia' dicas, ille vero 'post omnia'"? p. 203, 4. A subordinate difference was that the Samosatenes, Photinians, &c., considered our Lord to be really gifted with the true Word, whereas Arians did scarcely more than admit Him to be formed after its pattern.

The Sabellians agreed with the Arians, as far as words went, in considering the Logos as a creative attribute, vid. Sent D. 25. Ep. Ægypt. 14 fin. Epiph. Hær. 72, p. 835; but such of them as held that the Logos actually took flesh, escaped the mystery of God subsisting in Two Persons, only by

falling into the heterodox notion that His nature was
compounded of substance and attribute or quality,
σύνθετον τὸν θέον ἐκ ποιότητος καὶ οὐσίας. They virtually denied, with many Trinitarians outside the
Church in this day, that the Son and again the Spirit
is ὅλος θεός; but, if Each is not ὅλος θεὸς, God is
σύνθετος.

SANCTIFICATION.

ATHANASIUS insists earnestly on the merciful dispensation of God, who has not barely given us through Christ justification, but has made our sanctification to be included in the gift, and santification through the personal presence in us of the Son. After saying, Incarn. § 7, that to accept mere repentance from sinners would not have been fitting, εὔλογον, he continues, "Nor does repentance recover us from our state of nature, it does but arrest the course of sin. Had there been but a fault committed, and not a subsequent *corruption*, repentance had been well, but if," &c. vid. *Incarnation* and *Freedom*.

"While it is mere man who receives the gift, he is liable to lose it again (as was shown in the case of Adam, for he received and he lost), but that the grace may be irrevocable, and may be kept sure by men, therefore it is the Son who Himself appropriates the gift." Orat. iii. § 38.

He received gifts in order "that for His sake (δι᾽ αὐτὸν) men might henceforward upon earth have power against devils, as 'having become partakers of a divine nature,' and in heaven might, as 'being delivered from corruption,' reign everlastingly; . . . and, whereas the flesh received the gift in Him, henceforth by It for us also that gift might abide secure." Orat. iii. § 40.

"The Word of God, who loves man, put on Himself created flesh, at the Father's will, that, whereas the first man had made the flesh dead through the transgression, He Himself might quicken it in the Blood of His own body." Orat. ii. § 65. Vid. also Orat. i. § 48, 51, ii. § 56.

¶ "How could we be partakers of the adoption of sons, unless through the Son we had received from Him that communion with Him,—unless His Word had been made flesh, and had communicated that Flesh to us?" Iren. Hær. iii. 19. "He took part of flesh and blood, that is, He became man, whereas He was Life by nature, . . . that, uniting Himself to the corruptible flesh according to the measure of its own nature, ineffably and inexpressibly, and as He alone knows, He might bring it to His own life, and render it partaker through Himself of God and the Father. . . . For He bore our nature, re-fashioning it into His own life. . . . He is in us through the Spirit, turning our natural corruption into incorruption, and changing death to its contrary." Cyril. in Joan. ix. cir. fin.

¶ "The Word having appropriated the affections of the flesh, no longer do those affections touch the body, because of the Word who has come in it, but they are destroyed by Him, and henceforth men . . . abide ever immortal and incorruptible." Orat. iii. § 33. vid. also Incarn. c. Ar. § 12. contr. Apoll. i. § 17. ii. § 6. "Since God the Word willed to annul the passions, whose end is death, and His deathless nature was not capable of them, ... He is made flesh of the Virgin in the way He knoweth," &c. Procl. ad. Armen. p. 616.

Also Leon. Serm. 22, pp. 69, 71. Serm. 26, p. 88. Nyssen. contr. Apoll. t. 2, p. 696. Cyril. Epp. p. 138, 9. in Joan. p. 95. Chrysol. Serm. 148.

¶ " His body is none other than His, and is a natural recipient of grace; for He received grace as far as man's nature was exalted, which exaltation was its being deified." Orat. i. § 45. vid. arts. *Indwelling* and *Deification.*

SCRIPTURE CANON.

ATHAN. will not allow that the *Pastor* is canonical, Decr. § 18. "In the *Shepherd* it is written, since they [the Arians] allege this book also, though it is not in the Canon;" yet he uses the formula, "It is written."

¶ And so in Ep. Fest. fin. he enumerates it with Wisdom, Ecclesiasticus, Esther, Judith, Tobit, and others, "not canonised, but appointed by the Fathers to be read by recent converts and persons under teaching." He calls it elsewhere a most profitable book. Incarn. 3.

¶ As to the phrase, "it is written," or "he says," τάδε λέγει, the Douay renders such phrases by "he," διὸ λέγει, "wherefore *he* saith," Eph. v. 14; εἴρηκε περὶ τῆς ἑβδόμης οὕτω, "*he* spoke," Heb. iv. 4; and 7, "*he* limiteth." And we may take in explanation, "As the Holy Ghost saith, To-day," &c. Heb. iii. 7. Or understand with Athan. διελέγξει λέγων ὁ Παῦλος. Orat. i. § 57. ὡς εἶπεν ὁ Ἰωάννης. Orat. iii. § 30. vid. also iv. § 31. On the other hand, "doth not the *Scripture* say," John vii. 42; "what saith the *Scripture?*" Rom. iv. 3; "do you think that the *Scripture* saith in vain?" &c. James iv. 5. And so Athan. οἶδεν ἡ θεία γραφὴ λέγουσα. Orat. i. § 56. ἔθος τῇ θείῃ γραφῇ . . φησί. Orat. iv. § 27. λέγει ἡ γραφή, Decr. § 22. φησὶν ἡ γραφή, Syn. § 52.

AUTHORITY OF SCRIPTURE.

ATHANASIUS considers Scripture sufficient for the proof of such fundamental doctrines as came into controversy during the Arian troubles; but, while in consequence he ever appeals to Scripture, (and indeed has scarcely any other authoritative document to quote,) he ever speaks against interpreting it by a private rule instead of adhering to ecclesiastical tradition. Tradition is with him of supreme authority, including therein catechetical instruction, the teaching of the *schola*, ecumenical belief, the φρόνημα of Catholics, the ecclesiastical scope, the analogy of faith, &c.

" The holy and inspired Scriptures are sufficient of themselves for the preaching of the truth; yet there are also many treatises of our blessed teachers composed for this purpose." contr. Gent. init. " For studying and mastering the Scriptures, there is need of a good life and a pure soul, and virtue according to Christ," Incarn. 57. " Since divine Scripture is sufficient more than anything else, I recommend persons who wish to know fully concerning these things," (the doctrine of the Blessed Trinity,) " to read the divine oracles," ad Ep. Æg. 4. " The Scriptures are sufficient for teaching; but it is good for us to exhort each other in the faith, and to refresh each other with discourses." Vit. S. Ant. 16. " We must seek before

all things whether He is Son, and on this point
specially search the Scriptures, for this it was, when
the Apostles were questioned, that Peter answered,"
&c. Orat. ii. § 73. And passim in Athan. Vid.
Serap. i. 32 init. iv. fin. contr. Apoll. i. 6, 8, 9, 11,
22. ii. 8, 9, 13, 14, 17—19.

¶ "The doctrine of the Church should be proved,
not announced, (ἀποδεικτικῶς οὐκ ἀποφαντικῶς;) therefore show that Scripture thus teaches." Theod. Eran.
p. 199. "We have learned the rule of doctrine
(κανόνα) out of divine Scripture." ibid. p. 213.
"Do not believe me, let Scripture be recited. I
do not say of myself, 'In the beginning was the
Word,' but I hear it; I do not invent, but I read;
what we all read, but not all understand." Ambros.
de Incarn. 14. "Non recipio quod extra Scripturam
de tuo infers." Tertull. Carn. Christ. 7. vid. also 6.
"You departed from inspired Scripture, and therefore
did fall from grace." Max. de Trin. Dial. v. 29. "The
Children of the Church have received from their holy
Fathers, that is, the holy Apostles, to guard the faith;
and withal to deliver and preach it to their own
children. . . . Cease not, faithful and orthodox men,
thus to speak, and to teach the like from the divine
Scriptures, and to walk, and to catechise, to the confirmation of yourselves and those who hear you;
namely, that holy faith of the Catholic Church, as the
holy and only Virgin of God received its custody from
the holy Apostles of the Lord; and thus, in the case
of each of those who are under catechising, who are to
approach the Holy Bath, ye ought not only to preach

faith to your children in the Lord, but also to teach them expressly, as your common mother teaches, to say: 'We believe in One God,'" &c. Epiph. Ancor. 119, fin. who thereupon proceeds to give at length the Niceno-Constantinopolitan Creed. And so Athan. speaks of the orthódox faith, as " issuing from Apostolical teaching and the Fathers' tradition, and confirmed by New and Old Testament." ad Adelph. 6, init. Cyril Hier. too, as " declared by the Church and established from all Scripture." Cat. v. 12. "Let us guard with vigilance what we have *received*. . . . . What then have we received from the *Scriptures* but altogether this ? that God made the world by the Word," &c. &c. Procl. ad Armen. Ep. 2, p. 612. " That God the Word, after the union, remained such as He was, &c., so clearly hath divine Scripture, and moreover the doctors of the Churches, and the lights of the world taught us." Theodor. Eran. p. 175, init. " That it is the tradition of the Fathers is not the whole of our case; for they too followed the meaning of Scripture, starting from the testimonies, which just now we laid before you from Scripture." Basil de Sp. S. n. 16. vid. also a remarkable passage in Athan. Synod. § 6, fin.

¶ S. Gregory says in a well - known passage, " Why art thou such a slave to the letter, and takest up with Jewish wisdom, and pursuest syllables to the loss of things? For if thou wert to say, 'twice five,' or 'twice seven,' and I concluded 'ten' or 'fourteen' from your words, or from 'a reasonable mortal animal' I concluded 'man,' should I seem to you absurd? how so, if I did but give your meaning? for words belong as much to him who demands them as to him who utters." Orat. 31. 24. vid. also Hil. contr. Constant. 16. August. Ep. 238, n. 4—6. Cyril. Dial. i. p. 391. Petavius refers to other passages, de Trin. iv. 5, § 6.

¶ In interpreting Scripture, Athan. always assumes that the Catholic teaching is true, and the Scripture must be explained by it, vid. art. *Rule of Faith.* Thus he says, Orat. ii. 3, "If He be Son, as indeed He is, let them not question about the terms which the sacred writers use of Him. . . . For terms do not disparage His Nature, but rather that Nature draws to itself those terms and changes them." And presently, "Nature and truth draw the meaning to themselves; this being so, why ask, is He a work? it is proper to ask of them first, is He a Son?" ii. 5.

¶ The great and essential difference between Catholics and non-Catholics was that Catholics interpreted Scripture by Tradition, and non-Catholics by their own private judgment.

¶ That not only Arians, but heretics generally, professed to be guided by Scripture, we know from many witnesses.

¶ Heretics in particular professed to be guided by Scripture. Tertull. Præscr. 8. For Gnostics, vid. Tertullian's grave sarcasm, "Utantur hæretici omnes scripturis ejus, cujus utuntur etiam mundo." Carn. Christ. 6. For Arians, vid. supr. *Arian tenets.* And so Marcellus, "We consider it unsafe to lay down doctrine concerning things which we have not learned with exactness from the divine Scriptures." (leg.

περὶ ὧν . . . παρὰ τῶν.) Euseb. Eccl. Theol. p. 177. And Macedonians, vid. Leont. de Sect. iv. init. And Monophysites, "I have not learned this from Scripture; and I have a great fear of saying what it is silent about." Theod. Eran. p. 215. S. Hilary brings a number of these instances together with their respective texts, Marcellus, Photinus, Sabellius, Montanus, Manes; then he continues, "Omnes Scripturas sine Scripturæ sensu loquuntur, et fidem sine fide prætendunt. Scripturæ enim non in legendo sunt, sed in intelligendo, neque in prævaricatione sunt sed in caritate." ad Const. ii. 9. vid. also Hieron. c. Lucif. 27. August. Ep. 120, 13.

SCRIPTURE PASSAGES.

¶ 1. GEN. i. 26.—" Let us make man," &c.

The Catholic Fathers, as is well known, interpret such texts as this in the general sense which we find taken above (vol. i. de Syn. § 27, p. 112) by the first Sirmian Council convened against Photinus, Marcellus, &c. It is scarcely necessary to refer to instances; Petavius, however, cites the following: First, those in which the Eternal Father is considered in Gen. i. 26 to speak to the Son. Theophilus, ad Autol. ii. 18. Novatian, de Trin. 26. Tertullian, Prax. 12. Synod. Antioch. contr. Paul. Samos. ap. Routh, Reliqu. t. 2, p. 468. Basil. Hexaem. fin. Cyr. Hieros. Cat. x. 6. Cyril. Alex. Dial. iv. p. 516. Athan. contr. Gentes, 46. Orat. iii. § 29 fin. Chrysost. in Genes. Hom. viii. 3. Hilar. Trin. iv. 17, v. 8. Ambros. Hexaëm. vi. 7. Augustin. c. Maxim. ii. 26, n. 2. Next those in which Son and Spirit are considered as addressed. Theoph. ad Autol. ii. 18. Basil. contr. Eunom. v. 4, p. 315. Pseudo-Chrysost. de Trin. t. i. p. 832. Cyril. Thesaur. p. 12. Theodor. in Genes. 19. Hær. v. 3, and 9. But even here, where the Arians agree with Catholics, they differ in this remarkable respect, that in the Canons they pass in their Councils, they place certain interpretations of Scripture under the sanction of an anathema, showing how far less *free* the system of heretics is than that of the Church.

¶ 2. Gen. xviii. 1.—"The Lord appeared to Abraham," &c.

The same Sirmian Council anathematises those who say that Abraham saw "not the Son, but the Ingenerate God."

This again, in spite of the wording, which is directed against the Catholic doctrine, and is of an heretical implication, is a Catholic interpretation. vid. (besides Philo de Somniis, i. 12, p. 1139,) Justin. Tryph. 56, and 126. Iren. Hær. iv. 10, n. 1. Tertull. de Carn. Christ. 6. adv. Marc. iii. 9. adv. Prax. 16. Novat. de Trin. 18. Origen. in Gen. Hom. iv. 5. Cyprian. adv. Jud. ii. 5. Antioch. Syn. contr. Paul. apud Routh, Rell. t. 2, p. 469. Athan. Orat. ii. 13. Epiph. Ancor. 29 and 39. Hær. 71, 5. Chrysost. in Gen. Hom. 41, 6 and 7. These references are principally from Petavius; also from Dorscheus, who has written an elaborate commentary on this Council. The implication alluded to above is, that the Son is of a visible substance, and thus is naturally the manifestation of the Invisible God. Bull (Def. F. N. iv. 3) denies what Petavius maintains, that this doctrine is found in Justin, Origen, &c. The Catholic doctrine is that the Son manifests Himself (and thereby His Father) by means of material representations. Augustine seems to have been the first who changed the mode of viewing the texts in question, and considered the divine appearance, not God the Son, but a created Angel. vid. de Trin.

ii. passim. Jansenius considers that he did so from a suggestion of S. Ambrose, that the hitherto received view had been the "origo hæresis Arianæ," vid. his Augustinus, lib. prooem. c. 12, t. 2, p. 12.

¶ 3. Exodus xxxiii. 23.—"Thou shalt see My back, but My face," &c. τὰ ὀπίσω μου, and not τὸ πρόσωπον. Gregory Naz. interprets τὸ ὀπίσω (ὀπίσθια) to mean God's works in contrast with His εἶδος.

¶ 4. Deut. xxviii. 66.—"Thy Life shall be hanging before thee."

Athanasius says, "His crucifixion is denoted by 'Ye shall see your Life hanging.'" Orat. ii. 16, supr. vol. i. p. 270.

Vid. Iren. Hær. iv. 10, 2.   Tertull. in Jud. 11. Cyprian. Testim. ii. 20.   Lactant. Instit. iv. 18. Cyril. Catech. xiii. 19.   August. contr. Faust. xvi. 22, which are referred to in loc. Cypr. (Oxf. Tr.)   To which add Leon. Serm. 59, 6.   Isidor. Hisp. contr. Jud. i. 35, ii. 6.   Origen. in Cels. ii. 75.   Epiph. Hær. 24, p. 75.   Damasc. F. O. iv. 11. fin.   This interpretation I am told by a great authority is recommended even by the letter, which has תלאים לך מנגד, ἀπέναντι τῶν ὀφθαλμῶν σου, in Sept. "Pendebit tibi a regione," vid. Gesenius, who also says, "Since things which are à regione of a place, are necessarily a little removed from it, it follows that מנגד signifies at the same time to be at a small distance," referring to the case of Hagar, who was but a bow-shot from her child. Also, though the word here is תלא, yet תלה which is the same root,

is used for hanging on a stake, or crucifixion, e.g.
Gen. xl. 19. Deut. xxi. 22. Esth. v. 14 ; vii. 10.

¶ 5. Psalm xliv. 9.—"Therefore God, Thy God, hath
anointed Thee," &c.

" *Wherefore*," says Athan. " does not imply reward
of virtue or conduct in the Word, but the reason why
He came down to us, and of the Spirit's anointing
which took place in Him for our sakes. For he says
not, ' Wherefore He anointed Thee in order to Thy
being God or King or Son or Word ; ' for so He was
before and is for ever, as has been shown ; but rather,
' Since Thou art God and King, therefore Thou wast
anointed, since none but Thou couldest unite man to
the Holy Ghost, Thou the Image of the Father, in
which we were made in the beginning ; for Thine also
is the Spirit.' . . . That as through Him we have come
to be, so also in Him all men might be redeemed from
their sins, and by Him all things might be ruled."
Orat. i. § 49, supr. vol. i. p. 230.

The word " wherefore " denotes the fitness why the
Son of God should become the Son of man. His
Throne, as God, is for ever ; He has loved righteousness ; *therefore* He is *equal* to the anointing of the
Spirit, as man. And so S. Cyril in Joan. lib. v.
2. " In this ineffable unity," says St. Leo, " of the
Trinity, whose words and judgments are common in
all, the Person of the Son has fitly undertaken to
repair the race of man, that since He it is by whom
all things were made, and without whom nothing is
made, and who breathed the truth of rational life into

men fashioned of the dust of the earth, so He too should restore to its lost dignity our nature thus fallen from the citadel of eternity, and should be the reformer of that of which He had been the maker." Leon. Serm. 64, 2. vid. Athan. de Incarn. 7 fin. 10. In illud Omn. 2. Cyril. in Gen. i. p. 13.

¶ 6. Prov. viii. 22.—"The Lord created Me in the beginning of His ways, for His works."

The long and beautiful discourse left us by Athanasius on the First-born and His condescension, may be said to have grown out of what must be considered a wrong reading of this verse, *created* for *possessed*, ἔκτισε for ἔκτησατο being the Septuagint translation of the Hebrew קנה, as also in Gen. xiv. 19, 22. Such too is the sense of the word given in the Chaldee, Syriac, and Arabic versions, and the greater number of primitive writers. In consequence we find that it was one of the passages relied upon by the forerunners of the Arians in the 3rd century, vid. supr. vol. i. pp. 45—47. On the rise of Arianism, Eusebius of Nicomedia appealed to it against Alexander; also the other Eusebius in Demonstr. Evan v. p. 212, &c. It was still insisted on in A.D. 350.

On the other hand, Aquila translates ἔκτήσατο, and so read Basil c. Eunom. ii. 20, Nyssen c. Eunom i. p. 34, Jerome in Is. xxvi. 13; and the Vulgate translates *possedit*, vid. also Gen. iv. 1, and Deut. xxxii. 8. The Hebrew sense is also recognised by Eusebius, Eccl. Theol. iii. 2, p. 153, and Epiph. Hær. 69, 24.

Athanasius, assuming the word *created* to be correct, interprets it of our Lord's human nature, as do Epiph. Hær. 69, 20—25. Basil. Ep. viii. 8. Naz. Orat. 30. 2. Nyss. contr. Eunom. ut. supr. et al Cyril. Thesaur. p. 155. Hilar. de Trin. xii. 36—49. Ambros. de Fid. i. 15. August. de Fid. et Symb. 6.

¶ Our Lord is ἀρχὴ ὁδῶν, says Athan. Orat. ii. 47, fin. in contrast with His proper Sonship; and so Justin understands the phrase, according to the Benedictine Ed. vid. supr. art. *Indwelling*.

¶ 7. Isa. liii. 7.—"He shall be led as a sheep to the slaughter."

Athan. says, Orat. i. § 54, supr. vol. i. p. 234, as elsewhere, that the error of heretics in their interpretation of Scripture arises from their missing the person, time, circumstances, &c., which Scripture has in view, and which (as I understand him to imply) Tradition (that is, the continuous teaching of the Church,) supplies; just as the Jews, as regards Isa. liii. instead of learning from Philip, as he says, the meaning of the chapter, conjecture its words to be spoken of Jeremias or some other of the Prophets.

¶ The more common evasion on the part of the Jews was to interpret the prophecy of their own sufferings in captivity. - It was an idea of Grotius that the prophecy received a first fulfilment in Jeremiah. vid. Justin. Tryph. 72 et al. Iren. Hær. iv. 33. Tertull. in Jud. 9. Cyprian Testim. in Jud. ii. 13. Euseb. Dem. iii. 2, &c.

¶ 8. Jerem. xxxi. 22.—" The Lord hath created a new salvation," &c.

This is the Septuagint version, as Athan. notices Expos. F. § 3, Aquila's being " The Lord hath created a new thing in the woman." The Vulgate (" a new thing upon the earth, a woman shall compass a man,") is with the Hebrew. Athan. has preserved Aquila's version in three other places, Ps. xxx. 12, lix. 5, and lxv. 18.

¶ 9. Matt. i. 25.—"And he knew her not, *until*," &c., that is, until then when it became impossible, and need not be denied.

Supposing it was said, " He knew her not till her death," would not that mean, " He never knew her"? and in like manner, if she was "the Mother of God," it was an impossible idea, and the Evangelist would feel it to be so. They only can entertain the idea who in truth do not believe our Lord's divinity, who do not believe literally that the Son of Mary is God. Vid. art. *Mary*.

¶ 10. Matt. iii. 17.—" This is My well-beloved Son," ἀγαπητὸς, &c. " Only-begotten and Well-beloved are the same," says Athan. . . . " hence the Word, with a view of conveying to Abraham the idea ' Only-begotten,' says, ' Offer thy Son, thy Well-beloved.' " Orat. iv. § 24. He adds, ibid. iv. § 29, " The word ' Well-beloved ' even the Greeks, who are skilful in grammar, know to be equivalent with ' Only-be-gotten.' For Homer speaks thus of Telemachus,

who was the only-begotten of Ulysses, in the second
book of the Odyssey :—

> O'er the wide earth, dear youth, why seek to run,
> An only child, a well-beloved son? (μοῦνος ἐὼν ἀγαπητός.)
> He whom you mourn, divine Ulysses, fell,
> Far from his country, where the strangers dwell.

Therefore he who is the only son of his father is called
well-beloved."

Ἀγαπητὸς is explained by μονογενής by Hesychius,
Suidas, and Pollux; it is the version in the Sept.
equally with μονογενής of the Hebrew יָחִיד. Homer
calls Astyanax Ἑκτορίδην ἀγαπητόν; Plutarch notices
the instance of Telemachus, Ὅμηρος ἀγαπητὸν ὀνομάζει
μοῦνον τηλύγετον, τουτέστι μὴ ἔχουσι ἕτερον γονεῦσι
μήτε ἕξουσι γεγεννημένον, as quoted by Wetstein in
Matt. iii. 17. Vid. also Suicer in voc.

¶ 11. Matt. xii. 32.—" Whosoever shall speak a
word," &c.

This passage, which is commented on at Orat. i. § 50,
Athan. explains at some length in Serap. iv. 8, &c.,
supr. vol. i. p. 231. Origen, he says, and Theognostus
understand the sin against the Holy Ghost to be
apostasy from the grace of Baptism, referring to Heb.
vi. 4. So far the two agree; but Origen went on to say,
that the proper power or virtue of the Son extends
over rational natures alone, e.g. heathens, but that of
the Spirit only over Christians; those then who sin
against the Son or their reason, have a remedy in
Christianity and its baptism, but nothing remains for

those who sin against the Spirit. But Theognostus,
referring to the text, "I have many things to say, but
ye cannot bear them now; howbeit, when He, the
Spirit of Truth," &c., argued that to sin against the
Son was to sin against inferior light, but against the
Spirit was to reject the full truth of the Gospel.

¶ 12. Matt. xiii. 25.—"His enemy came and over-
sowed cockle," &c. ἐπίσπειρας, Decr. § 2. Orat. i. § ˈ1,
&c., &c. supr. vol. i. pp. 14, 155.   .

An allusion to this parable is very frequent in
Athan., chiefly with a reference to Arianism. He
draws it out at length, Orat. ii. § 34. "What is sown
in every soul from the beginning is that God has a
Son, the Word, the Wisdom, the. Power, that is,
His Image and Radiance; from which it at once
follows that He is always; that He is from the
Father; that He is like; that he is the eternal
offspring of His substance; and there is no idea
involved in these of creature or work. But when
the man who is an enemy, while men slept, made a
second sowing, of 'He is a creature,' and 'There
was once when He was not,' and 'How can it be?'
thenceforth the wicked heresy of Christ's enemies
rose." Elsewhere, he uses the parable for the evil
influences introduced into the soul upon Adam's fall,
contr. Apoll. i. § 15, as does S. Irenæus Hær. iv.
40, n. 3, using it of such as lead to backsliding in
Christians, ibid. v. 10, n. 1. Gregory Nyssen, of the
natural passions and of false reason misleading them, de
An. et Resurr. t. ii. p. 640. vid. also Leon, Ep. 156, c. 2.

¶ Tertullian uses the image in a similar but higher sense, when he applies it to Eve's temptation, and goes on to contrast it with Christ's birth from a Virgin : " In virginem adhuc Evam irrepserat verbum ædificatorium mortis; in Virginem æque introducendum erat Dei Verbum exstructorium vitæ. . . . Ut in doloribus pareret, verbum diaboli semen illi fuit; contra Maria," &c. de Carn. Christ. 17. S. Leo, as Athan., makes " seed " in the parable apply peculiarly to *faith* in contrast with *obedience,* Serm. 69, 5, init.

¶ 13. John i. 1.—" In the beginning," &c. vid. Orat. i. § 11, supr. vol. i. p. 167.

If " beginning " in this verse be taken, not to imply time, but origination, then the first verse of St. John's Gospel may be interpreted " In the Beginning," or Origin, i.e. in the Father, " was the Word." Thus Athan. himself understands the text. Orat. ii. 57. Orat. iv. § 1. vid. also Orat. iii. § 9. Origen. in Joan. tom. 1, 17. Method. ap. Phot. cod. 235, p. 940. Nyssen. contr. Eunom. iii. p. 106. Cyril. Thesaur. 32, p. 312. Euseb. Eccl. Theol. ii. 11 and 14, pp. 118, 123, and Jerome in Calmet on Ps. 109.

¶ 14. John i. 3.—" Without Him was nothing made that was made." Vid. Orat. i. § 19. supr. p. 179.

The words " that was made " which end this verse were omitted by the ancient citers of it, as Irenæus, Clement, Origen, Eusebius, Tertullian, nay, Augustine ; but because it was abused by the Eunomians, Macedonians, &c., as if derogatory to the divinity of the Holy Spirit, it was quoted in full, as by Epiphanius, Ancor. 75, who goes so far as to speak severely of the ancient mode of citation. vid. Fabric. and Routh, ad Hippol. contr. Noet. 12.

Also vid. Simon. Hist. Crit. Comment. pp. 7, 32, 52. Lampe in loc. Joann. Fabric. in Apocryph. N. T. t. 1, p. 384. Petav. de Trin. ii. 6, § 6. Ed. Ben. in Ambros. de Fid. iii. 6. Wetstein in loc. Wolf. Cur. Phil. in loc. The verse was not ended as we at present read it, especially in the East, till the time of S. Chrysostom, according to Simon, (vid. Ben. Præf. in Joann. § iv.) though, as has been said above, S. Epiphanius had spoken strongly against the ancient reading. S. Ambrose loc. cit. refers it to the Arians, Lampe refers it to the Valentinians on the strength of Iren. Hær. i. 8, n. 5. Theophilus in loc. (if the Commentary on the Gospels is his) understands by οὐδὲν "an idol," referring to 1 Cor. viii. 4. Augustine, even at so late a date, adopts the old reading, vid. de Gen. ad lit. v. 29—31. It was the reading of the Vulgate, even at the time it was ruled by the Council of Trent to be authentic, and of the Roman Missal. The verse is made to end after "in Him," (thus, οὐδ᾽ ἓν ὃ γέγονεν ἐν αὐτῷ) by Epiph. Ancor. 75. Hil. in Psalm. 148, 4. Ambros. de Fid. iii. 6. Nyssen in Eunom. i. p. 84, app., which favours the Arians. The counterpart of the ancient reading, which is very awkward, ("What was made in Him was life,") is found in August. loc. cit. and Ambrose in Psalm xxxvi. 35, but he also notices " What was made, was in Him," de Fid. loc. cit. It is remarkable that

St. Ambrose attributes the present punctuation to the Alexandrians (in loc. Psalm.) in spite of Athan.'s and Alexander's (Theod. Hist. i. 3, p. 733), nay, Cyril's (in loc. Joann.) adoption of the ancient.

¶ 15. John ii. 4.—"Woman," &c. "He chid His Mother," says Athan.

'Επέπληττε ; and so ἐπετίμησε, Chrysost. in loc. Joann. Hom. 21, 3, and Theophyl. ὡς δεσπότης ἐπιτιμᾷ, Theodor. Eran. ii. p. 106. ἐντρέπει, Anon. ap. Corder. Cat. in loc. μέμφεται, Alter Anon. ibid. ἐπιτιμᾶ οὐκ ἀτιμάζων ἀλλὰ διορθούμενος, Euthym. in loc. οὐκ ἐπέπληξεν, Pseudo-Justin. Quæst. ad Orthod. 136. It is remarkable that Athan. dwells on these words as implying our Lord's humanity, (i.e. because Christ appeared to *decline* a miracle,) when one reason assigned for them by the Fathers is that He wished, in the words τί μοι καί σοι, to remind our Lady that He was the Son of God and must be "in His Father's house." "Repellens ejus intempestivam festinationem," Iren. Hær. iii. 16, n. 7, who thinks she desired to drink of His cup; others that their entertainer was poor, and that she wished to befriend him. Nothing can be argued from S. Athan.'s particular word here commented on, how he would have taken the passage. That the tone of our Lord's words is indeed (judging humanly and speaking humanly) cold and distant, is a simple fact, but it may be explained variously. It is observable that ἐπιπλήττει and ἐπιτιμᾶ are the words used by Theophylact (in Joan. xi. 34, vid. infra, art. *Specialties*,) for our Lord's treatment of His own sacred body.

But they are very vague words, and have a strong meaning or not, as the case may be.

¶ 16. John x. 30.—"I and My Father are one." "They contend," says Athan., Orat. iii. § 10, supr. vol. i. p. 369, "that the Son and the Father are not in such wise one as the Church preaches . . but that, since what the Father wills, the Son wills also, and . . is in all respects concordant (σύμφωνος) with Him . . . therefore it is that He and the Father are one. And some of them have dared to write as well as to say this," viz. Asterius; vid. Orat. iii. § 2, supr. vol. i. p. 360.

We find the same doctrine in the Creed ascribed to Lucian, as translated above, Syn. § 23, supr. vol. i. p. 97, where vid. note 2; vid. also infra. art. ὅμοιον. Besides Origen, Novatian, the Creed of Lucian, and (if so) Hilary, (as mentioned in the note at vol. i. p. 97,) "one" is explained as oneness of will by S. Hippolytus, contr. Noet. 7, where he explains John x. 30, by xvii. 22, like the Arians; and, as might be expected, by Eusebius, Eccl. Theol. iii. 19, p. 193, and by Asterius ap. Euseb. contr. Marc. pp. 28, 37. The passages of the Fathers in which this text is adduced are collected by Maldonat. in loc.

¶ 17. John x. 30, 38. xiv. 9.—"I and the Father are One." "The Father is in Me, and," &c. "He that seeth Me," &c.

These three texts are found together frequently in Athan., particularly in Orat. iii., where he considers the doctrines of the "Image" and the περιχώρησις; vid.

de Decr. § 21, § 31. de Syn. § 45. Orat. iii. 3, 5, 6, 10, 16 fin. 17. Ep. Æg. 13. Sent D. 26. ad Afr. 7, 8, 9. vid. also Epiph. Hær. 64, 9. Basil. Hexaem. ix. fin. Cyr. Thes. xii. p. 111. Potam. Ep. ap. Dacher. t. 3, p. 299. Hil. Trin. vii. 41. Vid. also Animadv. in Eustath. Ep. ad Apoll. Rom. 1796, p. 58.

In Orat. iii. § 5, these three texts, which so often occur together, are recognised as "three;" so are they by Eusebius, Eccl. Theol. iii. 19, and he says that Marcellus and "those who Sabellianise with him," among whom he included Catholics, were in the practice of adducing them, θρυλλοῦντες; which bears incidental testimony to the fact that the doctrine of the περιχώρησις was the great criterion between orthodox and Arian. To the many instances of the joint use of the three which are given supr. may be added Orat. ii. 54 init. 67 fin. iv. 17, Serap. ii. 9, Serm. Maj. de fid. 29. Cyril. de Trin. p. 554, in Joann. p. 168. Origen, Periarch. p. 56. Hil. Trin. ix. 1. Ambros. Hexaem. vi. 7. August. de Cons. Ev. i. 7.

¶ 18. John xiv. 28.—"The Father is greater than I." Athan. explains these words by comparing them with "*Made so much better than the Angels*," Hebr. i. 1. "He says not '*the Father is better than I*,' lest we should conceive Him to be foreign to His Nature," as Angels are foreign in nature to the Son; "but greater, not indeed in greatness nor in time, but because of His generation from the Father Himself," Orat. i. § 58, that is, on account of the *principatus* of the Father, as the ἀρχή and πηγή θεότητος, and of His wn *filietas*.

¶ 19. Acts x. 36.—"God sent the word to the children of Israel. . . . You know the word," &c.

So the Vulgate, but the received Greek runs with Athan. Orat. iv. § 30. τὸν λόγον, ὃν ἀπέστειλε . . . οὗτός ἐστι . . . ὑμεῖς οἴδατε τὸ γενόμενον ῥῆμα. The followers of Paul of Samosata, with a view to their heresy, interpreted these words, as Hippolytus before them, as if τὸν λόγον were either governed by κατὰ or attracted by ὃν, οὗτος agreeing with ὁ λόγος understood. Dr. Routh in loc. Hipp. (vid. Noët 13) who at one time so construed it, refers to 1 Pet. ii. 7, John iii. 34, as parallel, also Matt. xxi. 42. And so 'Urbem quam statuo,' &c. vid. Raphel. in Luc. xxi. 6. vid. also τὴν ἀρχὴν ὅτι καὶ λαλῶ ὑμῖν, John viii. 25, with J. C. Wolf's remarks, who would understand by ἀρχὴν omnino, which Lennep however in Phalar. Ep. says it can only mean with a negative. The Vulgate is harsh in understanding λόγος and ῥῆμα as synonymous, and the latter as used merely to connect the clauses. Moreover, if λόγος be taken for ῥῆμα, τὸν λόγον ἀπέστειλε is a harsh phrase; however, it occurs Acts xiii. 26. If λόλος on the other hand has a theological sense, a primâ facie countenance is given to the distinction between " the Word " and " Jesus Christ," which the Samosatenes wished to deduce from the passage.

¶ 20. Rom. i. 20.—"His Eternal Power and Divinity."

Athanasius understands this of our Lord. Orat. i. § 11. Syn. § 49. vid. Justinian's Comment. in Paul.

Epp. for its various interpretations. It was either a received interpretation, or had been adduced at Nicæa, for Asterius had some years before these Discourses replied to it, vid. Syn. § 18, supr. vol. i. p. 88, and Orat. ii. § 37, p. 297.

SEMI-ARIANS.

THE Semi-Arian symbols admitted of an orthodox interpretation, but they also admitted of an heretical. They served as a shelter for virtual Arians, and as a refuge for those who feared the orthodox *homoüsion*, as either materialistic or Sabellian. In the first years of the controversy they were tokens of a falling short of the true faith, in the later years tokens of an approaching to it. Hence Athanasius is severe with Eusebius and Asterius, and kind in his treatment of Basil and his party.

Accordingly, these symbols in no way served the necessity of the time as a test to secure the Church against a dangerous and insidious heresy. Eusebius of Cæsarea could have no difficulty in professing our Lord was God, and like in His nature to the Father, yet his heterodoxy has been shown in art. *Eusebius.* Still more openly heterodox was Eusebius of Nicomedia; yet such statements as occur in the Semi-Arian Councils and Creeds would give him no annoyance. These men did but scruple at the one word *homoüsion*.

The Catholic Theologians taught, with our Lord, that " He and the Father are one ; " and, when asked in what sense one, they answered " numerically one, else were there two Gods ; " that is, they were ὁμοούσιοι. The Arians considered them numerically two, and only in agreement one with each other. Either then they held that there were two Gods, or that our Lord was God only in name and not true God. They would answer that that dilemma was none of their making; that is, the idea of incomprehensibility in the Infinite, and of mystery in what was predicated of Him, does not seem to have had a place in their reasonings.

So far Semi-Arians agreed with Arians, in holding a greater God and a less, a true God and a so-called God; a God of all, and a Divine Mediator and representative God; but when Catholics questioned them more closely on their belief, as, for instance, whether the Son was a creature, and what was meant by His being "like" the Father, the Arians proper said boldly that He was a creature, though the first of creatures and unlike other creatures, and not the Son of God except figuratively, as men were His sons, and that, moreover, as a creature He had been liable to fall, as the Angels fell and Adam; but from such blasphemy others shrank, and thus in consequence they were called Semi-Arians, holding that, though our Lord was not in being from everlasting, and though He had been brought into being at the will of the Father, still a *gennesis* was a divine act in kind different from a creation; not indeed an emanation, else, He was not only like, but the same as the Father in essence, and if so, why had Euseb. Nic. from the first protested against ἐξ ἀπορροίας and μέρος ὁμοούσιον, and why did Euseb. Cæs. so evidently evade the ἐξ οὐσίας (as shown supr. art. *Eusebius*)? In short they were driven by their remaining religiousness, unlike the Arians proper,

(who in the later shape of Eunomianism expressly denied that God was incomprehensible) into the admission that there was mystery in the revealed doctrine.
And this Eusebius confesses in a passage which will
be quoted infr. art. *Son of God.*

Recurring to the dilemma insisted on against
the Arian disputant, it will be observed that the
clear-headed Arians grasped fearlessly the conclusion
that our Lord was not God, while the more pious
and timid Semi-Arians could not extricate themselves from the charge of holding two Gods.

Eusebius (vid. art. *Euseb.*) calls our Lord a second
substance, another God, a second God. And it was in
this sense his co-religionists used such epithets as
τέλειος of our Lord, and called Him, as in Lucian's
creed, " perfect from perfect, king from king," &c. viz.
under the impression, or with the insinuation, that the
ὁμοούσιον diluted belief in His divinity into a sort
of Sabellianism. Whether in giving these high titles
to our Lord, Eusebius and his party used them in a
Catholic sense, would also be seen in their use and
interpretation of the word περιχώρησις, co-inherence,
(vid. art. *Coinherence*), which was a practical equivalent
to ὁμοούσιον, though it too they could explain away,
and did. Accordingly viewing Father and Son as
distinct substances, and rejecting both ὁμοούσιον and
περιχώρησις, they certainly considered them, as far as
words go, to be distinct Gods. Such strong expressions
as ὁμοιούσιος, and ἀπαράλλακτος εἴκων, which they used,
would but increase the evil, as Athanasius argues against
them. " If all that is the Father's is the Son's, as in

an Image and Impress," he says, "let it be considered dispassionately, whether a substance foreign to the Father's substance admits of such attributes; and whether such a one can possibly be other in nature and alien in substance, and not rather one in substance with the Father." Syn. § 50. vid. also Orat. iii. 16. vid. art. *Idolatry.*

However, Athan., and Hilary too, saw enough of what was good and promising in the second generation of Semi-Arians to adopt a kind tone towards them, which they could not use in speaking of the followers of Arius. Athan. calls certain of them " brethren " and " beloved," and Hilary "sanctissimi," and the events in many cases justified their anticipation.

They guard, however, their words, lest more should be understood by others than the language of charity and hope. Athan. speaks severely of Eustathius and Basil. Ep. Æg. 7, and Hilary explains himself in his notes upon his de Syn., from which it appears that he had been expostulated with on his conciliatory tone. Indeed all throughout he had betrayed a consciousness that he should offend some parties, e.g. § 6. In § 77, he had spoken of " having expounded the faithful and religious sense of 'like in substance,' which is called Homœüsion." On this he observes, note 3, " I think no one need be asked to consider why I have said in this place '*religious* sense of like in substance,' except that I meant that there was also an *irreligious;* and that therefore I said that ' like ' was not only *equal* but the ' same.' " vid. also supr. vol. i. p. 134, note. In the next note he speaks of them as not more than hopeful. Still it should be observed how careful the Fathers of the day were not to mix up the question of doctrine which rested on Catholic tradition, with that of the adoption of a certain term which rested on a Catholic injunction. Not that the term was not in duty to be received, but it was to be received mainly on account of its Catholic sense, and where the Catholic sense was held, the word might for a while by a sort of dispensation be waived. It is remarkable that Athanasius scarcely mentions the word "One in substance" in his three Orations, as has been already observed; nor does it occur in S. Cyril's Catecheses, of whom, as being suspected of Semi-Arianism, it might have been required, before his writings were received as of authority. The word was not imposed upon Ursacius and Valens, A.D. 349, by Pope Julius; nor, in the Council of Aquileia in 381, was it offered by St. Ambrose to Palladius and Secundianus. S. Jerome's account of the apology made by the Fathers of Arminum is of the same kind. "We thought," they said, "the sense corresponded to the words, nor in the Church of God, where there is simplicity, and a pure confession, did we fear that one thing would be concealed in the heart, another uttered by the lips. We were deceived by our good opinion of the bad." ad Lucif. 19. The same excuse avails for Liberius.

SON OF GOD.

I UNDERSTAND Athanasius (always, of course, after accepting and assuming the doctrine as true and indisputable on the ground of its being revealed,) to go on to argue about it thus:—

The Son of God must be God, granting that the human word "Son" is to guide us to the knowledge of what is heavenly; for on earth we understand by a son one who is the successor and heir to a given nature. A continuation or communication of nature enters into the very idea of γέννησις; if there is no participation of nature there is no sonship, "Μία ἡ φύσις, οὐ γὰρ ἀνόμοιον τὸ γέννημα τοῦ γεννήσαντος, εἰκὼν γάρ ἐστιν αὐτοῦ." Orat. iii. § 4. Hence he speaks of "οἰκειότης τῆς φύσεως," ibid. § 4, 16, &c.

This is the teaching also of the great theologians who followed Athanasius. Basil says that *Father* is "a term of relationship," οἰκειώσεως, in Eunom. ii. 24, init. and that a father may be defined, "one who gives to another the origin of being, *according to a nature like his own*," ibid. 22. And Gregory Nyssen, that "the title 'Son' does not simply express the being from another, but *relationship according to nature*," c. Eunom. ii. p. 91. And Cyril says that the term "Son" denotes the "*substantial* origin from the Father."

Dial. v. p. 573. This was why the Fathers at Nicæa were not content with "from the Father," but wrote "from the substance of the Father."

The Son then participates in the Divine Nature, and since the Divine Nature is none other than the One individual Living Personal True God, He too is that God, and since He is thus identical with that One True God, and since that One True God is eternal and never had a beginning of existence, therefore the Son is eternal and without beginning.

¶ Again, such a real Son is made necessary by considering what the very Nature of God, the existence of an Infinite, all-abounding, all-perfect Being, implies. We cannot be surprised to be told that the infinite Essence of God necessarily flows out, in consequence of His very immensity, into a reflection or perfect image or likeness of Himself, which in all respects is His reiteration, except in not being He. There are then at least two Selves (so to speak) in God, that is, a First and Second Person.

Now this infinite Image of God is not external to the First Person, because the First is infinite. The image is commensurate, but no more than commensurate, with the Original. The Second cannot extend beyond the First or be external to Him. The First and Second cannot become Two except as viewed in their relation of Father and Son. As eternity *a parte ante* is not doubled by being added to eternity *a parte post;* but *before* and *after* are two only when contrasted with each other, so, though God and His Image are relatively two, an Image of God does not make two Gods. Indeed we cannot apply ideas arising out of number to the Illimitable.

¶ This Image, as being the Effluence and Expression and Likeness of the Almighty, may equally well be called Word or Son, and, whether we use one of these names or the other, we mean to express, though under a distinct aspect in each of them, a Second Person in the Godhead. The name of Image teaches us that the Second is commensurate and co-equal with the First; that of Son, that He is co-eternal, for the nature of God cannot alter or vary; and the name of Word teaches us that in Him is represented and manifested the intelligence, living force, and operative energy of the Supreme Being. Hence it is that in the history (if I may use the word) of the Creator and His creatures, the Second Person of the Blessed Trinity is the chief Agent brought before us, and that the offices which are assigned to Him occupy a far larger portion of revealed teaching than even what belongs to His original Divine Nature.

¶ The Arians joined issue with Catholics on the question as to what was involved in the title " Son." They put aside Word, Image, &c., as figures of speech; said that Son was His real name, and then explained " Son " away, maintaining that, whatever else Sonship might teach us, even at first sight it was plain that a Son could not but be posterior in time to his Father; but if so, if our Lord was not eternal *a parte ante*, He was only a creature. The Catholics replied that that could not be the essential true meaning of a word which it did not always hold; now the Arian argument from the word " Son " involved the existence of *time*, that is, of a condition which did not always exist in the instance of the Almighty, of whom we are speaking; either then God had no Son, or else that Son was co-eval, co-eternal with Him. Moreover, there could be no change in the Divine Essence; what He was once, that He ever was. Once a Father, always a Father. The Arians replied that the Almighty was not always Creator, He became a Creator in time; and so as regards the *gennesis* of the Son, though in its very beginning it was not from eternity but in time, that *gennesis* was some unknown kind of creation, and that to connect it with the Divine οὐσία was to introduce material notions into the idea of God. The Catholics of course answered that the notion of materiality was quite as foreign to any right conception of God, as that of time was, and that as the Divine Sonship was eternal, so was it simply spiritual, being taught under material images, only because from the conditions of our knowledge we could not speak of it in any other way. vid. art. *Arian tenets.*

Here Eusebius makes an apposite remark, which ought to have led him farther:—As we do not know how God can create out of nothing, so, he says, we are utterly ignorant of the Divine Generation. We do not understand innumerable things which lie close to us; how the soul is joined to the body, how it enters and leaves it, what its nature, what the nature of Angels. It is written, " He who believes," not he who knows, " has eternal life." Divine Generation is as distinct from human as God from man. The sun's radiance itself is but an earthly image, and gives us no

true idea of that which is above all images. Eccl.
Theol. i. 12. So too S. Greg. Naz. Orat. 29. 8. vid.
also Hippol. in Noet. 16. Cyril, Cat. xi. 11 and 19,
and Origen, according to Mosheim, Ante-Const. p. 619.
And instances in Petav. de Trin. v. 6, § 2 and 3. vid.
arts. *Illustrations, Image*, &c.

¶ ".There are not many Words, but one only Word
of the one Father, and one Image of the one God."
Orat. ii. § 27.

¶ "The Son does not live by the *gift* of life, for He
is life, and does but give it, not receive." Orat. iii. § 1.
S. Hilary uses different language with the same meaning, "Vita viventis [Filii] in vivo [Patre] est," de
Trin. ii. 11. Other modes of expression for the
same mystery are found in art. *Coinherence*, "the
whole being of the Son is proper to the Father's substance;" Orat. iii. 3. "the Son's being, because
from the Father, is therefore in the Father;" ibid.
also 6 init. "the fulness of the Father's Godhead is
the being of the Son." 5. and Didymus, ἡ πατρικὴ
θεότης. Trin. i. 27, p. 82, and S. Basil, ἐξ οὗ ἔχει
τὸ εἶναι, contr. Eunom. ii. 12, fin. Thus the Father
is the Son's life because the Son is from Him, and
the Son the Father's because the Son is in Him.
All these are but different ways of signifying the
περιχώρησις.

¶ The Second Person in the Holy Trinity is not a
quality, or attribute, or a mere relation, but the One
Eternal Essence; not a part of the First Person, but
whole or entire God, all that God is; nor does the
gennesis impair the Father's Essence, which is already

v 2

whole and entire God. Thus there are two infinite Persons, in Each Other because They are infinite. Each of Them being wholly One and the Same Divine Being, yet not being merely separate aspects of the Same. Each is God as absolutely as if the Other were not. Such a statement indeed is not so much a contradiction in the terms used, as in our conceptions, from the inability of our minds to deal with infinities; yet not therefore a contradiction in fact, unless we would maintain that human words can express in one formula, or human thought can grasp and contemplate, the Incomprehensible, Self-existent First-Cause.

¶ " Man," says S. Cyril, " inasmuch as he had a beginning of being, also has of necessity a beginning of begetting, as what is from him is a thing generate, but . . . if God's substance transcend time, or origin, or interval, His generation too will transcend these; nor does it deprive the Divine Nature of the power of generating that He doth not this in time. For other than human is the manner of divine generation; and together with God's existing is implied His generating, and the Son was in Him by generation; nor did His generation precede His existence, but He was always, and that by generation." Thesaur. v. p. 35.

SPECIAL CHARACTERISTICS OF OUR LORD'S MANHOOD.

1. HIS manhood had no personality, but was taken up into His divinity as Second Person of the Holy Trinity.

That is, according to the words of the *Symbolum S. Athan.*, " Unus, non conversione divinitatis in carnem, sed assumptione humanitatis in Deum." That personality, which our Lord had had from eternity in the Holy Trinity, He had still after His incarnation. His human nature subsisted in His divine, not existing as we exist, but, so to say, grafted on Him, or as a garment in which He was clad. We cannot conceive of an incarnation, except in this way; for, if His manhood had not been thus after the manner of an attribute, if it had been a person, an individual, such as one of us, if it had been in existence before He united it to Himself, He would have been simply two beings under one name, or else, His divinity would have been nothing more than a special grace or presence or participation of divine glory, such as is the prerogative of saints.

He then is one, as He was from eternity,—the same " He" to whom also belong body and soul, and all their powers and affections, as well as the possession of divinity. He it is, God the Son, who was born, who had a mother, who shed His blood, who died and rose again.

His manhood loses the privilege of a personality of its own, in order to gain the special prerogative of belonging to the Second Person of the Divine Trinity, and all for our sake, that He may be the medium of a spiritual union between us and His Father.

¶ This was the question which came into discussion in the Nestorian controversy, when it was formally determined that all that took place in respect to the Eternal Word as man, belonged to His *Person*, and therefore might be predicated of Him; so that it was heretical not to confess the Word's body, (or the body of God in the Person of the Word,) the Word's death, the Word's blood, the Word's exaltation, and the Word's or God's Mother, who was in consequence called θεοτόκος, the tessera on which the controversy mainly turned. "The Godhead," says Athanasius, "dwelt in the flesh bodily; which is all one with saying, that, being God, He had a body proper to Him, (ἴδιον,) and using this as an instrument, ὀργάνῳ, He became man for our sakes; and because of this, things proper to the flesh are said to be His, since He was in it, as hunger, thirst, pain, fatigue, and the like, of which the flesh is capable, δεκτικὴ; while the works proper to the Word Himself, as raising the dead, and restoring sight to the blind, and curing the issue of blood, He did Himself through His body," &c. Orat. iii. 31. vid the whole passage, which is as precise as if it had been written after the Nestorian and Eutychian controversies, though without the technical words then adopted.

2. He took on Him our fallen nature, vid. art. *Flesh*, to which add here from Petavius, "Verbum corpus et

naturam hominis ex eâdem, quæ in corruptelam defluxerat, massâ sibi formare et assumere voluit; tametsi in eâ, unde genitus est Deus, carne Virginis repurgatum illud fuerit." Incarn. v. 14, 6. He says this, quoting Irenæus; and elsewhere quoting Leontius, " Recte Leontius ejusmodi assumpsisse carnem asserit Verbum, qualem habuit Adam post peccatum damnatus, et qualem nos habemus ex eâdem massâ procreati." Incarn. x. 3, 8. Vid. on this subject Perrone de Incarn. part. ii. c. 2. Corrol. iv.

3. His manhood was subject to death, and to the other laws of human nature.

¶ Athanasius, Orat. ii. 66, says that our Lord's body was subject to death; and so elsewhere, " His body, as having a common substance with all men, for it was a human body (though, by a new marvel, it subsisted of the Virgin alone), yet being mortal, died after the common course of the like natures." Incarn. 20, also 8, 18, init. Orat. iii. 56. And so τὸν ἄνθρωπον σαθρωθέντα. Orat. iv. 33. And so S. Leo. in his Tome lays down that in the Incarnation, " suscepta est ab æternitate mortalitas." Ep. xxviii. 3. And S. Austin, " Utique vulnerabile atque mortale corpus habuit" [Christus], contr. Faust. xiv. 2. A Eutychian sect denied this doctrine (the Aphthartodocetæ), and held that our Lord's manhood was naturally indeed corrupt, but became from its union with the Word incorrupt from the moment of conception; and in consequence they held that our Lord did not suffer and die, except by miracle. vid. Leont. c. Nest. ii. (Canis. t. i. pp. 563, 4 8.) vid. supr. art. *Adam*.

¶ It was a point in controversy with the extreme Monophysites, that is, the Eutychians, whether our Lord's body was naturally subject to death, the Catholics maintaining the affirmative, as Athanasius, Orat. i. § 44. Eutyches asserted that our Lord had not a human nature, by which he meant among other things that His manhood was not subject to the *laws* of a body, but so far as He submitted to them, did so by an act of will in each particular case; and this, lest it should seem that He was moved by the πάθη against His will ἀκουσίως ; and consequently that His manhood was not subject to death. But the Catholics maintained that He had voluntarily placed Himself *under* those laws, and died *naturally*, vid. Athan. contr. Apoll. i. 17, and that after the resurrection His body became incorruptible, not according to nature, but by grace. vid. Leont. de Sect. x. p. 530. Anast. Hodeg. c. 23. To express their doctrine of the ὑπερφυὲς of our Lord's manhood, the Eutychians made use of the Catholic expression "ut voluit," vid. Athan. l. c. Eutyches ap. Leon. Ep. 21. "quomodo voluit et scit" twice; vid. also Theod. Eranist. i. p. 10. ii. p. 105. Leont. contr. Nest. i. p. 544. Pseudo-Athan. Serm. adv. Div. Hær. § viii. (t. 2, p. 560.)

4. Yet He suspended those laws, when He pleased.

¶ This, our Lord's either suspense or permission, at His will, of the operations of His manhood, is a great principle in the doctrine of the Incarnation. "That He might give proof of His human nature," says Theophylact, on John xi. 34, "He allowed It to do its own work, and chides It and rebukes It by the

power of the Holy Spirit. The Flesh then, not bearing
the rebuke, is troubled and trembles, and thus gets the
better of Its grief." And S. Cyril: "When grief
began to be stirred in Him, and His sacred flesh was
on the verge of tears, He suffers it not to be affected
freely, as is our custom, but 'He was vehement
(ἐνεβριμήσατο) in the Spirit,' that is, He in some way
chides His own Flesh in the power of the Holy Ghost;
and It, not bearing the movement of the Godhead
united to It, trembles, &c. . . . For this I think is
the meaning of 'troubled Himself.'" fragm. in Joan.
p. 685. "Sensus corporei vigebant sine lege peccati, et
veritas affectionum sub moderamine Deitatis et mentis."
Leon. Ep. 35, 3. "Thou art troubled against thy
will; Christ is troubled, because He willed it. Jesus
hungered, yes, but because He willed it; Jesus slept,
yes, but because He willed it; Jesus sorrowed, yes,
but because He willed it; Jesus died, yes, but because
He willed it. It was in His power to be affected so or
so, or not to be affected." Aug. in Joan. xlix. 18. The
Eutychians perverted this doctrine, as if it implied that
our Lord was not subject to the laws of human nature;
and that He suffered *merely* "by permission of the
Word." Leont. ap. Canis. t. 1, p. 563. In like
manner, Marcion or Manes said that His "flesh appeared from heaven in resemblance, ὡς ἠθέλησεν."
Athan. contr. Apoll. ii. 3.

¶ "To be troubled was proper to the flesh," says
Athan., "but to have power to lay down His life, and
to take it again, when He will, was no property of
men, but of the Word's power. For man dies, not by

his own power, but by necessity of nature and against his will; but the Lord being Himself immortal, but having a mortal flesh, had power, as God, to become separate from the body and to take it again, when He would. Concerning this too speaks David in the Psalm, *Thou shalt not leave My soul in hell, neither shalt Thou suffer Thy Holy One to see corruption.* For it beseemed, that the flesh, corruptible as it was, should no longer after its own nature remain mortal, but, because of the Word who had put it on, should abide incorruptible." Orat. iii. § 57.

¶ This might be taken as an illustration of the "ut voluit," vid. supr. p. 296. And so the expressions in the Evangelists, "Into Thy hands I *commend* My Spirit," "He *bowed the head*," "He *gave up* the ghost," are taken to imply that His death was His free act. vid. Ambros. in loc. Luc. Hieron. in loc. Matt. also Athan. Serm. Maj. de Fid. 4. It is Catholic doctrine that our Lord, as man, submitted to death of His free will, and not as obeying an express command of the Father. "Who," says S. Chrysostom on John x. 18, Hom. 60, 2, "has not power to lay down his own life? for any one who will may kill himself. But He says not this, but how? 'I have power to lay it down in such sense that no one can do it against My will. . I alone have the disposal of My life,' which is not true of us." And still more appositely Theophylact, "It was open to Him not to suffer, not to die; for being without sin, He was not subject to death. . . . If then He had not been willing, He had not been crucified." in Hebr. xii. 2. "Since this punishment is contained in the death of the body, that the soul, because it has deserted God with its will, deserts the body against its will . . . the soul of the Mediator proved how utterly clear of the punishment of sin was its coming to the death of the flesh, in that it did not desert the flesh unwillingly, but because it willed, and when it willed, and as it willed. . . And this did they specially admire, who were present, says the Gospel, that after that work, in which He set forth a figure of our sin, He forthwith gave up the ghost. For crucified men were commonly tortured by a lingering death. . . . But He was a wonder, (miraculo fuit,) because He was found dead." August. de Trin. iv. n. 16.

5. Though His manhood was of created substance, He cannot be called a creature.

¶ Athan. seems to say, Orat. ii. § 45, that it is both true that "The Lord created Me," and yet that the Son was not created. Creatures alone are created, and He was not a creature. Rather something belonging or relating to Him, something short of His substance or nature, was created. However, it is a question in controversy whether even His manhood can be called a creature, though many of the Fathers, (including Athan. in several places,) seems so to call it. The difficulty may be viewed thus: that our Lord, even as to His human nature, is the natural, not the adopted, Son of God, (to deny which is the error of the Adoptionists,) whereas no creature can be His natural and true Son; and again, that His human nature is worshipped, which would be idolatry, if it were a creature. The question is discussed in Petav. de

Incarn. vii. 6, who determines that the human nature, though in itself a created substance, yet viewed as deified in the Word, does not in fact exist as a creature. Vasquez, however, considers that our Lord may be called creature, viewed as man, in 3 Thom. Disp. 66, and also Raynaud Opp. t. 2, p. 84, expressing his opinion strongly. And Berti de Theol. Disc. xxvii. 5, who adds, however, with Suarez after S. Thomas (in 3 Thom. Disput. 35. Opp. t. 16, p. 489,) that it is better to abstain from the use of the term. Of the Fathers, S. Jerome notices the doubt, and decides it in favour of the term: "Since," he says, "Wisdom in the Proverbs of Solomon speaks of Herself as created a beginning of the ways of God, and many through fear lest they should be obliged to call Christ a creature, deny the whole mystery of Christ, and say that not Christ, but the world's wisdom is meant by this Wisdom, we freely declare, that there is no hazard in calling Him creature, whom we confess with all the confidence of our hope to be 'worm,' and 'man,' and 'crucified,' and 'curse.'" In Eph. ii. 10. He is supported by Athan. Orat. ii. § 46. Ep. Æg. 17. Expos. F. 4 (perhaps), Serap. ii. 8, fin. Naz. Orat. 30. 2 fin. 38. 13. Nyss. in Cant. Hom. 13, t. i. p. 663, init. Cyr. Hom. Pasch. 17, p. 233. Max. Mart. t. 2, p. 265. Damasc. F. O. iii. 3. Hil. de Trin. xii. 48. Ambros. Psalm. 118. Serm. 5, 25. August. Ep. 187, n. 8. Leon. Serm. 77, 2. Greg. Mor. v. 63. The principal authority on the other side is S. Epiphanius, who ends his argument with the words, "The Holy Church of God worships not a creature, but the Son, who is begotten, Father in Son," &c. Hær. 69, 36. And S. Proclus too speaks of the child of the Virgin as being "Him who is worshipped, not the creature," Orat. v. fin.

¶ On the whole it would appear, (1.) that if " creature," like " Son," be a *personal* term, then He is not a creature; but if it be a word of (human) *nature*, He is a creature ; (2.) that our Lord is a creature in respect to the flesh (vid. Orat. ii. § 47); (3.) that since the flesh is infinitely beneath His divinity, it is neither natural nor safe to call Him a creature, (according to St. Thomas's example, "non dicimus, quod Æthiops est albus, sed quod est albus secundum dentes"); and (4.) that if the flesh is worshipped, still it is worshipped as in the Person of the Son, not by a separate act of worship. "A creature worship not we," says Athan., "perish the thought . . . but we worship the Lord of creation made flesh, the Word of God ; for though the flesh in itself be a part of creation, yet it has become God's body . . . who so senseless as to say to the Lord, Remove Thyself out of the body, that I may worship Thee ?" ad Adelph. 3. Epiphanius has imitated this passage, Ancor. 51, introducing the illustration of a king and his robe, &c.

¶ And hence Athanasius says, Orat. ii. § 47, that though our Lord's flesh is created, or He is created as to the flesh, it is not right to call Him a creature. This is very much what S. Thomas says above, that " Æthiops, albus secundum dentes," not " est albus." But why may not our Lord be so called upon the principle of the *communicatio Idiomatum,* (vid. infr. p.

367) as He is said to be born of a Virgin, to have suffered, &c.? The reason is this:—birth, passion, &c., confessedly belong to His human nature, without adding "according to the flesh;" but "creature," not implying humanity, might appear a simple attribute of His Person, if used without limitation. Thus, as S. Thomas adds, though we may not absolutely say "Æthiops iste albus," we may say "crispus est," or in like manner, "he is bald;" since "crispus," or "bald," can but refer to the hair. Still more does this remark apply in the case of "Sonship," which is a personal attribute altogether; as is proved, says Petav. de Incarn. vii. 6, fin. by the instance of Adam, who was in all respects a man like Seth, yet not a son. Accordingly, we may not call our Lord, even according to the manhood, an adopted Son.

6. In like manner we cannot call our Lord a servant.

¶ "The assumption of the flesh did not make of the Word a servant," says Athan. Orat. ii. § 14. οὐκ ἐδούλου τὸν λόγον, though, as he said, Orat. ii. § 11, the Word became a servant, as far as He was man. He says the same thing, Ep. Æg. 17. So say Naz. Orat. 32. 18. Nyssen. ad Simpl. (t. 2, p. 471). Cyril. Alex. adv. Theodor. p. 223. Hilar. de Trin. xi. 13, 14. Ambros. 1. Epp. 46, 3. Athan. however seems to modify the statement when he says, Orat. ii. § 50, "Not that He was servant, but because He took a servant's form." Theodoret also denies it, Eran. ii. fin. And Damasc. F. O. iii. 21, who says that our Lord "took on Him an ignorant and servile nature," but "that we may not call Him servant," though "the flesh is servile, had it not been united to God the Word." The parallel question of *ignorance*, here touched upon, has come under our notice already, vid. art. *Ignorance*. The latter view prevailed after the heresy of the Adoptionists, who seem to have made "servant" synonymous with "adopted son." Petavius, Incarn. vii. 9, distinguishes between the essence or (what is called) *actus primus* and the *actus secundus;* thus water may be considered in its *nature* cold, though certain springs are *in fact* always warm.

SPIRIT OF GOD.

THOUGH the Catholic doctrine of the Holy Trinity and the characteristics of the Three Persons have been taught from the first, there have been in the Church certain difficulties in determining what passages of Scripture belong to Each, what are the limits of Their respective offices, and what are the terms under which those offices and the acts of those offices are to be expressed. Thus the word "Spirit," if the Fathers are to be our expositors, sometimes means Almighty God, without distinction of Persons, sometimes the Son, and sometimes and more commonly the Holy Ghost. And, while the Son and Spirit divide, so to speak, the economy and mission of mercy between Them, it is not always clear how the line of division runs, and in what cases there is no assignable line.

It is with a view to remove some portion of this difficulty that Athan. observes, Serap. i. 4—7, that the Holy Ghost is never in Scripture called simply "Spirit" without the addition "of God," or "of the Father," or "from Me," or of the article, or of "Holy," or "The Paraclete," or "of truth," or unless He has been spoken of just before. This rule, however, goes but a little way to remove the difficulty, as it exists in fact. One important class of questions is suggested at once by the Holy Ghost being *another* Paraclete, which implies that that office is common to Him and the Son. It is hence, I suppose, that in St. Paul's words, "ὁ κύριος τὸ πνεῦμά ἐστιν," 2 Cor. iii. 17, Spirit is understood of the Third Divine Person by Origen. c. Cels. vi. 70. Basil de Spir. S. n. 52. Pseudo-Athan. Comm. Ess. 6. But there are more important instances than this. "Spirit" is used more or less distinctly of our Lord's divine nature, whether in itself or as incarnate, in John vi. 64, Rom. i. 4, 1 Cor. xv. 45, 1 Tim. iii. 16, Hebr. ix. 14, 1 Pet. iii. 18, &c. Indeed, the early Fathers speak as if the "Holy Ghost" which came down on Mary might be considered the Word, e.g. Tertullian against the Valentinians, "If the Spirit of God did not descend into the womb *to partake in flesh from the womb*, why did He descend at all?" de Carn. Chr. 19. vid. also ibid. 5 and 14. contr. Prax. 26. Just. Apol. i. 33. Iren. Hær. v. 1. Cypr. Idol. Van. 6. (p. 19, Oxf. Tr.) Lactant. Instit. iv. 12. vid. also Hilar. Trin. ii. 26. Athan. λόγος ἐν τῷ πνεύματι ἔπλαττε τὸ σῶμα. Serap. i. 31, fin. ἐν τῷ λόγῳ ἦν τὸ πνεῦμα. ibid. iii. 6. And more distinctly even as late as S. Maximus, αὐτὸν, ἄντι σπορᾶς συλλαβοῦσα τὸν λόγον, κεκύηκε. t. 2, p. 309. The earliest ecclesiastical authorities are S. Ignatius ad Smyrn. init. and S. Hermas (even though his date were A.D. 150), who also says plainly, "Filius autem Spiritus Sanctus est." Past. iii. 5, n. 5. The same use of "Spirit" for the Word or Godhead of the Word is also found in Tatian. adv. Græc. 7. Athenag. Leg. 10. Theoph. ad Autol. ii. 10. Tertull. Apol. 23. Lact. Inst. iv. 6, 8. Hilar. Trin. ix. 3 and 14. Eustath. apud Theod. Eran. iii. p. 235.

Athan. de Incarn. 22 (if it be Athanasius's), contr. Apol. i. 8. Apollinar. ap. Theod. Eran. i. p. 71, and the Apollinarists passim. Greg. Naz. Ep. 101. ad Cledon. p. 85. Ambros. Incarn. 63. Severian. ap. Theod. Eran. ii. p. 167. Vid. Grot. ad Marc. ii. 8. Bull. Def. F. N. i. 2, § 5. Coustant. Præf. in Hilar. 57, &c. Montfaucon in Athan. Serap. iv. 19.

Phœbadius too, in his remarks on 2nd Confession of Sirmium (the "blasphemia"), supr. vol. i. p. 116 note, in condemning the clause, "Hominem suscepisse per quem *compassus* est," as implying that our Lord's higher nature was not divine, but of the nature of a soul, uses the word "spiritus" in the sense of Hilary and the Ante-Nicene Fathers. "Impassibilis Deus," he says, "quia Deus *Spiritus* . . . non ergo passibilis Dei Spiritus, licet in homine suo passus."

¶ Again, Athan. says that our Lord's Godhead was the immediate anointing or chrism of the manhood He assumed. "God needed not the anointing, nor was the anointing made without God; but God both applied it, and also received it in that body which was capable of it." in Apollin. ii. 3. and τὸ χρῖσμα ἐγὼ ὁ λόγος, τὸ δὲ χρισθὲν ὑπ' ἐμοῦ ὁ ἄνθρωπος. Orat. iv. § 36. vid. Origen. Periarch. ii. 6. n. 4. And S. Greg. Naz. still more expressly, and from the same text as Athan., "The Father anointed Him 'with the oil of gladness above His fellows,' *anointing the manhood with the Godhead.*" Orat. 10. fin. Again, "This [the Godhead] is the anointing of the manhood, not sanctifying by an energy as the other Christs [anointed ones], but by a presence of that Whole who anointed, ὅλου τοῦ χρίοντος;

whence it came to pass that what anointed was called man, and what was anointed was made God." Orat. 30. 20. " He Himself anointed Himself; anointing as God the body with his Godhead, and anointed as man." Damasc. F. O. iii. 3. "Dei Filius, sicut pluvia in vellus, toto divinitatis unguento nostram se fudit in carnem." Chrysolog. Serm. 60. It is more common, however, to consider that the anointing was the descent of the Spirit, as Athan. says, Orat. i. § 47, according to Luke iv. 18. Acts x. 38.

¶ Again, in explaining Matt. xii. 32, "Quicunque dixerit verbum contra Filium," &c., he considers our Lord to contrast the Holy Ghost with His own humanity, vid. Orat. i. § 50, but he gives other expositions in Serap. iv. 6, vid. supr. art. *Scripture Passages*, No. 11.

¶ "The Spirit is God's gift," says Athan., θεοῦ δῶρον, Orat. ii. § 18. And so S. Basil, δῶρον τοῦ θεοῦ τὸ πνεῦμα. de Sp. S. 57, and more frequently the later Latins, as in the Hymn, "Altissimi Donum Dei;" also the earlier, e.g. Hil. de Trin. ii. 29, and August. Trin. xv. n. 29, who makes it a personal characteristic of the Third Person in the Holy Trinity: "non dicitur Verbum Dei, nisi Filius, nec Donum Dei, nisi Spiritus Sanctus." And elsewhere, "Exiit, non quomodo natus, sed quomodo datus, et ideo non dicitur Filius." ibid. v. 15, making it, as Petavius observes, His eternal property, "ut sic procedat, tanquam *donabile*," as being Love. Trin. vii. 13, § 20.

¶ It was an expedient of the Macedonians to deny that the Holy Spirit was God because it was not usual

w 2

to call Him Ingenerate; and perhaps to their form of heresy, which was always implied in Arianism, and which began to show itself formally among the Semi-Arians ten years later, the Sirmian anathematism may be traced: "Whoso speaking of the Holy Ghost as Paraclete, shall speak of the Ingenerate God," &c., supr. vol. i. p. 113. They asked the Catholics whether the Holy Spirit was *Ingenerate, generate,* or *created,* for into these three they divided all things. vid. Basil. in Sabell. et Ar. Hom. xxiv. 6. But, as the Arians had first made the alternative only between *Ingenerate* and *created,* and Athan. de Decr. § 28, supr. vol. i. p. 50, shows that *generate* is a third idea really distinct from one and the other, so S. Greg. Naz. adds *proceeding,* ἐκπορευτὸν, as an intermediate idea, contrasted with *Ingenerate,* yet distinct from *generate.* Orat. xxxi. 8. In other words, *Ingenerate* means, not only *not generate,* but *not from any origin.* vid. August. de Trin. xv. n. 47, 8.

¶ "If the Word be not from God," says Athan., "reasonably might they deny Him to be Son; but if He is from God, how see they not that what exists from any, is the son of that from whom it is?" Orat. iv. § 15. In consequence it is a very difficult question in theology, why the Holy Spirit is not called a " Son,' and His procession " generation." This was an objection of the Arians, vid. ad Serap. i. 15—17, and Athan. only answers it by denying that we may speculate. Other writers apply, as in other cases, the theological language of the Church to a solution of this question. It is carefully discussed in Petav. Trin. vii. 13, 14.

¶ As the Arians objected, Orat. i. § 14, that the

First and Second Persons of the Holy Trinity ought to be considered brothers, ἀδελφοὶ, so, in the course of the controversy, did they say the same as to the Second and Third. vid. Serap. i. § 15. iv. 2.

¶ "Is the Holy Spirit one," says Athan., "and the Paraclete another, and the Paraclete the later, as not mentioned in the Old Testament?" Orat. iv. § 29. A heresy of this kind is actually noticed by Origen, viz. of those "qui Spiritum Sanctum alium quidem dicant esse qui fuit in Prophetis, alium autem qui fuit in Apostolis Domini nostri Jesu Christi." In Tit. t. 4, p. 695. Hence in the Creed, "who spake by the prophets;" and hence the frequent epithet given by S. Justin to the Holy Spirit of προφητικόν; e.g. when speaking of baptism, Apol. i. 61, fin. Also Ap. i. 6, 13. Tryph. 49. On the other hand, he calls the Spirit of the Prophets "the Holy Spirit," e.g. Tryph. 54, 61. Vid. supr. art. *Coinherence.*

THEOGNOSTUS.

THEOGNOSTUS was Master of the Catechetical school of Alexandria towards the end of the 3rd century, being a scholar, or at least a follower, of Origen. He is quoted by Athanasius, as being one of those theologians who, before the Council of Nicæa, taught that the οὐσία of the Son was not created, but from the οὐσία of the Father. Athan. calls him a "learned man," Decr. § 25, and "the admirable and excellent," Serap. iv. 9. His seven books of Hypotyposes treated of the Holy Trinity, of angels, and evil spirits, of the Incarnation, and the Creation. Photius, who gives this account, Cod. 106, accuses him of heterodoxy on these points; which Athanasius in a measure admits, as far as the wording of his treatise went, speaking of his "investigating by way of exercise." Eusebius does not mention him at all.

TRADITION.

"SEE," says Athanasius, "we are proving that this view has been transmitted from Fathers to Fathers; but ye, O modern Jews and disciples of Caiaphas, whom can ye assign as Fathers to your phrases? Not one of the understanding and wise, (for all abhor you,) but the devil alone; none but he is your father in this apostasy, who both in the beginning scattered on you the seed of this irreligion, and now persuades you to slander the Ecumenical Council for committing to writing, not your doctrines, but that which 'from the beginning those who were eye-witnesses and ministers of the Word' have handed down to us. For the faith which the Council has confessed in writing, that is the faith of the Catholic Church; to assert this, the blessed Fathers so expressed themselves while condemning the Arian heresy; and this is a chief reason why these men apply themselves to calumniate the Council. For it is not the terms which trouble them, but that those terms prove them to be heretics, and presumptuous beyond other heresies." Decr. § 27.

¶ Elsewhere he speaks of the Arians "forcing on the divine oracles a misinterpretation according to their own private sense," Orat. i. § 37, and cries out, "Who heard in his first catechisings that God had a Son, without understanding it in our sense? who, on the rise of this odious heresy, was not at once startled at what he heard as being strange to him?" Orat. ii. § 34.

For parallel passages from Athan. and many others, vid. arts.on *Definitions, Heretics, Private Judgment, Rule of Faith*, and *Scripture*. From these it would appear that the two main sources of Revelation are Scripture and Tradition; that these constitute one Rule of Faith, and that, sometimes as a composite rule, sometimes as a double and co-ordinate, sometimes as an alternative, under the *magisterium*, of course, of the Church,.and without an appeal to the private judgment of individuals.

These articles, too, effectually refute the hypothesis of some Protestants, who, to destroy the force of the evidence in favour of our doctrine of Tradition, wish to maintain that by Tradition then was commonly meant Scripture; and that when the Fathers speak of "Evangelical Tradition" they mean the Gospels, and when they speak of "Apostolical" they mean the Epistles. This will not hold, and it may be right, perhaps, here to refer to several passages in illustration.

For instance, Irenæus says, "Polycarp, . . whom we have seen in our first youth, . . was taught those lessons which he learned from the Apostles, *which the Church also transmits*, which alone are true. All the Churches of Asia *bear witness* to them; and the *successors* of Polycarp, down to this day, who is a much more trustworthy and sure *witness* of truth than Valentinus," &c. Hær. iii. 3, § 4. Here is not a word about Scripture, not a hint that by "transmission" and "succession" Scripture is meant. And so Irenæus continues, contrasting "Traditio quæ est ab Apostolis" with Scripture: "Neque Scripturis neque Traditioni consentire;" "Apostolicam Ecclesiæ Traditionem;" "veterem Apostolorum Traditionem." Again, Theodoret says that the word θεοτόκος was used, κατὰ τὴν ἀποστολικὴν παράδοσιν; and no one would say that θεοτόκος was in Scripture. Hær. iv. 12. And S. Basil contrasts τὰ ἐκ τῆς ἐγγράφου διδασκαλίας with τὰ ἐκ τῆς τῶν ἀποστόλων παραδόσεως, de Sp. S. n. 66. Presently he speaks of οὔτε τῆς θεοπνεύστου γραφῆς, οὔτε τῶν ἀποστολικῶν παραδόσεων. n. 77. Origen speaks of a dogma, οὔτε παραδιδόμενον ὑπὸ τῶν ἀποστόλων, οὔτε ἐμφαινόμενόν που τῶν γραφῶν. Tom. in Matth. xiii. 1. Vid. also in Tit. t. 4, p. 696, and Periarchon. præf. 2, and Euseb. Hist. v. 23. So in S. Athanasius (de Synod. 21, fin.) we read of "the Apostolical Tradition and teaching which is acknowledged by all;" and soon after, of a believing conformably τῇ εὐαγγελικῇ καὶ ἀποστολικῇ παραδόσει." § 23, init. where παράδοσις means *doctrine*, not *books*, for the Greek would run τῇ εὐαγγ. καὶ τῇ ἀποστ. were the Gospels and Epistles intended. (Thus S. Leo, "secundum evangelicam apostolicamque *doctrinam*," Ep. 124, 1.) And he makes ἡ εὐαγγελικὴ παράδοσις and ἡ ἐκκλησιαστικὴ παρ. synonymous. Cf. Athan. contr. Apoll. i. 22, with ad Adelph. 2, init. In like manner, Neander speaks of two kinds of so-called Apostolical Traditions, doctrinal and ecclesiastical, Eccl. Hist. vol. ii. p. 333, transl. And Le Moyne considers the Apostolical Tradition of S. Hippolytus to be what S. Irenæus means by it, doctrine, as distinct from Scripture. Var. Sacr. t. 2, p. 1062. Vid.

also Pearson, Vindic. Ignat. i. 4, circ. fin. In like manner, S. Augustine contrasts Apostolical Tradition with writings, de Bapt. contr. Don. ii. 7, v. 23, and he calls Infant Baptism an Apostolical Tradition. De Peccat. Mer. i. 26. And S. Cyprian speaks of, not only wine, but the mixed Cup in the Holy Eucharist, as an "Evangelical truth" and "tradition of the Lord." Epist. 63. 14, 15.

Some instances indeed may be found in the Fathers of Scripture considered as a kind of Tradition, which it is: but these do not serve to make an unnatural (or rather an impossible) interpretation imperative in the case of such passages as the above. *E.g.* Athan. says, "The Apostolical Tradition teaches, blessed Peter saying, &c., and Paul writing," &c. Adelph. 6. Suicer refers to Greg. Nys. de Virg. xi. fin. Cyril in Is. lxvi. 5, p. 909. Balsamon, ad Can. vi. Nic. 2, Cyprian, Ep. 74, &c.

THE HOLY TRINITY IN UNITY.

WHEN the Church speaks of Three Persons in One Divine Essence, it seems at first sight that she must imply and mean, if she would avoid contradiction of ideas, either that the "Three" or that the "One" expresses an abstraction of our minds.

If God is numerically one, if the Divine Essence is undivided and simple in that strict sense in which we speak of each man as an individual, then the term Person must surely denote nothing more than some aspect, character, office, or assemblage of attributes, which belongs to the Almighty, as when our Lord is spoken of as Prophet, Priest, and King, which are mere titles or appellatives, not existing *re* but *ratione*. But this is Sabellianism.

On the other hand, we may consider the Three Persons actually to exist, not being mere ideas or modes of our viewing God, but as realities, intrinsically distinct from each other, separate and complete one by one, *re* as well as *ratione*, Persons as we men are persons, or at least in some analogous way. In that case we should go on to consider, as a necessary inference, that "One" expressed only a logical unity, *Ens unum in multis*, a nature or class, as when we say "*Man* is mortal;" but this conclusion brings us either to Arianism or to Tritheism.

There is no incompatibility of ideas involved in the doctrine of Sabellian, Arian, or Tritheist, that is, no mystery; but the Catholic believes and holds as an article of faith that the Divine Three, and again the Divine One, both as One and as Three, exist *re* not *ratione;* and therefore he has to answer the objection, " Either the word 'Trinity' denotes a mere abstraction, or the word ' Unity' does ; for how can it be at once a fact that Each of Three, who are eternally distinct one from another, is really God, and also a fact that there .really is but one God ? " This however is the doctrine of the creed of S. Athanasius, and certainly is to be received and held by every faithful member of the Church, viz., that the Father is God and all that God is, and so too is the Son, and so too is the Holy Ghost, yet there is but one God; that the word God may be predicated of an objective Triad, yet also belong to only One Being, to a Being individual and sole, all-perfect, self-existent, and everlasting.

To state this in the language of Petavius, who is the most learned expositor of the doctrine of the Fathers as distinct from the medieval Church, "Non omittendum Personas Tres, etsi invicem *reapse* distant, *re* tamen *idem* esse cum essentia, et ab eâ *non nisi ratione* discrepare." de Trin. iii. 11, 7. It is a Three or Triad, Each of whom is intrinsically and everlastingly distinct from Each, (as Prophet, Priest, and King are *not,* but as Priest and his people, King and his sub-jects, Teacher and taught *are,*) yet Each is One and the Same individual Divine Essence.

Let it be observed the mystery lies, not·in any one

of the statements which constitute the doctrine, but in their combination. The meaning of each proposition is on a level with our understanding. There is no intellectual difficulty in apprehending any one of them. "God is a Father; God is a Son; God is a Holy Spirit; the Father is not the Son; the Son is not the Holy Ghost; the Holy Ghost is not the Father; God is numerically One; there are not Three Gods." In which of these propositions do we not sufficiently understand what is meant to be told us? For devotion, then (and for devotion we may conceive these high truths to be revealed to us), the mystery is no difficulty; such understanding of its separate constituent propositions as we have is sufficient for devotion, which lives and thrives upon single objects rather than on a collection.

The difficulty then is not in understanding each sentence of which the doctrine consists, but in its incompatibility (taken as a whole, and in the only words possible for conveying it to our minds) with certain of our axioms of thought indisputable in themselves, but foreign and inapplicable to a sphere of existences of which we have no experience whatever.

What in fact do we know of pure spirit? What do we know of the infinite? Of the latter just a little, by means of mathematical science, that is, under the conditions of number, quantity, space, distance, direction, and shape; just enough to tell us how little we know, and how little we are able to draw arguments and inferences when infinites are in question. Mathematical science tells us that one and one infinite do not, put together, make two; that there may be innumerable infinites, and that all put together are not greater than one of them; that there are orders of infinites. It is plain we are utterly unable to determine what is possible and what is impossible in this high region of realities. And then again, in the case of infinitesimals, do not three lines become one line when one is placed upon another? yet how can we say, supposing them respectively coloured white, red, and blue, that they would not remain three, after they had coalesced into one, as entirely as they were really three before?

Nor in its doctrine of infinites only, does mathematical science illustrate the mysteries of Theology. Geometry, for instance, may be used to a certain point as an exponent of algebraical truth; but it would be irrational to deny the wider revelations of algebra, because they do not admit of a geometrical expression. The fourth power of a quantity may be received as a fact, though a fourth dimension in space is inconceivable. Again, a polygon or an ellipse is a figure different in kind from a circle; yet we may tend towards a conception of the latter by using what we know of either of the former. Thus it is by economical expedients that we teach and transmit the mysteries of religion, separating them into parts, viewing them in aspects, adumbrating them by analogies, and so approximating to them by means of words which say too much or too little. And if we consent to such ways of thought in our scientific treatment of "earthly things," is it wonderful that we should be forced to them in our investigation of "heavenly"?

¶ "You have the Son, you have the Father; fear not

duality. . . . . There is One God, because Father is
One, and Son· is God, having identity as Son towards
Father. . . . . The Father is the whole fulness of Godhead as Father, and the Son is the whole fulness of
Godhead as Son. . . . . The Father has Being perfect
and without defect, being root and fount of the Son
and the Spirit; and the Son is in the fulness of Godhead, a Living Word and Offspring of the Father
without defect. And the Spirit is full of the Son, not
being part of another, but whole in Himself. . . Let us
understand that the Face (nature εἶδος) is One of
Three truly subsisting, beginning in Father, beaming
in Son, and manifested through Spirit." Pseudo-Ath.
c. Sab. Greg. 5—12. "I hardly arrive at contemplating the One, when I am encircled with the radiance
of the Three ; I hardly arrive at distinguishing the
Three, when I am carried back to the One. When I
have imaged to myself One of the Three, I think It the
whole, and my sight is filled, and what is more escapes
me. . . . And when I embrace the Three in my contemplation, I see but One Luminary, being unable to distinguish or to measure the Light which becomes
One." Greg. Naz. Orat. 40. 41. "The fulness of Godhead is in the Father, and the fulness of Godhead
is in the Son, yet not differing, but one Godhead.
. . . . If of all believers there was one soul and one
heart, ... if every one who cleaves to the Lord
is one spirit, ... if man and wife are one flesh, if
all of us men in respect of nature are of one substance,
if Scripture thus speaks of human things, that many
are one, of which there can be no comparison with

things divine, how much more are Father and Son
one in Godhead, where there is no difference of substance or of will," &c. Ambros. de Fid. i. n. 18.
"This Trinity is of one and the same nature and substance, not less in Each than in All, nor greater in
All than in Each; but so great in Father alone or in
Son alone, as in Father and Son together . . . . For
the Father did not lessen Himself to have a Son for
Himself, but so begat of Himself another Self, as to
remain whole in Himself, and to be in the Son as great
as He is by Himself. And so the Holy Ghost, whole
from whole, doth not precede That whence He proceeds, but is as great with Him as He is from Him,
and neither lessens Him by proceeding nor increases
by adhering. . . . . Moreover, He who hath given to
so many hearts of His faithful to be one heart, how
much more doth He maintain in Himself that these
Three and Each of Them should be God, and yet all
together, not Three Gods, but One God?" August.
Ep. 170, 5.

¶ It is no inconsistency to say that the Father is first,
and the Son first also, for comparison or number is not
equal to the expression of this mystery. Since Each is
ὅλος θεὸς, Each, as contemplated by our finite reason,
at the moment of contemplation excludes the Other.
Though we profess Three Persons, Person cannot be
made one abstract *idea*, certainly not as containing
under it three individual subjects, but it is a *term* applied
to the One God in three ways. It is the doctrine of the
Fathers, that, though we use words expressive of a
Trinity, yet that God is beyond our numbering, and that

Father, Son, and Holy Ghost, though eternally distinct from each other, can scarcely be viewed together in common, except as *One* substance, as if they could not be generalised into Three Any-whatever; and as if it were, strictly speaking, incorrect to speak of *a* Person, or otherwise than of *the* Person, whether of Father, or of Son, or of Spirit. The question has almost been admitted by S. Austin, whether it is not possible to say that God is *One* Person (Trin. vii. 8), for He is wholly and entirely Father, and at the same time wholly and entirely Son, and wholly and entirely Holy Ghost. Vid. also Orat. iv. § 1 and 2, where Athan. argues against the Sabellian hypothesis as making the Divine Nature compound (the Word being a something in It), whereas the Catholic doctrine preserves unity because the Father is the One God simply and entirely, and the Son the One God simply and entirely (vid. next paragraph); the Word not a sound, he says, which is nothing, nor a quality which is unworthy of God, but a substantial Word and a substantial Wisdom. " As," he continues, " the Origin is One substance, so Its Word and Wisdom is One, substantial and subsistent; for as from God is God, and from Wise Wisdom, and from Rational (λογικοῦ) a Word, and from Father a Son, so from a subsistence is He subsistent, and from substance substantial and substantive, and from existing existent," &c. Vid. art. *Coinherence.*

¶ Nothing is more remarkable than the confident tone in which Athan. accuses Arians, as in Orat. ii. § 38, and Sabellians, Orat. iv. § 2, of considering the Divine Nature as compound, as if the Catholics were in no respect open to such a charge. Nor are they;

though in avoiding it, they are led to enunciate the most profound and ineffable mystery. vid. supr. art. *Son of God.* The Father is the One Simple Entire Divine Being, and so is the Son. They do in no sense share divinity between Them; Each is ὅλος Θεός. This is not ditheism or tritheism, for They are the same God; nor is it Sabellianism, for They are eternally distinct and substantive Persons; but it is a depth and height beyond our intellect, how what is Two in so full a sense can also in so full a sense be One, or how the Divine Nature does not come under number in the sense in which we have earthly experience of numbers. Thus, "being incomposite in nature," says Athan., "He is Father of One Only Son," Decr. § 11. In truth the distinction into Persons, as Petavius remarks, "avails especially towards the unity and simplicity of God," vid. de Deo ii. 4, 8.

¶ "The Father," says Athan., "having given all things to the Son, in the Son still hath all things; and the Son having, still the Father hath them; for the Son's Godhead is the Father's Godhead, and thus the Father in the Son takes the oversight of all things." Orat. iii. 36. Thus iteration is not duplication in respect to God; though *how* this is, is the inscrutable Mystery of the Trinity in Unity. Nothing can be named |which the Son is in Himself, as distinct from the Father; but we are told His relation towards the Father; and distinct from and beyond that relation, He is but the One God, who is also the Father. Such statements are not here intended to explain, but to bring home to the mind *what* it is which faith receives. We say, "Father, Son, and Spirit," a transcendent Three, but when we would abstract a general idea of Them in order to number Them as we number things on earth, our abstraction really does but carry us back to the One Substance. There will be different ways of expressing this, but such seems the meaning of such passages as the following: "Those who taunt us with tritheism," says St. Basil, "must be told that we confess One God not in number, but in nature. For what is one in number is not really one, nor single in nature; for instance, we call the world one in number, but not one in nature, for we divide it into its elements; and man again is one in number, but compounded of body and soul. . . . If then we say that God is in nature one, how do they impute number to us, who altogether banish it from that blessed and spiritual nature? For number belongs to quantity, and number is connected with matter," &c. Basil. Ep. 8, 2. "That which saveth us, is faith, but number has been devised to indicate quantity . . . . We pronounce Each of the Persons once, but when we would number them up, we do not proceed by an unlearned numeration to the notion of a polytheism." (vid. the whole passage,) ibid. de Sp. S. c. 18. "Why, passing by the First Cause, does he [S. John] at once discourse to us of the Second? We will decline to speak of 'first' and 'second;' for the Godhead is higher than number and succession of times." Chrysost. in Joan. Hom. ii. 3 fin. "In respect of the Adorable and most Royal Trinity, 'first' and 'second' have no place; for the Godhead is higher than number and times." Isid. Pel. Ep. 3, 18.

x 2

"He calls," says S. Maximus, commenting on Pseudo-
Dionysius, "fecundity, the Father's incomprehensible
progression to the production of the Son and the Holy
Ghost; and suitably does he say, '*as* a Trinity,' since
not number, but glory is expressed in 'The Lord God
is one Lord.'" in Dionys. Opp. t. 2, p. 101. "We do
not understand 'one' in the Divine Substance, as in
the creatures; in whom what is properly one is not to
be seen; for what is one in number, as in our case, is
not properly one. . . . It is not one in number, or as the
beginning of number, any more than It is as magnitude,
or as the beginning of magnitude. . . . That One is
ineffable and indescribable; since It is Itself the cause
of all that is one, πάσης ἑνάδος ἑνοποιόν." Eulog. ap.
Phot. 230, p. 864. "Three what? I answer, Father
and Son and Holy Ghost. See, he urges, you have
said Three; but explain Three what? Nay, do you
number, for I have said all about the Three, when I
say, Father and Son and Holy Ghost. Not, as there
are two men, so are They two Gods; for there is here
something ineffable, which cannot be put into words,
viz., that there should both be number, and not
number. For see if there does not seem to be number,
Father and Son and Holy Spirit, a Trinity. If Three,
Three what? number fails. Then God neither is
without number, nor is under number. . . . They
imply number, only relatively to Each Other, not in
Themselves." August. in Joan. 39, 3 and 4. "We
say Three 'Persons,' as many Latins of authority have
said in treating the subject, because they found no
more suitable way of declaring an idea in words which

they had without words. Since the Father is not the Son, and the Son not the Father, and the Holy Ghost neither Father nor Son, there are certainly Three; but when we ask, Three what? we feel the great poverty of human language. However, we say Three 'Persons,' not for the sake of saying that, but of not saying nothing." Aug. de Trin. v. 10. "Unity is not number, but is itself the principle of all things." Ambros. de Fid. i. n. 19. "That is truly one, in which there is no number, nothing in It beyond That which is. . . . There is no diversity in It, no plurality from diversity, no multitude from accidents, and therefore no number . . . . but unity only. For when God is thrice repeated, and Father, Son, and Holy Ghost is named, three Unities do not make plurality of number in That which They are (in eo quod ipsæ sunt).* . . . This repetition of Unities is iteration rather than numeration. . . . A trine numeration does not make number, which they rather run into who make some difference between the Three." Boeth. Trin. unus Deus, p. 959.

¶ The last remark is also found in Naz. Orat. 31. 18. Many of these passages are taken from Thomassin de Trin. 17. Petavius, de Trin. iv. 16, fin., quotes St. Anselm as saying, "Though there be not many eternities, yet, if we say eternity in eternity, there is but one eternity. And so whatever is said of God's essence, if returned into itself, does not increase quantity, nor admit number; since there is nothing out of God, when God is born of God." Infinity does not add to infinity; the treatment of infinities is above us. With this remark I end as I began.

---

* The words from Boethius here translated "in Him which They

UNITY OF EMMANUEL.

It is well known that the illustration in the Athan. Creed, "As the reasonable soul and flesh is one man, so God and man is one Christ," was taken by the Monophysites to imply that the Divine Nature was made dependent on the flesh, and was influenced and circumscribed by it. Man is partly soul and partly body; he is *of* body and soul, not body and soul; but Christ is wholly God, and wholly man, ὅλος Θεὸς, ὅλος ἄνθρωπος, Orat. iv. 35. He is as simply God as if He were not man, as simply man as if He were not God; "unus atque idem est," says S. Leo, "et totus hominis filius propter carnem, et totus Dei filius propter unam cum Patre deitatem," Ep. 165, 8. Athan. has anticipated the heresy which denied this doctrine in a very distinct passage written apparently even before the rise of Arianism. "It is the function of the soul," he says, "to contemplate in its thoughts what is within its own body; but not to operate in things beyond its own body, or to act by its presence on what is far from the body. Certainly man at a distance never moves or transposes such things; nor could a man sit at home and think of things in heaven, and thereby move the sun, or turn the heaven round. . . . Not thus is the

---

are," are in the original (p. 273, Ed. Lugd., and p. 1122, Ed. Basil.), "in eo quod ipsæ sunt," that is, rather, "in That which They are."

Word of God in man's nature; for He was not bound up with the body (συνεδέδετο), but rather He hath Himself dominion over it, so that He was not in it only, but in all things; nay, He was external to the whole universe and in the sole Father," Incarn. V. D. 17. The same passage occurs in Serm. Maj. de Fid. 11.

It could not be otherwise. The Divine Word was not a mere presence or manifestation of God in man, but He was God Himself incarnate. He was still what He had ever been, and will be from first to last, One,—one and the same, impassible, immutable, in His αὐτότης, so to speak, as being one of the Eternal Trinity. His Divine Nature carried with It on His incarnation that αὐτότης or Personality. So necessary, so cardinal is this truth for the right holding of the great doctrine under consideration, that the Alexandrians, St. Cyril at least, and perhaps St. Athanasius, spoke of there being only "One Nature" in the Incarnate Lord, meaning thereby one Person (for Person and Nature could not be divided; and, if our Lord's Nature was divine, His Person was divine also), and by saying "only one," was meant that, in comparison of the Divine Person who had taken flesh, what He had taken was not so much a nature, (though it was strictly a nature,) as the substance of a manhood which was not substantive.

Whereas the Apostle says, "One Lord Jesus Christ," that unity does not lie in the unity of two natures, (for they are two, not one,) but in His Person, which brings the two natures together, which is and ever has been indivisible from His Divine Nature, and has absorbed into Itself, and is sovereign over, not destroying thereby, but perpetuating, Its human nature.

¶ Hence, while it be true to say "Man is God," as well as to say "God is man," it is not true that "man became God," or "took on him divinity," as it is true to say "God became man," because from first to last the Son and Word is supreme, independent, and one and the same; and it is a first point in all orthodox teaching of the Incarnation to make this clear and definite. He is "Jesus Christ," indeed, but at the same time, "heri, et hodie, ipse et in sæcula;" He is now, and He was from everlasting.

¶ "While He received no hurt (οὐδὲν ἐβλάπτετο) Himself by bearing our sins in His body on the tree, we men were redeemed from our affections (παθῶν)," Orat. iii. § 31. And so ἐβλάπτετο μὲν αὐτὸς οὐδὲν, Incarn. § 54, μὴ βλαπτόμενος, ibid. § 34. In these passages αὐτὸς means "in that which is Himself," i.e., in His own Person or Divine Self, αὐτὸς being used when the next century would have used "Person." "For the sun, too, which He made, and we see, makes its circuit in the sky and is not defiled by touching," &c., Incarn. § 17. "As the rays of sun-light would not suffer at all, though filling all things and touching bodies dead and unclean, thus and much more the spiritual virtue of God the Word would suffer nothing in substance nor receive hurt," &c., Euseb. de Laud. Const. p. 536 and 538; also Dem. Evang. vii. p. 348. "The insults of the passion even the Godhead bore, but the passion His flesh alone felt; as we rightly say that a sunbeam or a body of flame can be cut indeed by a sword but not divided. . . . . I will speak yet more plainly: the Godhead [divinitas] was fixed with nails, but could not Itself be pierced, since the flesh was exposed and offered room for the wound, but God remained invisible," &c., Vigil. contr. Eutych. ii. 9, p. 503 (Bibl. Patrum, ed. 1624). "There were five together on the Cross, when Christ was nailed to it: the sun-light, which first received the nails and the spear, and remained undivided from the Cross and unhurt by the nails, next," &c., Anast. Hodeg. c. 12, p. 220 (ed. 1606); also p. 222; vid. also the beautiful passage in Pseudo-Basil: "God in flesh, not working with aught intervening as in the prophets, but having taken to Him a manhood con-natural with Himself (συμφυῆ, i.e. joined to His nature), and made one, and, through His flesh akin to us, drawing up to Him all humanity, ... What was the manner of the Godhead in flesh? as fire in iron, not transitively, but by communication. For the fire does not dart into the iron, but remains there and communicates to it of its own virtue, not impaired by the communication, yet filling wholly its recipient." Basil, t. 2, p. 596, ed. Ben. Also Ruffin. on Symb. 12; Cyril, *Quod unus*, t. v. p. 776 ; Dam. F.O., iii. 6 fin.; Aug. Serm. 7, p. 26, ed. 1842, Suppl. It is to show at once the intimacy of the union of natures and the absolute sovereignty of the divine, that such strong expressions are in use as God's body, God's death, God's mother, &c.

¶ θεοῦ ἦν σῶμα, Orat. iii. § 31; also ad Adelph. 3 ad Max. 2, and so τὴν πτωχεύσασαν φύσιν θεοῦ ὅλην γενομένην, c. Apoll. ii. 11. τὸ πάθος τοῦ λόγου, ibid. 16, σὰρξ τοῦ λόγου, Orat. iii. 34. σῶμα σοφίας, 53, also θεὸς

ἐν σαρκὶ, Orat. ii. § 10 ; θεὸς ἐν σώματι, ii. § 12 and 15 ;
λόγος ἐν σαρκὶ, iii. 54 ; λόγος ἐν σώματι, Sent. D. 8 fin.
πάθος Χριστοῦ τοῦ θεοῦ μου, Ignat. Rom. 6. ὁ θεὸς
πέπονθεν, Melit. ap. Anast. Hodeg. 12. Dei passiones,
Tertull. de Carn. Christ. 5. Dei interemptores, ibid.
caro Deitatis, Leon. Serm. 65 fin. Deus mortuus et
sepultus, Virgil. c. Eut. ii. p. 502. Vid. supr. p. 294.
Yet Athan. objects to the phrase, " God suffered in the
flesh," i.e. as used by the Apollinarians. Vid. contr.
Apoll. ii. 13 fin. Vid. article μία φύσις.

VAPOUR.

Vid. art. ἀπορρυή.

TWO WILLS IN CHRIST.

THE Monothelite tenet does not come into the range of subjects included in the foregoing Treatises; but as far as I understand it, it argued as follows :—
It was faulty in considering that no distinction was to be drawn between the physical and psychical emotions and volitions which belong to our nature, and which are not sinful, (such as the horror of death,) and those two acts of will, good and bad, which proceed from deliberate purpose and determination, and, as in the case in question, are of an ethical character. The Monothelites held mere volition to be an act of will, and to have the nature of sin, or at least to be inconsistent with that moral perfection which is possible to human nature, and was realised in our Lord. It follows that He could not have among His special constituents as man one which was of so dubious a complexion; in other words, He had no human will, and therefore He had but one will, viz., that which He had by being God.

Such a resolution of the true doctrine led by a few steps to Eutychianism, that is, to a confusion of the received teaching on the Incarnation, and was seen to be dangerous when it came before the Schools and Councils of the Church, but till then it serves as an

instance of the verbal mistakes into which the clearest
and most saintly intellects may fall by living a little too
early to have the experience necessary for a judgment
on dogmatic questions.   Athanasius says:—

"And as to His saying, *If it be possible, let the cup
pass,* observe how, though He thus spake, He rebuked
Peter, saying, *Thou savourest not the things that be of
God, but those that be of men.*   For He willed what
He deprecated, for therefore had He come; but His
was the willing, (since for it He came,) but the terror.be-
longed to the flesh.   Wherefore as man He utters this
speech also, and yet both were said by the Same, to
show that He was God, willing in Himself, but when
He had become man, having a flesh that was in terror.
For the sake of this flesh He combined His own will
with human weakness, that destroying this affection He
might in turn make man undaunted in the thought of
death." Orat. iii. § 57.

¶ Several centuries later Anastasius says:—"I
say not, perish the thought, that there are two wills
in Christ at variance with each other, as you consider,
and in opposition; nor at all a will of flesh, or of
passion, or evil. . . But, since it was perfect man
that He took on Him, that He might save him whole,
and He is perfect in manhood, therefore we call that
sovereign disposal of His orders and commands by the
name of the Divine will in Christ, and we understand
by human will the intellectual soul's power of willing,
given it after the image and likeness of God, and
breathed into it by God, when it was made, by means
of this power to prefer and to obey, and to do the

divine will and the divine orders. If then the soul
of Christ was destitute of the power of reason,
will, and preference, it is not indeed after the image
of God, nor consubstantial with our souls . . . . and
Christ cannot be called perfect in manhood. Christ
then, being in the form of God, has, according to the
Godhead, that lordly will which is common to Father
and Holy Ghost; and, as having taken the form of a
servant, He does also the will of His intellectual and
immaculate soul, &c. . . . . Else if this will be taken
away, He will according to the Godhead be subject,
and fulfil the Father's will as a servant . . . . as if there
were two wills in the Godhead of Father and of Son,
the Father's that of a Lord, the Son's that of a servant."
Anast. Hodeg. i. p. 12.

WISDOM.

¶ ATHAN. considers that the Eternal Wisdom, one of the proper appellatives of the Son, is that Wisdom which in Prov. ix. 1, viii. 22, &c., is said to be created, and that this creation is to be understood of His taking on Him a created nature.　He says, " *Wisdom has made herself a house;* it is plain that our body, which it took upon itself to become man, is Wisdom's House."　Orat. ii. § 44.　And he is followed by St. Leo, "ut intra intemerata viscera ædificante sibi sapentia domum, Verbum caro fieret." Leon. Epist. 31, 2.　Also Didymus de Trin. iii. 3, p. 337 (ed. 1769).　August. Civ. D. xvii. 20.　Cyril. in Joann. iv. 4, p. 384, 5.　Max. Dial. iii. p. 1029 (ap. Theod. ed. Schulz).　Hence Clem. Alex. ὁ λόγος ἑαυτὸν γεννᾷ.　Strom. v. 3.　vid. art. *Holy Spirit.*

But without denying that our Lord is signified in the above passage, as the Prototype, Author, and Pattern of all wisdom, it is more natural to apply it, as Athan. also does, to the attribute or grace called wisdom as displayed in the creation, whether in the original creation or in the new.　Hence he says, " The Only-begotten and very Wisdom of God is Creator and Framer of all things ; for *in Wisdom hast Thou made them all,* he says, and *the earth is full of Thy creation.*　But that what came into being might not only be, but be good, it pleased God that His own Wisdom should condescend to the creatures, so as to introduce an impress and semblance of Its Image on all in common and on each, that what was made might be manifestly wise works and worthy of God. For, as of the Son of God, considered as the Word, our word is an image, so of the same Son, considered as Wisdom, is the wisdom which is implanted in us an image; in which wisdom we, having the power of knowledge and thought, become recipients of the All-framing Wisdom, and through It we are able to know Its Father." Orat. ii. § 78.

¶ As Athan. in the above passage considers wisdom as the image of the Creator in the Universe, so elsewhere he explains it of the Church, de Incarn. contr. Ar. 6, if it be his (and so Didym. Trin. iii. 3 fin.), where his teaching about the Word is very much the same as in Orat. ii. § 56. S. Jerome understands by it the creation of the new man in holiness, "'Put ye on Christ Jesus;' for He is the new man, in whom all we believers ought to be clad and attired. For what was not new in the man which was taken on Him by our Saviour? . . . He therefore who can imitate His conversation and bring out in himself all virtues, he has put on the new man, and can say with the Apostle, 'Not I, but Christ liveth in me.' . . . Only in great deeds and works the word 'creation' is used. . . The new man is the great work of God, and excels all other creatures, since he is said to be framed, as the world is said to be, and is created the beginning of God's ways, and in the commencement of all the elements." in Eph. iv. 23, 24. Naz. alludes to the interpretation by which Wisdom is the plan, system,

or the laws of the Universe, Orat. 30. 2, though he does
not so explain it himself. Epiphanius says, "Scripture has nowhere confirmed this application of Prov.
viii. 22, nor has any Apostle referred it to Christ." (vid.
also Basil. contr. Eunom. ii. 20.) He adds, "How
many wisdoms of God are there, improperly so called!
but One Wisdom is the Only-begotten, not improperly
so called, but in truth . . . . The very word 'wisdom'
does not oblige me to speak of the Son of God." Hær.
69, pp. 743—745. He proceeds to show how it may
apply to Him.

¶ Didymus argues at length in favour of interpreting the passage of created wisdom, Trin. iii. 1. c. He
says that the context makes this interpretation necessary, as speaking of "the fear of God" being the
"beginning" of it, of "doing it," and of "kings and
rulers" reigning by means of it. Again it is said that
wisdom was with the Creator, who was Himself the
Son and Word. "The Son and Word, the Framer of all,
seeing and being able from the first, long suffering and
waiting for repentance in the unrighteous and wrong-
thinking multitude, when He had finished all, delighted
in wisdom which was in His creatures, and was glad in
it, rejoicing in His own work." p. 336. He contrasts
with this the more solemn style used by the sacred
writer when he speaks of the Uncreated Wisdom:
ὑπερφυῶς καὶ ὥσπερ ὑπ' ἐκπλήξεως θαυμάζων ἀναφθέγ-
γεται, e.g. Prov. xxx. 3, p. 338.

THE WORD OF GOD.

LOGOS, *verbum*, being a term already used in the schools of heathen philosophy, was open to various misunderstandings on its appearance in the theology of Revealed teaching. In the Church it was both synonymous with and corrective of the term "Son;" but heretics had almost as many senses of the term as they had sects.

¶ It is a view familiar to the Fathers that in this consists our Lord's Sonship, viz., that He is the Word, or as S. Augustine says, "Christum ideo Filium quia Verbum." Aug. Ep. 102, n. 11. "If God is the Father of a Word, why is not He who is begotten a Son?" de Decr. § 17; Orat. iv. § 12. "If I speak of Wisdom, I speak of His Offspring." Theoph. ad Autolyc. i. 3. "The Word, the genuine Son of Mind." Clem. Protrept. p. 78; and Dionysius, "ἔστιν ὁ μὲν οἷον πατὴρ ὁ νοῦς τοῦ λόγου," Sent. Dion. § 23, fin. Petavius discusses this subject accurately with reference to the distinction between Divine Generation and Divine Procession, de Trin. vii. 14.

¶ But the heretics, says Athan., "dare to separate Word and Son, and to say that the Word is one and the Son another, and that first was the Word and then the Son. Now their presumption takes various forms; for some say that the man whom the Saviour assumed is the Son; and others, that both the man and the Word then became Son when they were united. And others say that the Word Himself then became Son when He became man; for from being Word, they say, He became Son, not being Son before, but only Word." Orat. iv. § 15. The Valentinians, in their system of Eons, had already divided the Son from the Word; but they considered the μονογενής first, the λόγος next.

The title "Word" implies the ineffable mode of the Son's generation, as distinct from material parallels, vid. Gregory Nyssen, contr. Eunom. iii. p. 107; Chrysostom in Joan. Hom. 2, § 4; Cyril Alex. Thesaur. 5, p. 37. Also it implies that there is but *One* Son.

¶ "As there is one Origin," says Athan., "and therefore one God, so one is that Substance and Subsistence (οὐσία καὶ ὑπόστασις) which indeed and truly and really is, and which said *I am that I am*, and not two, lest there be two Origins; and from the One, a Son in nature and truth is Its proper Word, Its Wisdom, Its Power, and inseparable from It. And as there is not another substance, lest there be two Origins, so the Word which is from that One Substance has no dissolution, is not a sound significative, but is a substantial Word and substantial Wisdom, which is the true Son. For were He not substantial, God would be speaking into the air, and having a body in nothing different from that of men; but since He is not man, neither is His Word according to the infirmity of man. For as the Origin is one Substance, so Its Word is one, substantial, and subsisting, and Its Wisdom. For as He is God from God, and Wisdom from the Wise, and Word from the

Rational, and Son from Father, so is He from Subsistence Subsistent, and from Substance Substantial and Substantive, and Being from Being." Orat. iv. § 1.

For the contrast between the Divine Word and the human which is Its shadow, vid. also Orat. iv. 1, above; Iren. Hær. ii. 13, n. 8; Origen. in Joan. t. i., p. 23, 25; Euseb. Demonstr. v. 5, p. 230; Cyril. Cat. xi. 10; Basil, Hom. div. xvi. 3; Nyssen contr. Eunom. xii. p. 350; Orat. Cat. i. p. 478; Damasc. F. O. i. 6; August. in Psalm. 44, 5.

¶ " Men have many words, and after those many, not any one of them all; for the speaker has ceased, and thereupon his word fails. But God's Word is one and the same, and as it is written, *remaineth for ever*, not changed, not first one and then another, but existing the same always. For it behoved that, God being one, one should be His Image, one His Word, one His Wisdom." Orat. ii. § 36. vid. contr. Gent. 41. ad Ep. Æg. 16. Epiph. Hær. 65, 3. Nyss. in Eun. xii. p. 349. Origen. (in a passage, however, of questionable doctrine) says, " as there are gods many, but to us one God the Father, and many lords, but to us one Lord Jesus Christ, so there are many words, but we pray that in us may exist the Word that was in the beginning, with God, and was God," in Joan. tom. ii. 3. " Many things, it is acknowledged, does the Father speak to the Son," say the Semi-Arians at Ancyra, " but the words which God speaks to the Son are not sons. They are not substances of God, but vocal energies; but the Son, though a Word, is not such, but, being a Son, is a substance." Epiph. Hær. 73, 12. The Semi-Arians are

Y 2

here speaking against Sabellianism, which took the same ground here as Arianism.

¶ Vid. the article on the *Nicene Tests* for those ante-Nicene theologians, who, though they undoubtedly were upholders of the Homoüsion and good Catholics when they wrote, nevertheless seem to have held that the Word, after existing from eternity, was born to be a Son at " the beginning," and on the beginning of time, and then became the Creator, the Pattern, the conservative power of the whole universe :—these writers were such as Tatian, Tertullian, Novatian, &c. There was a parallel theory to theirs, and by which they were apparently influenced, in the heathen and Jewish schools. The view of the Logos as ἐνδιάθετος and as προφορικὸς, as the Word conceived and the Word uttered, the Word mental and the Word active and effectual—to distinguish the two senses of Logos, thought and speech—came from the Stoics, and is found in Philo, and was, under certain limitations, allowed in Catholic theology. Damasc. F. O. ii. 21. To use, indeed, either of the two absolutely and to the exclusion of the other, would have involved some form of Sabellianism, or Arianism, as the case might be ; but each term might correct the defective sense of the other. That the use was not oversafe would appear from its history in the Church, into which the above theologians, by their mode of teaching the γέννησις of the Word, introduce us. Theophilus does not scruple, in teaching it, to use the very terms, endiathetic and prophoric. God made all things out of nothing, he says. . . . " Having His own Word *endiathetic* in His own womb, He begat Him together with His own Wisdom, bringing Him forth before the universe was." Again he speaks of "the Word of God, who also is His Son, who was ever (διαπαντός) *endiathetic* in the heart of God, . . . God begat Him to be *prophoric,* the first-born of all creation." ad Autol. ii. 10, 22.

While S. Theophilus speaks of our Lord as both endiathetic and prophoric, S. Cyril seems to consider Him endiathetic, in Joan. i. 4, p. 39, though he also says, "This word of ours, προφορικὸς, is generated from mind and unto mind, and seems to be other than that which stirs in the heart, &c., &c. . . . so too the Son of God, proceeding from the Father without division, is the *expression* and likeness of what is proper to Him, being a subsistent Word, and living from a Living Father." Thesaur. p. 47. When the Fathers deny that our Lord is the προφορικὸς λόγος, they only mean that that title is not, even in the fulness of its philosophical idea, an adequate representative of Him, a word spoken being insubstantive, vid. Athan. Orat. ii. 35. Hil. de Syn. 46. Cyr. Catech. xi. 10. Damas. Ep. ii. p. 203, "nec prolativum, ut generationem ei demas," for this was the Arian doctrine. The first Sirmian Council of the Arians anathematises those who use of the Son either name. So does the Arian Macrostich. "The Son," said Eunomius, " is other than the endiathetic Word, or Word in intellectual action, of which partaking and being filled He is called the Prophoric Word, and expressive of the Father's substance, that is, the Son." Cyril in Joan. p. 31. The Gnostics seem to have held the λόγος προφορικὸς. Iren. Hær. ii. 12, n. 5. Marcellus is said by

Eusebius to have considered our Lord as first the one and then the other. Eccl. Theol. ii. 15. Sabellius thought our Lord the προφορικὸς, according to Epiph. Hær. p. 398. cf. Damasc. Hær. 62. Paul of Samosata, the ἐνδιάθετος. Epiph. Hær. 65, passim. Eusebius, Eccles. Theol. ii. 17, describes our Lord as the προφορικὸς while disowning the word.

¶ Athan. speaks, contr. Gent., of man as "having, besides grace, from the Giver, also his own natural virtue proper from the Father's Word;" of the mind "seeing the Word, and in Him the Word's Father also," 2; of "the way to God being, not as God Himself, above us and far off, or external to us, but in us," 30, &c., &c. vid. also Basil. de Sp. S. n. 19. Athan. also speaks of the seed of Wisdom as being "a reason combined and connatural with everything that came into being, which some are wont to call seminal, inanimate indeed and unreasoning and unintelligent, but operating only by external art according to the science of Him who sowed it." contr. Gent. 40.

This is drawn out somewhat differently, and very strikingly, in contr. Gent. 43, &c. The Word indeed is regarded more as the Governor than as the Life of the world, but He is said to be, ὁ παραδοξοποιὸς καὶ θαυμα-τοποιὸς τοῦ θεοῦ λόγος φωτίζων καὶ ζωοποιῶν . . . . ἑκάστῳ τὴν ἰδίαν ἐνέργειαν ἀποδιδούς, &c. 44. Shortly before the Word is spoken of as the Principle of permanence, 41 fin.

¶ "For it was fitting," says Ath. elsewhere, "whereas God is One, that His Image should be One also, and

His Word One, and One His Wisdom. Wherefore I am in wonder how, whereas God is One, these men, after their private notions, introduce many images and wisdoms and words, and say that the Father's proper and natural Word is other than the Son, by whom He even made the Son, and that He who is really Son is but notionally called Word, as vine, and way, and door, and tree of life; and that He is called Wisdom also only in name, the proper and true Wisdom of the Father, which co-exists ingenerately with Him, being other than the Son, by which He even made the Son, and named Him Wisdom as partaking of Wisdom." Orat. ii. § 37. That is, they allowed Him to be really the Son, though they went on to explain away the name, and argued that He was but by a figure the Word, πολλοὶ λόγοι since there were, and He was not οὐδ' ἐκ πολλῶν εἷς, Sent. D. 25. Also Ep. Æg. 14; Origen in Joan. tom. ii. 3; Euseb. Demonstr. v. 5, p. 229, fin.; contr. Marc. p. 4, fin.; contr. Sabell. i. p. 4; August. in Joan. Tract. i. 8. Also vid. Philo's use of λόγοι for Angels, as commented on by Burton, Bampt. Lect. p. 556. The heathens called Mercury by the name of λόγος. Vid. Benedictine note f. in Justin, Ap. i. 21.

¶ "If the Wisdom which is in the Father is other than the Lord, Wisdom came into being in Wisdom; and if God's Word is Wisdom, the Word too has come into being in a Word; and if God's Word is the Son, the Son too has been made in the Son." Ep. Æg. 14. vid. also Decr. § 8, and Orat. iii. 2, 64. And so S. Austin, "If the Word of God was

Himself made, by what other Word was He made? If you say, that it is the Word of the Word, by whom that Word is made, this I say is the only Son of God. But if you say the Word of the Word, grant that He is not made by whom all things are made; for He could not be made by means of Himself, by whom are made all things," in Joan. Tract. i. 11. Vid. a parallel argument with reference to the Holy Spirit, Athan. Serap. i. 25.

Index of Annotations on Theological Terms in the foregoing Treatises alphabetically arranged.

346

Annotations on Theological Terms in the foregoing Treatises alphabetically arranged.

The Ἀγέννητον, *or Ingenerate.*

IT had been usual in the Schools of Philosophy, as we contrast Creator and creatures, the Infinite and the finite, the Eternal and the temporal, so in like manner to divide all beings into the Unoriginate or Ingenerate, the ἄναρχα or ἀγένητα, on the one hand, and those on the other which have an origin or beginning. Under the ingenerate, which was a term equivalent to "uncreate," fell—according as particular philosophies or heresies determined—the universe, matter, the soul of man, as well as the Supreme Being, and the Platonic *ideas.* Again, the Neoplatonists spoke of Three Principles as beyond time, that is, eternal: the Good, Intellect, and the Soul of the world. (Theod. Affect. Cur. ii. p. 750.) Plotinus, however, in his Enneads, seems to make Good the sole ἀρχή; ἡ ἀρχὴ ἀγέννητος, (5. Enn. iv. 1,) while Plato says, εἴτε ἀρχὴν εἴτε ἀρχάς (Theod. ibid. p. 749, Tim. p. 48), and in his Phædrus, p. 246, he calls the soul of man ingenerate or ἀγένητον. The Valentinians (Tertull. contr. Valent. 7, and Epiph. Hær. 31, 10) and Basilides (Epiph. Hær. 24) applied the term to the

Supreme God. The word thus selected to denote the
First Principle or Cause, seems to have been spelt sometimes with one ν, sometimes with two. Vid. art. γένητος.
¶ And so too with Christian writers, and with like
variety in the spelling, this was the word expressing
the contrast between the First Cause or causes, and all
things besides. Ignatius distinctly applies it to our
Lord in His Divine Nature, doubling the ν in the *Cod.
Med.* "There is One Physician, generate and ingenerate, . . . from Mary and from God." (Ephes. 7,) vid.
Athan. Syn. § 47. Theophilus says, ὁ γενητὸς καὶ
προσδεής ἐστι· ὁ δὲ ἀγένητος οὐδενὸς προσδεῖται, (ad
Autol. ii. 10.) Clement of Alexandria, ἓν τὸ ἀγένητον, in
contrast to our Lord (Strom. vi. 7, p. 769). Dionysius
Alex. even entertains the hypothesis that ἀγεννησία
is the very οὐσία of God (Euseb. Præp. vii. 19), which
the Arians took advantage of for the purposes of their
heresy, (vid. Epiph. Hær. 76,) laying it down as a
fundamental axiom that nothing γεννητὸν could be
God. Hence Eusebius of Nicomedia, in the beginning
of the controversy, rested his heresy on the *dictum*,
ἓν τὸ ἀγέννητον, adding ἓν δὲ τὸ ὑπ' αὐτοῦ ἀληθῶς, καὶ
οὐκ ἐξ' οὐσίας αὐτοῦ. Theod. Hist. i. 5. Eusebius of
Cæsarea too speaks of the Supreme Being as ἀγεννητὸς
καὶ τῶν ὅλων ποίητης θεός. (Ev. Dem. iv. 7, p. 167.)

The word ἀρχὴ expressed the same attribute of the
Divine Being, and furnished the same handle to the
Arian disputant for his denial of our Lord's Divinity.
The ἀρχὴ of all was ἄναρχος; how then could our
Lord be the ἀρχὴ, that is, God, if He was a Son ?
But the solution of both forms of the question was

obvious, being as easy as that of the stock fallacies inserted, half as exercises, half as diversions for the student, to relieve a dry treatise on Logic. It was enough for Catholics to answer that ἀρχὴ had notoriously two meanings, origin and beginning; that in the philosophical schools these senses were understood to go together, but that Christianity had introduced a separation of them; that our Lord's Sonship involved His having no beginning because He was God, but His having an origin, because He was Son. And in like manner, the Son of God was, as God, ingenerate, that is, without a beginning, and as Son generate, that is, with an origin.

Thus Clement calls Him ἄναρχος ἀρχὴ, and Arius scoffingly ἀγεννητογενής.

As to the assumption that nothing generate could be God, Athan. maintains on the contrary that our Lord cannot but be God because He is generate. vid. art. *Son*.

The 'Αειγεννές.

ATHAN., as the other Fathers, insists strongly on the
perfection and the immutability of the Divine Being;
from which it follows that the birth of the Son must
have been from eternity, for, if He exists now, He must
have existed ever. " I am the Lord, I change not." It
was from dimness and inaccuracy even in orthodox
minds, in apprehending this truth, that Arianism arose
and had its successes.

Athan. says, " Never was the substance of the
Father incomplete, so that what belonged to it should
be added afterwards; on the contrary, whereas it
belongs to men to beget in time, from the imperfection
of their nature, God's Offspring is eternal, for God's
nature is ever perfect."   Orat. i. § 14. (Disc. n. 24.)
" Though a parent be distinct in time from his son, as
being man, who himself has come into being in time,
yet he too would have had his child ever co-existent
with him except that his nature was a restraint, and
made it impossible.   Let these say what is to restrain
God from being always Father of the Son?" Orat. i.
§ 26, 27; iv. § 15.

" Man," says S. Cyril, " inasmuch as he had a
beginning of being, also has of necessity a beginning
of begetting, as what is from him is a thing generate;
but . . . . if God's substance transcend time, or

origin, or interval, His generation also will transcend these; nor does it deprive the Divine Nature of the power of generating, that He doth not generate in time. For other than human is the manner of divine generation; and together with God's existing is His generating implied, and the Son was in Him by generation, nor did His generation precede His existence, but He was always, and that by generation." Thesaur. v. p. 35. vid. also p. 42, and Dialog. ii. fin. This was retorting the objection; the Arians said, "How can God be ever perfect, who added to Himself a Son?" Athan. answers, "How can the Son not be eternal, since God is ever perfect?" vid. Greg. Nyssen. contr. Eunom. Append. p. 142. Cyrl. Thesaur. x. p. 78. As to the Son's perfection, Aetius objects, ap. Epiph. Hær. 76, p. 925, 6, that growth and consequent accession from without were essentially involved in the idea of Sonship; whereas S. Greg. Naz. speaks of the Son as not ἀτελῆ πρότερον, εἶτα τέλειον, ὥσπερ νόμος· τῆς ἡμετέρας γενέσεως. Orat. 20. 9, fin. In like manner, S. Basil argues against Eunomius, that the Son is τέλειος, because He is the Image, not as if copied, which is a gradual work, but as a χαρακτὴρ, or impression of a seal, or as the knowledge communicated from master to scholar, which comes to the latter and exists in him perfect, without being lost to the former. contr. Eunom. ii. 16 fin.

It follows from this perfection and unchangeableness of the Divine Nature, that, if there is in the beginning a gennesis of the Son, it is continual:—that is the doctrine of the ἀειγεννές. Athan. says that there is no

παῦλα τῆς γεννήσεως. Orat. iv. § 12. Again, " Now man,
begotten in time, in time also himself begets the
child; and whereas from nothing he came to be,
therefore his word also is over and continues not. But
God is not as man, as Scripture has said; but is
existing and is ever; therefore also His Word is
existing and is everlastingly with the Father, as
radiance from light." vid. Orat. ii. § 35.

¶ In other words, by the Divine γέννησις is not meant
so much an act, as an eternal and unchangeable faċt, in
the Divine Essence. Arius, not admitting this, objected
at the outset of the controversy to the phrase "always,
Father, always Son," Theod. Hist. i. 4, p. 749, and
Eunomius argues that, "if the Son is co-eternal with
the Father, the Father was never a Father in act, ἐνεργὸς,
but was ἀργός." Cyril. Thesaur. v. p. 41. S. Cyril
answers that it is works, ἔργα, that are made ἔξωθεν,
from without; but that our Lord is neither a " work " nor
"from without." And hence, he says elsewhere, that,
while men are fathers first in posse then in act, God is
δυνάμει τε καὶ ἐνεργείᾳ πατήρ. Dial. 2, p. 458. Victo-
rinus in like manner says that God is "potentiâ et
actione Deus sed in æternâ," Adv. Ar. i. 33; and he
quotes S. Alexander, speaking apparently in answer to
Arius, of a "semper generans generatio." And Arius
scoffs at ἀειγεννὴς and ἀγεννητογενής. Theod. Hist. i.
4, p. 749. And Origen had said, ὁ σωτὴρ ἀεὶ γεννᾶται.
ap. Routh. Reliq. t. 4, p. 304, and S. Dionysius calls
Him the Radiance, ἄναρχον καὶ ἀειγενές. Athan. S. D.
15. And Athan., " As the Father is good always and by
nature, so is He always generative by nature." Orat.

iii. § 66. S. Augustine too says, "Semper gignit Pater, et semper nascitur Filius." Ep. 238, n. 24. Petav. de Trin. ii. 5, n. 7, quotes the following passage from Theodorus Abucara, "Since the Son's generation does but signify His having His existence from the Father, which He has ever, therefore He is ever begotten. For it became Him, who is properly (κυρίως) the Son, ever to be deriving His existence from the Father, and not as we who derive its commencement only. In us generation is a way to existence; in the Son of God it denotes the existence itself; in Him it has not existence for its end, but it is itself an end, τέλος, and is perfect, τέλειον." Opusc. 26. Vid. art. *Father Almighty*.

Didymus however says, οὐκ ἔτι γεννᾶται, de Trin. iii. 3, p. 338, but with the intention of maintaining our Lord's perfection and eternity, as Hil. Trin. ii. 20. Naz. Orat. 20. 9 fin. Basil. de Sp. S. n. 20 fin. It is remarkable that Pope Gregory too objects to "Semper nascitur" as implying imperfection, and prefers "Semper natus est." Moral. 29, 1; but this is a question of words.

Ἄθεος, ἀθεότης.

THIS epithet, in its passive sense, as used by St. Paul, Eph. ii. 12, (not in the sense of disowning or denying God, but of being disowned by Him,) is familiar with the Fathers in their denunciation of heretics and heathen, and with the heathen against Christians and others, who refused to worship their country's gods. Of course the active sense of the word is here and there more or less implied in the passive.

Thus Athan. says of Arius that "he is on all sides recognised as godless (atheist) Arius," Orat. i. § 4. And of the Anomœan Aetius, "Aetius who was surnamed godless," Syn. § 6. Asterius too he seems to call atheist, including Valentinus and the heathen, Orat. iii. § 64. Eustathius calls the Arians ἀνθρώπους ἀθέους, who were attempting κρατῆσαι τοῦ θείου. Theod. Hist. i. 7, p. 760. And Arius complains that Alexander had expelled him and his from Alexandria, ὡς ἀνθρώπους ἀθέους, ibid. i. 4.

¶ Since Christ was God, to deny Him was to deny God; but again, whereas the Son had revealed the "unknown God," and destroyed the reign of idols, the denial of the Son was bringing back idolatry and its attendant spiritual ignorance. Thus in the Orat. contr. Gent. § 29 fin., written before the Arian controversy, he speaks of "the Greek idolatry as full of all Atheism" or ungodliness, and contrasts with it the knowledge of "the Guide and Framer of the Universe, the Father's Word," "that through Him we may discern His Father, and the Greeks may know how far they have separated themselves from the truth." And, Orat. ii. § 43, he classes Arians with the Greeks, who, "though they have the name of God in their mouths, incur the charge of *Atheism*, because they know not the real and true God, *the Father of our Lord Jesus Christ.*" (vid. also Basil. in Eunom. ii. 22.) Shortly afterwards Athan. gives a further reason for the title, observing that Arianism was worse than previous heresies, such as Manicheism, inasmuch as the latter denied the Incarnation, but Arianism tore from God's substance His connatural Word, and, as far as its words went, infringed the perfections and being of the First Cause. And so ad Ep. Æg. § 17 fin. he says, that it alone, beyond other heresies, "has been bold against the Godhead Itself in a mad way, (μανικώτερον,) denying that there is a Word, and that the Father was always Father."

¶ In like manner he says, ad Serap. iii. 2, that if a man says "that the Son is a creature, who is Word and Wisdom, and the Impress, and the Radiance, whom whoso seeth seeth the Father," he falls under the text, "Whoso denieth the Son, the same hath not the Father." "Such a one," he continues, "will in no long time say, *as the fool, there is no God.*" In like manner he speaks of those who think the Son to be the Spirit, as "without (ἔξω) the Holy Trinity, and

atheists," Serap. iv. 6, "because they do not really
believe in the God that is, and there is none other but
He." And so again, "As the faith delivered [in the
Holy Trinity] is one, and this unites us to God, and he
who takes aught from the Trinity, and is baptised in
the sole name of the Father or of the Son, or in Father
and Son without the Spirit, gains nothing, but remains
empty and incomplete, both he and the professed
administrator, (for in the Trinity is the perfection,)
[initiation,] so whoso divides the Son from the Father,
or degrades the Spirit to the creatures, hath neither
the Son nor the Father, but is an atheist and worse than
an infidel, and anything but a Christian." Serap. i. 30.

¶ Elsewhere, he speaks more generally, as if Arianism introduced "an Atheism or rather Judaism
against the Scriptures, being next door to Heathenism,
so that its disciple cannot be even named Christian,
for all such tenets are *contrary to the Scriptures;*" and
he makes this the reason why the Nicene Fathers
stopped their ears and condemned it, Ep. Æg. § 13.
Moreover, he calls the Arian persecution worse than the
pagan *cruelties*, and therefore "a Babylonian Atheism,"
Ep. Encycl. § 5, as not allowing the Catholics the use
of prayer and baptism, with a reference to Dan. vi.
11, &c. Thus too he calls Constantius atheist, for his
treatment of Hosius, οὔτε τὸν θεὸν φοβηθεὶς ὁ ἄθεος,
Hist. Arian. 45 ; and Nazianzen calls Lucius, on account
of his cruelties in Alexandria, "this second Arius,
the most copious river of the atheistic fountain." Orat.
25. 11. And Palladius, the Imperial officer, is ἀνὴρ
ἄθεος. ibid. 12.

¶ Another reason for the title seems to have lain in the idolatrous character of Arian worship *on its own showing*, viz., as paying divine honours to One whom they yet maintained to be a creature.

¶ As to other heresies, Eusebius uses the word of the Sabellian, Eccl. Theol. p. 63; of Marcellus, p. 80; of Phantasiasts, p. 64; of Valentinus, p. 114. Basil applies it to Eunomius.

¶ As to the heathen, Athan. speaks of the εἰδώλων ἀθεότητα, contr. Gent. § 14 and 46 init. Orat. iii. § 67, though elsewhere he contrasts apparently atheism with polytheism, Orat. iii. § 15 and 16. Nazianz. speaks of the πολύθεος ἀθεΐα, Orat. 25. 15. vid. also Euseb. Eccl. Theol. p. 73.

¶ On the other hand, Julian says that Christians preferred " atheism to godliness." vid. Suicer. Thes. in voc. It was a popular imputation upon Christians, as it had been before on philosphers and poets, some of whom better deserved it. On the word as a term of reproach, vid. Voet. Disput. 9, t. 1, pp. 115, &c. 195.

Αἰών.

BY αἰών, age, seems to be meant duration, or the
measure of duration, before or independent of the
existence of motion, which is the measure of time. As
motion, and therefore time, are creatures, so are the
ages. Considered as the measure of duration, an age
has a sort of positive existence, though not an οὐσία or
substance, and means the same as "world," or an
existing system of things viewed apart from time and
motion. vid. Theodor. in Hebr. i. 2. Our Lord then
is the Maker of the ages, thus considered, as the
Apostle also tells us, Hebr. xi. 3, and God is the King
of the ages, 1 Tim. i. 17, or is before all ages, as being
eternal, or προαιώνιος. However, sometimes the word
is synonymous with eternity: "as time is to things
which are under time, so ages to things which are
everlasting," Damasc. Fid. Orth. ii. 1, and "ages of
ages" stands for eternity; and then the "ages," or
measures of duration, may be supposed to stand for
the ἴδεαι or ideas in the Divine Mind, which seems
to have been a Platonic or Gnostic notion. Hence
Synesius, Hymn. iii., addresses the Almighty as αἰωνό-
τοκε, Parent of the Ages. Hence sometimes God
Himself is called the Age, Clem. Alex. Hymn. Pæd. iii.
fin., or the Age of ages, Pseudo-Dion. de Div. Nom. 5,
p. 581, or again, αἰώνιος. Theodoret sums up what
has been said thus: " Age is not any subsisting sub-

stance, but is an interval indicative of time, now infinite, when God is spoken of, now commensurate with creation, now with human life." Hær. v. 6. If then, as St. Paul says in Hebr. xi. 3, the Word is Maker of the ages, He is independent of duration altogether; He does not come to be in time, but is above and beyond it, or eternal. vid. Decr. 18. Elsewhere he says, "The words addressed to the Son in the 144th Psalm, 'Thy kingdom is a kingdom of all ages,' forbid any one to imagine any interval at all in which the Word did not exist. For if every interval is measured by ages, and of all the ages the Word is King and Maker, therefore, whereas no interval at all exists prior to Him, it were madness to say, 'There was once when the Everlasting (αἰώνιος) was not.'" Orat. i. 12. And so Alexander: "Is it not unreasonable that He who made times, and ages, and seasons, to all of which belongs 'was not,' should be said not to be? for, if so, that interval in which they say the Son was not yet begotten by the Father, precedes that Wisdom of God which framed *all* things." Theod. Hist. i. 3, p. 736. vid. also Basil. de Sp. S. n. 14. Hilar. de Trin. xii. 34.

The subject is treated of at length in Greg. Nyssen. contr. Eunom. i. t. 2. Append. p. 93—101. vid. also Ambros. de Fid. i. 8—11. As time measures the material creation, so "ages" were considered to measure the immaterial, as the duration of Angels. This had been a philosophical distinction. Timæus says, εἰκών ἐστι χρόνος τῷ ἀγεννάτῳ χρόνῳ, ὃν αἰῶνα πυταγορεύομες. Vid. also Philo, p. 298, Quod Deus Immort. 6. Euseb. Laud. C. p. 501. Naz. Orat. 38. 8.

″Ακρατος,

SIMPLE, absolute, untempered, direct ; an epithet applied
both by Catholics and Arians to the creative Hand of
God, as if the very contact of the Infinite with the finite,
which creation involves, would extinguish the nascent
creature which it was bringing into being. The
Arians attempted to find in this doctrine an argument
in favour of their own account of our Lord's nature.
They said that our Lord was created to be the instrument whereby the world could be created without that
perilous intervention of the Almighty Hand, which made
creation almost impossible. Decr. § 8, Orat. ii. § 25, 30.
Epiph. Hær. 76, p. 951. Cyril. Thes. pp. 150, 241. de
Trin. iv. p. 523. Basil. contr. Eunom. ii. 21, Orat. ii. 29.
But how was it, asked Catholics, that creation was possible at all, that is, in the case of our Lord Himself, on
supposing Him a creature ? vid. Decr. § 8. Catholics on
their side had no difficulty to overcome : they considered that the Creator, by a special and extraor-
dinary grace, supplied whatever was necessary for
bearing the mighty Hand of God, as also a parallel
grace is supplied for receiving safely the great privileges of the Gospel, especially the Holy Eucharist.

" Not as if He were a creature, nor as having any
relation in substance with the universe, is He called
Firstborn of it ; but because, when at the beginning

He framed the creatures, He condescended to them
that it might be possible for them to come into being.
For they could not have endured His untempered
nature and His splendour from the Father, unless,
condescending by the Father's love for man, He had
supported them and taken hold of them and brought
them into substance." Orat. ii. § 64.

¶ He does not here say with Asterius that God could
not create man immediately, . . . but that He did not
create him without at the same time infusing a grace
or presence from Himself into his created nature, to
enable it to endure His external plastic hand; in other
words, that man was created *in Him*, not as something
external to Him (in spite of the διὰ and ἐν in reference
to the first and second creation, In Illud omn. 2). Vid.
art. *Arian Tenets*, &c., and Gent. 47, where the
συγκατάβασις is spoken of.

'Αλήθεια,

TRUTH, whether true doctrine or true reasoning, means the objective truth in contrast to subjective opinion or private judgment. Sometimes ἀλήθεια is used by itself, sometimes ἀληθείας λόγος, sometimes λόγος (vid. arts. *Rule of Faith* and ὀρθός). E.g. ὁ τῆς ἀληθείας λόγος ἐλέγχει, Orat. ii. 35. ὡς ὁ τῆς ἀληθείας ἀπῄτει λόγος, Ap. c. Ar. 36, where it is contrasted with ὡς ἤθελον (vid. above, art. *Private Judgment*); also Serap. ii. 2. Epiphanius: ὁ τῆς ἀλ. λ. ἀντιπίπτει αὐτῷ, Hær. 71, p. 830. Eusebius: ὁ τῆς ἀλ. λ. βοᾷ, Eccl. Theol. i. p. 62, and ἀντιφθέγξεται αὐτῷ μέγα βοήσας ὁ τῆς ἀλ. λ. ibid. iii. p. 164. And the Council of Sardica: κατὰ τὸν τῆς ἀλ. λ. ap. Athan. Apol. contr. Ar. 46, where it seems equivalent to "fairness" or "impartiality." Asterius: οἱ τῆς ἀλ. ἀποφαίνονται λογισμοί, Orat. ii. 37, i. 32. de Syn. § 18 cir. fin., and so also τοῖς ἀλ. λογισμοῖς, Sent. D. 19. And so also, ἡ ἀλ. διήλεγξε, Orat. ii. § 18. ἡ φύσις καὶ ἡ ἀλ. "draw the meaning to themselves," § 5 init. τοῦ λόγου δεικνύντος, ibid. 3 init. ἐδείκνυεν ὁ λόγος, 13 fin. τῆς ἀλ. δειξάσης, 65 init. 60, ἐλέγχονται παρὰ τῆς ἀληθείας, 63, ἡ ἀλήθεια δείκνυσι, 70 init. τῆς ἀλ. μαρτυρησάσης, 1 init. τὸ τῆς ἀλ. φρόνημα μεγαληγορεῖν πρεπεῖ, § 31 init. and Decr. 17 fin. In some of these instances the words ἀλήθεια, λόγος, &c., are almost synonymous with the Regula Fidei; vid. παρὰ τὴν ἀλήθειαν, Orat. ii. § 36, and Origen de Princ. Præf. 1 and 2.

¶ "Had these expositions proceeded from orthodox men (ὀρθυδόξων), Hosius," &c., &c. Ep. Æg. 8. And, "Terms do not disparage His Nature; rather that Nature draws to Itself those terms, and changes them." Orat. ii. § 3. Also de Mort. Ar. fin. And vid. Leont. contr. Nest. iii. 41. (p. 581, Canis.) He here seems alluding to the Semi-Arians, Origen, and perhaps the earlier Fathers.

¶ One of the characteristic points in Athanasius is his constant attention to the *sense* of doctrine, or the *meaning* of writers, in preference to the very words used. Thus he scarcely uses the symbol ὁμοούσιον, (one in substance,) throughout his Orations, and in the de Synod. acknowledges the Semi-Arians as brethren. Hence, Decr. § 18, he says that orthodox doctrine "is revered by all, though expressed in strange language, provided the speaker means religiously, and wishes to convey by it a religious sense." vid. also § 21. He says that Catholics are able to "speak freely," or to expatiate, παρρησιαζόμεθα, "out of Divine Scripture." Orat. i. § 9. vid. de Sent. Dionys. § 20 init. Again: "The devil spoke from Scripture, but was silenced by the Saviour; Paul spoke from profane writers, yet, being a saint, he has a religious meaning." de Syn. § 39. Again, speaking of the apparent contrariety between two Councils, "It were unseemly to make the one conflict with the other, for all their members are Fathers; and it were profane to decide that these spoke well and those ill, for all of them have slept in Christ." § 43; also § 47. Again: "Not the phrase, but the meaning and the religious life, is the recommendation of the faithful." ad Ep. Æg. § 9.

'Αλογία, Άλογος.

THIS epithet is used by Athan. against the Arians, as if, by denying the eternity of the Logos (Reason or Word), first, they were denying the Intellectual nature of the Divine Essence; and, secondly, were forfeiting the source and channel of their own rational nature.

1. As to the first of these, he says, " Imputing to God's nature an absence of His Word, ἀλογίαν, . . . they are most impious." Orat. i. § 14. Again, " Is the God, *who is*, ever without His rational Word?" Orat. i. § 24, iv. § 4 and 14. Also Sent. D. 16, 23, &c. Serap. ii. 2. Athenag. Leg. 11. Tat. contr. Græc. 5. Hippol. contr. Noet. 10. Nyssen. contr. Eunom. vii. p. 216. Orat. Catech. 1. Naz. Orat. 29. 17 fin. Cyril. Thesaur. xiv. p. 145. (vid. Petav. de Trin. vi. 9.)

¶ It must not be supposed from these instances that the Fathers meant that our Lord was literally what is called the *attribute* of reason or wisdom in the Divine Essence, or in other words that He was God merely viewed as God is wise; which would be a kind of Sabellianism. But, whereas their opponents said that He was but *called* Word and Wisdom *after* the attribute, they said that such titles marked, not only a typical resemblance to the attribute, but so full a correspondence and (as it were) coincidence in *character* with it, that

whatever relation that attribute had to God, such in kind
had the Son;—that the attribute was the Son's symbol. and not His mere archetype;—that our Lord was
eternal and proper to God, because that attribute was
so, which was His title, vid. Athan. Ep. Æg. 14;—that
our Lord was that Essential Reason and Wisdom, not
by which the Father *is* wise, but *without* which the
Father was *not* wise;—not, that is, in the way of a
formal cause, but in *fact*. Or, whereas the Father
Himself is Reason and Wisdom, the Son is the necessary issue of that Reason and Wisdom, so that, to say
that there was no Word, would imply there was no
Divine Reason; just as a radiance supposes a light; or,
as Petavius remarks, Trin. vi. 9, as the eternity of the
Original involves that of the Image: τῆς ὑποστάσεως
ὑπαρχούσης, πάντως εὐθὺς εἶναι δεῖ τὸν χαρακτῆρα καὶ
εἰκόνα ταύτης. Orat. i. § 20. vid. also § 31. Decr. § 13.
Theod. Hist. i. 3, p. 737.

¶ Secondly, he says of the Arians themselves,
" Denying the Word of God, Divine Reason have they
forfeited." Decr. § 2. And again, " If they impute
change to the Word, their own reason is in peril." Orat.
i. § 35. Hence Arianism, as denying the Word, is
essentially madness. " Has not a man lost his mind
who entertains the thought that God is Wordless and
Wisdomless?" Orat. ii. § 32. This will help us to
understand how it is he calls them ἀρειομανῖται. vid.
art. *in voc.*

Ἄνθρωπος

In Greek, and *homo* in Latin, are used 'by the Fathers
to signify our Lord's manhood, and again, human
nature, with an abruptness which, were it not so frequent, would be taken to give some sanction to
Nestorianism.

Thus Athan., speaking of His receipt of grace, says,
" The Word being united to *the man*," Orat. iv. § 7.
" Separating the hypostasis of God's Word from the
Man from Mary," ibid. § 35. "I, the Word, am the
Chrism, and that which has the Chrism from Me is the
man," ibid. It illustrates this use of the word, that it
is also used for human nature; e.g., " Of that was
ὁ ἄνθρωπος in want, because of . . . the flesh and of
death," Orat. i. § 41, vid. also iv. § 6.

¶ I will set down one or two specimens of the parallel
use of *homo* among the Latins : " Deus cum homine mis-
cetur; hominem induit," Cypr. Idol. ed. Ven. p. 538.
" Assumptus homo in Filium Dei," Leon. Serm. 28, p. 101.
" Suus [the Word's] homo," ibid. 22, p. 70. " Hic homo,"
Ep. 31, p. 855. " Hic homo, quem Deus suscepit." Aug.
Ep. 24, 3. vid. the author's Tract. Theol. μία φύσις, fin.

'Αντίδοσις τῶν Ἰδιωμάτων.

SINCE God and man are one Person, we are saved from the confusion which would otherwise follow from the union of two contrary natures. We may say intelligibly that God is man and man is God, because the attributes of those two contrary natures of Christ do not rest and abide in, and thereby destroy, each other, but belong to the one Person, and become one because they are His; and when we say that God becomes man, we mean that the Divine Person becomes man; and when we say that a man is the object of our worship, we mean that He is worshipped who is Himself also truly a man.

The word "Person," as the received term for expressing this union of natures, is later than Athan., who uses instead "He" and "His," the personal pronouns; but no writer can bring out the theological idea more forcibly than he.

¶ οὐκ ἄλλου, ἀλλὰ τοῦ κυρίου· and so οὐκ ἑτέρου τινὸς, Incarn. 18; also Orat. i. § 45, and iv. 35. Cyril. Thes. p. 197, and Anathem. 11, who defends this phrase against the Orientals.

¶ ἴδιον is another word by which Athan. signifies the later word "Person." "For when the flesh suffered, the Word was not external to it; and therefore is the passion said to be His: and when He did divinely His

Father's works, the flesh was not external to Him, but in the body itself did the Lord do them," &c. . . . μετα τῶν ἰδίων παθῶν, &c. Orat. iii. § 31, 32, 3.

For ἴδιον, which occurs so frequently in Athan., vid. also Cyril. Anathem. 11. ἰδιοποιούμενον, Orat. iii. § 33 and 38. ad Epict. 6. fragm. ex Euthym. (t. i. p. 1275, ed. Ben.) Cyril. in Joann. p. 151. And οἰκείωται, contr. Apoll. ii. 16, Cyril. Schol. de Incarn. t. v. p. 782, Concil. Eph. t. 1, pp. 1644, 1697, (Hard.) Damasc. F. O. iii. 3, p. 208, (ed. Ven.) Vid. Petav. de Incarn. iv. 15.

For κοινόν, opposed to ἴδιον, vid. Orat. iii. § 32, 51. Cyril. Epp. p. 23; " communem," Ambros. de Fid. i. 94.

Vid. Orat. iv. 6. This interchange is called theologically the ἀντίδοσις or communicatio ἰδιωμάτων. " Because of the perfect union of the flesh which was assumed, and of the Godhead which assumed it, the names are interchanged, so that the human is called from the divine and the divine from the human. Wherefore He who was crucified is called by Paul, Lord of glory, and He who is worshipped by all creation of things in heaven, in earth, and under the earth, is named Jesus," &c. Nyssen. in Apoll. t. 2, pp. 697, 8.

" And on account of this, the properties of the flesh are said to be His, since He was in it, such as to hunger, to thirst, to suffer, to weary, and the like, of which the flesh is capable; while on the other hand the works proper to the Word Himself, such as to raise the dead, to restore sight to the blind, and to cure the woman with an issue of blood, He did through His own body. The Word bore the infirmities of the flesh,

as His own, for His was the flesh ; and the flesh ministered to the works of the Godhead, because the Godhead
was in it, for the body was God's." Orat. iii. § 31.
"The birth of the flesh is a manifestation of human
nature, the bearing of the Virgin a token of divine
power. The infancy of a little one is shown in the
lowliness of the cradle, the greatness of the Highest is
proclaimed by the voices of Angels. He has the rudiments of men whom Herod impiously plots to kill, He
is the Lord of all whom the Magi delight suppliantly
to adore, &c., &c. To hunger, thirst, weary, and sleep
are evidently human ; but to satisfy five thousand on
five loaves, and to give the Samaritan living water,"
&c., &c. . . Leon. Ep. 28, 4. Serm. 51. Ambros. de Fid.
ii. n. 58. Nyssen. de Beat. t. 1, p. 767. Cassian. Incarn.
vi. 22. Aug. contr. Serm. Ar. c. 8. Plain and easy as
such statements seem in this and some parallel notes,
they are of the utmost importance in the Nestorian
and Eutychian controversies.

¶ " If any happen to be scandalised by the swathing
bands, and His lying in a manger, and the gradual
increase according to the flesh, and the sleeping in a
vessel, and the wearying in journeying, and the hungering in due time, and whatever else happen to one who
has become really man, let them know that, making a
mock of the sufferings, they are denying the nature ;
and denying the nature, they do not believe in the
economy; and not believing in the economy, they
forfeit the salvation." Procl. ad Armen. p. 2, p. 615, ed.
1630.

The 'Απαράλλακτον.

Unvarying or *exact*, i.e. Image. This was a word
used by the Fathers in the Nicene Council to express
the relation of the Son to the Father, and if they eventually went farther, and adopted the formula of the
Homoüsion, this was only when they found that the
Arians explained its force away. "When the Bishops
said that the Word . . . was the Image of the Father,
like to Him in all things and ἀπαράλλακτον, &c. . . .
the party of Eusebius were caught whispering to each
other that 'like' &c. were common to us and to the
Son, and that it was no difficulty to agree to these . . .
So the Bishops were compelled to concentrate the sense
of the Scriptures, and to say that the Son is 'consubstantial,' or 'one in substance,' that is, the same in
likeness with the Father." Decr. § 20.

¶ The Eusebian party allowed that our Lord was
like, and the image of, the Father, but in the sense in
which a picture is like the original, differing from it in
substance and in fact. In this sense they even allowed
the strong word ἀπαράλλακτος, *exact* image, which, as
I have said, had been used by the Catholics, (vid.
Alexander, ap. Theod. Hist. i. 3, p. 740,) as by the
Semi-Arians afterwards, who even added the words κατ'
οὐσίαν, or "according to substance." Even this strong
phrase, however, κατ' οὐσίαν ἀπαράλλακτος εἰκὼν, or

ἀπαραλλάκτως ὅμοιος, or ἀπαράλλακτος ταυτότης, did not appear to the Council an adequate safeguard of the doctrine. Athan. notices, Syn. § 53, that "like" applies to qualities rather than to substance. Also Basil. Ep. 8, n. 3. "In itself it is frequently used of faint similitudes, and falling very far short of the original." Ep. 9, n. 3. Accordingly, the Council determined on the word ὁμοούσιον as implying, as Athan. Decr. § 20 expresses it, "the same in likeness," ταυτὸν τῇ ὁμοιώσει, that the likeness might not be analogical. vid. Cyril. in Joan. l. iii. p. 302.

¶ Athan. says that in consistency those who professed the ἀπαράλλακτον should go further one way or the other. Syn. § 38. When they spoke of "like," Athan. says, they could not consistently mean anything short of "likeness of substance," for this is the only true likeness; and while they used the words ἀπαράλλακτος εἰκὼν, unvarying image, to exclude all essential likeness, they were imagining instead an image varying utterly from its original. While then he allows it, he is far from satisfied with the phrase ὅμοιος κατ' οὐσίαν or ὁμοιούσιος; he rejects it on the very ground that when we speak of "like," we imply qualities, not substance. Every image varies from the original, because it is an image. Yet he himself frequently uses it, as do other Fathers; vid. Orat. i. § 26, ὅμοιος τῆς οὐσίας. And all human terms are imperfect; and "image" itself is used in Scripture.

¶ 'Απαράλλακτος εἰκὼν κατ' οὐσίαν was practically the symbol of Semi-Arianism, not because it did not admit of a religious explanation, but because it did admit of a wrong one. It marked the limit of Semi-Arian approximation to the absolute truth. It was in order to secure the true sense of ἀπαράλλακτον that the Council adopted the word ὁμοούσιόν. Ἀπαράλλακτον is accordingly used as a familiar word by Athan. de Decr. supr. § 20, 24. Orat. iii. § 36. contr. Gent. 41, 46 fin. Provided with a safe evasion of its force, the Arians had no difficulty in saying it after him. Philostorgius ascribes it to Asterius, and Acacius quotes a passage from his writings containing it. (vid. Epiph. Hær. 72, 6.) Acacius at the same time forcibly expresses what is meant by the word, τὸ ἔκτυπον καὶ τρανὲς ἐκμαγεῖον τοῦ θεοῦ τῆς οὐσίας. In this he speaks as S. Alexander, τὴν κατὰ πάντα ὁμοιότητα αὐτοῦ ἐκ φύσεως ἀπομαξάμενος, Theod. Hist. i. 3, p. 740. Χαρακτὴρ, Hebr. i. 3, contains the same idea. "An image not inanimate, not framed by the hand, nor work of art and imagination, (ἐπινοίας,) but a living image, yea, the very life (αὐτοοῦσα); ever preserving the unvarying (τὸ ἀπαράλλακτον), not in likeness of fashion, but in its very substance." Basil. contr. Eunom. i. 18. The Auctor de Trinitate says, speaking of the word in the Creed of the Dedication, "Will in nothing varying from will (ἀπαράλλακτος) is the *same* will; and power nothing varying from power is the *same* power; and glory nothing varying from glory is the *same* glory." The Macedonian replies, "Unvarying I say, the same I say not." Dial. iii. p. 993 (Theod. t. v.); Athan. de Decr. l. c. seems to say the same. That is, in the Catholic sense, the image was not ἀπαράλλακτος, if there was *any* difference, if He was not one with Him of whom He was the image. vid. Hil. de Syn. 91. ad Const. ii. 5. And the heretical party saw that it was impossible to deny the ὁμοούσιον and περιχώρησις, and yet maintain the ἀπαράλλακτον, without holding two Gods. Hence the ultimate resolution of the Semi-Arians, partly into orthodox, partly into Anomœans.

¶ " What sort of faith have they who stand neither to word nor writing, but alter and change everything according to the season? For if, O Acacius and Eudoxius, you do not decline the faith published at the Dedication, and in it is written that the Son is ' Exact Image of God's substance,' why is it ye write in Isauria, We reject ' the Like in substance ' ? for if the Son is not like the Father in respect of substance, how is He ' exact image of the substance? ' But if you are dissatisfied at having written ' Exact Image of the substance,' how is it that ye anathematise those who say that the Son is unlike? for if He be not according to substance like, He is altogether unlike : and the Unlike cannot be an Image. And if so, then it does not hold that *he that hath seen* the Son, *hath seen the Father*, there being then the greatest difference possi- ble between Them, or rather the One being wholly Unlike the Other. And Unlike cannot possibly be called Like. By what artifice then do ye call unlike like, and consider Like to be unlike, and so pretend to say that the Son is the Father's Image? for if the Son be not like the Father in substance, something is wanting to the Image." Syn. § 38.

Ἀπαύγασμα,

RADIANCE or shine. This is St. Paul's word, Hebr. i. 3, taken from Wisdom vii. 26, and suggesting the "Light from Light" of the Nicene Creed. It is the familiar illustration used by Athan. to convey the idea of the Divine Sonship, as consubstantial and from eternity. He sometimes uses the image of fire, Orat. iv. § 2 and 10, but it is still fire and its *radiance*. However, we find the illustration of fire from fire, Justin. Tryph. 61, Tatian. contr. Græc. 5. At this early day the illustration of radiance might have a Sabellian bearing, as that of fire in Athan.'s had an Arian. Hence Justin protests against those who considered the Son as "like the sun's light in the heaven," which "when it sets, goes away with it," whereas it is as "fire kindled from fire." Tryph. 128. Athenagoras, however, like Athanasius, says "as Light from Fire," using also the word ἀπόρροια, *effluence*. Vid. also Orig. Periarchon, i. 2, n. 4. Tertull. Apol. 21. Theogn. ap. Athan. Decr. § 25.

Απορροή.

THIS word, though in itself unobjectionable as an expression of the divine γέννησις, is generally avoided by the Fathers, as being interpreted by the Arians in a material sense. "The offspring of men are portions of their fathers," says Athanasius, "and men ἀπορρέουσι in begetting, and gain substance in taking food; but God, being without parts, is Father of a Son without partition or passion, for there is neither ἀπορροή in the Immaterial nor ἐπιρροὴ, and, being uncompounded by nature, He is Father of One only Son. And He too is the Father's Word, from which may be understood the impassible nature of the Father, in that not even a human word is begotten with passion, much less the Word of God." Decr. § 11.

¶ S. Cyril, Dial. iv. init. p. 505, speaks of the θρυλλουμένη ἀπορροή; and disclaims it, Thesaur. 6, p. 43. Athanasius disclaims it, Expos. § i. Orat. i. § 21. So does Alexander, ap. Theod. Hist. i. 3, p. 743. On the other hand, Athanasius quotes it in a passage which he adduces from Theognostus, Decr. § 25, and from Dionysius, de Sent. D. § 22, and Origen uses it, Periarchon, i. 2. It is derived from Wisd. vii. 25.

The passage of Theognostus is as follows:—

¶ "The substance of the Son is not anything gained

from without, nor provided out of nothing, but it sprang from the Father's substance, as the radiance of light, as the vapour of water; for neither the radiance, nor the vapour, is the water itself or the sun itself, nor is it alien; but it is an effluence of the Father's substance, which, however, suffers no partition. For as the sun remains the same, and is not impaired by the rays poured forth by it, so neither does the Father's substance suffer change, though it has the Son as an Image of Itself." Decr. § 25. "Vapour" is also used in Wisdom vii., Origen, &c., as referred to supr.

¶ Hieracas the Manichæan compared the Two Divine Persons to the two lights of one lamp, where the oil is common and the flame double, thus implying a substance distinct from Father and Son of which each partook, or to a flame divided into two by (for instance) the papyrus which was commonly used instead of a wick. vid. Hilar. de Trin. vi. 12.

'Αρειομανῖται,

A TITLE of the Arians. "The dumb ass forbade the *madness* of the prophet," παραφρονίαν. On the word 'Αρειομανῖται, Gibbon observes, "The ordinary appellation with which Athanasius and his followers chose to compliment the Arians, was that of Ariomanites," ch. xxi. note 61. Rather, the name originally was a state title, enjoined by Constantine, vid. Petav. de Trin. i. 8 fin. Naz. Orat. 43. 30, p. 794, note *e.*, and thenceforth used by the general Church, e.g. Eustathius of Antioch, ap. Theod. Hist. i. 7. Constant. ap. Concil. t. i. p. 456. Hilar. de Trin. vii. n. 7, note. Julius ap. Athan. Apol. c. Ar. 23. Council of Egypt, ibid. 77, vid. also 6. Phœbadius contr. Arian. 22. Epiph. Hær. 69, 19. (ὁ μανιώδης "Αρειος.) Greg. Naz. Orat. 2. 37, τὴν 'Αρείου καλῶς ὀνομασθεῖσαν μανίαν, and so ὁ τῆς μανίας ἐπώνυμος, Orat. 43. 30, vid. also Orat. 20. 5 ; and so Proclus, τὴν 'Αρείου μανίαν, ad Armen. p. 618 fin. And Athan. e.g. μανίαν διαβόλου, ad Serap. i. 1 ; also ad Serap. i. 17 fin. 19 init. 20, 24, 29. ii. 1 fin. iv. 5 init. 6 fin. 15 fin. 16 fin. In some of these the denial of the divinity of the Holy Ghost is the madness. In like manner Hilary speaks continually of their "furor," de Trin. i. 17.

¶ Several meanings are implied in this title ; the real reason for it was the fanatical fury with which it

spread and maintained itself; (cf. on the other
hand, ὁ μανικὸς ἐραστὴς τοῦ χριστοῦ, enthusiastic.
Chrysost. in Esai. vi. 1. Hom. iv. 3, t. 6, p. 124.) Thus
Athan. contrasts the Arian hatred of the truth with
the mere worldliness of the Meletians, Ep. Æg. 22.
Hence they are ἀσεβεῖς, χριστομάχοι, and governed by
κακόνοια and κακοφροσύνη.

Again, Socrates speaks of it as a flame which
ravaged, ἐπενέμετο, provinces and cities. i. 6. And
Alexander cries out, ὦ ἀνοσίου τύφου καὶ ἀμέτρου
μανίας. Theod. Hist. i. 3, p. 741. vid. also pp.
735, 6. 747. And we read much of their eager
spirit of proselytism. Theod. ibid. The word *mania*
may be taken to express one aspect of it in English.
Their cruelty came into this idea of their "mania;"
hence Athan. in one place calls the Arian women, in
the tumult under George of Cappadocia, *Mænades*.
"They, running up and down like Bacchantes and
furies, μαινάδες καὶ ἐριννύες, thought it a misfortune
not to find opportunity for injury, and passed that day
in grief in which they could do no harm." Hist. Arian.
59. Also, "profana Arianorum novitas velut quædam
Bellona aut Furia." Vincent. Common. 4., Eustathius
speaks of οἱ παράδοξοι τῆς ἀρείου θυμέλης μεσόχοροι.
ap. Phot. 225, p. 759. And hence the strange parono-
masia of Constantine, "Αρες, ἄρειε, with an allusion to
Hom. Il. v. 31.

¶ A second reason, or rather sense, of the appellation was what is noted supr. art. ἀλογία, that,
denying the Word, they have forfeited the gift of
reason, e.g. τῶν 'Αρειομανιτῶν τὴν ἀλογίαν, de Sent.

Dion. init. vid. ibid. 24 fin. Orat. ii. § 32. iii.
§ 63 throughout. Hence in like manner Athan.
speaks of the heathen as mad who did not acknowledge God and His Word. contr. Gent. fin., also 23
fin. Hence he speaks of εἰδωλυμανία. contr. Gent. 10,
and 21 fin. Again, Incarn. 47, he speaks of the
mania of oracles, which belongs rather to the former
sense of the word.

¶ Other heresies had the word *mania* applied
to them, e.g. that of Valentinus, Athan. Orat. ii. § 70,
κἂν μαινῆται. Epiphanius speaks of the ἐμμανὴς
διδασκαλία of the Noetians. Hær. 57, 2. Nazianzen contrasts the sickness, νόσος, of Sabellius with
the madness of Arius, Orat. 20. 5; but Athan.
says, μαίνεται μὲν Ἄρειος, μαίνεται δὲ Σαβέλλιος, Orat.
iv. 25. Manes also was called mad: "Thou must
hate all heretics, but especially him who even in name
is a maniac." Cyril. Catech. vi. 20. vid. also ibid. 24
fin.—a play upon the name. But this note might be
prolonged indefinitely.

'Αρχὴ,

First principle or the *beginning*. This is a term employed both in expounding the doctrine of the Holy Trinity and in that of the Incarnation. For its employment in the former of these, vid. supr. art. *Father Almighty.* As to the second, it expresses the great providential office of the Second Person towards the universe, spiritual and material, which He has created. The creature, as such, is insufficient for itself; and He, who gave it being, gives it also a grace above its nature to enable it to use and enjoy that being well and happily. Nor is it a mere gift of power or health, as a quality, but it is the very Presence of the Word, the Second Person of the Blessed Trinity, in the creature, of which Presence a certain perfection of being and a continuous life is the result. A still more wonderful dispensation or Economy is revealed to us pre-eminently in the Gospel, vid. *Deification, Grace, Sanctification, Indwelling,* &c.; but such a gift above nature has been and is exercised in the first instance towards the material and Angelic world, and the title given to the Word in exercising this high Providential office is that of ἀρχὴ. Vid. also arts. ἄκρατος, συγκατάβασις, πρωτότοκος.

This office of the Word, it is plain, commences from the first moment of creation, and in its very nature implies divinity. It is spoken of in Scripture, viz. in the Proverbs,—"Dominus possedit Me in *initio* viarum suarum;" a passage to which the Arians appealed in the controversy more than to any other place in Scripture. It is in refutation of their arguments that Athan. introduces his own grand dissertation upon the sense of ἀρχὴ. The Arians interpreted it as meaning that the Personal Word and Son of God was the work with which creation commenced, that is, He was the first creature. Athan. lays it down that He was not the beginning in the sense of being the first of the whole number of creatures, but as heading the creation of God. He could not have been the first of all, if He had been one of all. As being an *efficax initium*, or an *initium* that initiates, He is more than a beginning; He is a cause: He could not initiate, unless He were divine. He entered creation by an act of condescension, in order to associate it with His own greatness. Vid. Orat. ii. § 49. And ibid. § 60, "He who is before all is not a beginning of all, but is other than all." Yet again, He is a beginning, because He begins the beginning.

In this there is an analogy to the circumstances of His Incarnation. His inhabiting and vivifying the creation implies attributes of the Supreme Being: He could not be by office πρωτότοκος (first-born) without first being μονογενής (only-begotten); and in like manner in the Gospel He is able to stoop to be our Mediator, and to be a Priest making atonement for us, and to be our Brother gaining blessings for us, because, though man, He is more than mere man. vid. *Priesthood*. Such is the force, as Athan. says, of the "wherefore" in Ps. xliv.; *because* He is by nature God, *therefore* He was able to be exalted as Mediator.

In consequence of this close analogy between the circumstances of Creation and Redemption, our Lord is called ἀρχὴ by Athan. in both dispensations. There is an initial grace necessary for the redeemed, if they are to partake of the redemption, as well as for their having their place in creation. Vid. the passages quoted under *Spiritual Freedom*.

The ᾿Ατρεπτος,

THAT is, of a nature capable of change in ethical character. Arius maintained this of our Lord in the strongest terms in the earlier statements of his heresy. " On being asked (says Alexander) whether the Word of God is capable of altering, as the devil altered, they scrupled not to say, ' Yes, He is capable.' " Socr. i. 6. vid. the anathema at Sirmium on those who said τὸν λόγον τροπὴν ὑπομεμενηκότα. supr. vol. i. p. 111, note 4.

It was indeed difficult, with their opinions, to exclude the notion that change of some kind belonged to Him ; nay, that He was not only in nature τρεπτὸς, but in fact ἀλλοιούμενος. (vid. Decr. § 23. Orat. ii. § 6.) It would be strange if they stopped short of this, as soon as they came to hold that our Lord's superhuman nature took the place of a soul, and was dependent on the body; and they scarcely would encumber themselves with the mystery of a double ἡγεμονικόν, when they had thrown aside the " mysterium pietatis." This they seem to have done even in S. Athanasius's lifetime ; for he speaks of them in contr. Apoll. i. 15, as supposing that the Saviour took flesh only, and thus imputing suffering to the impassible Godhead. Vid. also Ambros. de Fid. iii. n. 38. Also an assumption of this tenet seems involved (vid. Macrostich 6) in the ground assigned for condemning the Sabellians. vid. supr. vol. i. p. 106.

This tenet was the connecting point between Arians and Apollinarians. Both held that our Lord was a sort of man made up of a divine being and what resembles a creature, and what Athan. and other Fathers say against the Apollinarians serves against the Arians also. Ἄτρεπτος μένων, &c., he says, Orat. ii. § 6, against the Arians, and so against Apollinaris he says, ὁ λόγος ἄνθρωπος γέγονε, μένων θεός. ii. 7. vid. also ibid. 3 circ. init. So ὃ μὲν ἦν, διέμεινεν· ὃ δὲ οὐκ ἦν, πρυσέλαβεν. Naz. Orat. 29. 19. οὐσία μένουσα ὅπερ ἐστί. Chrysost. ap. Theodor. Eran. p. 47. ὃ ἦν ἔμεινε δι' ἑαυτὸν, καὶ ὃ ἠθέλησε γέγονε δι' ἡμᾶς. Procl. ad Arm. Ep. ii. p. 615, ed. 1630. vid. also Maxim. Opp. t. 2, ed. 1675. ὅπερ ἦν διαμένων, καὶ γενόμενος ὅπερ οὐκ ἦν. p. 286. vid. also p. 264. "Manens id quod erat, factus quod non erat." August. cons. Ev. i. n. 53 fin. "Non omiserat quod erat, sed cœperat esse quod non erat." Hilar. Trin. iii. 16. "Non amittendo quod suum erat, sed suscipiendo quod nostrum erat." Vigil. contr. Eut. i. 13, p. 498, (Bibl. P. ed. 1624,) and so Leo.

Βουλὴ, κατὰ βούλησιν.

ONE of the arguments, on which the Arians laid most stress in controversy, was the received doctrine, as it may be considered, that our Lord's *gennesis* was κατὰ τὸ βούλημα of the Father. Athanasius says that the doctrine is not only heretical in its application, but in its source, though still not necessarily heretical, viewed in itself. "The phrase," he says, "is from the heretics, and the words of heretics are suspicious." Orat. iii. § 59, supr. vol. i. p. 192; and in corroboration he might allege various heterodox writers. E.g. of these, Tatian had said θελήματι προπηδᾷ ὁ λόγος. Gent. 5. Tertullian had said, "Ut primum voluit Deus ea edere, ipsum primum protulit Sermonem." adv. Prax. 6. Novatian, "Ex quo, quando ipse voluit, Sermo filius natus est." de Trin. 31. And Constit. Apost. τὸν πρὸ αἰώνων εὐδοκίᾳ τοῦ πατρὸς γεννηθέντα. vii. 41. Also Pseudo-Clem. "Genuit Deus voluntate præcedente." Recognit. iii. 10. And Eusebius, κατὰ γνώμην καὶ προαίρεσιν βουληθεὶς ὁ θεὸς and ἐκ τῆς τοῦ πατρὸς βουλῆς καὶ δυνάμεως. Dem. iv. 3. Arius, of course, θελήματι καὶ βουλῇ ὑπέστη, ap. Theod. Hist. i. 4, p. 750, and supr. vol. i. p. 84, Arius's Creed.

This is true, but far higher authorities can be cited in favour of the phrase, so that Athan. feels it necessary to guard and soften his adverse judgment upon it. Hence he says, "If any orthodox believer were to use these words in simplicity, there would be no cause to be suspicious of them, the orthodox intention prevailing over that somewhat simple use of words." Orat. iii. § 59 (as supra). And, " Had these expositions of theirs proceeded from the great confessor Hosius, Maximinus, Philogonius, Eustathius, Julius," &c. &c. Ep. Æg. 8. But, after all, his admissions in favour of the phrase do not go far enough, as the following specimens of the use of it will show:—

S. Ignatius speaks of our Lord as "Son of God according to the will (θέλημα) and power of God." ad. Smyrn. 1. S. Justin as "God and Son according to His will, βουλήν," Tryph. 127; and " begotten from the Father at His will, θελήσει," ibid. 61; and he says, δυνάμει καὶ βουλῇ αὐτοῦ, ibid. 128. S. Clement, "issuing from the Father's will itself quicker than light." Gent. 10 fin. S. Hippolytus, " Whom God the Father, having willed, βουληθεὶς, begat as He willed, ὡς ἠθέλησεν." contr. Noet. 16. Origen, ἐκ θελήματος. ap. Justin ad Menn. (in Concil. Const. ii. p. 274, Hard.) vid. also "cum filius charitatis etiam voluntatis." Periarch. iv. 28.

But what is more to the purpose still, Athan. uses the phrase himself, and thereby necessarily sanctions the doctrine which it represents, in one passage in his Discourses, viz. in Orat. iii. § 31. " Our Lord was ever God," he says, " and hallowed those to whom He came, arranging all things κατὰ τὸ βούλημα τοῦ πατρός." And similarly he says, " Men came into being through the Word, ὅτε αὐτὸς ὁ πατὴρ ἠθέλησε." Orat. i. § 63.

¶ Now let us consider what the argument was which

the Arians founded on this phrase, and how it was to be refuted.

They threw it into the form of a dilemma thus: " Was our Lord's *gennesis* with or without the Father's will? If with, then He who willed the Son's existence, could have not willed it, or could unwill it now; if without, then it is the blind action of some unknown cause or fate, not the act of the Living Almighty God." If the first of these alternatives was accepted, then followed two conclusions, both contradictory of our Lord's divinity. " God is self-existent; but a son depends on his father's will :— God is eternal; but a son is posterior to his father's will. For both reasons the Son is not God." If the second alternative is taken, then Necessity is sovereign, and God ceases to be.

This reasoning, which in the first instance they applied to our Lord's *gennesis*, they proceeded to apply to all His divine acts also. As He was a being depending for His being, life, and powers on the will of the Supreme God, His Maker, so His great works in creation, conservation, and moral governance, in redemption and sanctification, were all done in obedience to definite commands and fiats of His Almighty Father.

Such was the Arian argument, yet it was not very difficult to expose its fallacy, while admitting the κατὰ τὸ βούλημα to be orthodox; and one can only suppose that Athan. in fact found Catholics perplexed and disturbed by the use the Arians made of it, and felt tender towards those who were not clear-headed. It was scarcely more than another form of the original objec-

tion that a son must be posterior to his father, as if
the conditions of time existed in eternity. "Sooner"
and "later" imply succession, and vanish when time is
no longer. It is customary to lay down that with Omnipo-
tence to say is to do: "He spake and it was done;" and
if in creation, which is a work in time, to determine and
to effect is one act, how much more really is succession
as regards His own nature foreign to the Ancient of
days, who is at once the Alpha and Omega, the Beginning and the End! Then as to the alternative of the
Divine acts being subject to necessity or fate, it is
obvious to ask whether the Supreme Being is not good
and just, omnipotent, and all-blessed, κατὰ τὸ βούλημα,
yet could He change His nature? could He make
virtue vice, and vice virtue? If He cannot destroy
Himself, and would not be God if He could or would,
why should He cease to be God, if He cannot be, nor can
will to be, without a Son? Such thoughts are as profane as they are unmeaning; and in the presence of
them, Athanasius begs God to pardon him, if his Arian
opponents force him to entertain them.

The gennesis, he says, belongs to the Divine Nature,
as the Divine Attributes do, and, as we cannot explain
why and how the moral law is what it is, so neither
can we understand how Father and Son are what They
are. "They say," he observes, "'Unless the Son has
by the Father's will come into being, it follows that
the Father had a Son of necessity and against His
good pleasure.' Who is it who imposes necessity on
Him? . . . What is contrary to will they see; but what is
greater and transcends it, has escaped their perception.

For, as what is besides purpose is contrary to will, so what is according to nature transcends and precedes counselling. . . . The Son is not external to the Father, wherefore neither does [the Father] counsel concerning Him, lest He appear to counsel about Himself. As far then as the Son transcends the creature, by so much does what is by nature in God transcend the will. . . . For let them tell us, that God is good and merciful, does this attach to Him by will or not? if by will, we must consider that He began to be good, and that His not being good is possible. . . . Moreover, the Father Himself, does He exist, first having counselled, then being pleased, to exist, or before counselling?" Orat. iii. § 62, 63, supr. vol. i. p. 197.

¶ Thus he makes the question a nugatory one, as if it did not go to the point, and could not be answered, or might be answered either way, as the case might be. Really Nature and Will go together in the Divine Being, but in order, as we regard Him, Nature is first, Will second, and the generation belongs to Nature, not to Will. He says, "Whereas they deny what is by nature, do they not blush to place before it what is by will? If they attribute to God the willing about things which are not, why recognise they not what in God lies above the will? Now it is a something that surpasses will that He should exist by nature, and should be Father of His proper Word." Orat. ii. § 2. In like manner S. Epiphanius: "He begat Him neither willing, θέλων, nor not willing, but in nature, which is above will, βουλήν. For He has the nature of the Godhead, neither needing will, nor acting without

will." Hær. 69, 26. vid. also Ancor. 51, and Ambros.
de Fid. iv. 4. Vid. others, as collected in Petav.
Trin. vi. 8, § 14—16.

¶ It would seem then that the phrase " by the
Father's will," is only objectionable, as giving rise
to interpretations erroneous and dangerous. vid. Decr.
§ 18. Hence Athan. says, "It is all one to say 'at
will,' and 'once He was not.'" Orat. iii. § 61. But
as this needed not be the interpretation of the phrase,
and it is well to keep to what has been received, therefore as the earlier Fathers had used it, so did those
who came after Arius. Thus Nyssen in the passage
in contr. Eun. vii. referred to lower down. And S.
Hilary, " Nativitatis perfecta natura est, ut qui ex sub-
stantiâ Dei natus est, etiam ex consilio ejus et voluntate nascatur." Hilar. Syn. 37. The same Father says,
" charitate Patris et virtute," in Psalm. xci. 8, and " ut
voluit qui potuit, ut scit qui genuit." Trin. iii. 4. And
he addresses Him as " non invidum bonorum tuorum in
Unigeniti tui nativitate." ibid. vi. 21. S. Basil too
speaks of our Lord as αὐτοζωὴν καὶ αὐτοάγαθον, " from
the quickening Fountain, the Father's goodness,
ἀγαθότητος." contr. Eun. ii. 25. And Cæsarius calls
the Son ἀγάπην πατρός. Quæst. 39. Vid. Ephrem. Syr.
adv. Scrut. R. vi. 1, Oxf. Trans. and note there. Maximus Taurin. says, that God is " per omnipotentiam
Pater." Hom. de Trad. Symb. p. 270, ed. 1784. vid. also
Chrysol. Serm. 61. Ambros. de Fid. iv. 8. Petavius
in addition refers to such passages as one just quoted
from S. Hilary, speaking of God as not " invidus," so as
not to communicate Himself, since He was· able. " Si

non potuit, infirmus; si noluit, invidus." August. contr. Maxim. ii. 7.

Hence, in order to secure the phrase from an heretical tendency, the Fathers adopted two safeguards, both of which are recognised by Athanasius. (1) As regards the relation between the βούλημα and the γέννησις, they made a distinction between the βουλὴ προηγουμένη and the σύνδρομος, the precedent and the concomitant will; and (2) as to the relation between the βούλημα and creation &c., they took care that the Son Himself should be called the βουλὴ or βούλημα of the Father. vid. supr. *Mediation*, p. 220.

¶ (1) As to the *precedent* will, which Athan. notices, Orat. iii. § 60, supr. vol. i. p. 192 &c., it has been mentioned in Recogn. Clem. supr. p. 385. For Ptolemy vid. Epiph. Hær. p. 215. Those Catholics who allowed that our Lord was θελήσει, explained it as a σύνδρομος θέλησις, and not a προηγουμένη; as Cyril. Trin. ii. p. 450. And with the same meaning S. Ambrose, " nec voluntas ante Filium nec potestas." de Fid. v. n. 224. And S. Gregory Nyssen, " His immediate union, ἄμεσος συνάφεια, does not exclude the Father's will, βούλησιν, nor does that will separate the Son from the Father." contr. Eunom. vii. p. 206, 7. vid. the whole passage. The alternative which these words, σύνδρομός and προηγουμένη, expressed was this: whether an act of Divine Purpose or Will took place *before* the gennesis of the Son, or whether both the Will and the gennesis were eternal, as the Divine Nature was eternal. Hence Bull says, with the view of exculpating Novatian, " Cum Filius dicitur ex Patre, quando ipse voluit, nasci, *velle* illud

Patris æternum fuisse intelligendum," Defens. F. N. iii. 8, § 8, though Novatian's word *quando* is against this interpretation.

¶ Two distinct meanings may be attached to "by will," (as Dr. Clarke observes, Script. Doct. vol. iv. p. 142, ed. 1738,) either a concurrence or acquiescence, or a positive act. S. Cyril uses it in the former sense, when he calls it σύνδρομος, as referred to above; in the latter, when he says that "the Father wills His own subsistence, θελητής ἐστι, but is not what He is from any will, ἐκ βουλήσεως τινὸς," Thes. p. 56; Dr. Clarke would apply to the *gennesis* the ἐκ βουλήσεως, with a view of inferring that the Son was subsequent to a Divine act, i.e. not eternal; but what Athan. says leads to the conclusion, that it does not matter which sense is taken. He does not meet the Arian objection, "if not by will therefore by necessity," by speaking of a concomitant will, or by merely saying that the Almighty exists or is good, by will, with S. Cyril, but he says that "nature *transcends* will and necessity also." Accordingly, Petavius is even willing to allow that the ἐκ βουλῆς is to be ascribed to the γέννησις in the sense which Dr. Clarke wishes, i.e. he grants that it may precede the γέννησις, i.e. in *order*, not in time, viz. the succession of our ideas, Trin. vi. 8, § 20, 21; and follows S. Austin, Trin. xv. 20, in preferring to speak of our Lord rather as "voluntas de voluntate," than, as Athan. is led to do, as the "voluntas Dei."

¶ (2) As to our Lord being the Father's βουλὴ, and thereby the concomitant βούλημα, Athan. declares it, Orat. ii. § 31. iii. § 63. Thus in the first of these places, " Since the Word is the Son of God by nature, and is from Him and in Him, so the Father without Him works nothing. *God said, Let there be light. . . He spoke and it was done.* . . . He spoke, not that some under-worker might hear and learn His will who spoke, and go away and do it, for the Word is the Father's Will."

¶ ζῶσα βουλή, supr. Orat. ii. 2. Cyril. in Joan. p. 213. ζῶσα δύναμις, Sabell. Greg. 5. ζῶσα εἰκὼν, Naz. Orat. 30. 20. ζῶσα ἐνέργεια, Syn. Antioch. ap. Routh, Reliqu. t. 2, p. 469. ζῶσα ἰσχὺς, Cyril. in Joan. p. 951. ζῶσα σοφία, Origen. contr. Cels. iii. fin. ζῶν λόγος, Origen. ibid.

¶ ἀγαθοῦ πατρὸς ἀγαθὸν βούλημα. Clem. Pæd. iii. p. 309. σοφία, χρηστότης, δύναμις, θέλημα παντοκρατορικόν. Strom. v. p. 546. " Voluntas et potestas patris." Tertull. Orat. 4. " Natus ex Patre velut quædam voluntas ejus ex mente procedens." Origen. Periarch. i. 2, § 6. S. Jerome notices the same interpretation of " by the will of God," in the beginning of Comment. in Ephes. S. Austin on the other hand, as just now referred to, says, " Some divines, to avoid saying that the Only-begotten Word is the Son of the counsel or will of God, have named Him the very Counsel or Will of the Father. But I think it better to speak of Him as Counsel from Counsel, Will from Will, as Substance from Substance, Wisdom from Wisdom." Trin. xv. 20. And so Cæsarius, ἀγάπη ἐξ ἀγάπης. Qu. 39, supr. vid. for other instances Tertullian's Works, Oxf. Tr. Note I.

¶ And so Cyril. Thes. p. 54, who uses it expressly, (as has been said above, p. 220,) in contrast to the κατὰ βούλησιν of the Arians, though Athan. uses κατὰ τὸ βούλημα, also (as in Orat. iii. 31):—αὐτὸς τοῦ πατρὸς θέλημα, says Nyss. contr. Eunom. xii. p. 345. The principle to be observed in the use of such words is this: that we must ever speak of the Father's will, command, &c., and the Son's fulfilment, assent, &c., as if one act.

¶ Vid. de Decr. 9. contr. Gent. 46. Iren. Hær. iii. 8, n. 3. Origen contr. Cels. ii. 9. Tertull. adv. Prax. 12 fin. Patres Antioch. ap. Routh. t. 2, p. 468. Prosper in Psalm. 148. (149.) Basil. de Sp. S. n. 20. Hilar. Trin. iv. 16. vid. art. *Mediation.* " That the Father speaks and the Son hears, or contrariwise, that the Son speaks and the Father hears, are expressions for the sameness of nature and the agreement of Father and Son." Didym. de Sp. S. 36. " The Father's bidding is not other than His Word; so that 'I have not spoken of Myself' He perhaps meant to be equivalent to 'I was not born from Myself.' For if the Word of the Father speaks, He pronounces Himself, for He is the Father's Word," &c. August. de Trin. i. 26. On this mystery, vid. Petav. Trin. vi. 4.

¶ " When God commands others, . . . then the hearer answers, . . . for each of these receives the Mediator Word which makes known the will of the Father; but when the Word Himself works and creates, there is no questioning and answer, for the Father is in Him, and the Word in the Father; but it suffices to will, and the work is done." Orat. ii. § 31. Such is the Catholic doctrine. For the contrary Arian view, even when it is highest, vid. Euseb. Eccl. Theol. iii. 3; also vid. supra, art. *Eusebius*, in which passage, p. 164,

the Father's νεύματα are spoken of, a word common
with the Arians. Euseb. ibid. p. 75. de Laud. Const.
p. 528. Eunom. Apol. 20 fin. The word is used of
the Son's command given to the creation, in Athan.
contr. Gent. e.g. 42, 44, &c. S. Cyril. Hier. frequently,
as the Arians, uses it of the Father. Catech. x. 5. xi.
passim. xv. 25, &c. The difference between the orthodox and Arian views on this point is clearly drawn
out by S. Basil. contr. Eunom. ii. 21.

Γέννημα,

Offspring. This word is of very frequent occurrence
in Athan. He speaks of it, Orat. iv. 3, as virtually
Scriptural. " If any one declines to say ' offspring,'
and only says that the Word exists with God, let such
a one fear lest, *declining an expression of Scripture,*
(τὸ λεγόμενον,) he fall into extravagance," &c. Yet
Basil, contr. Eunom. ii. 6—8, explicitly disavows the
word, as an unscriptural invention of Eunomius.
" That the Father begat we are taught in many places:
that the Son is an offspring we never heard up to this
day, for Scripture says, ' unto us a *child* is born, unto
us a *son* is given.' " c. 7. He goes on to say that " it
is fearful to give Him names of our own, to whom God
has given a name which is above every name ; " and
observes that offspring is not the word which even a
human father would apply to his son, as for instance
we read, " Child, (τέκνον,) go into the vineyard," and
" Who art thou, my son ? " moreover that fruits of the
earth are called offspring, (" I will not drink of the
offspring of this vine,") rarely animated things, except
indeed in such instances as, " O generation (offspring)
of vipers." Nyssen defends his brother, contr. Eunom.
Orat. iii. p. 105. In the Arian formula " an offspring,
but not as *one of the offsprings,*" it is synonymous with
" work " or " creature." On the other hand Epiph

nius uses it, e.g. Hær. 76, 8, and Naz. Orat. 29. 2.
Eusebius, Demonstr. Ev. iv. 2. Pseudo-Basil. adv.
Eunom. iv. p. 280 fin. It may be added, too, that S.
Basil seems to have changed his mind, for he uses the
word in Hom. contr. Sabell. t. 2, p. 192. It is
remarkable that this Homily in substance (i.e. the
" contr. Sabell. Greg." which is so like it that it cannot
really be another, unless S. Basil copies it) is also given
to S. Athan.

THE Γενητὸν, Γεννητόν.

The Γενητὸν, Γεννητόν.

IN these Treatises γενητὸν and γεννητὸν seem to be one word, whatever distinction was made at a later date. So they were considered by S. Ignatius, by the Neo-Platonists, and by the Arians, who availed themselves of the *equivoque* of meaning, in order to pronounce our Lord a creature, γέννημα, though not as *other* creatures. So also by Athan. and Basil. Hence perhaps it is that Basil is severe on the application of γέννημα to our Lord, his brother Gregory supporting him. Athanasius on the other hand uses it of our Lord with an explanation. After a time the distinction was made, and this will account for other Fathers, Nazianz. &c., following Athanasius. vid. supr. art. γέννημα. Also Damasc. F. O. i. 8, p. 135, and Le Quien's note; also note in Cotelerius, in Ign. Eph. t. 2, p. 13.

¶ Athanasius considers that Scripture sanctions both the one and the two uses; and he considers the one and the same word, in its two forms, to have the meaning of Son, but that " Son " admits of a primary sense and of a secondary. He virtually says, " It is true that the Word of God and the creatures whom He has made may both be called γεννήματα, but both in a very different sense. Both may be called ' Sons of God,' but the Word of God is true γέννημα by nature, whereas creatures are sons, γεννήματα, only by adoption,

and that adoption through a mere μετουσία or participation of the divine nature, which is a gift of grace;
but our Lord possesses the very οὐσία of the Father,
and is thereby His fulness, and has all His attributes."
Hence Athan. says, " Things generate, γεννητὰ, cannot
receive this name, (God's handiwork though they be,)
except so far as, *after* their making, they partake of
the Son who is the True Generate, and are therefore
said to have been generated also, not at all in their
own nature, but because of their participation of the
Son in the Spirit." Orat. i. § 56. Vid. art. 'Αρχή.

¶ It is by a like neglect of the one ν and the two, that
our Lord is called μονογενής with a single ν. And Athan.
speaks of the γένεσις of human sons, and of the Divine, de
Decr. § 11 ; and in de Syn. § 47, he observes that S. Ignatius calls the Son γενητὸς καὶ ἀγένητος, without a hint
about the distinction of roots. Again, one of the original
Arian positions was that our Lord was a· γέννημα ἀλλ'
οὐκ ὡς ἓν τῶν γεννημάτων, which Athan. frequently
notices and combats, vid. Orat. ii. 19. But instead of
answering it by showing that our Lord's epithet should
have a double ν and creatures a single, he allows
γεννημάτων to be applied to creatures improperly, and
only argues that there is a proper sense of it in which
it applies to the Word, not *as one of a number*, as the
Arians said, but solely, incommunicably, as being the
μονογενής. It may be admitted, as evident even from
this passage, that though Athan. does not distinguish between γενητὸν and γεννητὸν, yet he considers
γεγεννῆσθαι and γέννημα as especially appropriate to the
Son. γεγονέναι and γενόμενος to the creation.

Δημιουργός.

THE γέννησις of the Eternal Son is intimately connected with the idea of creation; so much so that Origen
thought that the creation was eternal because the Son
was so; and Tertullian thought that the Son was not
eternal because the creation was not.

These were erroneous conclusions, but Catholic
theologians allow thus much of truth in them, not that
the Creator and the creation were co-eval, but that the
mission of the Son to create is included in the eternal
gennesis; so that, as by the Father's teaching the Son
is meant " doctum et scientem genuisse," and, as His
committing judgment to Him is " judicem ipsum gig-
nere," so the mission to create signifies the *gennesis* of
a Son in eternity who is in time to be Creator. vid.
Petav. de Trin. viii. 1, § 10. Hence S. Augustine says,
" In Verbo Unico Dei omnia præcepta sunt Dei, quæ
ille *gignens* dedit nascenti." contr. Max. ii. 14, 9, and
still more definitely I understand S. Thomas to say,
" Importatur in Verbo ratio factiva eorum quæ Deus
facit." Summ. 1, qu. 34, art. 3.

Immediately upon the creation follows the second
act, viz. of conservation; for the Divine Hand is of such
incomprehensible force and intensity in operation, that
the thing created needs, by the intervention of its
Creator, to be enabled to bear creation. " Things

created," says Athanasius, " could not have endured
His absolute nature and His splendour from the
Father, unless, condescending by the Father's love for
man, He had supported them and taken hold of them,
and brought them into substance," &c. Orat. ii. § 61.
vid. ἄκρατος.

Διαβολικὸς,

Diabolical. This is Athan.'s judgment about the Arians.
vid. Decr. § 5 fin. Orat. ii. § 38, 74. iii. § 17. Ep.
Æg. § 4—6. de Sent. Dion. 27 fin., where he says,
" Who then will continue to call these men Christians,
whose leader is the devil, and not rather diabolical ? " and
he adds, " not only Christ's foes in fight, χριστομάχοι,
but diabolical also." Again, " though the diabolical
men rave," Orat. iii. § 8 ; " friends of the devil, and
his spirits." ad Ep. Æg. 5.

¶ In Orat. iii. § 8, there seems an allusion to false
accusation or lying (which is the proper meaning of the
word διαβάλλων), as occurring shortly before. And so in
Apol. ad Const. when he calls Magnentius διάβολος, it
is as being a traitor, 17 ; and soon after he says that his
accuser was τὸν διαβόλου τρόπον ἀναλαβὼν, where the
word has no article, and διαβέβλημαι and διεβλήθην
have preceded ; vid. also Hist. Ar. 52 fin. And so in
Sent. D. 3, 4, his speaking of the Arians' " father the
devil," is explained by τοὺς πατέρας διαβαλλόντων and
τῆς εἰς τὸν ἐπίσκοπον διαβολῆς.

¶ Another reason of his so accounting them, was
their atrocious cruelty towards Catholics ; this leads
him elsewhere to break out, " O new heresy, that has
put on the whole devil in irreligious doctrine *and conduct !* " Hist. Arian. § 66 ; also Alexander, " diabolical,"
ap. Theod. Hist. 1. 3, p. 731 ; " satanical," ibid. p. 741.
vid. also Socr. i. 9, p. 30 fin.   Hilar. contr. Const. 17.

Εἶδος.

'Ενὸς ὄντος εἴδους θεότητος, says Athan. Syn. § 52.
The word εἶδος, face, cast of countenance, assemblage
of features, is generally applied to the Son, and is
synonymous with *hypostasis*; but it is remarkable that
here as elsewhere it is almost synonymous with οὐσία
or φύσις. Indeed in one sense nature, substance, and
hypostasis, are all synonymous, i.e. as one and all
denoting the Una Res, which is Almighty God.
They differed, in that the word *hypostasis* regards
the One God *as* He is the Son. The apparent confusion
is useful then as reminding us of this great truth, that
God is One; vid. infr. art. Μία φύσις.

In Orat. iii. § 6, first the Son's εἶδος is the εἶδος of the
Father, then the Son is the εἶδος of the Father's Godhead, and then in the Son is the εἶδος of the Father.
These expressions are equivalent, if Father and Son
are, Each separately, ὅλος θεός. S. Greg. Naz. uses the
word ὀπίσθια, (Exod. xxxiii. 23, which forms a contrast
to εἶδος,) for the Divine Works. Orat. 28. 3.

¶ Vid. also in Gen. xxxii. 30, 31, Sept., where it is
translated "face," in Vulg., though in John v. 37
"species." vid. Justin Tryph. 126. In Orat. iii. § 15,
εἶδος is also used in composition for "kind." Athan.
says as above, "there is but one face of Godhead;" yet
the word is used of the Son as synonymous with "image."

It would seem as if there were a certain class of words, all expressive of the One Divine Substance, which admit of more appropriate application, either ordinarily or under circumstances, to This or That Divine Person who is also that One Substance. Thus "Being" is more descriptive of the Father as the πηγὴ θεότητος, and He is said to be "the Being of the Son;" yet the Son is really the One Supreme Being also. On the other hand the word "form," μορφὴ, and "face," εἶδος, are rather descriptive of the Divine Substance in the Person of the Son, and He is called "the form" and "the face of the Father," yet there is but one Form and Face of God, who is at once Each of Three Persons; while "Spirit" is appropriated to the Third Person, though God is a Spirit. Thus again S. Hippolytus says ἐκ [τοῦ πατρὸς] δύναμις λόγος, yet shortly before, after mentioning the Two Persons, he adds, δύναμιν δὲ μίαν. contr. Noet. 7 and 11. And thus the word "Subsistence," ὑπόστασις, which expresses the One Divine Substance, has been found more appropriate to express that Substance viewed personally. Other words may be used correlatively of either Father or Son; thus the Father is the Life of the Son, the Son the Life of the Father; or, again, the Father is in the Son and the Son in the Father. Others in common, as "the Father's Godhead is the Son's," ἡ πατρικὴ υἱοῦ θεότης, as indeed the word οὐσία itself. Other words on the contrary express the Substance in This or That Person only, as "Word," "Image," &c. The word εἶδος also occurs Orat. i. 20. Ep. Æg. 17. contr. Sabell. Greg. 8 and 12.

Ἔνσαρκος παρουσία.

THIS phrase or its equivalent is very frequent with
Athan. vid. Orat. i. § 8, 53, 59, 62 fin. ii. 6, 10, 55,
66 twice, 72 fin. iii. 28, 35. Incarn. 20. Sent. D.
9. Ep. Æg. 4. Serap. i. 3, 9. Vid. also Cyril. Catech. iii.
11. xii. 15. xiv. 27, 30. Epiph. Hær. 77, 17. The
Eutychians avail themselves of it at the Council of
Constantinople, vid. Hard. Conc. t. 2, pp. 164, 236.
Instead of it ἐπιδημία is used Orat. i. § 59, three times;
(ἐπεδήμησεν, iii. 30, and ἐνσώρατον, i. § 53.)

'Εξαίρετον,

Or *prerogative*, Orat. ii. § 19, iii. 3, iv. § 28, literally
special, singular. Vid. also Euseb. Eccl. Th. pp. 47,
73, 89, 124, 129. Theod. Hist. p. 732. Nyssen. c.
Eunom. iii. p. 133. Epiph. Hær. 76, p. 970. Cyr. Thes.
p. 160.

The 'Εξουκόντιον,

A TITLE of the Arians, from ἐξ οὐκ ὄντων, "out of nothing," one of their original positions concerning the Son.   Theodoret says that they were also called Exacionitæ, from the name of their place of meeting, Hær. iv. 3, and Du Cange confirms it so far as to show that there was a place or quarter of Constantinople called Exocionium or Exacionium.   Some have thought that Exucontians and Exocionites are perhaps the same word corrupted.   At the same time, since the Arians of Constantinople were of the violent sort who were called by various names, Anomœans, Aetians, Eunomians, Acacians, as well as pure Arians, it is not improbable that, in order to distinguish them from the more moderate heretics, they were also called in Constantinople from Exocionium, the district of the great metropolis to which they belonged.

'Επίνοια,

Κατ' ἐπίνοιαν, ἐπινοεῖν, *conception*. This is a word
very common with Athanasius. It expresses the view
taken by the mind of theological realities, whether
that view be the true view or not; thus it is used both
in reference to heretical error and to Catholic faith.
Thus Athan., Orat. i. init., speaks of heresies as ἐπινοή-
σασαι μανίαν, implying that there is no objective truth
corresponding to those conceptions which they so
vehemently insist upon. And Socrates, speaking of
the decree of the Council of Alexandria, 362, against
Apollinaris: "for, not as originating, ἐπινοήσαντες, any
novel devotion, did they introduce it into the Church,
but what from the beginning the *Ecclesiastical Tradition* declared." Hist. iii. 7. And the Arians allowed
what was imputed to them as far as this, that they
were strenuous from the first in maintaining that the
titles given to our Lord, viz. Word, Wisdom, &c.,
were not to be taken as expressing literal facts, but
were mere names given to Him in honour and as a
reward. Thus in the Thalia, "He is conceived in num-
berless conceptions, ἐπινοίαις." de Syn. § 15. Hence
Athan. says they held that "He who is really Son is
but κατ' ἐπίνοιαν Word, as He is Vine, and Way, and
Door, and Tree of Life, and that He is called Wisdom
also only in name (vid. art. 'Ονόματα), the proper and

true Wisdom of the Father, which co-exists ingenerately with Him, being other than the Son, by which
He even made the Son, and named Him Wisdom as
partaking of Wisdom." Orat. ii. § 37. Not that they even
allowed Him really to be Son, except in the sense that
we are sons of God, that is, because adoption involves
a gift of the Spirit, which is a real principle of a new
birth. Thus Athan. quotes or charges Arius elsewhere
as saying, "He is not the very and only Word of the
Father, but is in name only called Word and Wisdom,
and is called by grace Son and Power." Orat. i. § 9;
and just after he contrasts "true" Son with the Arian
tenet, Son "by adoption, which is from participation"
of the Spirit "and κατ' ἐπίνοιαν." vid. also de Sent.
D. 2. Ep. Æg. 12, 13, 14. Orat. iv. § 2.

The word, however, has also a good meaning and
use, as expressive of the nearest approximation in
human thought to the supernatural truths of Revelation,
and thus equivalent to *economical*. (vid. art. in voc.)
Thus in our thoughts of the Almighty, though He is
in reality most simple and uncompounded, without
parts, passions, attributes, or properties, we consider
Him as good or holy, or as angry or pleased, denoting
some particular aspect in which our infirmity views—in
which alone it can view—what is infinite and incomprehensible. That is, He is κατ' ἐπίνοιαν holy or merciful, being in reality a Unity which is all mercifulness
and also all holiness, not in the way of qualities, but as
one indivisible Perfection, which is too great for us to
conceive as It is. And for the very reason that we
cannot conceive It simply, we are bound to, use thank-

fully these conceptions, which are true as far as they go, and our best possible; since some conceptions, however imperfect, are better than none. They stand for realities which they do not reach, and must be accepted for what they do not adequately represent. But when the mind comes to recognise this existing inadequacy, and to distrust itself, it is tempted to rush into the opposite extreme, and to conclude that because it cannot understand fully, it does not realise anything, or that its ἐπίνοιαι are but ὀνόματα.

'Επισπείρας.   .

Vid. *Scripture Passages.*

Εὐσέβεια.

Εὐσέβεια, ἀσέβεια, &c., here translated *piety*, &c.,
stand for *orthodoxy* and *heterodoxy*, &c., throughout,
being taken from St. Paul's text, μέγα τὸ τῆς εὐσεβείας
μυστήριον, 1 Tim. iii. 16, iv. 8. "Magnum *pietatis*
mysterium," Vulg.

E.g. τὴν τῆς αἱρέσεως ἀσέβειαν, Decr. *init.* ὅσον
εὐσεβοῦς φρονήσεως ἡ 'Αρειανὴ αἵρεσις ἐστέρηται. *ibid.*
§ 2. τί ἔλειπε διδασκαλίας εἰς εὐσέβειαν τῇ καθολικῇ
ἐκκλησίᾳ; Syn. § 3. ἡ οἰκουμενικὴ σύνοδος τὸν "Αρειον
ἐξέβαλε οὐ φέρουσα τὴν ἀσέβειαν. Orat. i. § 7, *et
passim.* Hence Arius ends his letter to Eusebius Nic.
with ἀληθῶς Εὐσέβιε. Theod. Hist. i. 4.

¶ A curious instance of the force of the word as a
turning-point in controversy occurs in a Homily,
(given to S. Basil by Petavius, Fronto Ducæus, Com-
befis, Du Pin, Fabricius, and Oudin, doubted of by
Tillemont, and rejected by Cave and Garnier,) where it
is said that the denial of our Lady's perpetual virginity,
though "lovers of Christ do not bear to hear that
God's Mother ever ceased to be Virgin," yet "does
no injury to the doctrine of *religion*," μηδὲν τῷ τῆς
εὐσεβείας παραλυμαίνεται λόγῳ, i.e. (according to the
above explanation of the word) to the orthodox view of
the *Incarnation.* vid. Basil. Opp. t. 2, p. 599. vid. on the
passage Petav. de Incarn. xiv. 3, § 7, and Fronto-Duc. in
loc. Pearson refers to this passage, and almost trans-

lates the λόγος εὐσεβείας by "mystery," Apost. Creed, Art. 3. "Although it may be thought *sufficient as to the mystery of the Incarnation*, that, when our Saviour was conceived and born, His Mother was a Virgin, though whatsoever should have followed after could have no reflective operation upon the first-fruit of her womb, . . . yet the peculiar eminency," &c.

¶ John of Antioch, however, furnishes us with a definition of *pietas*, as meaning obedience to the word of God. He speaks, writing to Proclus, of a letter which evidenced caution and piety, i.e. orthodoxy: "piety, because you went along the royal way of *Divine Scripture* in your remarks, rightly confessing the word of truth, not venturing to declare anything of *your own authority without Scripture testimonies;* caution, because *together with* divine Scripture you propounded also *statements of the Fathers*, in order to prove what you advanced." ap. Facund. i. 1.

Θεανδρικὴ ἐνέργεια,

Operatio Deivirilis, "the Man-God's action." By the word ἐνέργεια is meant in theology the action or operation, the family of acts, which naturally belongs to and discriminates the substance or nature of a thing from that of other things; and not only the mere operation, but also inclusively the faculty of such operation; as certain nutritive or medicinal qualities adhere, and serve as definitions, to certain plants and minerals, or as the ἐνέργεια and the ἔργον of a seraph may be viewed as being the adoration of the Holy Trinity.

This being laid down, it would seem to follow that our Lord, having two natures, has two attendant ἔργα and two ἐνέργειαι, and this in fact is the Catholic doctrine; whereas the Monothelites maintained He had but one, as if, with the Monophysites, they held but one nature of Christ, the divine and human energies making up one single third energy, neither divine nor human,—for, in the Monophysite creed, God and man made one third and compound being, who would necessarily have one compound energy, and, as will is one kind of energy, one only will.

This one and only energy of our Lord, as proceeding from what they considered His one composite nature, they denoted by the orthodox phrase, " ἐνέργεια θεανδρικὴ," diverting it from its true sense. Catholic theologians, holding two energies, one for each nature, speak of them in three ways, viz. as a divine energy, a human, and a union or concurrence of the two; this last they call θεανδρικὴ, but in a sense quite distinct from the use of the word by the Monothelites. Sometimes our Lord exerts His divine *energia*, as when He protects His people; sometimes His human, as when He underwent hunger and thirst; sometimes both at once, as in making clay and restoring sight, or in His suffering for His people; but in this last instance, there is no intermingling of the divine and the human, and, though it may be spoken of as a double energy, still there are in fact two, not one.

It is this θεανδρικὴ ἐνέργεια that is spoken of in the following passages:—

"And thus when there was need to raise Peter's wife's mother who was sick of a fever, He stretched forth His hand humanly, but He stopped the illness divinely. And in the case of the man blind from the birth, human was the spittle which he gave forth from the flesh, but divinely did He open the eyes through the clay. And in the case of Lazarus, He gave forth a human voice, as man; but divinely, as God, did He raise Lazarus from the dead." Orat. iii. 32.

"When He is said to hunger and thirst, and to toil, and not to know, and to sleep, and to weep, and to ask, and to flee, and to be born, and to deprecate the chalice, and in a word to undergo all that belongs to the flesh, let it be said, as is congruous, in each case, 'Christ's then hungering or thirsting *for us in the flesh*, and saying He did not know, and being buffeted and toiling *for us in the flesh*, and being exalted too, and born and growing *in the flesh*, and fearing and hiding *in the flesh*, and saying, *If it be possible let this* chalice pass from Me, and being beaten and receiving gifts *for us in the flesh*; and in a word, all such things *for us in the flesh*,'" &c. Orat. iii. § 34.

"When He touched the leper, it was the man that was seen; but something beyond man, when He cleansed him," &c. Ambros. Epist. i. 46, n. 7. Hil. Trin. x. 23 fin. vid. *Incarnation* and *Two Natures*, and S. Leo's extracts in his Ep. 165. Chrysol. Serm. 34 and 35. Paul. ap Conc. Eph. t. iii. (p. 1620, Labbe.)

Θεομάχος, Χριστομάχος.

VID. Acts v. 39. xxiii. 9. text. rec. These epithets are in very frequent use in Athan., in speaking of the Arians; also ἀντιμαχόμενοι τῷ σωτῆρι. Ep. Encycl. § 5. And in the beginning of the controversy, Alexander ap. Socr. i. 6, p. 10, p. 11, p. 13. Theod. Hist. i. 3, p. 729. And so θεομάχος γλῶσσα. Basil. contr. Eunom. ii. 27 fin. χριστομάχων, in his Ep. 236 init. Vid. also Cyril. Thesaur. p. 19, p. 24. Θεομάχοι is used of other heretics, e.g. the Manichees, by Greg. Naz. Orat. 45. § 8.

¶ The title contains, in Athan.'s use of it, an allusion to the antediluvian giants; e.g. γίγαντας θεομαχοῦντας, Orat. iii. § 42. vid. also Naz., of the disorderly bishops during the Arian ascendency. Orat. 43. 26, and Socr. v. 10. Sometimes the mythological giants are spoken of. Orat. ii. § 32. In Hist. Arian. 74, he calls Constantius a γίλας.

¶ λογομαχία too is used with reference to the divine λόγος and the fight against Him, as χριστομαχεῖν and θεομαχεῖν. Thus λογομαχεῖν μελετήσαντες, καὶ λοιπὸν πνευματομαχοῦντες, ἔσονται μετ᾽ ὀλίγον νεκροὶ τῇ ἀλογίᾳ. Serap. iv. 1.

Θεότης (vid. *Trinity*).

IF the doctrine of the Holy Trinity admits of being
called contrary to reason, this must be on the ground
of its being incompatible with some eternal truth,
necessary axiom, &c., or with some distinct experience,
and not merely because it is in its nature inconceivable
and unimaginable; for if to be inconceivable makes it
untrue, then we shall be obliged to deny facts of daily
experience, e.g. the action of the muscles which follows upon an act of the will.

However, clear as this is, the language by which we
logically express the doctrine will be difficult to interpret and to use intelligently, unless we keep in mind
the fundamental truths which constitute the mystery,
and use them as a key to such language.

E.g. the Father's Godhead is the Son's, or is in the
Son. Orat. i. § 52. Ἡ πατρικὴ αὐτοῦ θεότης. Orat. i.
§ 45, 49. ii. § 18, 73. iii. § 26. ἡ πατρικὴ φύσις αὐτοῦ.
i. § 40. τὸ πατρικὸν φῶς ὁ υἱός. iii. § 53. ἡ θεότης καὶ
ἡ ἰδιότης τοῦ πατρὸς τὸ εἶναι τοῦ υἱοῦ ἐστι. iii. § 5.
The Son is worshipped κατὰ τὴν πατρικὴν ἰδιότητα. i.
§ 42. He has τὴν τῆς ὁμοιώσεως ἑνότητα. Syn. § 45.
He is, ὁ αὐτὸς τῇ ὁμοιώσει to the Father. Decr. § 20.
He has τὴν ἑνότητα τῆς φύσεως καὶ τὴν ταυτότητα
τοῦ φωτός. Decr. § 24. ταυτότητα τῆς φύσεως, Basil, Ep.
8, 3. τῆς οὐσίας, Cyril. in Joan. iii. p. 302. He is ἐξ οὐσίας

οὐσιώδης. Orat. iv. § 1. ἡ οὐσία αὕτη τῆς οὐσίας τῆς πατρικῆς ἐστι γέννημα. Syn. § 48. And we are told of the prophet ἐκβοήσαντος τὴν πατρικὴν ὑπόστασιν περὶ αὐτοῦ. Orat. iv. § 33. vid. the present author's Tract, μία φύσις, §. 6 fin.

¶ φύσις seems sometimes in Athanasius to be used, not for οὐσία, as would be the ordinary application of the word, but for ὑπόστασις or person. Thus he says, "whereas the *nature* of the Son is less divisible relatively to the Father" than radiance is relatively to the sun, . . . "wherefore should not He be called consubstantial?" de Syn. § 52. And at least this is an Alexandrian use of the word. It is found in Alexander ap. Theod. Hist. i. 3, p. 740, and it gives rise to a celebrated question in the Monophysite controversy, is used in S. Cyril's phrase, μία φύσις σεσαρκωμένη. S. Cyril uses the word both for person and for substance successively in the following passage: "Perhaps some one will say, 'How is the Holy and Adorable Trinity distinguished into three Hypostases, yet issues in *one nature* of Godhead?' Because, the Same in substance, necessarily following the *difference of natures*, recalls the minds of believers to *one nature* of Godhead." contr. Nest. iii. p. 91. In this passage "One Nature" stands for one substance; but "three Natures" is the One Eternal Divine Nature viewed in that respect in which He is Three. And so S. Hilary, "naturæ ex naturâ gignente nativitas," de Syn. 17; and "essentia de essentiâ," August de Trin. vii. n. 3, and "de seipso genuit Deus id quod est," de Fid. et Symb. 4: i.e. He is the Adorable Θεότης viewed as begotten. These phrases

mean that the Son *who is* the Divine Substance, is from
the Father *who is* the [same] Divine Substance. As (to
speak of what is *analogous*, not parallel) we might say
that " man is father of man," not meaning by man the
same individual in both cases, but the same nature, so
here we speak, not of the same Person in the two cases,
but the same Individuum. All these expressions resolve
themselves into the original mystery of the Holy Trinity,
that Person and Individuum are not equivalent terms,
and we understand them neither more nor less than we
understand it. In like manner as regards the Incarnation, when St. Paul says, " God was in Christ," he does
not mean absolutely the Divine Nature, which is the
proper sense of the word, but the Divine Nature as
existing in the Person of the Son. Hence too (vid.
Petav. de Trin. vi. 10, § 6) such phrases as "the Father
begat the Son from *His* substance." And in like manner Athan. just afterwards speaks of "the Father's
Godhead *being in* the Son." Orat. i. § 52.

The μονὰς θεότητος is ἀδιαίρετος. Orat. iv. § 1, 2.
Though in Three Persons, they are not μεμερισμέναι,
Doin. ap. Basil. Sp. S. n. 72. Athan. Expos. F. § 2;
not ἀπερρηγμέναι, Naz. Orat. 20. 6 ; not ἀπεξενωμέναι
καὶ διεσπασμέναι, Orat. 23. 6, &c.; but ἀμέριστος
ἐν μεμερισμένοις ἡ θεότης. Orat. 31. 14.

¶ Though the Divine Substance is both the Father
lngenerate and also the Only-begotten Son, it is not
itself ἀγέννητος or γεννητή; which was the objection
urged against the Catholics by Aetius, Epiph. Hær.
76, 10. Thus Athen. says de Decr. § 30, "He has
given the authority of all things to the· Son, and,

having given it, is *once more*, πάλιν, the Lord of all things through the Word." vol. i. p. 52. Again, "the Father having given all things to the Son, has all things *once again*, πάλιν . . . for the Son's Godhead is the Godhead of the Father." Orat. iii. § 36 fin. Hence ἡ ἐκ τοῦ πατρὸς εἰς τὸν υἱὸν θεότης ἀῤῥεύστως καὶ ἀδιαιρέτως τυγχάνει. Expos. F. 2. " Vera et æterna substantia, in se tota permanens, totam se coæternæ veritati nativitatis indulsit." Fulgent. Resp. 7. And S. Hilary, " Filius in Patre est et in Filio Pater, non per transfusionem, refusionemque mutuam, sed per viventis naturæ perfectam nativitatem." Trin. vii. 31.

Θεοτόκος.

Vid. *Mary*.

Καταπέτασμα.

" As Aaron did not change," says Athanasius,
Orat. ii. 8, " by putting on his High-priest's dress, so
that, had any one said, ' Lo, Aaron has this day become High-priest,' he had not implied that he then had
been born man, . . . so in the Lord's instance the
words, ' He became' and ' He was made' must not be
understood of the Word, considered as the Word,"
&c. &c.

This is one of those protests by anticipation against
Nestorianism, which in consequence may be abused
to the purposes of the opposite heresy. Such expressions as περιτιθέμενος τὴν ἐσθῆτα, ἐκαλύπτετο,
ἐνδυσάμενος σῶμα, were familiar with the Apollinarians,
against whom S. Athanasius is, if possible, even more
decided. Theodoret objects, Hær. v. 11, p. 422, to the
word προκάλυμμα, when applied to our Lord's manhood,
as implying that He had no soul; vid. also Naz. Ep.
102 fin. (ed. 1840). In Naz. Ep. 101, p. 90, παραπέτασμα is used to denote an Apollinarian idea. Such
expressions were taken to imply that Christ was not
in nature man, only in some sense human; not a substance, but an appearance; yet S. Athan. (if Athan.)
contr. Sabell. Greg. 4, has παραπεπετασμένην, and
κάλυμμα, ibid. init.; S. Cyril Hieros. καταπέτασμα,
Catech. xii. 26, xiii. 32, after Hebr. x. 20; and Athan.

ad Adelph. 5; Theodor. παραπετασμα, Eran. 1, p. 22,
and προκάλυμμα, ibid. p. 23, and adv. Gent. vi. p. 877;
and στολὴ, Eran. l. c. S. Leo has "caro Christi
velamen," Ep. 59, p. 979. vid. also Serm. 22, p. 7C;
Serm. 25, p. 84.

Κύριος, Κυρίως.

THE meaning of κυρίως, when applied to language, on
the whole presents no difficulty. It answers to the
Latin *propriè*, and is the contrary to *impropriè*. Thus
Athan. says, " When the thing is a work or creature,
the words ' He made ' &c. are used of it properly,
κυρίως ; when an offspring, then they are no longer
used κυρίως." Orat. ii. § 3.

But the word has an inconvenient latitude (vid. art.
Father Almighty, fin.) Sometimes it is used in the sense
of archetypal or transcendent, as when Athan. says,
" The Father is κυρίως Father, and the Son κυρίως Son,"
Orat. i. § 21 ; and in consequence in Their instance alone
is the Father always Father and the Son always Son,
ibid. Sometimes the word is used of us as sons,
and opposed to *figuratively*, ἐκ μεταφορᾶς, as in Basil c.
Eunom. ii. 23 ; while Hilary seems to deny that we are
sons *propriè*. Justin says, ὁ μόνος λεγόμενος κυρίως υἱὸς,
Apol. ii. 6, but here κυρίως seems to be used in reference
to the word κύριος, Lord, which he has just been using,
κυριολογεῖν being sometimes used by him as by others
in the sense of " naming as Lord," like θεολογεῖν. vid.
Tryph. 56. There is a passage in Justin's ad Græc. 21,
where he (or the anon. writer), when speaking of ἐγώ εἰμι
ὁ ὤν, uses the word in the same ambiguous sense ; οὐδὲν
γὰρ ὄνομα ἐπὶ θεοῦ κυριολογεῖσθαι δυνατόν ; as if κύριος,

the Lord, by which " I am " is translated, were a sort of symbol of that proper name of God which cannot be given.

¶ On κυριολογία, vid. Lumper, Hist. Theol. t. 2, p. 478.

Λόγος,

ἐνδιάθετος καὶ προφορικός.

Vid. rt. *Word*.

Μετουσία.

To all creatures in different ways or degrees is it given
to participate in the Divine attributes. In these it is
that they are able or wise or great or good; in these
they have life, health, strength, well-being, as the case
may be. And the All-abounding Son is He through
whom this exuberance of blessing comes to them
severally.

They are partakers, in their measure, of what He
possesses in fulness. From the Father's οὐσία, which is
His too, they have through Him a μετουσία. Here lies
the cardinal difference of doctrine between the Catholic
and Arian: Arians maintain that the Son has only
that μετουσία of God, which we too have. Catholics
hold Him to be God, and the Source of all divine
gifts. The antagonism between Athanasius and
Eusebius is the more pointed, by the very strength of
the language of the latter. He considers the Son
ἐξ αὐτῆς τῆς πατρικῆς ⌊not οὐσίας, but⌋ μετουσίας,
ὥσπερ ἀπὸ πηγῆς, ἐπ' [vid. supr. *Eusebius*] αὐτὸν
προχεομένης, πληρούμενον. Eccl. Theol. i. 2. But Athanasius, οὐδὲ κατὰ μετουσίαν αὐτοῦ, ἀλλ' ὅλον ἴδιον αὐτοῦ
γέννημα. Orat. iii. § 4.

¶ Athanasius considers this attribute of communication to be one of the prerogatives of the Second
Person in the Divine Trinity. He enlarges on this

doctrine in many places: e.g. "if, as we have said before, the Son is not such by participation, but, while all things generated have, by participation, the grace of God, He is the Father's Wisdom and Word, of which all things partake, if so, it follows that He, as the deifying and enlightening power of the Father, in which all things are deified and quickened, is not alien in substance from the Father, but one in substance. For by partaking of Him, we partake of the Father; inasmuch as the Word is proper to the Father. Whence, if He was Himself too from participation, and not the substantial Godhead and Image of the Father, He would not deify, being deified Himself. For it is not possible that he who but possesses from participation, should impart of that portion to others, since what he has is not his own, but the Giver's; as what he has received is barely the grace sufficient for himself." Syn. § 51.

¶ " As the Father has life in Himself, so has He also given to the Son to have life in Himself," *not by participation*, but in Himself. What the Father gives to the Son is a *communication* of Himself; what He gives to His creatures is a participation. Vid. supr. Orat. i. § 16. "To say that God is *wholly partaken* is equivalent to saying that *He begets*."

Μία φύσις,

(of our Lord's Godhead and of His Manhood).

Two natures are united in One Christ, but it does
not follow that their union is like any other union of
which we have cognisance, such, for instance, as the
union of body and soul. Beyond the general fact, that
both the Incarnation and other unions are of substances
not homogeneous, there is no likeness between it and
them. The characteristics and circumstances of the Incarnation are determined by its history. The One Self-
existing Personal God created, moulded, assumed, a
manhood truly such. He, being from eternity, was in
possession and in the fulness of His Godhead before mankind had being. Much more was He already in existence,
and in all His attributes, when He became man, and
He lost nothing by becoming. All that He ever had
continued to be His ; what He took on Himself · was
only an addition. There was no change ; in His
Incarnation, He did but put on a garment. That
garment was not *He*, or, as Athan. speaks, αὐτὸς, or,
as the next century worded it, " His Person." That
αὐτὸς was, as it had ever been, one and the same with
His Divinity, οὐσία, or φύσις ; it was this φύσις, as one
with His Person, which took to Itself a manhood. He
had no other Person than He had had from the beginning ; His manhood had no Personality of its own ;

it was a second φύσις, but not a second Person; it never existed till it was His; for its integrity and completeness it depended on Him, the Divine Word. It was one with Him, and, through and in Him, the Divine Word, it was one with the Divine Nature; it was but indirectly united to It, for the medium of union was the Person of the Word. And thus being without personality of its own, His human nature was relatively to Himself really what the Arians falsely said that His divinity was relatively to the Father, a περὶ αὐτὸν, a περιβολὴ, a συμβεβηκὸς, a "something else besides His substance," Orat. ii. § 45, e.g. an ὄργανον. Such was His human nature; it might be called an additional attribute; the Word was "made man," not was made a man.

¶ Thus Athanasius almost confines the word οὐσία to denote the Word, and seldom speaks of His manhood as a nature; and Cyril, to denote the dependence of the manhood upon His Divine Nature, has even used of the Incarnate Lord the celebrated dictum, μία φύσις τοῦ θεοῦ λόγου σεσαρκωμένη. This was Cyril's strong form of protesting against Nestorianism, which maintained that our Lord's humanity had a person as well as the Divine Word, who assumed it.

¶ Athan.'s language is remarkable: he says, Orat. ii. § 45, that our Lord is not a creature, though God, in Prov. viii. 22, is said to have created Him, because to be a creature, He ought to have taken a created substance, which He did not. Does not this imply that he did not consider His manhood an οὐσία or φύσις? He says that He who is said to be created, is not at once in His

Nature and *Substance* a creature : ἡ λέξις τι ἕτερον δηλοῖ περὶ ἐκεῖνον, καὶ οὐ τὸ λεγόμενον κτίζεσθαι ἤδη τῇ φύσει καὶ τῇ οὐσίᾳ κτίσμα. As the complement of this peculiarity, vid. his constant use of the οὐσία τοῦ λόγου, when we should use the word " Person." Does not this corroborate St. Cyril in his statement that the saying, "μία φύσις σεσαρκωμένη" belongs to Athanasius? for whether we say one φύσις or one οὐσία does not seem to matter.   Observe, too, he speaks of something taking place in Him, περὶ ἐκεῖνον, i.e. some adjunct or accident, (vid. art. περιβολὴ and συμβεβηκὸς,) or, as he says, Orat. ii. § 8, envelopment or dress.   In like manner he presently, ii. § 46, speaks of the creation of the Word as like the new-creation of the soul, which is a creation not in substance but in qualities, &c.   And ibid. § 51, he contrasts the οὐσία and the ἀνθρώπινον of the Word; as in Orat. i. 41, οὐσία and ἡ ἀνθρωπότης; and φύσις with σάρξ, iii. 34, init.; and λόγος with σάρξ, 38, init.   And he speaks of the Son "taking on Him the *economy*," ii. § 76, and of the ὑπόστασις τοῦ λόγου being one with ὁ ἄνθρωπος, iv. 35; why does he not, instead of ἀνθρώπινον, use the word φύσις?

It is plain that this line of teaching might be wrested to the purposes of the Apollinarian and Eutychian heresies; but, considering Athan.'s most emphatic protests against those errors in his later works, as well as his strong statements in Orat. iii., there is no hazard in this admission.   We thus understand how Eutyches came to deny the "two natures."   He said that such a doctrine was a new one; this is not true, for, not to mention other Fathers, Athan. Orat. iv. fin. speaks of our Lord's "invisible nature *and visible*," (vid. also contr. Apoll. ii. 11, Orat. ii. 70, iii. 43,) and his ordinary use of ἄνθρωπος for the manhood might quite as plausibly be perverted on the other hand into a defence of Nestorianism; but still the above peculiarities in his style may be taken to account for the heresy, though they do not excuse the heretic. Vid. also the Ed. Ben. on S. Hilary (præf. p. xliii.), who uses *natura* absolutely for our Lord's Divinity, as contrasted to the *dispensatio*, and divides His titles into *naturalia* and *assumpta*.

¶ St. Leo secured at Chalcedon this definition of the "Two Natures" of Christ, instead of the Alexandrian "One Nature Incarnate." In this he did but follow the precedent of the Nicene Fathers, who recalled the dogmatic authority of the ὁμοούσιον, which in the preceding century had been superseded at Antioch.

Μοναρχία.

Vid. *Father Almighty*.

Μονογενής.

THE Arians had a difficulty as to the meaning, in their
theology, of the word μονογενής. Eunomius decided
that it meant, not μόνος γεννηθεὶς, but γεννηθεὶς παρὰ
μόνου. And of the first Arians also Athan. apparently
reports that they considered the Son Only-begotten
because He μόνος was brought into being by God
μόνος. Decr. § 7. The Macrostich Confession in like
manner interprets μονογενὴς by μόνος and μόνως, Syn.
§ 26, (supr. vol. i. p. 107,) i.e. the only one of the
creatures who was named "Son," and the Son of
one Father (with Eunomius above), in opposition to
the προβολὴ of the Gnostics. (vid. Acacius in Epiph.
Hær. p. 839.) Naz., however, explains μόνως by οὐχ ὡς
τὰ σώματα. Orat. 25. 16. vid. the Eusebian distinction
between ὁμοούσιος and ὁμοιούσιος, Soz. iii. 18, in art.
ὁμοούσιος infr. It seems, however, that Basil and
Gregory Nyssen, (if I understand Petav. rightly, Trin.
vii. 11, § 3,) consider μονογενὴς to include ὑπὸ μόνου, as if
in contrast to the Holy Spirit, whose procession is not
from the Father only, or again not a *gennesis*.

¶ If it be asked, what the *distinctive* words are
which are incommunicably the Son's, since so many of
His names are given also to the creature, it is obvious
to answer, ἴδιος υἱὸς and μονογ νὴς, which are in
Scripture, and the symbols "of the substance," and

"one in substance," used by the Council; and this is the value of the Council's phrases, that, while they guard the Son's divinity, they allow full scope, without risk of trenching on it, to the Catholic doctrine of the fulness of the Christian privileges. vid. art. *Son.* For ʼΑγαπητὸς, vid. Matt. iii. in *Scripture Passages.*

The "Ὁμοιον.

GOD is both One and Three: neither as One nor as
Three can we speak of likeness in connection with
Him; for likeness, as Athan. says, relates not to
things but to their qualities, and to speak of likeness
between Father, Son, and Spirit, is to imply that
instead of being One and the Same, They are three
distinct beings. Again, so far as They are three, They
do but differ from each other, and are not merely
unlike; They are ke in nothing, viewed as Persons;
They have not so much likeness as to admit (in the
ordinary sense) of numbering. Those things, strictly
speaking, alone are like or equal which are not the
same: the Three Divine Persons are not like Each
Other, whether viewed as Three or One.

However, in the difficulty of finding terms, which
will serve as a common measure of theological thought
for the expression of ideas as to which there is no
experimental knowledge or power of conception, and
in the necessary use of economical language, both
these terms, likeness and equality, have been received
in orthodox teaching concerning the Supreme Being.
The Athanasian Creed declares that the Three Persons
in the Godhead have "æqualis gloria," and are
"co-æquales," and S. Athanasius himself in various
places uses the word "like," though he condemns its

adoption in the mouth of Arians, as being insufficient to exclude error.

That is, he accepts it as a word of orthodoxy as far as it goes, while he rejects it as sufficient to serve as a symbol and test. Sufficient it is not, even with the strong additions, which the Semi-Arians made, of ὅμοιος κατὰ πάντα, ὅμοιος κατ᾽ οὐσίαν or ὁμοιούσιος, and ἀπαράλλακτος εἰκὼν, because what is like, is, by the very force of the term, not equivalent to the same. Thus he says, Syn. § 41 and 53, "Only to say ' Like according to substance,' is very far from signifying ' Of the substance ' (vid. art. Eusebius); thus tin is only like silver, and gilt brass like gold. . . No one disputes that like is not predicated of substances, but of habits and of qualities. Therefore in speaking of Like in substance, we mean Like by participation, κατὰ μετουσίαν, and this belongs to creatures, for they, by partaking, are made like to God . . . not in substance, but in sonship, which we shall partake from Him. . . . If then ye speak of the Son as being such by participation, then indeed call Him like God in substance and not in nature God, . . . but if this be extravagant, He must be, not by participation, but in nature and truth, Son, Light, Wisdom, God; and being so by nature and not by sharing, therefore He is properly called, not Like in substance with the Father, but One in substance,"—that is, not ὁμοιούσιος, but ὁμοούσιος, Consubstantial.

Yet clear and decided as is his language here, nevertheless, for some reason (probably from a feeling of charity, as judging it best to inculcate first the revealed truth itself as a mode of introducing to the faithful and defending the orthodox symbol, and showing its meaning and its necessity,) he uses the phrases ὅμοιος κατὰ πάντα, and ὁμοιούσιος more commonly than ὁμοούσιος: this I have noted elsewhere.

¶ E.g. ὅμοιος κατὰ πάντα. "He who is in the Father, and like the Father in all things." Orat. i. § 40. "Being the Son of God, He must be like Him." Orat. ii. § 17. "The Word is unlike us, and like the Father." Orat. iii. § 20 ; also i. § 21, 40 ; ii. § 18, 22. Ep. Ægypt. 17.

¶ And ὅμοιος κατ' οὐσίαν. " . . Unless indeed they give up shame, and say that 'Image' is not a token of similar substance, but His name only." Orat. i. § 21. Vid. also Orat. i. § 20 init. 26 ; iii. § 11, 26, 67. Syn. § 38. Alex. Enc. § 2.

¶ Also Athan. says that the Holy Trias is ὅμοια ἑαυτῇ, instead of using the word ὁμοούσια. Serap. i. 17, 20, 38 ; also Cyril. Catech. vi. 7.

¶ In some of the Arian Creeds we have this almost Catholic formula, ὅμοιον κατὰ πάντα, introduced by the bye, marking the presence of what may be called the new Semi-Arian school. Of course it might admit of evasion, but in its fulness it included "substance." At Sirmium Constantius inserted the above (Epiph. Hær. 73, 22) in the Confession which occurs supr. vol. i. p. 72. On this occasion Basil subscribed in this form : "I, Basil, Bishop of Ancyra, believe and assent to what is aforewritten, confessing that the Son is like the Father in all things ; and by 'in all things,' not only that He is like in will, but in subsistence, and existence, and being ; as divine Scripture teaches, spirit from spirit, life from life, light from light, God from God, true Son from true, Wisdom from the Wise God and Father; and once for all, like the Father in all things, as a son is to a father. And if any one says that He is like in a certain respect, κατά τι, as is written afore, he is alien from the Catholic Church, as not confessing the likeness according to divine Scripture." Epiph. Hær. 73, 22. S. Cyril of Jerusalem uses the κατὰ πάντα or ἐν πᾶσιν ὅμοιον, Catech. iv. 7; xi. 4 and 18; and Damasc. F. O. i. 8, p. 135.

¶ S. Athanasius, in saying that like is not used of ·substance, implies that the common Arian senses of ὅμοιον are more natural, and therefore the more probable, and therefore also the less admissible by Catholics, if the word came into use. These were, 1. likeness in *will* and *action*, as συμφωνία, of which vid. Orat. iii. 11. 2. likeness to the *idea* in God's mind in which the Son was created. Cyril. Thesaur. p. 134. 3. likeness to the divine *act* or *energy* by which He was created. Basil. contr. Eun. iv. p. 282. Cyril. in Joan. c. 5. iii. p. 304. 4. like according to the Scriptures, which of course was but an evasion. 5. like κατὰ πάντα, which was, as they understood it, an evasion also.

¶ According to Athanasius, supr. p. 371, the phrase "unvarying image" was, in truth, self-contradictory, for every image varies from the original because it is an image. Still he himself frequently uses it, as other Fathers, and Orat. i. § 26, uses ὅμοιος τῆς οὐσίας.

¶ As "of the substance" declared that our Lord was *uncreate*, so "one in substance" declared that He was *equal* with the Father; no term derived from "likeness," even "like in substance," answering for this purpose, for such phrases might all be understood of *resemblance* or *representation*. vid. Decr. § 23, Hyp. Mel. and Hil. Syn. 89. Things that are like cannot be the same; whereas Athan. contends for the ταὐτὸν τῇ ὁμοιώσει, the same in likeness, Decr. § 20. "Una substantia religiose prædicabitur, quæ ex nativitatis proprietate et ex naturæ similitudine ita indifferens sit, ut una dicatur." Hil. Syn. § 67.

¶ By "the Son being *equal* to the Father," is but meant that He is His "unvarying image;" it does not imply any distinction of substance. "Perfectæ. æqualitatis significantiam habet similitudo." Hil. de Syn. 73. But though He is in all things the Father's Image, this implies some exception, for else He would not be an Image, merely like or equal, as I said just now, but the same. "Non est æqualitas in dissimilibus, nec similitudo est intra unum." ibid. 72. Hence He is the Father's image in all things except in being the Father, εἰκὼν φυσικὴ καὶ ἀπαράλλακτος κατὰ πάντα ὅμοια τῷ πατρὶ, πλὴν τῆς ἀγεννησίας καὶ τῆς πατρότητος. Damasc. de Imag. iii. 18, p. 354. vid. also Basil contr. Eun. ii. 28. Theod. Inconfus. p. 91. Basil. Ep. 38, 7 fin. For the Son is the Image of the Father, not as Father, but as God. The Arians on the other hand, objecting to the phrase "unvarying image," asked why the Son was not in consequence a Father, and the beginning of a θεογονία. vid. Athan. Orat. i. § 14, 21. Eunom. in Cyril. Thes. pp. 22, 23.

¶ The characteristic of Arianism in all its shapes was the absolute separation of Father from Son. It considered Them as two οὐσίαι, like perhaps, but not really one; this was their version of the phrase τέλειος ἐκ τελείου. Semi-Arians here agreed with Arians. When the Semi-Arians came nearest to orthodoxy in words, it was the περιχώρησις that was the test whether they fell short in words alone, or in their theological view.

Ὁμοούσιος.

THE term ὁμοούσιος, *one in substance* or *consubstantial*,
was accepted as a symbol, for securing the doctrine of
our Lord's divinity, first by the infallible authority of
the Nicene Council, and next by the experimental
assent and consent of Christendom, wrought out in its
behalf by the events of the prolonged Arian controversy.

It had had the mischance in the previous century of
being used by heretics in their own sense, and of in-
curring more or less of suspicion and dislike from the
Fathers in the great Council of Antioch, A.D. 264—272,
though it had been already in use in the Alexandrian
Church; but, when the momentous point in dispute, the
divinity of the Son, was once thoroughly discussed and
understood, it was forced upon the mind of theologians
that the reception or rejection of this term was the
difference between Catholic truth and Arianism.

¶ "We were aware," says Eusebius to his people,
"that, even among the ancients, some learned and
illustrious Bishops and writers have used the term
'one in substance,' in their theological teaching concerning the Father and Son." And Athanasius in like
manner, ad Afros 6, speaks of "testimony of ancient
Bishops about 130 years since;" and in de Syn. § 43,
of "long before" the Council of Antioch, Tertullian,

Prax. 13 fin., has the translation "unius substantiæ," as he also has "de substantia Patris," in Prax. 4; and Origen perhaps used the word, vid. Pamph. Apol. 5, and Theognostus and the two Dionysius's, Decr. § 25, 26. And before them Clement had spoken of the ἕνωσις τῆς μοναδικῆς οὐσίας, "the union of the single substance," vid. Le Quien in Damasc. Fid. Orth. i. 8. Novatian too has "per substantiæ communionem," de Trin. 31. Vid. Athan. ad Afros 5, 6; ad Serap. ii. 5. S. Ambrose tells us, that a Letter written by Eusebius of Nicomedia, in which he said, "If we call Him true Son of the Father and uncreate, then are we granting that He is one in substance, ὁμοούσιον," determined the Council on the adoption of the term. de Fid. iii. n. 125. He had disclaimed "of the substance," in his Letter to Paulinus. Theod. Hist. i. 4. Arius, however, had disclaimed ὁμοούσιον already, Epiph. Hær. 69, 7, and again in the Thalia. Gibbon's untenable assertion has been already observed upon (vid. *Nicene Tests*) supr., viz., that the Council was at a loss for a test, and that on Eusebius's "ingenuously confessing that his ὁμοούσιος was incompatible with the principles of [his] theological system, the *fortunate opportunity* was eagerly embraced by the Bishops," as if they were bent at all hazards, and without reference to the real and substantial agreement or disagreement of themselves and the Arians, to find some word which might accidentally serve to exclude the latter from communion.

¶ When the Semi-Arians objected that the Council of Antioch, 264—272, determined that the Son is not

consubstantial with the Father, de Syn. supr. 49—52,
Athan. answered in explanation that Paul of Samosata took the word in a material sense, as indeed
Arius did, calling it the doctrine of Manes and Hieracas. S. Basil, contr. Eunom. i. 19, agrees with Athan.,
but S. Hilary on the contrary reports that Paul himself accepted it, i.e. in a Sabellian sense, and therefore
the Council rejected it. " Male homoüsion Samo-
satenus confessus est, sed numquid melius Arii nega-
verunt ? " de Syn. 86. Doubtless, however, both reasons
told in causing its rejection. But Montfaucon and
Bull consider it a difficulty. Hence, it would seem, the
former, in his *Nova Collectio*, t. ii. p. 19, renders οὐκοῦν
by *ergo non ;* he had not inserted *non* in his addition of
Athanasius.

¶ The objections made to the word ὁμοούσιον were, 1.
that it was not in Scripture ; 2. that it had been disowned by the Antiochene Council against Paul of
Samosata ; 3. that it was of a material nature, and belonged to the Manichees ; 4. or else that it was of a
Sabellian tendency ; 5. that it implied that the divine
substance was distinct from God.

¶ The Eusebians tried to establish a distinction between ὁμοούσιον and ὁμοιούςιον, " one in substance "
and " like in substance," of this sort : that the former
belonged to things material, and the latter to immaterial, Soz. iii. 18, a remark which in itself was quite
sufficient to justify the Catholics in insisting on the
former term. For the heretical party, starting with the
notion in which their heresy in all its shades consisted,
that the Son was a distinct being from the Father,

and appealing to a doctrine which might be plausibly maintained, that spirits are incommensurable with one another, or that each is at most not more than *sui similis*, concluded that "*like* in substance" was the only term which would express the relation of the Son to the Father. Here then the word "one in substance" did just enable the Catholics to join issue with them, as exactly expressing what Catholics wished to express, viz. that there was no such distinction between Them as made the term "like" necessary, or even possible, but that Their relation to Each Other was *analogous* to that of a material offspring to a material parent, or that, as material parent and offspring are individuals under one existing correlation, so the Eternal Father and Son are Persons under one common *individual substance*.

"The East," says Sozomen, "in spite of its being in dissension after the Antiochene Council" of the Dedication, "and thenceforth openly dissenting from the Nicene faith, in reality, I think, concurred in the sentiment of the majority, and with them confessed the Son to be of the Father's substance; but from contentiousness certain of them fought against the term 'One in substance;' some, as I conjecture, having originally objected to the word . . . others from habit . . . others, aware that the resistance was unsuitable, leaned to this side or that to gratify parties; and many thought it weak to waste themselves in such strife of words, and peaceably held to the Nicene decision." Hist. iii. 13.

Athan. is very reserved in his use of the, word ὁμοούσιον in these three Orations. Indeed I do not recollect his using it but once, Orat. i. § 9, and that in what is almost a confession of faith. Instead he uses ὅμοιος κατὰ πάντα, ὅμοιος κατ' οὐσίαν, ὁμοφυὴς, &c.

'Ονόματα.

THE various titles of the Second Divine Person are at once equivalent and complementary to each other. Son, Word, Image, all imply relation, and suggest and teach that attribute of supereffluence which is one of the perfections of the Divine Being. (vid. *Father Almighty.*)

" The Son of God, as may be learnt from the divine oracles themselves, is Himself the Word of God, and the Wisdom, and the Image, and the Hand, and the Power; for God's Offspring is one, and of the generation from the Father these titles are tokens. For if you say the Son, you have declared what is from the Father by nature; and if you imagine the Word, you are thinking again of what is from Him, and what is inseparable; and, speaking of Wisdom, again you mean nothing less, what is not from without, but from Him and in Him ; and if you name the Power and the Hand, again you speak of what is proper to substance; and, speaking of the Image, you signify the Son; for what else is like God but the Offspring from Him ? Doubtless the things which came to be through *the Word*, these are *founded in Wisdom;* and what are *laid in Wisdom*, these are all made by the Hand, and came to be through the Son." Decr. § 17.

¶ As Sonship is implied in " Image " (art. *Son*), so it

is implied in "Word" and "Wisdom." For instance,
"Especially is it absurd to name the Word, yet deny
Him to be Son, for, if the Word be not from God,
reasonably might they deny Him to be Son; but if He
is from God, how see they not that what exists from
anything is son of him from whom it is?" Orat. iv.
15. Again, ἀεὶ θεὸς ἦν καὶ υἱός ἐστι, λόγος ὤν. Orat.
iii. 29 init. υἱὸς τίς ἦ ὁ λόγος; de Decr. 17. And still
more pointedly, εἰ μὴ υἱός, οὐδὲ λόγος, Orat. iv. 24 fin.
And so "Image" is implied in Sonship: "being Son
of God, He must be like Him," ii. § 17. It is implied
in "Word:" ἐν τῇ ἰδίᾳ εἰκόνι, ἥτις ἐστὶν ὁ λόγος αὐτοῦ.
§ 82, also 34 fin. On the contrary, the very root
of heretical error was the denial that these titles implied each other.

¶ All the titles of the Son of God are consistent
with each other, and variously represent one and the
same Person. "Son" and "Word" denote His de-
rivation; "Word" and "Image," His Likeness;
"Word" and "Wisdom," His immateriality; "Wisdom" and "Hand," His co-existence. "What else is
Like God, but His Offspring from Him?" de Decr. § 17.
"If He is not Son, neither is He Image." Orat. ii.
§ 2. "How is there Word and Wisdom, unless there
be a proper Offspring of His substance?" ii. § 22. vid.
also Orat. i. § 20, 21, and at great length Orat. iv.
§ 20, &c. vid. also Naz. Orat. 30. 20. Basil. contr.
Eunom. i. 18. Hilar. de Trin. vii. 11. August. in
Joann. xlviii. 6, and in Psalm. 44, (45,) 5.

¶ It is sometimes erroneously supposed that such
illustrations as these are intended to *explain* how the

Sacred Mystery in question is possible, whereas they are merely intended to show that the words we use concerning it are not *self-contradictory*, which is the objection most commonly brought against them. To say that the doctrine of the Son's generation does not trench upon the Father's perfection and immutability, or negative the Son's eternity, seems at first sight inconsistent with what the words Father and Son mean, till another image is adduced, such as the sun and radiance, in which that alleged inconsistency can be conceived to exist in fact. Here one image corrects another; and the accumulation of images is not, as is often thought, the restless and fruitless effort of the mind to *enter into the Mystery*, but is a *safeguard* against any one image, nay, any collection of images, being supposed *adequate*. If it be said that the language used concerning the sun and its radiance is but popular, not philosophical, so again the Catholic language concerning the Holy Trinity may, nay, must be economical, not exact, conveying the truth, not in the tongues of angels, but under human modes of thought and speech. vid. supr. articles *Illustrations*, p. 174, and *Economical Language*, p. 94.

¶ It is usual with the Fathers to use the two terms "Son" and "Word" to guard and complete the ordinary sense of each other. Their doctrine is that our Lord is both, in a certain transcendent, prototypical, and singular sense; that in that high sense they are coincident with one another; that they are applied to human things by an accommodation, as far as these are shadows of Him to whom properly they really

belong ; that, being but partially realised on earth, the
ideas gained from the earthly types are but imperfect;
that in consequence, if any one of them is used exclu-
sively of Him, it tends to introduce wrong ideas re-
specting Him; but that their respective imperfections,
as lying on different sides, when used together correct
each other. The term Son, used by itself, was abused
into Arianism, and the term Word into Sabellianism;
the term Son might be accused of introducing material
notions, and the term Word of suggesting imperfection
and transitoriness. Each of them corrected the other.
" Scripture," says Athan., " joining the two, has said
' Son,' that the natural and true Offspring of the Substance may be preached; but, that no one may understand a human offspring, therefore, signifying His
substance a second time, it calls Him Word, and
Wisdom, and Radiance." Orat. i. § 28.

Vid. also iv. § 8. Euseb. contr. Marc. ii. 4, p. 54.
Isid. Pel. Ep. iv. 141. So S. Cyril says that we
learn " from His being called Son that He is from
Him, τὸ ἐξ αὐτοῦ; from His being called Wisdom and
Word, that He is in Him," τὸ ἐν αὐτῷ. Thesaur. iv.
p. 31. However, S. Athanasius observes, that properly speaking the one term implies the other, i.e. in
its fulness. " Since the Son's Being is from the Father,
therefore It is in the Father." Orat. iii. § 3. " If
not Son, not Word either; and if not Word, not Son.
For what is from the Father is Son; and what is from
the Father, but the Word ? " &c. Orat. iv. § 24 fin.
On the other hand, the heretics accused Catholics of
inconsistency, or of a union of opposite errors, because

they accepted all the Scripture images together. But Vigilius of Thapsus says, that "error bears testimony to truth, and the discordant opinions of misbelievers blend into concordance in the rule of orthodoxy." contr. Eutych. ii. init. "Grande miraculum, ut expugnatione sui veritas confirmetur." ibid. 3. vid. also i. init. and Eulogius, ap. Phot. 225, p. 759.

¶ Every illustration, as being incomplete on one or other side of it, taken by itself, tends to heresy. The title Son by itself suggests a second God, as the title Word a mere attribute, and the title Minister a creature. All heresies are partial views of the truth, and are wrong, not so much in what they say, as in what they deny. The truth, on the other hand, is a positive and comprehensive doctrine, and in consequence necessarily mysterious and open to misconception. When Athan. implies that the Eternal Father is in the Son, though remaining what He is, as a man is in his child, he is intent only upon the point of the Son's connaturality and co-equality, which the Arians denied. In like manner he says in a later Discourse, "In the Son the Father's Godhead is beheld. The Emperor's countenance and form are in his image, and the countenance of his image is in the Emperor. For the Emperor's likeness in his image is a definitive likeness, ἀπαράλλακτος, so that he who looks upon the image, in it sees the Emperor, and again he who sees the Emperor recognises that he is in the image. The image then might say, 'I and the Emperor are one.'" Orat. iii. § 5. And thus the Auctor de Trin. refers to "Peter, Paul, and Timothy having three subsistencies

and one humanity." i. p. 918. S. Cyril even seems to
deny that each individual man may be considered a
separate substance, except as the Three Persons are
such, Dial. i. p. 409; and S. Gregory Nyssen is led to
say that, strictly speaking, the abstract *man*, which is
predicated of separate individuals, is still one, and this
with a view of illustrating the Divine Unity. ad Ablab.
t. 2, p. 449. vid. Petav. de Trin. iv. 9.

¶ The title "Word" implies the ineffable mode of
the Son's generation, as distinct from *material* parallels,
vid. Gregory Nyssen, contr. Eunom. iii. p. 107. Chrysostom in Joan. Hom. 2, § 4. Cyril Alex. Thesaur. 5,
p. 37. Also it implies that there is but *One* Son. vid.
Orat. i. § 16. "As the Origin is one substance, so its
Word and Wisdom are one, substantial and subsisting."
Athan. Orat. iv. 1 fin.

¶ Vid. passim. All these titles, "Word, Wisdom,
Light," &c., serve to guard the title "Son" from
any notions of parts or dimensions, e.g. "He is not
composed of parts, but being impassible and single,
He is impassibly and indivisibly Father of the Son . . .
for . . . the Word and Wisdom is neither creature, nor
part of Him whose Word He is, nor an offspring
passibly begotten." Orat. i. § 28.

¶ As the Arians took the title Son in that part of
its earthly sense in which it did not apply to our Lord,
so they misinterpreted the title Word also; which denoted the Son's immateriality and indivisible presence
in the Father, but did not express His perfection. vid.
Orat. ii. § 34—36. "As our word belongs to us and
is from us, and not a work external to us, so also the

Word of God is proper to Him and from Him, and is not made, *yet not as the word of man,* else one must consider God as man. Men have many words," &c. Orat. ii. § 36. vid. art. *Word.*

¶ The name of Image was of great importance in correcting heterodox opinions as to the words Son and Word, which were propagated in the Ante-Nicene times, and in keeping their economical sense in the right direction. A son who had a beginning, and a word which was spoken and over, were in no sense an "Image" of the Eternal and All-perfect God.

Ὄργανον,

Instrument. This word, which is rightly used of our Lord's manhood relatively to His Divine Person (τούτῳ χρώμενος ὀργάνῳ, Orat. iii. § 31, and ὄργανον πρὸς τὴν ἐνέργειαν καὶ τὴν ἔκλαμψιν τῆς θεότητος,˙53), is simply heretical if taken to express the relation of His Divine Person towards His Father. In the latter relation the term is inapplicable,˙ unless He "was different from the Father in nature and substance." Decr. § 23. vid. Basil. de Sp. S. 19 fin. In this Arians, Socr. i. 6, Eusebius, Eccl. Theol. i. 8, and Anomœans would agree. At the same time, doubtless, some early writers use it of our Lord's Divine Nature, though not in a heretical sense. vid. art. *Mediation.*

¶ As it was abused by the Arians to mean a servant or ὑπουργὸς, as if our Lord was a mere creature, so it was afterwards used heretically in the doctrine of the Incarnation by the Apollinarians, who looked on our Lord's manhood as merely a *manifestation* of God. vid. καταπέτασμα. Thus σχῆμα ὀργανικὸν in Athan. in Apol. i. 2, 15, also a parallel in Euseb. Laud. Const. 13, p. 536. However, it is used freely even by Athan., e.g. Orat. iii. 31, 53, as above, and Incarn. 8, 9, 43, 44. And he uses the words πρὸς φανέρωσιν καὶ γνῶσιν, 41 fin., but he also insists upon our Lord's coming being not merely for manifestation, else He might have come in a higher nature. ibid. 8. vid. also 44. It may be added that φανέρωσις is a Nestorian as well as Eutychian idea; vid. Orat. iii. § 30, Facund. Tr. Cap. ix. 2, 3, and the Syrian use of *parsopa*, Asseman. Bibl. Orient. t. 4. p. 219. Thus both parties really denied the Atonement.

'Ορθός.

WHAT is strange to ears accustomed to Protestant modes of arguing, S. Athanasius does not simply expound Scripture, rather he vindicates it from the imputation of its teaching any but true doctrine. It is ever ὀρθός, he says, that is, orthodox; I mean, he takes it for granted that there is an existing doctrinal tradition, as a standard, with which Scripture must, and with which it doubtless does agree, and of which it is the written confirmation and record. Vid. Oxf. Trans. note, p. 431.

In Orat. ii. § 44, he says, " We have gone through thus much before coming to the passage in the Proverbs, that they may rightly read what admits in truth of a sound (ὀρθὴν) interpretation," as if the authoritative interpretation required to be applied to Scripture, before we could assume that the doctrine conveyed by it was orthodox. And so μετ' εὐσεβείας just below. Such phrases are frequent in Athan., e.g. τὴν διάνοιαν εὐσεβῆ καὶ λίαν ὀρθὴν, de Decr. 13. καλῶς καὶ ὀρθῶς, Orat. iv. 31. γέγραπται μάλα ἀναγκαίως, de Decr. 14. εἰκότως, Orat. ii. 44, iii. 53. τὴν διάνοιαν ἐκκλησιαστικὴν, Orat. i. 44 init. τὸν σκοπὸν τὸν ἐκκλησιαστικὸν, Orat. iii. 58. ἡ διάνοια ἔχει τὴν αἰτίαν εὔλογον, iii. 7 fin. vid. also Orat. i. 37 init. 46; ii. 1, 9 init. 12, 53; iii. 1, 18, 19, 35, 37; iv. 30.

¶ Vid. art. *Rule of Faith.* This illustrates what he means when he says that certain texts have a "good," "pious," "orthodox" sense, i.e. they can be interpreted (in spite, if so be, of appearances) in harmony with the Regula Fidei. And so, τὸ ἐν ταῖς παροιμίαις ῥητὸν, ὀρθὴν ἔχον καὶ αὐτὸ τὴν διάνοιαν. Orat. ii. § 44. ἤρκει ταῦτα πρὸς ἀπόδειξιν ὀρθὴν εἶναι τὴν τοῦ ῥητοῦ διάνοιαν. ibid. § 77. τὸ τοίνυν λεγόμενον ὑπὸ τοῦ μακαρίου Πέτρου ὀρθόν. iv. § 35. vid. also iii. 7, &c. &c.

Οὐσία, ὄν.

Usia, *substance.* The word οὐσία in its Greek or
Aristotelic sense seems to have stood for an individual
substance, numerically one, which is predicable of
nothing but itself. Improperiy, it stood for a species or
genus, vid. Petav. de Trin. iv. 1, § 2, but, as Anastasius
observes in many places of his *Viæ dux,* Christian
theology innovated on the sense of Aristotelic terms.
vid. c. 1, p. 20; c. 6, p. 96; c. 9, p. 150; c. 17, p. 308.
There is some difficulty in determining *how* it innovated. Anastasius and Theorian, (Hodeg. 6, Legat. ad
Arm. pp. 441, 2,) say that it takes οὐσία to mean an
universal or species, but this is nothing else than the
second or improper Greek use. Rather, in speaking of
God, it takes the word in a sense of its own, such as we
have no example of in creation, of a Being numerically
one, subsisting in three persons; so that the word is a
predicable, or in one sense *universal,* without ceasing
to be individual; in which consists the mystery of the
Holy Trinity. However, heretics, who refused the
mystery, objected it to Catholics in its primary philosophical sense; and then, standing simply for an individual
substance, when applied to Father and Son, it either
implied the parts of a *material* subject, or it involved
no *real* distinction of persons, i.e. Sabellianism. The
former of these two alternatives is implied in Athan.'s
text by the "Greek use;" the latter by the same phrase

as used by the conforming Semi-Arians, A.D. 363. "Nor, as if any passion were supposed of the ineffable generation, is the term 'substance' taken by the Fathers, &c., nor *according to any Greek use*," &c. Socr. iii. 25. Hence came such charges against Catholicism on the part of Arians as Alexander protests against, of *either* Sabellianism *or* Valentinianism, οὐκ . . . ὥσπερ Σαβελλίῳ καὶ Βαλεντίνῳ δοκεῖ, &c. Theod. Hist. i. 3, p. 743. Hence Paul's argument against the Antiochene Council in Athan.'s and in Hilary's report.

¶ By the substance of God we mean nothing more or less than God Himself. "If God be simple, as He is, it follows that in saying 'God' and naming 'Father,' we name nothing as if about (περὶ) Him, but signify His substance, and that alone." Decr. § 22.

In like manner de Synod. § 34. Also Basil, "The substance is not any one of things which do not attach, but is the very being of God." contr. Eunom. i. 10 fin. "The nature of God is no other than Himself, for He is simple and uncompounded." Cyril Thesaur. p. 59. "When we say the person of the Father, we say nothing else than the substance of the Father." August. de Trin. vii. 6. And so Numenius in Eusebius, "Let no one deride, if I say that the name of the Immaterial is substance and being." Præp. Evang. xi. 10.

¶ In many passages Athan. seems to make *usia* synonymous with *hypostasis*, but this mode of speaking only shows that the two terms had not their respective meanings so definitely settled and so familiarly received as afterwards. Its *direct* meaning is usually substance, though *indirectly* it came to imply subsistence. He speaks of that Divine Essence which, though also the Almighty Father's, is as simply and entirely the Word's as if it were only His. Nay, even when the Substance of the Father is spoken of in a sort of contrast to that of the Son, as in the phrase οὐσία ἐξ οὐσίας, (e.g. "His substance is the offspring of the Father's substance," Syn. § 48, and ἐξ οὐσίας οὐσιώδης καὶ ἐνούσιος, Orat. iv. 1,) harsh as such expressions are, it is not accurate to say that οὐσία is used for subsistence or person, or that two οὐσίαι are spoken of (vid. art. φύσις), except, that is, by Arians, as Eusebius (art. *Eusebius*). We find φύσις τοῦ λόγου, Orat. i. § 51 init., meaning His *usia* without including the idea of His Person. vid. art. εἶδος.

Other passages may be brought, in which *usia* and *hypostasis* seem to be synonymous, as Orat. iii. § 65. "The Apostle proclaims the Son to be the very impress, not of the Father's will, but of His *usia*, saying, 'the impress of His *hypostasis*;' and if the Father's *usia* and *hypostasis* is not from will, it is very plain neither is from will what belongs to the Father's *hypostasis*." And so Orat. iv. § 1: "As there is one Origin, and therefore one God, so one is that substance and subsistence which indeed and truly and really exists." And "The Prophet has long since ascribed the Father's *hypostasis* to Him." Orat. iv. § 33. And ἡ ὑπόστασις οὐσία ἐστὶ, καὶ οὐδὲν ἄλλο σημαινόμενον ἔχει ἢ αὐτὸ τὸ ὄν. . . . . ἡ γὰρ ὑπόστασις καὶ ἡ οὐσία ὕπαρξίς ἐστι. ad Afros, 4.

For the meaning in the early Fathers of οὐσία, ὑπόστασις, φύσις, and εἶδος, vid. the author's "Theological Tracts," art. Μία φύσις.

Περιβολή.

ATHAN. seems to say, Decret. § 22, and so de Synod. § 34, which is very much the same passage, that there is nothing of quality (περὶ αὐτὸν) in God. Some Fathers, however, seem to say the reverse. E.g. Nazianzen lays down that "neither the immateriality of God, nor the ingenerateness, present to us His substance." Orat. 28. 9. And S. Augustine, arguing on the word *ingenitus*, says, that "not everything which is said to be in God is said according to substance." de Trin. v. 6. And hence, while Athan. in the text denies that there are qualities or the like belonging to Him, περὶ αὐτὸν, it is still common in the Fathers to speak of qualities, as in the passage of S. Gregory, just cited, in which the words περὶ θεὸν occur. There is no difficulty in reconciling these statements, though it would require more words than could be given to it here. Petavius has treated the subject fully in his work de Deo, i. 7—11, and especially ii. 3. When the Fathers say that there is no difference between the divine 'proprietates' and essence, they speak of the fact considering the Almighty as He is; when they affirm a difference, they speak of Him as contemplated by us, who are unable to grasp the idea of Him as one and simple, but view His Divine Nature as if *in projection*, (if such a word may be used,) and thus divided into substance and quality as man may be divided into genus and difference.

Πηγή.

Vid. *Father Almighty.*

Προβολή.

WHAT the Valentinian προβολὴ was, is described in Epiph. Hær. 31, 13. The Æons, wishing to show thankfulness to God, contributed together (ἐράνισα-μένους) whatever was most beautiful of each of them, and moulding these several excellences into one, formed this Issue, προβαλλέσθαι πρόβλημα, to the honour and glory of the Profound, βύθος, and they called this star and flower of the Pleroma, Jesus, &c. And so Tertullian, "a joint contribution, ex ære collatitio, to the honour and glory of the Father, ex omnium defloratione constructum," contr. Valent. 12. Accordingly Origen protests against the notion of προβολὴ, Periarch. iv. 28, p. 190, and Athanasius Expos. § 1. The Arian Asterius too considers προβολὴ to introduce the notion of τεκνογονία, Euseb. contr. Marc. i. 4, p. 20. vid. also Epiph. Hær. 72, 7. Yet Eusebius uses the word προβάλλεσθαι, Eccles. Theol. i. 8. On the other hand, Tertullian uses it with a protest against the Valentinian sense. Justin has προβληθὲν γέννημα, Tryph. 62. And Nazianzen calls the Almighty Father προβολεὺς of the Holy Spirit. Orat. 29. 2. Arius introduces the word into his creed, Syn. § 14, as an *argumentum ad invidiam.* Hil. de Trin. vi. 9.

Πρωτότοκος.

Primogenitus, " First-born."

¶ Πρωτότοκος and *Primogenitus* are not exact equivalents, though Homer may use τίκτω for *gigno*. Primogenitus is never used in Scripture for Unigenitus. We never read there of the First-born of God, of the Father; but of the First-born of the creation, whether of the original creation or of the new.

¶ First-born, or the beginning, is used as an epithet of our Lord five times in Scripture, and in each case it is distinct in meaning from Only-begotten. It is a word of office, not of nature. 1. St. Paul speaks of His becoming, in His incarnation, the " First-born among many brethren," Rom. viii. 29; and he connects this act of mercy with their being conformed to His Image, and gifted with grace and glory. 2. He is " the First-born of the dead," Apoc. i. 5. 3. As also in Col. i. 18. 4. Col. i. 15. " The First-born of all creation," as *quasi* the efficient and the formal cause whereby the universe is born into a divine adoption. 5. St. Paul speaks of the Father's " bringing the First-born into the world." To these may be added, Apoc. iii. 14, " the beginning of the [new] creation of God." In none of these passages does the phrase " First-born of God " occur.

¶ Our Lord is in three distinct respects πρωτότοκος, First-born or Beginning, as the animating Presence of the Universe, as the Life of the Christian Church, as the first-fruit and pledge and earnest of the Resurrection.

The word never intimates in Scripture His divine nature itself. "It is nowhere written of Him in the Scriptures 'the First-born of God,' nor 'the creation of God,' but it is the words ' the Only-begotten,' and 'Son,' and 'Word,' and 'Wisdom,' that signify His relation and His belonging to the Father. But 'First-born' implies descent to the creation. . . . The same cannot be both Only-begotten and First-born, except in different relations ; that is, Only-begotten, because of His generation from the Father, and First-born, because of His condescension to the creation, and to the brotherhood which He has extended to many." Orat. ii. § 62.

In like manner Augustine says that we must distinguish between the two titles " Only-begotten and First-born," that the Son may be with the Father Only-begotten, and First-born towards us. vid. - the author's Theol. Tracts, *Arianism*, § 9, circ. fin. And St. Thomas says, " In quantum solus est verus et naturalis Dei Filius, dicitur Unigenitus, .. in quantum vero per assimilationem ad ipsum alii dicuntur filii adoptivi, quasi metaphoricè dicitur esse Primogenitus." Part I. 41, art. 3 (t. 20).

¶ It would be perhaps better to translate " first-born *to* the creature," to give Athan.'s idea ; τῆς κτίσεως not being a partitive genitive, or πρωτότοκος a

superlative, (though he so considers it also,) but a
simple appellative and τῆς κτίσεως a common genitive
of relation, as "the king of a country," "the owner of
a house." "First-born of creation" is like "author,
type, life of creation." As, after calling our Lord in
His own nature "a light," we might proceed to say
that He was also "a light to the creation," or "Arch-
luminary," so He was not only the Eternal Son, but a
"Son to creation," an "archetypal Son." Hence St.
Paul goes on at once to say, "for *in* Him all things
were made," not simply "by and for," as at the end
of the verse; or as Athan. says, Orat. ii. § 63, "because
in Him the creation came to be." On the distinction of
διὰ and ἐν, referring respectively to the first and
second creations, vid. In illud Omn. 2.

¶ "His coming into the world," says Athan., "is
what makes Him called 'First-born' of all; and thus
the Son is the Father's 'Only-begotten,' because He
alone is from Him, and He is the 'First-born of creation,' because of this adoption of all as sons." Thus
he considers that "first-born" is mainly a title, connected with the incarnation, and also connected with our
Lord's office at the creation. (vid. parallel of Priesthood, art. *in voc.*) In each economy it has the same
meaning; it belongs to Him as the type, idea, or
rule on which the creature was made or new-made,
and the life by which it is sustained. Both economies
are mentioned, Incarn. 13, 14. And so εἴκων καὶ τύπος
πρὸς ἀρετήν, Orat. i. 51. (vid. art. *Freedom*, supr. p. 127.)
And τύπον τινὰ λαβόντες and ὑπογραμμόν, iii. 20. vid.
also 21. ἐν αὐτῷ ἦμεν προτετυπωμένοι. ii. 76, init.

He came τύπον εἰκόνος ἐνθεῖναι. 78, init. τὴν τοῦ ἀρχετύπον πλάσιν ἀναστήσασθαι ἑαυτῷ. contr. Apol. ii. 5. Also κατεσφραγίσθημεν εἰς τὸ ἀρχέτυπον τῆς εἰκόνος. Cyr. in Joan. v. 12, p. 91. οἷον ἀπὸ τινὸς ἀρχῆς, Nyss. Catech. 16, p. 504, fin. And so again, as to the original creation, the Word is ἰδέα καὶ ἐνέργεια of all material things. Athen. Leg. 10. ἡ ἰδέα . . ὅπερ λόγον εἰρήκασι. Clem. Strom. v. 3. ἰδέαν ἰδεῶν καὶ ἀρχὴν λεκτέον τὸν πρωτότοκον πάσης κτίσεως. Origen. contr. Cels. vi. 64, fin. " Whatever God was about to make in the creature, was already in the Word, nor would be in the things, were it not in the Word." August. in Psalm. 44, 5. He elsewhere calls the Son, "ars quædam omnipotentis atque sapientis Dei, plena omnium rationum viventium incommutabilium." de Trin. vi. 11. And so Athan. says πρωτότοκος εἰς ἀπόδειξιν τῆς τῶν πάντων διὰ τοῦ υἱοῦ δημιουργίας καὶ υἱοποιήσεως. iii. 9, fin. vid. the contrast presented to us by the Semi-Arian Eusebius on the passage which Athan. is discussing, (Prov. viii. 22,) as making the Son, not the ἰδέα, but the external minister of the Father's ἰδέα (in art. *Eusebius*, supra). S. Cyril says on the contrary, " The Father shows the Son what He does Himself, *not* as if setting it before Him drawn out on a tablet, or teaching Him as ignorant; for He knows all things as God; but as depicting Himself whole in the nature of the Offspring," &c., in Joann. v. 20, p. 222.

ʽΡευστός.

Vᴵᴰ. Decr. § 11. de Synod. § 51. Orat. i. § 15, 16. vid.
also Orat. i. § 28. Bas. in Eun. ii. 23. ῥύσιν. ibid. ii. 6.
Greg. Naz. Orat. 28. 22. Vid. contr. Gentes, § 41,
where Athan., without reference to the Arian controversy, draws out the contrast between the Godhead
and human nature. "The nature of things generated,"
as having its subsistence from nothing, "is of a
transitory (ῥευστός, melting, dissolving, dissoluble)
and feeble and mortal sort, considered by itself.
Seeing then that it was *transitory* and had no stay, lest
this should come into effect, and it should be resolved
into its original nothing, God governs and sustains it
all by His own Word, who is Himself God," and who,
he proceeds, § 42, "remaining Himself immovable with
the Father, moves all things in His own consistence,
as in each case it may seem fit to His Father." vid.
Μετουσία, &c.

Συγκατάβασις.

"CONDESCENSION" of the Son. Vid. the author's
"Tracts, Theological, &c.," to which, on a subject
too large for a Note, the reader is referred.
By this term Athanasius expresses that (so to say)
stooping from the height of His Infinite Majesty,
which is involved in the act of the Almighty's sur-
rounding Himself with a created universe. This may
of course be sometimes spoken of as the act of the
Eternal Father, but is commonly and more naturally
ascribed to the Only-begotten Son. Creation was the
beginning of this condescension; but creation was but
an inchoate act if without conservation accompanying it.
The universe would have come into being one moment
only to have come to nought the next, from its intrinsic
impotence, and moreover from the unendurableness on
the part of the finite of contact with the Infinite, had
not the Creator come to it also as a conservator.

"The Word," says Athanasius, "when in the beginning He framed the creatures, *condescended* to them,
that it might be possible for them to come into being.
For they could not have endured His absolute, unmi-
tigated nature, and His splendour from the Father,
unless, condescending with the Father's love for man,
He had supported them, and brought them into subsistence." Orat. ii. 64. vid. art. ἄκρατος.

This conservation lay in a gift over and above nature, a gift of grace, a presence of God throughout the vast universe, as a principle of life and strength; and that Presence is in truth the indwelling in it of the Divine Word and Son, who thereby took His place permanently as if in the rank of creatures, and as their First-born and Head, thereby drawing up the whole circle of creatures into a divine adoption, whereby they are mere works no longer, but sons of God. He has thus, as it were, stamped His Image, His Sonship, upon all things according to their several measures, and became the archetype of creation and its life and goodness.

As then He is in His nature the Only Son of God, so is He by office First-born of all things and Eldest Son in the world of creatures. Vid. Πρωτότοκος.

Συμβεβηκός,

Or Accident. The point in which Arians and Sabellians agreed was that Wisdom was only an attribute, not a Person, in the Divine Nature, for both denied the mystery of a Trinity in Unity. Hence St. Athanasius charges them with holding the Divine Nature to be compounded of substance and quality or accident, the latter being an envelopment or περιβολὴ or περὶ τὸν θεόν. Vid. as quoted below. Decr. § 22, and so Syn. § 34, ἕξιν συμβαίνουσαν καὶ ἀποσυμβαίνουσαν. Orat. iii. § 65. σύμβαμα. Euseb. Eccl. Theol. iii. p. 150. Also Or. ii. § 38. Serap. i. 26. Naz. Orat. 31. 15 fin. For περὶ τὸν θεὸν, vid. Decr. § 22, de Syn. § 34. Orat. i. § 14, 27; ii. 45; iii. § 65.

¶ Thus Eusebius calls our Lord " the light throughout the universe, moving round (ἄμφι) the Father." de Laud. Const. i. p. 501. It was a Platonic idea, which he gained from Plotinus, whom he quotes speaking of his second Principle as " radiance around, from Him indeed, but from one who remains what He was ; as the sun's bright light circling around it, (περίθεον,) ever generated from it, while the sun itself nevertheless remains." Evang. Præp. xi. 17. vid. Plotin. 4. Ennead. iv. c. 16.

Eusebius could afford to use Platonic language, because he considered our Lord to be external to the

Divine Nature; hence he can say, (as Marcellus could not,) by way of accusation against him, σύνθετον εἰσῆγεν τὸν θεὸν, οὐσίαν· δίχα λόγου συμβεβηκὸς δὲ τῇ οὐσίᾳ τὸν λόγον. Eccl. Theol. ii. 14, p. 121. However, Athan. says the same of the Arians, vid. references, supr. in this article; also ad Afros. 8. Basil. Ep. 8, 3. Cyril. Thes. p. 134. For the Sabellians vid. Ath. Orat. iv. 2; perhaps Epiph. Hær. 73, p. 852; and Cyril. Thes. p. 145. Basil. contr. Sabell. 1. Nyssen. App. contr. Eunom. i. p. 67, &c. Max. Cap. de Carit. t. i. p. 445. Damasc. F. O. i. 13, p. 151.

"If then any man conceives as if God were composite, so as to have accidents in His substance, or any external envelopment, and to be encompassed, or as if there were aught about Him which completes the substance, so that when we say 'God,' or name 'Father,' we do not signify the invisible and incomprehensible substance, but something about it, then let them complain of the Council's stating that the Son was from the substance of God; but let them reflect, that in thus considering they commit two blasphemies; for they make God material, and they falsely say that the Lord is not Son of the very Father, but of what is about Him. But if God be simple, as He is, it follows that in saying 'God' and naming 'Father,' we name nothing as if about Him, but signify His substance itself." Athan. Decr. § 22.

And so elsewhere, he says, when resisting the Arian and Sabellian notion that the wisdom of God is only a quality in the Divine Nature, "In that case God will be compounded of substance and quality; for

every quality is in a substance. And at this rate,
whereas the Divine Monad is indivisible, it will be
considered compound, being separated into substance
and accident." Orat. iv. 2. vid. also Orat. i. 36. This
is the common doctrine of the Fathers. Athenagoras,
however, speaks of God's goodness as an accident,
"as colour to the body," "as flame is ruddy and the
sky blue," Legat. 24. This, however, is but a verbal
difference, for shortly before (23) he speaks of His
being, τὸ ὄντως ὄν, and His unity of nature, τὸ μονοφυὲς,
as in the number of ἐπισυμβεβηκότα αὐτῷ. Eusebius
uses the word συμβεβηκὸς in the same way, Demonstr.
Evang. iv. 3. And hence St. Cyril, in controversy
with the Arians, is led by the course of their objections
to observe, "There are cogent reasons for considering
these things *as accidents*, συμβεβηκότα, in God, though
they be not." Thesaur. p. 263.

The Τέλειον.

"Perfect from Perfect" is often found in Catholic Creeds, and also (with an evasion) in Arian. "The Word who is perfect from the perfect Father." Orat. iii. § 52. "As radiance from light, so is He perfect Offspring from perfect." ii. § 35, also iii. § 1 circ. fin. "One from One, Perfect from Perfect," &c. Hil. Trin. ii. 8. τέλειος τέλειον γεγέννηκεν, Epiph. Hær. 76, p. 945. Not only the Son but the Father was ἀτελὴς, says Athan., if the Son were not eternal. "He is rightly called the eternal Offspring of the Father, for never was the substance of the Father imperfect, that what belongs to it should be added afterwards. . . . God's Offspring is eternal, because His nature is ever perfect." Orat. i. 14. A similar passage is found in Cyril. Thesaur. v. p. 42. Dial. ii. fin. This was retorting the objection : the Arians said, "How can God be ever perfect, who added to Himself a Son ? " Athan. answers, " How can the Son be a later addition, since God is ever perfect ? " vid. Greg. Nyssen. contr. Eunom. Append. p. 142. Cyril. Thesaur. x. p. 78. Also Origen, as quoted by Marcellus in Euseb. c. Marc. p. 22, εἰ γὰρ ἀεὶ τέλειος ὁ θεὸς . . . . τί ἀναβάλλεται; &c. As to the Son's perfection, Aetius objects, ap. Epiph. Hær. 76, p. 925, 6, that growth and consequent accession from without are essentially involved in the idea of Sonship;

whereas S. Greg. Naz. speaks of the Son as not ἀτελῆ πρότερον, εἶτα τέλειον, ὥσπερ νόμος τῆς ἡμετέρας γενέσεως. Orat. 20. 9 fin. In like manner, S. Basil argues against Eunomius, that the Son is τέλειος, because He is the Image, not as if copied, which is a gradual work, but as a χαρακτὴρ, or impression of a seal, or as the knowledge communicated from master to scholar, which comes to the latter and exists in him perfect, without being lost to the former. contr. Eunom. ii. 16. fin.

¶ It need scarcely be said, that "perfect from perfect" is a symbol on which the Catholics laid stress, Athan. Orat. ii. 35; Epiph. Hær. 76, p. 945; but it admitted of an evasion. An especial reason for insisting on it in the previous centuries had been the Sabellian doctrine, which considered the title "Word," when applied to our Lord, to be adequately explained by the ordinary sense of the term, as a word spoken by us. Vid. on the λόγος προφορικὸς, art. Word, a doctrine which led to the dangerous, often heretical, hypothesis that our Lord was first Word, and then Son. In consequence they insisted on His τὸ τέλειον, perfection, which became almost synonymous with His personality. Thus the Apollinarians e.g. denied that our Lord was perfect man, because his personality was not human. Athan. contr. Apoll. i. 2. Hence Justin, and Tatian, are earnest in denying that our Lord was a portion divided from the Divine substance, οὐ κατ' ἀποτομὴν, &c. &c. Just. Tryph. 128. Tatian. contr. Græc. 5. And Athan. condemns the notion of the λόγος ἐν τῷ θεῷ ἀτελὴς, γεννηθεὶς τέλειος. Orat. iv. 11. The Arians then, as

being the especial opponents of the Sabellians, insisted
on nothing so much as our Lord's being a real, living,
substantial, Word, (vid. Eusebius passim,) and they
explained τέλειον as they explained away "real," art.
supr. *Arian tenets*. "The Father," says Acacius against
Marcellus, "begat the Only-begotten, alone alone, and
perfect perfect; for there is nothing imperfect in the
Father, wherefore neither is there in the Son, but the
Son's perfection is the genuine offspring of His
perfection, and superperfection." ap. Epiph. Hær.
72, 7. Τέλειος then was a relative word, varying
with the subject-matter, vid. Damasc. F. O. i. 8,
p. 138.

¶ The Arians considered Father and Son to be two
οὐσίαι, ὅμοιαι, but not ὁμοούσιαι. Their characteristic
explanation of the word τέλειος was, "distinct," and
"independent." When they said that our Lord was
perfect God, they meant, "perfect, *in that sense in
which* He is God"—i.e. as a secondary divinity.—
Nay, in one point of view they would use the term of
His Divine Nature more freely than the Catholics sometimes used it. Thus Hippolytus e.g. though really
holding His perfection from eternity as the Son, yet
speaks of His *condescension* in coming upon earth as
if a kind of complement of His Sonship, He becoming
thus a Son a second time; whereas the Arians holding
no real condescension or assumption of a really new
state, could not hold that our Lord was in any respect
essentially other than He had been before the Incarnation. "Nor was the Word," says Hippolytus, "before
the flesh and by Himself, perfect Son, though being

perfect Word [as] being Only-begotten ; nor could the
flesh subsist by itself without the Word, because that in
the Word it has its consistence : thus then He was
manifested One perfect Son of God." contr. Noet. 15.

Τριάς,

Vid. *Trinity*.

THE word τριάς, translated Trinity, is first used by Theophilus ad Autol. ii. 15. Gibbon remarks that the doctrine of "a numerical rather than a generical unity," which has been explicitly put forth by the Latin Church, is "favoured by the Latin language; τριὰς seems to excite the idea of substance, *trinitas* of qualities." ch. 21, note 74. It is certain that the Latin view of the sacred truth, when perverted, becomes Sabellianism; and that the Greek, when perverted, becomes Arianism; and we find Arius arising in the East, Sabellius in the West. It is also certain that the word Trinitas is properly abstract; and only in an ecclesiastical sense expresses τριὰς or "a three." But Gibbon does not seem to observe that Unitas is abstract as well as Trinitas; and that we might just as well say in consequence, that the Latins held an abstract unity or a unity of qualities, while the Greeks by μονὰς taught the doctrine of "a one" or a numerical unity. "Singularitatem hanc dico," says S. Ambrose, "quod Græcè μονότης dicitur; singularitas ad personam pertinet, unitas ad naturam." de Fid. v. 3. It is important, however, to understand, that "Trinity" does not mean the *state* or *condition* of being three, as humanity is the condition of being man, but is synonymous with "three persons." Humanity does not exist and cannot be addressed, but the Holy Trinity is a three, or a unity which exists in three. Apparently from not considering this, Luther and Calvin objected to the word Trinity. "It is a common prayer," says Calvin, "'Holy Trinity, one God, have mercy on us.' It displeases me, and savours throughout of barbarism." Ep. ad Polon. p. 796. Tract. Theol.

Υἱοπάτωρ.

THIS word is made the symbol of the Noetians or
Sabellians by both Catholics and Arians, as if their
doctrine involved or avowed Patripassianism, or that
the Father suffered. Without entering upon the
controversy on the subject raised by Beausobre (Hist.
Manich. iii. 6, § 7, &c.), Mosheim (Ant. Constant. sæc.
ii. § 68, iii. 32), and Lardner (Cred. part ii. ch. 41),
we may refer to the following passages for the use
of the term. It is ascribed to Sabellius, Ammon. in
Caten. Joan. i. 1, p. 14; to Sabellius and perhaps
Marcellus, Euseb. Eccl. Theol. ii. 5; to Marcellus,
Cyr. Hier. Catech. xv. 9, also iv. 8, xi. 16; to
Sabellians, Athan. Expos. F. 2, and 7 Can. Con-
stant. and Greg. Nyssen. contr. Eun. xii. p. 305; to
certain heretics, Cyril Alex. in Joann. v. 31, p. 243;
Epiph. Hær. 73, 11 fin.; to Praxeas and Montanus, Mar.
Merc. p. 128; to Sabellius, Cæsar. Dial. i. p. 550; to
Noetus, Damasc. Hær. 57.

αὐτὸς ἑαυτοῦ πατὴρ is used by Athan. Orat. iv.
§ 2. also vid. Hipp. contr. Noet. 7. Euseb. in Marc.
pp. 42, 61, 106, 119, υἱὸν ἑαυτοῦ γίνεσθαι. supr.
Orat. iii. 4 init. "Ipsum sibi patrem," &c. Auct.
Præd. (ap. Sirmond. Opp. t. i. p. 278, ed. Ven.)
Mar. Merc. t. 2, p. 128, ed. 1673 as above. Greg.
Boet. (ap. Worm. Hist. Sabell. p. 17.) Consult Zach.

et Apoll. ii. 11 (ap. Dach. Spicil. t. i. p. 25). Porphyry uses αὐτοπάτωρ, but by a strong figure, Cyril. contr. Julian. i. p. 32. vid. Epiphan. in answer to Aetius on this subject, Hær. 76, p. 937. It must be observed that several Catholic Fathers seem to countenance such expressions, as Zeno Ver. and Marius Vict., not to say S. Hilary and S. Augustine. vid. Thomassin de Trin. 9. For υἱοπάτωρ, add to the above references, Nestor. Serm. 12. ap. Mar. Merc. t. 2, p. 87. and Ep. ad Martyr. ap. Bevereg. Synod. t. 2. Not. p. 100.

Χριστομάχος.

Vid. θεομάχος.

THE END.

A SELECT LIST

OF

THEOLOGICAL BOOKS

(MAINLY ROMAN CATHOLIC)

PUBLISHED BY

LONGMANS, GREEN, & CO.

LONDON, NEW YORK, AND BOMBAY.

MESSRS. LONGMANS, GREEN, & CO.

Issue the undermentioned Catalogues and Lists of their Publications, any of which may be had post free on application:—

1. MONTHLY LIST OF NEW BOOKS AND NEW EDITIONS.
2. QUARTERLY LIST OF ANNOUNCEMENTS AND NEW BOOKS.
3. NOTES ON BOOKS: BEING AN ANALYSIS OF THE WORKS PUBLISHED BY MESSRS. LONGMANS, GREEN & CO. DURING EACH QUARTER.
4. SCIENTIFIC AND TECHNICAL BOOKS.
5. MEDICAL AND SURGICAL BOOKS.
6. EDUCATIONAL AND SCHOOL BOOKS.
7. EDUCATIONAL BOOKS RECENTLY PUBLISHED.

8. BOOKS FOR ELEMENTARY SCHOOLS AND PUPIL TEACHERS.
9. BOOKS FOR SCHOOL PRIZES.
10. BOOKS FOR CHRISTMAS AND NEW YEAR PRESENTS.
11. THEOLOGICAL BOOKS (CHURCH OF ENGLAND).
12. THEOLOGICAL BOOKS (MAINLY ROMAN CATHOLIC).
13. BOOKS IN GENERAL LITERATURE AND GENERAL THEOLOGY.
14. A CLASSIFIED CATALOGUE (144 pp.) (GENERAL LITERATURE, SCIENCE, THEOLOGY, EDUCATION.

CARDINAL NEWMAN'S WORKS.

Letters and Correspondence of John Henry Newman during his Life in the English Church. With a brief Autobiograpy. Edited, at Cardinal Newman's request, by ANNE MOZLEY. 2 vols. Cr. 8vo. 7s.

Parochial and Plain Sermons. Edited by REV. W. J. COPELAND, B.D., late Rector of Farnham, Essex. 8 vols. Sold separately. Crown 8vo. Cabinet Edition, 5s. each; Popular Edition, 3s. 6d. each.

CONTENTS OF VOL. I.:—Holiness necessary for Future Blessedness—The Immortality of the Soul—Knowledge of God's Will without Obedience—Secret Faults—Self-Denial the Test of Religious Earnestness—The Spiritual Mind—Sins of Ignorance and Weakness—God's Commandments not Grievous—The Religious Use of Excited Feelings—Profession without Practice—Profession without Hypocrisy—Profession without Ostentation—Promising without Doing—Religious Emotion—Religious Faith Rational—The Christian Mysteries—The Self-Wise Inquirer—Obedience the Remedy for Religious Perplexity—Times of Private Prayer—Forms of Private Prayer—The Resurrection of the Body—Witnesses of the Resurrection—Christian Reverence—The Religion of the Day—Scripture a Record of Human Sorrow—Christian Manhood.

CONTENTS OF VOL. II.:—The World's Benefactors—Faith without Sight—The Incarnation—Martyrdom—Love of Relations and Friends—The Mind of Little Children—Ceremonies of the Church—The Glory of the Christian Church—St. Paul's Conversion viewed in Reference to his Office—Secrecy and Suddenness of Divine Visitations—Divine Decrees—The Reverence Due to the Blessed Virgin Mary—Christ, a Quickening Spirit—Saving Knowledge—Self-Contemplation—Religious Cowardice—The Gospel Witnesses—Mysteries in Religion—The Indwelling Spirit—The Kingdom of the Saints—The Gospel, a Trust Committed to us—Tolerance of Religious Error—Rebuking Sin—The Christian Ministry—Human Responsibility—Guilelessness—The Danger of Riches—The Powers of Nature—The Danger of Accomplishments—Christian Zeal—Use of Saints' Days.

CARDINAL NEWMAN'S WORKS.

Parochial and Plain Sermons.—*Continued.*

Sermons Preached on Various Occasions. Crown 8vo. Cabinet
Edition, 6s. ; Popular Edition, 3s. 6d.

CARDINAL NEWMAN'S WORKS.

Selection, Adapted to the Seasons of the Ecclesiastical Year,

from the 'Parochial and Plain Sermons.' Edited by the REV. W. J. COPELAND, B.D. Crown 8vo. Cabinet Edition, 5s.; Popular Edition, 3s. 6d.

CONTENTS :—*Advent:* Self-Denial the Test of Religious Earnestness—Divine Calls—The Ventures of Faith—Watching. *Christmas Day:* Religious Joy. *New Year's Sunday:* The Lapse of Time. *Epiphany:* Remembrance of Past Mercies — Equanimity — The Immortality of the Soul — Christian Manhood—Sincerity and Hypocrisy—Christian Sympathy. *Septuagesima:* Present Blessings. *Sexagesima:* Endurance, the Christian's Portion. *Quinquagesima:* Love, the One Thing Needful. *Lent:* The Individuality of the Soul—Life the Season of Repentance—Bodily Suffering—Tears of Christ at the Grave of Lazarus—Christ's Privations, a Meditation for Christians—The Cross of Christ the Measure of the World. *Good Friday:* The Crucifixion. *Easter Day:* Keeping Fast and Festival. *Easter Tide:* Witnesses of the Resurrection—A Particular Providence as Revealed in the Gospel—Christ Manifested in Remembrance—The Invisible World—Waiting for Christ. *Ascension:* Warfare the Condition of Victory. *Sunday after Ascension:* Rising with Christ. *Whitsun Day:* The Weapons of Saints. *Trinity Sunday:* The Mysteriousness of Our Present Being. *Sundays after Trinity:* Holiness Necessary for Future Blessedness—The Religious Use of Excited Feelings—The Self-Wise Inquirer—Scripture a Record of Human Sorrow—The Danger of Riches—Obedience without Love, as instanced in the Character of Balaam—Moral Consequences of Single Sins—The Greatness and Littleness of Human Life—Moral Effects of Communion with God—The Thought of God the Stay of the Soul—The Power of the Will—The Gospel Palaces—Religion a Weariness to the Natural Man—The World our Enemy—The Praise of Men—Religion Pleasant to the Religious—Mental Prayer—Curiosity a Temptation to Sin—Miracles no Remedy for Unbelief—Jeremiah, a Lesson for the Disappointed—The Shepherd of our Souls—Doing Glory to God in Pursuits of the World.

Sermons Bearing upon Subjects of the Day. Edited by the REV.

W. J. COPELAND, B.D., late Rector of Farnham, Essex. Crown 8vo. Cabinet Edition, 5s.; Popular Edition, 3s. 6d.

CONTENTS :—The Work of the Christian—Saintliness not Forfeited by the Penitent—Our Lord's Last Supper and His First—Dangers to the Penitent—The Three Offices of Christ—Faith and Experience—Faith unto the World—The Church and the World—Indulgence in Religious Privileges—Connection between Personal and Public Improvement—Christian Nobleness—Joshua a Type of Christ and His Followers—Elisha a Type of Christ and His Followers—The Christian Church a Continuation of the Jewish—The Principles of Continuity between the Jewish and Christian Churches—The Christian Church an Imperial Power—Sanctity the Token of the Christian Empire—Condition of the Members of the Christian Empire—The Apostolic Christian—Wisdom and Innocence—Invisible Presence of Christ—Outward and Inward Notes of the Church—Grounds for Steadfastness in our Religious Profession—Elijah the Prophet of the Latter Days—Feasting in Captivity—The Parting of Friends.

Fifteen Sermons Preached before the University of Oxford,

between A.D. 1826 and 1843. Crown 8vo. Cabinet Edition, 5s.; Popular Edition, 3s. 6d.

CONTENTS :—The Philosophical Temper, first enjoined by the Gospel—The Influence of Natural and Revealed Religion respectively—Evangelical Sanctity the Perfection of Natural Virtue—The Usurpations of Reason—Personal Influence, the Means of Propagating the Truth—On Justice as a Principle of Divine Governance—Contest between Faith and Sight—Human Responsibility, as independent of Circumstances—Wilfulness, the Sin of Saul—Faith and Reason, contrasted as Habits of Mind—The Nature of Faith in Relation to Reason—Love, the Safeguard of Faith against Superstition—Implicit and Explicit Reason—Wisdom, as contrasted with Faith and with Bigotry—The Theory of Developments in Religious Doctrine.

CARDINAL NEWMAN'S WORKS.

Apologia Pro Vita Sua. Crown 8vo. Cabinet Edition, 6s. ; Popular Edition, 3s. 6d.

Verses on Various Occasions. Crown 8vo. Cabinet Edition, 6s. ; Popular Edition, 3s. 6d.

Discourses Addressed to Mixed Congregations. Crown 8vo. Cabinet Edition, 6s.; Popular Edition, 3s. 6d.

CONTENTS :—The Salvation of the Hearer the Motive of the Preacher—Neglect of Divine Calls and Warnings—Men not Angels—The Priests of the Gospel—Purity and Love—Saintliness the Standard of Christian Principle—God's Will the End of Life—Perseverance in Grace—Nature and Grace—Illuminating Grace—Faith and Private Judgment—Faith and Doubt—Prospects of the Catholic Missioner—Mysteries of Nature and of Grace—The Mystery of Divine Condescension—The Infinitude of Divine Attributes—Mental Sufferings of Our Lord in His Passion—The Glories of Mary for the Sake of Her Son—On the Fitness of the Glories of Mary.

Lectures on the Doctrine of Justification. Crown 8vo. Cabinet Edition, 5s. ; Popular Edition, 3s. 6d.

CONTENTS :—Faith considered as the Instrumental Cause of Justification—Love considered as the Formal Cause of Justification—Primary Sense of the term 'Justification'—Secondary Senses of the term 'Justification'—Misuse of the term 'Just' or 'Righteous'—The Gift of Righteousness—The Characteristics of the Gift of Righteousness—Righteousness viewed as a Gift and as a Quality—Righteousness the Fruit of our Lord's Resurrection—The Office of Justifying Faith—The Nature of Justifying Faith—Faith viewed relatively to Rites and Works—On Preaching the Gospel—Appendix.

On the Development of Christian Doctrine. Crown 8vo. Cabinet Edition, 6s.; Popular Edition, 3s. 6d.

On the Idea of a University. Crown 8vo. Cabinet Edition, 7s.; Popular Edition, 3s. 6d.

An Essay in Aid of a Grammar of Assent. Crown 8vo. Cabinet Edition, 7s. 6d.; Popular Edition, 3s. 6d.

Two Essays on Miracles. 1. Of Scripture. 2. Of Ecclesiastical History. Crown 8vo. Cabinet Edition, 6s. ; Popular Edition, 3s. 6d.

Discussions and Arguments. Crown 8vo. Cabinet Edition, 6s.; Popular Edition, 3s. 6d.

1. How to accomplish it. 2. The Antichrist of the Fathers. 3. Scripture and the Creed. 4. Tamworth Reading-room. 5. Who's to Blame? 6. An Argument for Christianity.

Essays, Critical and Historical. 2 vols. Crown 8vo. Cabinet Edition, 12s.; Popular Edition, 7s.

1. Poetry. 2. Rationalism. 3. Apostolic Tradition. 4. De la Mennais. 5. Palmer on Faith and Unity. 6. St. Ignatius. 7. Prospects of the Anglican Church. 8. The Anglo-American Church. 9. Countess of Huntingdon. 10. Catholicity of the Anglican Church. 11. The Antichrist of Protestants. 12. Milman's Christianity. 13. Rèformation of the XI. Century. 14. Private Judgment. 15. Davison. 16. Keble.

CARDINAL NEWMAN'S WORKS.

Historical Sketches. 3 vols. Crown 8vo. Cabinet Edition, 6s. each; Popular Edition, 3s. 6d.

1. The Turks. 2. Cicero. 3. Apollonius. 4. Primitive Christianity. 5. Church of the Fathers. 6. St. Chrysostom. 7. Theodoret. 8. St. Benedict. 9. Benedictine Schools. 10. Universities. 11. Northmen and Normans. 12. Mediæval Oxford. 13. Convocation of Canterbury.

The Arians of the Fourth Century. Crown 8vo. Cabinet Edition, 6s.; Popular Edition, 3s. 6d.

Select Treatises of St. Athanasius in Controversy with the Arians. Freely translated. 2 vols. Crown 8vo. Cabinet Edition, 15s.; Popular Edition, 7s.

Theological Tracts. Crown 8vo. Cabinet Edition, 8s.; Popular Edition, 3s. 6d.

1. Dissertatiunculæ. 2. On the Text of the Seven Epistles of St. Ignatius. 3. Doctrinal Causes of Arianism. 4. Apollinarianism. 5. St. Cyril's Formula. 6. Ordo de Tempore. 7. Douay Version of Scriptures.

The Via Media of the Anglican Church. 2 vols. Crown 8vo. Cabinet Edition, 6s. each ; Popular Edition, 3s. 6d. each.

Vol. I. Prophetical Office of the Church.

Vol. II. Occasional Letters and Tracts.

Certain Difficulties felt by Anglicans in Catholic Teaching Con-sidered. 2 vols.

Vol. I. Twelve Lectures. Crown 8vo. Cabinet Edition, 7s. 6d.; Popular Edition, 3s. 6d.

Vol. II. Letters to Dr. Pusey concerning the Blessed Virgin, and to the Duke of Norfolk in defence of the Pope and Council. Crown 8vo. Cabinet Edition, 5s. 6d. ; Popular Edition, 3s. 6d.

Present Position of Catholics in England. Crown 8vo. Cabinet Edition, 7s. 6d. ; Popular Edition, 3s. 6d.

Loss and Gain. The Story of a Convert. Crown 8vo. Cabinet Edition, 6s. ;. Popular Edition, 3s. 6d.

Callista. A Tale of the Third Century. Crown 8vo. Cabinet Edition, 6s. ; Popular Edition, 3s. 6d.

The Dream of Gerontius. 16mo, sewed, 6d.; cloth, 1s.

Meditations and Devotions. Part I. Meditations for the Month of May. Novena of St. Philip. Part II. The Stations of the Cross. Meditations and Intercessions for Good Friday. Litanies, etc. Part III. Meditations on Christan Doctrine. Conclusion. Oblong Crown 8vo. 5s. *net.*

CARDINAL NEWMAN'S WORKS.

COMPLETION OF THE POPULAR EDITION.

BATIFFOL.—**History of the Roman Breviary.** By PIERRE BATIF-FOL, Litt.D. Translated by ATWELL M. Y. BAYLAY, M.A., Vicar of Thurgarton, Notts. With a New Preface by the Author. Crown 8vo. 7s. 6d.

DOBRÈE.—**Stories on the Rosary.** By LOUISA EMILY DOBRÈE, Author of 'Stories of the Seven Sacraments.' Parts I. and II. Crown 8vo. 1s. 6d. each.

FOUARD.—**The Christ, The Son of God.** A Life of Our Lord and Saviour Jesus Christ. By the ABBÉ CONSTANT FOUARD, Honorary Cathedral Canon, Professor of the Faculty of Theology at Rouen, etc., etc. Translated from the Fifth Edition with the Author's sanction. By GEORGE F. X. GRIFFITH. With an Introduction by CARDINAL MANNING. Third Edition. With 3 Maps. 2 vols. Crown 8vo. 14s.

Saint Peter and the First Years of Christianity. By the ABBÉ CONSTANT FOUARD. Translated by GEORGE F. X. GRIFFITH. Crown 8vo. 9s.

St. Paul and His Missions. By the ABBÉ CONSTANT FOUARD. Translated, with the Author's sanction and co-operation, by GEORGE F. X. GRIFFITH. With 2 Maps. Crown 8vo. 9s.

CHRISTIAN BIOGRAPHIES:

Henri Dominique Lacordaire. A Biographical Sketch. By H. L. SIDNEY LEAR. With Frontispiece. Crown 8vo. 3s. 6d.

A Christian Painter of the Nineteenth Century; being the Life of Hippolyte Flandrin. By H. L. SIDNEY LEAR. Crown 8vo. 3s. 6d.

Bossuet and his Contemporaries. By H. L. SIDNEY LEAR. Crown 8vo. 3s. 6d.

Fénelon, Archbishop of Cambrai. A Biographical Sketch. By H. L. SIDNEY LEAR. Crown 8vo. 3s. 6d.

A Dominican Artist. A Sketch of the Life of the Rev. Père Besson, of the Order of St. Dominic. By H. L. SIDNEY LEAR. Crown 8vo. 3s. 6d.

The Life of Madame Louise de France, Daughter of Louis XV., also known as the Mother Thérèse de S. Augustin. By H. L. SIDNEY LEAR. Crown 8vo. 3s. 6d.

The Revival of Priestly Life in the Seventeenth Century in France. Charles de Condren—S. Philip Neri and Cardinal de Berulle—S. Vincent de Paul—S. Sulpice and Jean Jacques Olier. By H. L. SIDNEY LEAR. Crown 8vo. 3s. 6d.

Life of S. Francis de Sales, Bishop and Prince of Geneva. By H. L. SIDNEY LEAR. Crown 8vo. 3s. 6d.

Henri Perreyve. By A. GRATRY, PRÊTRE DE L'ORATOIRE, Professeur de Morale Evangélique à la Sorbonne, et Membre de l'Académie Française. Translated, by special permission, by H. L. SIDNEY LEAR. With Portrait. Crown 8vo. 3s. 6d.

DRANE.—A Memoir of Mother Francis Raphael O.S.D. (Agusta Theodosia Drane), some time Prioress Provincial of the Congregation of Dominican Sisters of S. Catherine of Siena, Stone. With some of her Spiritual Notes and Letters. Edited by Rev. Father BERTRAND WILBERFORCE, O.P. With Portrait. Crown 8vo. 7s. 6d.

The History of St. Dominic, Founder of the Friar Preachers. By AUGUSTA THEODOSIA DRANE, author of 'The History of St. Catherine of Siena and her Companions. With 32 Illustrations. 8vo. 15s.

FÉNELON.—Spiritual Letters to Men. By ARCHBISHOP FÉNELON. Translated by H. L. SIDNEY LEAR, author of 'Life of Fénelon,' 'Life of S. Francis de Sales,' etc. etc. 16mo. 2s. 6d.

Spiritual Letters to Women. — By ARCHBISHOP FÉNELON. Translated by H. L. SIDNEY LEAR, author of 'Life of Fénelon,' 'Life of S. Francis de Sales,' etc. etc. 16mo. 2s. 6d.

GIBSON.—The Abbé de Lamennais and the Liberal Catholic Movement in France. By the HON. W. GIBSON. With Portrait. 8vo. 12s. 6d.

JAMESON—Works by MRS. JAMESON:

Sacred and Legendary Art. With 19 Etchings and 197 Woodcuts. 2 vols. Cloth, gilt top. 20s. *net.*

Legends of the Madonna : The Virgin Mary as Represented in Sacred and Legendary Art. With 27 Etchings and 165 Woodcuts. 1 vol. Cloth, gilt top. 10s. *net.*

Legends of the Monastic Orders. With 11 Etchings and 88 Woodcuts. 1 vol. Cloth, gilt top. 10s. *net.*

History of the Saviour, His Types and Precúrsors. Completed by LADY EASTLAKE. With 13 Etchings and 281 Woodcuts. 2 vols. Cloth, gilt top. 20s. *net.*

LYONS.—Christianity or Infallibility. Both or Neither. By the Rev. DANIEL LYONS. Crown 8vo. 5s.

RIVINGTON.—The Primitive Church and the See of Peter. By the Rev. LUKE RIVINGTON, D.D. With an Introduction by the CARDINAL ARCHBISHOP OF WESTMINSTER. 8vo. 16s.

TYRRELL.—Nova et Vetera : Informal Meditations for Times of Spiritual Dryness. By GEORGE TYRRELL, S.J. Crown 8vo. 6s.

WISEMAN.— The Life and Times of Cardinal Wiseman. By WILFRID WARD, Author of 'William George Ward and the Catholic Revival.' With 3 Portraits. 2 vols. Crown 8vo. 24s.

MANUALS OF CATHOLIC PHILOSOPHY.

(Stonyhurst Series.)

EDITED BY RICHARD F. CLARKE, S.J.

Logic. By RICHARD F. CLARKE, S.J., D.D. Crown 8vo. 5s.

First Principles of Knowledge. By JOHN RICKABY, S.J. Crown 8vo. 5s.

Moral Philosophy (Ethics and Natural Law). By JOSEPH RICKABY, S.J. Crown 8vo. 5s.

General Metaphysics. By JOHN RICKABY, S.J. Crown 8vo. 5s.

Psychology. By MICHAEL MAHER, S.J. Crown 8vo. 6s. 6d.

Natural Theology. By BERNARD BOEDDER, S.J. Crown 8vo. 6s. 6d.

Political Economy. By CHARLES S. DEVAS. Crown 8vo. 6s. 6d.

ENGLISH MANUALS OF CATHOLIC THEOLOGY.

Outlines of Dogmatic Theology. By SYLVESTER JOSEPH HUNTER, of the Society of Jesus. Crown 8vo. 3 vols., 6s. 6d. each.

www.ingramcontent.com/pod-product-compliance
Lightning Source LLC
Chambersburg PA
CBHW031348290326
41932CB00044B/365